The Hobbit and
Tolkien's Mythology

ALSO EDITED BY BRADFORD LEE EDEN

Middle-earth Minstrel: Essays on Music in Tolkien (McFarland, 2010)

The Hobbit and Tolkien's Mythology

Essays on Revisions and Influences

Edited by BRADFORD LEE EDEN

McFarland & Company, Inc., Publishers
Jefferson, North Carolina

LIBRARY OF CONGRESS CATALOGUING-IN-PUBLICATION DATA

The Hobbit and Tolkien's mythology : essays on
revisions and influences / edited by Bradford Lee Eden.
p. cm.
Includes bibliographical references and index.

ISBN 978-0-7864-7960-3 (softcover : acid free paper) ∞
ISBN 978-1-4766-1795-4 (ebook)

1. Tolkien, J. R. R. (John Ronald Reuel), 1892–1973—Criticism and interpretation. 2. Tolkien, J. R. R. (John Ronald Reuel), 1892–1973. Hobbit. I. Eden, Bradford Lee, editor.
PR6039.O32Z66125 2014   823'.912—dc23   2014034213

BRITISH LIBRARY CATALOGUING DATA ARE AVAILABLE

© 2014 Bradford Lee Eden. All rights reserved

*No part of this book may be reproduced or transmitted in any form
or by any means, electronic or mechanical, including photocopying
or recording, or by any information storage and retrieval system,
without permission in writing from the publisher.*

On the cover: "The Fight Between
Thingol and Boldog" (artwork courtesy Tom Loback)

Printed in the United States of America

*McFarland & Company, Inc., Publishers
Box 611, Jefferson, North Carolina 28640
www.mcfarlandpub.com*

This book is dedicated to
the three most important girls in my life:
Sonja, Noëlle, and Crystal.

Table of Contents

Introduction
    BRADFORD LEE EDEN   1

Part I: The Evolution of the Dwarven Race

Anchoring the Myth: The Impact of *The Hobbit* on Tolkien's Legendarium
    JOHN D. RATELIFF   6

From Nauglath to Durin's Folk: *The Hobbit* and Tolkien's Dwarves
    GERARD HYNES   20

Part II: Durin's Day

"It passes our skill in these days": Primary World Influences on the Evolution of Durin's Day
    KRISTINE LARSEN   40

A Scientific Examination of Durin's Day
    SUMNER GARY HUNNEWELL   59

Part III: Themes

Tolkien's French Connection
    VERLYN FLIEGER   70

Tolkien's Hybrid Mythology: *The Hobbit* as Old Norse "Fairy-Story"
    JANE CHANCE   78

From "The Silmarillion" to *The Hobbit* and Back Again: An Onomastic Foray
    DAMIEN BADOR   97

Civilized Goblins and Talking Animals: How *The Hobbit* Created Problems of Sentience for Tolkien
    GREGORY HARTLEY   113

Seeing in the Dark, Seeing by the Dark: How Bilbo's Invisibility Defined Tolkien's Vision
    MICHAEL A. WODZAK   136

A Victorian in Valhalla: Bilbo Baggins as the Link Between England and Middle-earth
    WILLIAM CHRISTIAN KLARNER   152

Beorn and Bombadil: Mythology, Place and Landscape in Middle-earth
    JUSTIN T. NOETZEL   161

Travel, Redemption and Peacemaking: Hobbits, Dwarves and Elves and the
Transformative Power of Pilgrimage
    VICKIE L. HOLTZ-WODZAK   181

A Baggins Back Yard: Environmentalism, Authorship and the Elves in Tolkien's
Legendarium
    DAVID THIESSEN   195

Polytemporality and Epic Characterization in *The Hobbit: An Unexpected
Journey*: Reflecting *The Lord of the Ring*'s Modernism and Medievalism
    JUDY ANN FORD *and* ROBIN ANNE REID   208

The Wisdom of the Crowd: Internet Memes and *The Hobbit: An Unexpected
Journey*
    MICHELLE MARKEY BUTLER   222

About the Contributors   233

Index   235

Introduction

Bradford Lee Eden

The idea for this book began with the "Celebrating *The Hobbit*" conference held at Valparaiso University in Valparaiso, Indiana, in March 2013. The conference celebrated the seventy-fifth anniversary of the publication of *The Hobbit*, as well as the first installment of new *Hobbit* movies by Peter Jackson. The conference was anchored by two plenary papers, one by John D. Rateliff which provided numerous examples of *The Hobbit*'s influence on Tolkien's legendarium titled "Anchoring the Myth: The Impact of *The Hobbit* on Tolkien's Legendarium," and one by Verlyn Flieger which discussed French influences on the development of Bilbo Baggins and his adventure titled "Tolkien's French Connections." In discussions with the plenary speakers and other presenters, it became apparent that a book focusing on how *The Hobbit* influenced the subsequent development of Tolkien's legendarium was sorely needed. This set of essays provides that perspective.

The book is divided into three parts: "The Evolution of the Dwarven Race," "Durin's Day," and "Themes." The first of two essays in Part I is by John D. Rateliff, whose significant documentation on the major versions and revisions leading up to the publication of *The Hobbit* is well-known (Rateliff, 2007). In his contribution to this volume, he indicates that the most significant departure that *The Hobbit* makes from the earlier "Silmarillion" material is Tolkien's reinterpretation of the dwarves. In the previous "Silmarillion" material, dwarves are presented as prone to evil if not outright evil, treacherous, and avaricious, not unlike their depiction in Germanic mythology and nineteenth-century works and adaptations of those myths by the Brothers Grimm, Andrew Lang, and William Morris. In *The Hobbit*, however, the reader meets a race that is honorable, fun-loving, musical, proud, and ultimately dependable. Rateliff documents in copious detail Tolkien's depictions of dwarves in his writings pre–*Hobbit*, contemporary with *The Hobbit*, and post–*Hobbit*, thus providing a timeline of Tolkien's thoughts and opinions in his unpublished and published works on how he wrote about the dwarven race throughout his life. Gerard Hynes builds off of Rateliff's superb essay by focusing on dwarven song and poetry and linking Tolkien's dwarves with their depictions in Germanic and Old Norse mythology. Nineteenth-century influences such as William Morris, Andrew Lang, the Brothers Grimm, and Richard Wagner are mentioned, along with a brief discussion of similarities between the dwarven race and the Jewish people. Hynes mentions that the depiction of dwarves in *The Lord of the Rings* provides the reader with viewpoints of Middle-earth from their own perspective, rather than from those of Elves or Men; a distinct break from Tolkien's previous writings. It is this perspective that makes the dwarves both believable and understandable, heroic and epic, especially through the development of Gimli's character. Hynes mentions Tolkien's late writings on dwarves, specifically the concept of the Nibin-Noeg of the late 1950s through early 1960s.

Part II contains two essays that focus on one particular and unique event mentioned in *The Hobbit*: Durin's Day. Kristine Larsen does an excellent job of documenting the main scientific hypotheses regarding the creation of the moon in the early twentieth century, especially the research and work of John Knight Fotheringham (1874–1936). According to Larsen, Tolkien would have been well aware of Fotheringham's research through his 1930 article "Ancient Astronomy and Cosmology" in *The Oxford Magazine* (where Tolkien published in the previous term), as well as Fotheringham's 1931 application to succeed H. H. Turner as Savilian Professor of Astronomy (since Tolkien was an elected member of the General Board of the Faculties at Oxford from 1929 to 1932, and would have known of his application for the position). Documentation on Tolkien's various drafts to align Durin's Day with the chronology of events in *The Hobbit* eventually resulted in the construction of a many-columned timeline cheat-sheet for novel-wide consistency, which still survives in the Tolkien archive at Marquette University. Sumner Gary Hunnewell's contribution on Durin's Day examines this anomaly from the perspective of various book and jacket illustrations that depict the "new moon" in various positions (some of which are Tolkien's own illustrations of the event), along with Hunnewell's attempts to observe "the youngest moon relative to the time of the astronomical new moon" himself. Hunnewell also provides evidence that Tolkien was drawing from the Jewish tradition of a lunar calendar in his construction of Durin's Day.

Part III contains a number of essays on various themes regarding the construction of *The Hobbit* and its influence on the writing of *The Lord of the Rings* and "The Silmarillion" material. Each of these themes brings out important challenges and influences that the publication of *The Hobbit* placed on Tolkien's continual construction of his legendarium and *The Lord of the Rings*, as well as his attempt to reconcile and revise subsequent published versions of *The Hobbit* and "The Silmarillion" material due to linkages and anomalies between and among all of these works. Verlyn Flieger does an excellent job of illustrating the differences between Bilbo's *aventures* and Frodo's quest, and how Tolkien's scholarly and linguistic background supports a strong French connection to the construction and story line of *The Hobbit*. The French Arthurian connection is even stronger, now that we have Tolkien's *The Fall of Arthur* available for reference (Houghton Mifflin, 2013). Jane Chance indicates that *The Hobbit* (1938) has often been dismissed as a simple children's story. Given its final publication after a period when Tolkien had worked on his Old Norse poem *Legend of Sigurd and Gudrún,* his seminal lecture "On Fairy-Stories," and what became *The Silmarillion*, however, Chance will argue that the work constitutes a pivot on which his medievalized mythology of magic is balanced. As an example of his favorite genre, the "fairy-story," *The Hobbit* borrows and transforms magical elements from his beloved fairy-story of Andrew Lang's Old Norse Sigurd to help create a "mythology for England" through the filter of his own "Silmarillion." By examining early drafts of "On Fairy-Stories" as a gloss on *The Hobbit,* this essay provides a taxonomy for the Hobbit anti-hero Bilbo, the Elves (Fairies), and humankind and stamps it as a "fairy-story" in his hybrid mythology.

Damien Bador's contribution investigates the onomastic content of proper names appearing in *The Hobbit*, illustrating how Tolkien not only reused the names of races already present in his legendarium, but specific names of places and peoples as well. Names and places original to *The Hobbit* were incorporated into the legendarium, including that most original character Bilbo Baggins and the new race of hobbits, who eventually become the linchpin of the entire re-telling of the mythology to future generations.

Gregory Hartley then addresses one of the major issues arising from the publication of *The Hobbit* that seriously challenged the validity of much of Tolkien's legendarium: the concept of animal sentience, and hence the many theological and eschatological issues surrounding that sentience in relation to orthodox doctrine via Plato and Thomas Aquinas. Hartley indicates that monsters within folklore come in two general categories: altered humanoid and oversized animals. Tolkien follows these categories, and Hartley fits trolls, giants (Treebeard was originally a giant; ent means "giant" in Old English), goblins, and orcs into the altered humanoid area, and puts eagles, spiders, and Smaug into the oversized animals area. Hartley also mentions personified animals such as Beorn's livestock and the ravens of Erebor, including Roac, old Carc's son. *The Hobbit's* popularity required Tolkien to bring its characters and races, and thus his legendarium, into line with Roman Catholic orthodoxy in order to address issues of Providence and salvation, topics that became of great concern for Tolkien towards the end of his life.

Michael A. Wodzak examines the importance of Bilbo's ring becoming The Ring, and how the concept of invisibility is explained in Tolkien's works, and how that concept relates to modern optics, mirrors, light refraction, and physics. Wodzak indicates that there is strong circumstantial evidence as well as very strong textual evidence that Tolkien had an awareness of modern optics, and describes in detail the many instances of this evidence in Tolkien's correspondence and in drafts. Wodzak discusses interesting topics such as Gollum's and Smaug's eyes, the Black Riders/Nazgul, the concept of extramission, reflected light, and the question "What does an invisible person see?" William Christian Klarner postulates that Bilbo is Tolkien personified in his own story, the Victorian gentleman living in the world of ancient Norse mythology. Bilbo provides the role of sympathetic friend to the reader, a link between our comfortable world and the Victorian Shire, between modern-day society and Norse Middle-earth. As the transmitter and writer of the adventures and quests of the later Third Age to subsequent generations, Bilbo also fulfills Tolkien's role as storyteller and historian of his legendarium to the modern reader. Justin T. Noetzel discusses two key yet very enigmatic figures: Beorn and Tom Bombadil. These two figures are taken from the Soup of Story and meld together various attributes and characteristics from many cultures and myths, as well as Tolkien's personal life. They are singular entities that possess profound but geographically focused power, and are intricately linked to their landscape and the natural world. Noetzel documents the origins and backgrounds of these two characters in Tolkien's life and scholarship, and how they stand out in a world full of communities, races, and events as enigmas of the world around them.

Vickie L. Holtz-Wodzak examines the pilgrimage motif in Tolkien's works, illustrating how Bilbo's journey was to find treasure, while Frodo's was to lose one. She documents Tolkien's references to the meditational and mystical aspects of pilgrimage in his correspondence, and how much of his scholarship was based on the Old English theme of the exile and the Middle English theme of the pilgrim's journey. Even Bilbo's and Tolkien's use of the word *holiday* (along with present-day society) proceeds etymologically from the Old English *halig daeg*, or holy day. Peregrin Took's name means *pilgrim* as well, from the Latin *peregrinus*, one who is on a journey. Finally, pilgrimage transforms and changes a person, and Bilbo's adventure and Frodo's quest take them through different lands and peoples towards the goal of self-enlightenment and self-discovery for all involved. David Thiessen works around the themes of environmentalism and authorship, showing how Tolkien weaves the Elves' love of nature, song, and words throughout his legendarium, using their perspective as the primary authors of the historical record of Middle-earth to convey his own thoughts and views on these topics. The ecological perspectives of the hobbits and other races are occasionally interspersed, but it is the Elvish "voice" that dominates in the tales and stories of Middle-earth.

The final two essays center around the theme of contemporary interpretations of

The Hobbit, specifically the Peter Jackson movie trilogy. Judy Ann Ford and Robin Anne Reid examine the polytemporality and medieval epic that Jackson has infused into *The Hobbit: An Unexpected Journey*, the first movie in the trilogy. They situate the mood of the film into the time period between the two world wars of the twentieth century (roughly 1920 to 1940), and that Jackson draws on Tolkien's later revisions of *The Hobbit* as a prequel to *The Lord of the Rings* rather than a children's story unrelated to the larger legendarium. One must remember as well that *The Lord of the Rings* movie trilogy has proceeded *The Hobbit* trilogy, and thus many of the main characters and subplots are already well-known, including Saruman's eventual treachery even as he is depicted as the head of the order of wizards in *The Hobbit* movie. One interesting term that Ford and Reid mention is "retconning," known in the comics industry as creating retroactive continuity between two works, something that Tolkien obviously did between the 1937 publication and the 1951 revised edition of *The Hobbit*. Peter Jackson has obviously incorporated the same technique in *The Hobbit* film trilogy, making his interpretation much closer to his own *Lord of the Rings* film trilogy than to the original book itself. Michelle Markey Butler then takes the reader through the world of Internet memes—recurring images with different captions—that have spread over the Internet since the premiere of *The Hobbit: An Unexpected Journey*. Butler comments on some of more popular Internet memes related to *The Hobbit* film version thus far, including ones on making a film trilogy out of one book (whereas a film trilogy out of three books make sense), and depictions of Thorin as epic hero and of his "Never have I been so wrong" statement. Social media at its finest!

John D. Rateliff sums up best the influence of *The Hobbit* on Tolkien's larger legendarium at the end of his contribution to this volume:

> In the end, *The Hobbit* and *The Silmarillion* are very different expressions of the same mythology, the same "mythology for England" project that was Tolkien's life's work. To return to my earlier analogy, *The Hobbit* and the *Silmarillion* texts do indeed swim in the same ocean, but occupy different ecological niches within that sea of story, the one in the sunlit shallows, the other in the abyssal deeps. Exploring the connections between these diverse zones gives us insights into the ecosystem as a whole in all its wonderful entangled complexity—"alive at once and in all its parts."

Work Cited

Rateliff, John D. 2007. *The History of* The Hobbit. 2 vols. London: HarperCollins.

PART I

The Evolution of the Dwarven Race

Anchoring the Myth
The Impact of *The Hobbit* on Tolkien's Legendarium

JOHN D. RATELIFF

> "I had a mind to make a body of more or less connected legend, ranging from the large and cosmogonic to the level of romantic fairy-story—the larger founded on the lesser in contact with the earth, the lesser drawing splendour from the vast backcloths."
>
> —J.R.R. Tolkien, *Letter to Waldman* [1951]
> (*Letters* 144)

In *The History of* The Hobbit, my edition (with copious commentary) of the original draft manuscripts of *The Hobbit*, I took fairly emphatic positions on two controversial issues relating to *The Hobbit*: when it was written, and what its relation to the larger legendarium was. On the first of these, I'm pleased to see that my argument seems well on its way to being adopted by the community of Tolkien scholars at large (though by no means universally); I often see my proposed dates (summer 1930 to the 1932/33 Christmas vacation) repeated by others with no reference back to me: they seem to be becoming genericized "known facts." On the second, I took what was then very much the minority view, arguing that *The Hobbit* was deeply influenced by *The Silmarillion* and from its very inception had been part of Tolkien's larger mythology—in Tolkien's own phrase, a "fairy-story ... drawing splendour from the vast backcloths." To me it seemed and seems Mr. Baggins' world so clearly shares a history with that in which Eärendil the Mariner (whose son they meet), and Turgon of Gondolin (whose sword they find), and Beren and Luthien (who are mentioned by name in the original draft) had all had their adventures that to insist otherwise—i.e., to claim that *The Hobbit* was originally an independent tale only later drawn into the mythos—is to deny the evidence of the manuscript. And to argue that all those shared details existed, right down to the three races of the Eldar (Light Elves [Vanyar] and Deep Elves [Noldor] and Sea Elves [Teleri]) and the use of Noldorin (or Sindarin, as we call it today) in a number of personal and place-names (Bladorthin, Esgaroth), but only in a casual and inconsequential way seems, to me at least, special pleading.

Recently I wrote up the argument for considering *The Hobbit* as part of "The Silmarillion" (in the larger sense: that is, the ongoing project comprised of the *Quenta*, the *Annals*, the *Ambarkanta*, the *Lhammas*, et al.) in a piece called *Un Fragment détaché: Bilbo le Hobbit et le Silmarillion* (or, to put it in plain English, "'A Fragment, Detached': *The Hobbit* and *The Silmarillion*").[1] And having done that, I thought it'd be an interesting experiment to back up and approach the problem from the opposite direction. In other words, having made the argument that *The Silmarillion* greatly influenced *The Hobbit*, both in general (a world populated by elves, dwarves, the half-elven, giant eagles, goblins, giant spiders, evil wolves, blood-sucking bats, etc., with a Fairyland in the far West reachable only by sea-voyaging) and in specific detail (e.g., shared characters playing a role in both works such as Elrond Half-elven and Thû the Necromancer), now I wanted to go back and see if I could discover evidence of ways in which *The Hobbit* influenced *The Silmarillion* in turn. I'd made a first foray into this topic in *Return to Bag-End* in my discussion of the Arkenstone and the ways in which it resembles a Silmaril (which are many), concluding by noting that one detail in the Arkenstone's description later appeared in a description of the Silmarils as well (HoH, 607)[2]: one small but clear example of *The Silmarillion* being influenced by *The Hobbit*. Of course *The Hobbit* set the stage and, early on, the tone of *The Lord of the Rings*, which began as its direct sequel, and *Lord of the Rings* in turn had considerable impact on the older mythology—but that's a topic for another paper. What I'd like to look for in this piece are examples of direct influence, unmediated by *The Lord of the Rings*, from *The Hobbit* to the latter versions of *The Silmarillion*.

Thus it becomes necessary to identify the various layers of *The Silmarillion* and the points at which specific elements entered into it, or when significant changes took place. For my purposes, it's sufficient to distinguish between those versions of the mythology that pre-date *The Hobbit* (*The Book of Lost Tales*, the 1926 *Sketch of the Mythology*, the *Túrin* Lay) from those that are contemporaneous with its writing (the 1930 *Quenta*, the earliest *Annals of Beleriand*, *The Lay of Leithian*) from those that postdate it, either coming from around the time of its publication (the 1937 *Quenta Silmarillion*, the later *Annals*, the *Lhammas*) or afterwards (the 1951 *Silmarillion*, *The Grey Annals*). And, contrasting the earlier from the later works, one major shift involving an element of the legendarium featured prominently in *The Hobbit* is immediately apparent: Tolkien's treatment of the Dwarves.

Pre-Hobbit

> *dwarf-natured: Mean, avaricious*
> —the *Gnomish Lexicon* [1917]

As Christopher Tolkien observes, with admirable concision and directness, "In the early writings the Dwarves are always portrayed as an evil people" (BLT I, 236). So far as I know, no hint of them appears in the earliest layer of the mythology (1914–1915): the Earendil poems (*The Trumpets of Faerie*) plus the early mythological paintings (e.g. *Tanaqui* and *The Shores of Faery*) included in *The Book of Ishness* (H&S #43 & #44), plus the creation of his first Elvish language (Qenya). But they had clearly emerged by the time of the next layer, represented by *The Book of Lost Tales* (1916–1920) and the advent of Gnomish (circa 1917). The very earliest mentions of them portray very traditional dwarves entirely in accord with what is glimpsed of such beings in old legends of the North. First, there is Mîm the Fatherless, guardian of abandoned dragon-treasure, whose name comes directly from Eddic lore (Mímr the Wise)[3] and who has clear analogues to the Norse Andvari (or, for that matter, Wagner's Alberich), whose curse bedevils all who lay claim to his stolen hoard (cmp. BLT II, 113–114 and the Eldar Edda's *Reginsmál*). Second, an early outline of the Thingol story tells how Gongs (an obscure evil people unrepresented in the later mythology) pillage Linwë's halls (better known to us as Thingol's Menegroth), carry the gold away, and are destroyed by Beren at a river-crossing. Dwarves that dwell nearby dive for the gold but recover only the Silmaril-necklace, which therefore becomes known as "the necklace of the dwarves" (BLT II, 137). Thus, in this earliest version of the Nauglamir story (in which the dwarves play no part in the attack on the elvenking's halls), the analogues to Icelandic legend are much nearer the surface and the borrowings more direct, even to details such as the dwarves' unlikely association with water (a motif soon dropped in Tolkien's developing conception).[4]

Tolkien soon developed this story so that it became the dwarves themselves who had killed the elvenking and sacked his halls (cf. *The Tale of the Nauglafring*; BLT II, 221–251), an event that had such dire ramifications for elf-dwarf relations that its echoes are felt in *The Hobbit* itself, where the quarrel is specifically referred to and is shown as still having an inimical effect centuries later (H 155). And in so doing, he departed from his analogues in real-world myth and ventured into new territory: the personalities and complex knot of motivations and betrayals and battles that make up *The Tale of the Nauglafring* are all Tolkien's own, as is signaled by his shift here into using names from his invented language for these dwarves: Naugladur, lord of the Nauglath of Nogrod, advised by Fangluin the Aged, allied with Bodruith king of the Indrafangs (*or* Longbeards) of Belegost. In the story of how the dwarves went to war with the elves, disastrously for both sides, Tolkien introduces another element original to his mythos: the dwarves as great warriors, whose battles often end in catastrophic losses whether in defeat or victory.[5]

Given the importance of Tolkien's invented languages in inspiring and shaping his legendarium, the glossary of names in the back of *The Book of Lost Tales* is revealing. In addition to learning that the elven word for *dwarf* is *naug* or *naugli* (hence *Nauglafring*, "the Necklace of the Dwarves," and *Naugladur*, "King [of the] Dwarves [of Nogrod]," or simply The Dwarven King), we discover that the elves had a related word, *nauglafel*, which is glossed as "dwarf-natured, i.e. mean, avaricious" (BLT I, 261).[6] It turns out that this gloss as it appears in *The Book of Lost Tales* is somewhat abbreviated; the original, full entry in the *Gnomish Lexicon* (published in *Parma Eldalamberon* Vol. XI) adds a third gloss: *eschrokerdos*, a Greek word meaning "shameful profit" (*Parma* XI 59). Interestingly enough, the more usual form of the word, *eschrokerdia*, is often used in the context of "war profiteering."[7] And neutral, nonbelligerent war-profiteers is just how Tolkien portrays them at the start of *The Tale of the Nauglafring*: we are told that the Dwarves made "swords and coats of mail and other smithyings of exquisite skill in which the Nauglath in those days did great traffic with the free Noldoli, and, 'tis said, with the Orcs and soldiers of Melko also" (BLT II, 224).[8]

This motif of the dwarves as makers of superb weaponry and unmatched armor proved to be enduring within the mythos: even Curufin the Fëanorean carries a dwarf-made knife in the 1930 *Quenta*, and in *The Hobbit* itself one of the items recovered from Thror's treasure is a suit of dwarf-mail made for an elven princeling (suggesting that even the elves believed dwarves made armor better than they did).

Aside from the *Nauglafring*, a necklace so beautiful it improves upon the beauty of the Silmaril set within it, we also learn in *The Lay of the Children of Húrin* [circa 1921–1925; cf. HME III, 3] that the great dragon-helm of Túrin is dwarf-made:

> ... his sire's heirloom,
> o'er-written with runes **by wrights of yore
> in dark dwarfland   in the deeps of time,**
> ere Men to Mithrim   and misty Hithlum
> o'er the world wandered
>   —lines 670b–674a [HME III, 114–115; emphasis mine].

Thus Tolkien combines a thoroughly traditional motif—the dwarves as makers of fabulous treasures (Odin's spear, Freya's necklace) and cursed weapons (Angantyr's *Tyrfing*)—with new thoroughly modern associations all his own (World War I era war profiteers).

So far as the elven tellers of the tales are concerned (and all the Lost Tales are explicitly narrated by individual elves to a human listener, Eriol the Wanderer), the dwarves remain beyond the pale: neutral non-combatant war profiteers selling their goods to elves and orcs alike, who eventually enter the wars of Beleriand on the wrong side. And while it may be unclear from *The Tale of the Nauglafring* whether Ufedhin the renegade Noldoli has been corrupted by contact with the Dwarves or that association is merely outward confirmation of his inner corruption, there can be no doubt that elsewhere association with Dwarves is directly linked to inculcating elves and men with treachery and avarice. Thus in the Túrin lay we are told of Blodrin Bor's son, one of Túrin's men, who sells out and betrays the rest to an Orc-patrol:

> Now tales have told   that **trapped as a child**
> **he was dragged by the Dwarves**   **to their deep mansions,**
> **and in Nogrod nurtured,**   and in nought was like,
> spite blood and birth,   to the blissful Elves.
> —lines 666–669, revised version [HME III, 32; emphasis mine]

The implication is clearly that Blodrin is evil and treacherous, and filled with avarice, *because* he was raised by Dwarves. Through such references, the malign influence of the dwarves spreads beyond their relatively few actual appearances within the tales, and they come to be inextricably linked to malice and treachery (it is perhaps worth noting that in each case in the *Lost Tales* where the Dwarves go to war, they attack suddenly, ambushing their enemy without open declaration of war).

Aside from the episode with the *Nauglafring*, Dwarves mainly appear on the fringes of the stories of what came to be know as the First Age. It seems that they would have featured prominently in one other story, *Gilfanon's Tale*, but that story of "The Awakening of Men" remained unwritten and exists only in a series of shifting outlines. Through these, we can see that the Dwarves were once again to play a villainous role, attacking the people of Palisor (the early legendarium's Eden) as the host of one Fangli, a minion of Melko the Morgoth (BLT I, 236–237). Sometimes we even hear of them fighting alongside goblins, or hiring orc mercenaries and arming them with the best dwarven weaponry. Thus, for the assault against the elvenking

> [Naugladur] gathered about him a great host of the Orcs, and wandering goblins, promising them a good wage, and the pleasure of their Master moreover, and a rich booty at the end; **and all these he armed with his own weapons** [BLT II, 230; emphasis mine].

See also the description of Dior's brief reign:

> those were days of happiness ... for there was peace with Melko and the Dwarves who had but one thought as they plotted against Gondolin [BLT II, 241].

From this it seems clear Tolkien was thinking of having the Dwarves take part in the assault on Turgon's realm as well, though no Dwarven troops appear in the actual *Lost Tales* account of that battle (*The Fall of Gondolin*, BLT II, 144–220), nor have I been able to find any mention of dwarven involvement in succeeding or subsequent accounts of that episode, such as the 1926 *Sketch* or the 1930 *Quenta* (cf. HME IV, 36–37 and 144, respectively).

Thus we see the Dwarves go from bad to worse; in *The Nauglafring* they were at least strongly motivated by the elf-king's cheats and insults, as well as seeking vengeance for Mîm's murder and to reclaim what they see as dwarven treasure. But they can have no such grievance against Gondolin, which has held itself aloof through the centuries of the wars between Melko and the Elves, nor against the newly-awakened Men of Palisor. Indeed, at one point Tolkien refers to them as *Uvanimor*, thus signaling that they belong to a group that includes giants and ogres; the term is elsewhere glossed simply as "monsters" (*Qenya Lexicon*; *Parma* XII 98).

And—as if war profiteering, hiring and arming Orc mercenaries, kidnapping human children, and associations with malice and avarice and treachery were not enough—there is one more remarkable statement about the Dwarves in the early legendarium that paints them in a uniquely unfavorable light. We are told in the *Lost Tales* that the Nauglath are atheists: "they serve not Melko nor Manwë ... and some say that they have not heard of Ilúvatar, or hearing disbelieve" (BLT II, 223). So we see that Christopher Tolkien's characterization of Dwarves as an evil people in the early legendarium is fully borne out by a wide array of texts.

And, in later versions of these texts contemporary with *The Hobbit*'s publication, it gets worse.

Contemporary with The Hobbit

> *"I will give you one piece of advice...:*
> *don't have more to do with dwarves than you can help!*
> *...You'll come to a bad end, if you go with such friends."*
> —Smaug, the Chiefest and Greatest of Calamities,
> [H 205–206]

Such was Tolkien's conception of the Dwarves in the tales predating Mr. Baggins' story. And much of that portrayal is carried over into works contemporary with *The Hobbit*.[9] For example, the idea of dwarves as creators of magnificent armor and weaponry is not just retained but greatly expanded. Thus in *The Lay of Leithian* much is made of "The dwarvish knife of Curufin" (Synopsis V, HME III, 305), with which Beren cut the Silmaril from Morgoth's crown. In *The Tale of Tinúviel* this had been merely a kitchen-knife Beren had snatched up in Telvido's kitchen, and hence its snapping when prying the jewel loose isn't particularly surprising (BLT II, 29 & 33). In the *Lay*, however, its stasis is much enhanced. We are told that Beren took from the defeated Curufin

> ... his knife there gleaming pale,
> hanging sheathless, wrought of steel.
> **No flesh could leeches ever heal**
> **that point had pierced; for long ago**
> **the dwarves had made it,** singing slow
> enchantments, where their hammers fell
> in Nogrod ...
> Iron as tender wood it cleft,
> and sundered mail like woollen weft.
> —lines 3053–3061, Canto x
> [HME III, 264; emphasis mine]

So far as I can tell, the motif of an evil knife that inflicts a wound that never heals enters the legendarium here; the later familiar Morgul knife wielded by the Lord of the Nazgul to inflict on Frodo a wound that never truly heals derives, as a motif within the mythology, from a dwarf-made weapon.[10]

When Beren comes to actually use Curufin's wonderful knife

> The **dwarvish** steel of **cunning** blade
> by **treacherous** smiths of Nogrod made
> snapped; then ringing sharp and clear
> in twain it sprang, and like a spear
> or errant shaft the brow it grazed
> of Morgoth's sleeping head ...
> —ll.4160–4165, Canto XIII [HME III, 303]

The juxtaposition of *dwarvish* and *cunning* and *treacherous* here is clearly deliberate—which is all the more remarkable when we remember that this passage was written in September 1931 or shortly thereafter (HME III, 304), while *The Hobbit* was still being drafted. And the more concise, less expansive 1930 *Quenta* agrees: here when Beren decides to cut a second and third Silmaril free of the crown we are told: "Then **the knife of the treacherous Dwarves** snapped, and the ringing sound of it stirred the sleeping hosts and Morgoth groaned" (HME IV, 113; emphasis mine).

In *The History of* The Hobbit, I wrote that

> The most significant departure in *The Hobbit* from the old mythology of the Silmarillion texts lies in the new story's more or less sympathetic treatment of Durin's Folk ... [T]heir characterization here is totally at variance with what is said and shown of them in the old legends. And the break is both sudden and complete: no intermediate stages prepare the way. For them to be treated sympathetically ... [in] the new story is ... no less surprising than if a company of goblin wolf-riders had ridden up to Bag-End seeking a really first-class burglar [HoH, 76].

Allowing for some exaggeration for effect (the dwarves are unreliable neutrals before they go altogether bad; the goblins are always bad through and through), I nonetheless stand by this. If by 1930 the Dwarves had become less actively malevolent than they had been in the writings of a decade before, they were still sinister and espoused an untenable position as self-proclaimed neutrals in an all-out war between good and evil. Some might see this sudden break in the treatment of the Dwarves between *The Hobbit* and the *Silmarillion* tradition as evidence for the idea that *The Hobbit* was not conceived as taking place in the same fictive universe as the *Silmarillion* tales: they are fish who swim in different oceans. That may seem the case at first glance, until closer scrutiny reveals how Tolkien emphasized the links and continuity between the two. Now that the *History of Middle-earth* series has been published, in hindsight we can see that within *The Hobbit* itself Tolkien refers to his earlier depiction of the Dwarves on at least three separate occasions.

1. Alliances w. Goblins

They [the goblins] did not hate dwarves especially; **in some parts wicked dwarves had even made alliances with them.** But goblins do not care who they caught as long as it was done smart and secret, and the prisoners were not able to defend themselves [HoH, 131; emphasis mine]

To this, in the published text, is added an additional sentence: "**But they had a special grudge against Thorin's people**, because of the [Dwarf-Goblin] war which you have heard mentioned, but which does not come into this tale" (H 59; emphasis mine).[11] Thus we see that the text of *The Hobbit* acknowledges the dwarf-orc alliances described in the older texts, taking pains to include mention of them within the new story, while at the same time distancing Bilbo's dwarven companions from such behavior.

> 2. Dispute w. the Elvenking
>
> They [the wood-elves] did not love dwarves. They had had wars in ancient days with dwarves, and accused them of stealing their treasure (& the dwarves accused them of the same, and of hiring dwarves to shape their gold & silver, and refusing to pay them after!) [HoH, 315].

This is clearly an allusion to *The Tale of the Nauglafring*, as Tolkien himself made clear when in a letter he described this passage as a "**referenc[e] ... to ...** the quarrel of king Thingol, Lúthien's father, with the Dwarves" (*Letters* 346). And again, the published text adds two mentions exempting Thorin's people from this quarrel, saying first that "they [the wood-elves] did not love dwarves, **and thought he [Thorin] was an enemy**" and, of the dispute "All this was well known to every dwarf, though **Thorin's family had had nothing to do with the old quarrel** I have spoken of" (H 155; emphasis mine).[12]

This last statement is all the more remarkable because we have already been told (in *The Hobbit*) that Thorin's people are the Longbeards (H 50), described in the first and second editions of the published book as "one of the two races of dwarves" (*Hobbit*, 1st edition text, 64; cf. *Annotated Hobbit* 98)—the other, unnamed race obviously being the Nauglar—while we have also been told (in the *Silmarillion* texts) that the *Indrafang* or 'Longbeards' most certainly *did* take part—indeed, played a prominent and dishonorable role—in those events. As the 1930 *Quenta* puts it, Nauglir the Gnomes called them, and those who dwelt in Nogrod they called Indrafangs, the Longbeards, because their beards swept the floor before their feet [HME IV, 104].

And, as we've seen *The Tale of the Nauglafring* is explicit that it's a joint force of the Nauglar and Indrafangs (Longbeards), the dwarves of Nogrod and Belegost, who treacherously attack Tinwelint/Thingol's realm (cf. BLT II. 247).[13] So, in the *Silmarillion* text immediately preceding *The Hobbit*—i.e., the 1930 *Quenta*—we are explicitly told the Longbeards took part in the war against the wood-elves. Then in *The Hobbit* itself, in a passage probably written in 1931–32, we are emphatically told that the Longbeards had "nothing to do with" that war. And yet a *Silmarillion* text that immediately follows *The Hobbit*, dating from the time of the book's publication (the *Later Annals* of circa 1937), once again asserts that both the Dwarves of Nogrod and Belegost took part. And the 1937 *Quenta Silmarillion* tells us that these Dwarves of Nogrod are known as the Longbeards, and call their home *Khazad-Dûm* (1937 QS; HME V, 274). Thus both the name by which Thorin identifies his people (the Longbeards) and what becomes the iconic name for their home (*Khazad-dûm*) originate with the Dwarves of Nogrod.

> 3. Decent Enough Folk
>
> There it is: dwarves aren't heroes, but commercial-minded; some are tricky and treacherous and pretty bad lots; some are not, but are decent enough people like Thorin and Co. if not over high-minded [HoH, 505].

The published version of this passage, which corresponds exactly to the First Typescript (Marq. Ms. 1/1/62:1), differs from the draft in replacing "commercial-minded" with "calculating folk with a great idea of the value of money" and "decent enough ... if not over high-minded" with the more comical "decent enough ... if you don't expect too much" (H 196). This description puts a more positive spin on the old concept of Dwarves as neutrals regarding the great events taking place around them, replacing the image of treacherous war-profiteers with warriors-merchants who, if not 'heroes,' at least look after their own—which of course is very much not the case in *The Tale of the Nauglafring*, where an alliance between Dwarven houses ends in internecine war: "the agelong feud between those kindreds of the Dwarves that has spread to many lands and caused many a tale" (BLT II, 235).[14]

In all three of these passages, Tolkien takes pains to distance the dwarves of *The Hobbit*, Durin's folk, from the Nauglath and Indrafang, even while using the same name (the Longbeards) for dwarves on both sides of that divide. And yet the need for such accommodation is only necessary if we take the new story as rising from, and sharing the same background as, the older myths and legends. And it presupposes that we, when first reading *The Hobbit*, are approaching that book from the point of view of a reader familiar with the older *Silmarillion* texts. To most readers, who begin with *The Hobbit*, Thorin's succumbing to the dragon-sickness is a shock; it seems like a trusted and reliable ally has gone mad.

After all, this is the same Thorin who sent Bilbo and Balin, Fili and Kili to safety while risking sudden death himself to organize the rescue of Bofur and Bombur from Smaug's attack (H 200–201), and whose troupe had earlier refused to leave Bombur behind when he fell into enchanted slumber (H 136). This Thorin even spells out, in explicit refutal of Smaug's insinuations about Bilbo's fourteenth share, that he and his fellow dwarves intend to "take our share of the costs" (H 211)—i.e., the expense of conveying Bilbo's treasure back to his distant home will come under the heading of "travelling expenses" as provided for in the original contract (see H 28) and thus not affect Bilbo's share of the "total profits" disproportionately.

But to a reader experiencing Tolkien's stories in the order he'd been writing them (i.e., Tolkien's own perspective when he was writing the story), Thorin's radically shifting behavior once others begin to lay claim to the dragon-hoard he suddenly found himself in possession of after the dragon's departure (with all its echoes of Glorund and Mîm) would seem less a shock and more a reverting to form: this, the elves had written, is how a Longbeard behaves in the presence of dragon-gold.

Post-Hobbit

> The Dwarfs [sic] ... derive their thought and being ... from only one of the Powers... Therefore the works of the Dwarfs have great skill, but small beauty, save where they imitate the arts of the Eldar; and the Dwarfs return to the earth and the stone of the hills of which they were fashioned.
> —1937 *Quenta Silmarillion* [HME V, 273]

We might think that, having evolved a new conception of his dwarves for the purposes of his new story, Tolkien would, in the immediate aftermath of getting that new story accepted and into print, go back and re-cast his earlier portrayals to better match this new conception. Instead, the *Silmarillion* texts continue under their own momentum, with the old conceptions still fully in play. I said earlier that in some ways Tolkien's depiction of the dwarves became even more negative in works dating from around the time of *The Hobbit*'s publication; this trend reached its peak circa 1937, the same year *The Hobbit* (drafted 1930–1932/33, text finalized 1936) was published. Earlier we had learned that Dwarves are atheists (BLT II, 223).

Now it turns out they have good reason for this: Dwarves, this new set of texts reveal, are soul-less. In the words of the *Lhammas*, "Dwarves have no spirit indwelling" (HME V, 178)—unlike Elves and Men, but like the Orcs, they are living but derive their sentience from a single Vala (Aulë and Morgoth, respectively). They are not Children of Ilúvatar (that came later) nor Children of Morgoth (a step up, at least, from their earlier description/depiction/classification as 'uvanimor') but hold an anomalous position. Having no souls, they have no afterlife: as the 1937 *Later Annals* puts it, drawing details from both the *Lhammas* and *Quenta Silmarillion*'s versions of what we may call the 'Dwarven Origins' paragraph together, Dwarves have no spirit indwelling ... and they go back into the stone of the mountains of which they were made [HME V, 129].

Having no afterlife, it's no surprise they show little concern for the Powers: with different fates than Elves or Men, it's no wonder they sought a neutral position in Wars between the Children of Ilúvatar and the minions of Morgoth.

All this is in stark contrast to what is said in *The Hobbit* about the fate of dwarves. The dying Thorin Oakenshield is clear and confident about the afterlife that awaits him:

> **I go now to the halls of waiting** to sit beside my fathers **until the world is renewed** ... I leave now all gold and silver and go where it is of little worth ... I wish to part in friendship with you, and would take back my words and deeds at the Gate [HoH, 679, emphasis mine; cf. H 262].

We might consider that the inclusion in all three versions of the 'Dwarven Origins' paragraph of some such phrase as "it is said" (*QS*), "it is said by some" (*A*), "I ... have heard it said by some" (*Lh*) might mitigate the glaring contradiction between these accounts and that in *The Hobbit* (the only one which comes from a Dwarf), were it not that the 'Dwarven Origins' paragraph is demonstrably wrong on other, related points. All three versions of the latter state that because the Dwarves were created and animated by only one Vala acting alone, therefore "they have skill but not art" (*A*), "the works of the Dwarfs have great skill, but small beauty, save where they imitate the arts of the Eldar" (*QS*), "the Dwarves have skill and craft, but no art, and **they make no poetry**" (*Lh*; emphasis mine). This we know to be false: the whole Thingol quarrel story was predicated on the elvenking's asking the Dwarves to turn his raw treasure into beautiful works of art. And as for "make no poetry," anyone who has ever read *The Hobbit* knows this to be patently untrue: the dwarves sing and play and make music on many occasions (at Bag-End, in Beorn's Hall, even in Smaug's lair).

Take, for example, "Far Over the Misty Mountains Cold" (H 14–16). Not only is the song's very existence refutation of the claim, but the poem contains within itself more evidence not just of the dwarves' skill but of the elves' recognition thereof:

> *For ancient king and elvish lord*
> *There many a gleaming golden hoard*
> *They shaped and wrought, and light they caught*
> *To hide in gems on hilt of sword*
>   —it's only a few stanzas later that we get to the cups and
>   harps the dwarves made "for themselves" (H 15).

Thus we have texts in the *Silmarillion* tradition that clearly lag behind developments elsewhere in Tolkien's legendarium. It was not until 1951, when *The Lord of the Rings* had been completed and the second edition of *The Hobbit* was released, that Tolkien granted the dwarves an afterlife in the *Silmarillion* texts, specifically in the 1951 *Silmarillion* (what would have been the Collins *Silmarillion*, had Milton Waldman's plans not fallen through). Although the actual dramatic account of their creation by Aulë and adoption by Ilúvatar seems to come several years later (in 1958, curiously enough in a draft letter to enquiring reader Rhona Beare; cf. HME XI, 212–213), the Dwarves' fate is now altogether otherwise than stated in the 1937 texts:

> Aforetime the Noldor held that dying they [the Dwarves] returned unto the earth and the stone of which they were made; yet that is not their own belief. For they say that Aulë cares for them and gathers then in Mandos in halls set apart for them,

> and there they wait, not in idleness but in the practice of crafts and the learning of yet deeper lore.... Ilúvatar will hallow them and give them a place among the Children in the End. Then their part shall be to serve Aulë and to aid him in the re-making of Arda after the Last Battle.
>
> —HME XI, 204

This, of course, accords perfectly with Thorin's dying words, written almost twenty years before, aside from the refinement that the dwarves now do not simply sit and wait, but instead busily devote their time to mastering their craft. And since there is no mention of Aulë or the creation of the Dwarves in *The Lord of the Rings* at all,[15] it seems likely that this passage represents Tolkien's development of the original passage in *The Hobbit*—the first place, so far as I have been able to discover, where any description of a dwarven afterlife occurs—to fit the grander tone of the later *Silmarillion* before incorporating it into the larger work. If so, then we have found a prime example of what we're searching for: *The Hobbit* directly influencing *The Silmarillion*.

Also in the 1951 *Silmarillion* appears for the first time the account of Dwarves fighting alongside Elves and Men against the evil of Morgoth: something which would have been unthinkable in the context of the *Lost Tales* or the 1930 *Quenta* or even the 1937 *Quenta Silmarillion*, but which had formed the climax of *The Hobbit*, The Battle of Five Armies. Thus in *The Grey Annals* we read, in the entry for Year 468, that even though Thingol and Nargothrond refused to join his cause, "Maidros had the help of the Naugrim, **both in armed force and** in great store of weapons" (HME XI, 70; emphasis mine). As for the battle itself, described in Year 472 as the *Nírnaeth Arnediad* ("The Battle of Unnumbered Tears"), consider the heroic behavior of the Longbeard's king as he battles alongside his Elven allies:

[Azaghâl's battle against Glaurung]

> Last of all the eastern forces to stand firm were the Enfeng [Longbeards] of Nogrod [>Belegost],[16] and thus won renown... And but for them Glaurung and his brood would have withered all that was left of the Noldor. But the Naugrim made a circle about him when he assailed them, and even his mighty armour was not full proof against the blows of their great axes; and when in his rage he turned and struck down Azaghâl of Belegost and crawled over him, with his last stroke Azaghâl drove a knife into his belly and so wounded him that he fled the field and the beasts of Angband in dismay followed after him ... then the Enfeng raised up the body of Azaghâl and bore it away ... and gave no heed more to their foes; and indeed none dared to stay them [HME XI, 75].

Although it is easy to overlook amid the high drama of the scene, I suspect here we have an unused idea from *The Hobbit* working its way into the *Silmarillion* texts. In two outlines for Mr. Baggins' story, Tolkien sketched out the idea that Bilbo himself would be the dragon-slayer. In the first of these, Plot Notes B, he uses a spear he finds in the hoard (HoH, 364), but in the second, Plot Notes C, he kills the dragon with "his little magic knife," which plunges into the wound and disappears (HoH, 496). In the end Tolkien decided to shift the dragon-slaying in *The Hobbit* to a suitable hero, Bard, but given Tolkien's penchant for internal borrowing ("auto-plagiarism") it may be that the unused idea resurfaced twenty years later and worked its way into this *Silmarillion* text.

And, for anyone today trying to read Tolkien's works in order of their internal chronology, I think this scene should be kept in mind when reading the passage in *The Hobbit* where Thorin and Company "began discussing dragon-slayings historical, dubious, and mythical, and the various sorts of stabs and jabs and undercuts, and the different arts devices and stratagems by which they had been accomplished. The general opinion was that catching a dragon napping was not as easy as it sounded, and the attempts to stick one or prod one asleep was more likely to end in disaster than a bold frontal attack" (H 210). In retrospect, I think we may assume that Azaghâl's battle with Glaurung would not have been forgotten by his descendants and must have weighed heavily in their discussion.

Conclusion

If, as I have argued, the early *Silmarillion* texts had an influence on *The Hobbit*, the extent and significance of that influence will no doubt be the subject of debate for some time to come. In Tolkien's own words, Bilbo's story was "consciously based on ... the 'Silmarillion,' a history of the Elves, to which frequent allusion is made" (HoH, 857). In this paper I have tried to make the case that *The Hobbit* had a demonstrable influence back on the older tale as well. Curiously enough, where we might expect to see part of the legendarium getting into print as having an effect of anchoring portions of the myth, establishing fixed points from which Tolkien could build to stabilize the ever-shifting *Silmarillion* texts (hence my original title for this paper), the exact opposite seems to have been the case. Instead, it bifurcated the legendarium at a number of points: "the Elvenking" became not Thingol appearing in a new story (as he had already appeared in differing roles in the stories of Lúthien, of Túrin, and of the Quarrel), but Thranduil, a parallel figure who plays a similar role in a similar quarrel, but one with an different ending, making him ultimately a distinct character in his own right. The Arkenstone is not revealed as a long-lost Silmaril but remains a silmaril-like gemstone. The dwarves were so transformed that the epitome of their race in the old legend, Mîm the Fatherless, had to be recast as belonging to a non-representative subrace, the petty-dwarves, and a figure like Durin created to fill the role of honored ancient. Such multiplicity enriches the text but also makes Tolkien's task of finishing it ever more difficult, adding yet another to the many challenges he was ultimately unable to overcome.

In the end, *The Hobbit* and *The Silmarillion* are very different expressions of the same mythology, the same 'mythology for England' project that was Tolkien's life's work. To return to my earlier analogy, *The Hobbit* and the *Silmarillion* texts do indeed swim in the same ocean, but occupy different ecological niches within that sea of story, the one in the sunlit shallows, the other in the abyssal deeps. Exploring the connections between these diverse zones gives us insights into the ecosystem as a whole in all its wonderful entangled complexity—"alive at once and in all its parts."

Notes

1. This piece was delivered at the 47th International Congress on Medieval Studies at Kalamazoo in May 2012, and has since been published (in French, tr. Vivien Stocker) as "Un Fragment détaché: Bilbo le Hobbit et le Silmarillion." For the original English text, see http://www.tolkiendil.com/essais/tolkien_1892–2012/john_d_rateliff.

2. This detail is that the Arkenstone magnifies reflected light, so that it shines back more brightly than the original source—a feature in later descriptions of the Silmarils not found in pre–*Hobbit* texts. For the full discussion of the Arkenstone/Silmaril affinity, see "The Arkenstone as Silmaril" (HoH 603–609 & 614–617). Jason Fisher has since (Fisher 2008) pointed out that I failed to take into account images Tolkien drew or painted of the Silmarils in the various badges and family crests (dated by Hammond & Skull to 1960–61; cf. *Artist and Illustrator* [191]) published in *Pictures by Tolkien* (Plate 47); to these should also be added the illustration of the Arkenstone in *The Hobbit* itself (HoH Plate XI), shining brightly from the topmost point of Smaug's pile of treasure. All of these are many-faceted glowing jewels.

3. I should note that Mímir is not named as a dwarf in the Eddas; the linkage between name and dwarf here is Tolkien's own. The original Mímr, an ancient figure about whom little is known, is variously identified as a giant or one of the Æsir, depending on the source (see Dronke p.137). In any case, he had been reduced

to an oracular severed head by the time of the *Voluspa* (stanzas 28 and 45) whose magical well at the roots of the Yggdrasil conveys wisdom and visions on those who drink from it.

    4. Note on the one hand Andvari's living in pike-form in a pool (and Mímir's well, assuming that Tolkien had indeed chosen to re-interpret the latter as a dwarf; cf. the similarity between the dwarf Alvis in *Alvíssmál* and the giant Vafthrúthnir in *Vafthruthnismál*) and on the other the statement that "in crafts and sciences and in the knowledge of the virtues of all things that are in the earth **or under the water** none excel them" (BLT II, 224; emphasis mine). Similarly, according to an entry in the *Gnomish Lexicon* Mim's curse on the Nauglafring is not broken or "appeased" until Elwing "sank ... to the bottom of the sea" (*Gnomish Lexicon* 59).

    A final echo of this conception linking water and dwarves may lay behind the great spring welling up beneath the Lonely Mountain and flowing forth through the Front Gate to become the River Running, and the Gate Stream outside the West-gate of Moria.

    5. Tolkien might have been partly inspired here by Dunsany's story "A Pretty Quarrel" (1919), which tells how the dwarfs go to war against the demi-gods (the immortal but otherwise powerless mixed-race children of gods and human maidens), especially since we are told the dwarfs are "contemptuous of all things savouring of heaven, and of everything that was even partly divine" (Dunsany 32).

    6. In addition to the stated glosses, Andrew Higgins suggests (http://dir.groups.yahoo.com/group/mythsoc/message/24134) that the Qenya root NAQA—("steal, take, get by stealth") and its derivatives *naqa* (steal) and *naqar* (thief) might also be relevant; Jason Fisher, in the same online discussion, drew attention to the later Quenya *nauko* as well (http://dir.groups.yahoo.com/group/mythsoc/message/24135). My thanks to Andrew, Jason, and Pat Wynne (who also participated in this online discussion in February 21–24, 2013) for their elucidation.

    7. I am grateful to Dimitra Fimi for help in transliterating the Greek original and for informing me of its "war profiteering" associations.

    8. I have recently discovered that I am not the first to associate the *Lost Tales* Dwarves with war profiteers: John Garth made this same identification in a section cut from the final draft of his book *Tolkien and the Great War* [2003]. I am grateful to John Garth for sharing the relevant unpublished passage with me.

    9. For example, in the 1930 *Quenta*'s version of the Turin story, we are told of the treacherous Blodrin son of Ban that "**he had lived long with the Dwarves and was of evil heart** and joined Turin for the love of plunder. He loved little the new life in which wounds were more plentiful than booty. **In the end he betrayed** the hiding-places of **Turin to the Orcs** ... " (HME IV, 123; emphasis mine)

Similarly, compare the account in the 1930 *Quenta*

> Skill they had well-nigh to rival that of the Gnomes, but less beauty was in their works, and iron they wrought rather than gold and silver, and mail and weapons were their chief craft [HME IV, 104].

with the cognate passage in *The Tale of the Nauglafring*

> in crafts and sciences ... none excel them ... these creatures Men called 'Dwarves', and say that their crafts and cunning surpass that of the Gnomes in marvellous contrivance, but of a truth there is little beauty in their works of themselves, for in those things of loveliness that they have wrought in ages past ... renegade Gnomes ... have ever had a hand ... swords and coats of mail and other smithyings of exquisite skill [BLT II, 224].

Finally, the 1930 *Quenta* has this to say about The Union of Maidros: "The smithies of Nogrod and Belegost were busy in those days making mail and sword and spear for many armies, and much of the wealth and jewelry of Elves and Men they got into their keeping in that time, though they went not themselves to war. 'For we do not know the rights of this quarrel,' they said, 'and we are friends of neither side—until it hath the mastery'" (HME IV, 116).

    10. The motif of a dwarf-made weapon, superlatively sharp yet cursed, clearly derives from the dwarf-made sword Tyrfing in *Heidrek's Saga*, which is fated to kill a man every time it is drawn (*The Saga of King Heidrek the Wise*, p. 2). Tyrfing had already obviously furnished the inspiration for Turin's black sword Gurtholfin, a similar (but elf-made [cf. BLT II, 83, which describes its forging by the Rodothlim (who later came to be called the people of the hidden city of Nargothrond)] weapon of which it is said "all things died, or man or beast, whom once its edges bit" (BLT II, 108). The elven sword, dwarven knife, and Morgul-blade are all three similar but not quite the same; with Curufin's knife and Morgul-blade making the closer pairing of the group.

    11. The passage about Thorin and his family first appears in the First Typescript version of this passage (Marq. Ms. 1/1/54:5), and thus probably dates from the latter half of 1932. The war in question is, of course, "the dwarf and goblin war" referred to by Elrond (H 49) and more obliquely by Thorin himself (H 24–25).

    12. In full, the typescript for this passage reads "they did not love dwarves and thought he [Thorin] was an enemy. In ancient days they had had wars with some of the dwarves whom they accused of stealing their

treasure. It is only fair to say that the dwarves gave a different account and said that they only took what was their due, for the elf-king had bargained with them to shape his raw gold and silver and had after refused to give them their pay. If the elf-king had a weakness it was for treasure... All this was well known to every dwarf, though Thorin's family had had nothing to do with the old quarrel I have spoken of" (Marq. Ms. 1/1/30:4). Aside from the addition of punctuation and the emendation of "after" to "afterwards," this corresponds exactly to the published text (H 155).

13. Although, confusingly enough, the Indrafang are originally the dwarves of Belegost (BLT II, 230) and the Nauglath the dwarves of Nogrod (ibid., 224–225), whereas in the 1930 *Quenta* (HME IV, 104) and 1937 *Quenta Silmarillion* (HME V, 274) these had been reversed so that the Indrafangs' home is now the tunneled city of Nogrod, "the Dwarf-Mine" (HME V, 274). In *The Lord of the Rings* Tolkien changed this to make the Longbeards or Durin's Folk the Dwarves of Moria or Khazad-Dûm — itself a name originally applied to Nogrod (1937 QS; HME V, 274). Much later (circa 1969) Tolkien gave new names to the Dwarves of the Blue Mountains: the Broadbeams of Belegost and the Firebeards of Nogrod (HME XII, 322).

14. This idea of a great war lasting year after year involving the Dwarves soon disappears from the mythos, but I suspect it inspired the great Dwarf-Goblin war which is mentioned repeatedly in *The Hobbit*.

15. "Concerning the beginning of the Dwarves strange tales are told both by the Eldar and by the Dwarves themselves; but since these things lie far back beyond our days little is said of them here." — *The Lord of the Rings*, Appendix A, part iii: Durin's Folk (*LotR* 1108).

16. Note that here the home of the Enfeng, as the Indrafang have now come to be called, shifts yet again, from Nogrod back to Belegost; see Note 13, above, and Christopher Tolkien's discussion of the shift in *The War of the Jewels* (HME XI, 108). In the published 1977 *Silmarillion*, it is the Dwarves of Nogrod who attack Doriath; we are told that "they asked aid from Belegost, but it was denied them, and the Dwarves of Belegost sought to dissuade them from their purpose; but their counsel was unavailing" (*Silm* 233). Douglas Kane describes this division between the dwarves, with only those of Nogrod taking part in the invasion as "editorial invention" (Kane 216); Christopher Tolkien notes that this motif is based on a suggestion by his father, "proposed rather than stated" (HME XI, 353).

Works Cited

Note: Abbreviations for citations used in the essay follow some entries in brackets.

Anderson, Douglas A. 2002. *The Annotated Hobbit*. rev. ed. Boston and New York: Houghton Mifflin Co.
Dronke, Ursula. 1997. *The Poetic Edda. Volume II: Mythological Poems*. Oxford, Clarendon Press.
Dunsany, Lord. 1919. "A Pretty Quarrel." *Tales of Three Hemispheres*. Boston: John W. Luce. pp 31–35.
Fisher, Jason. 2008. "Visualizing the Silmarils." *Lingwe: The Musing of a Fish*. Blogpost, Monday March 3, 2008. http://lingwe.blogspot.com/2008/03/visualizing-silmarils.html.
Garth, John. 2003. *Tolkien and the Great War: The Threshold of Middle-earth*. London: HarperCollins.
Hammond, Wayne G., and Christina Scull. 1995. *J.R.R. Tolkien: Artist & Illustrator*. Boston and New York: Houghton Mifflin. [H&S]
Kane, Douglas Charles. 2009. *Arda Reconstructed: The Creation of the Published Silmarillion*. Bethlehem, PA: Lehigh University Press.
Rateliff, John D. 2007. *The History of* The Hobbit. *Part One: Mr. Baggins*. London: HarperCollins.
_____. 2007. *The History of* The Hobbit. *Part Two: Return to Bag-End*. London: HarperCollins.
_____. 2011. *The History of* The Hobbit. revised and expanded one-volume edition. London: HarperCollins. [HoH]
_____. 2012. "Un Fragment détaché: *Bilbo le Hobbit* et *le Silmarillion*." tr. Vivien Stocker. *L'Arc et le Heaume: Le Mag de Tolkiendil*. Hors-series, Juillet, pp 45–57. English text available online at http://www.tolkiendil.com/essais/tolkien_1892–2012/john_d_rateliff.
Terry, Patricia, tr., 1990. *Poems of the Elder Edda,* rev. ed. Philadelphia: University of Pennsylvania Press. cf. *Alvíssmál* (90–96), *Reginsmál* (145–151), *Vafthruthnismál* (36–45).
Tolkien, Christopher, ed. and tr. 1960. *The Saga of King Heidrek the Wise*. London: Thomas Nelson and Sons.
Tolkien, J.R.R. 1977. *The Silmarillion*. Ed. Christopher Tolkien. Boston: Houghton Mifflin. [Silm]
_____. 1979. *Pictures by Tolkien*. Ed. Christopher Tolkien. Boston: Houghton Mifflin.
_____. 1981. *Letters of J.R.R. Tolkien*. Ed. Humphrey Carpenter, with the assistance of Christopher Tolkien. Boston: Houghton Mifflin. [*Letters*]
_____. 1984. *The Book of Lost Tales*. Part One. Ed. Christopher Tolkien Boston: Houghton Mifflin. [BLT I]
_____. 1984. *The Book of Lost Tales*. Part Two. Ed. Christopher Tolkien London: George Allen and Unwin. [BLT II]

_____. 1985. *The Lays of Beleriand*. Ed. Christopher Tolkien. London: George Allen and Unwin. [HME III]
_____. 1986. *The Shaping of Middle-earth*. Ed. Christopher Tolkien. London: George Allen and Unwin. [HME IV]
_____. 1987. *The Lost Road and other writings*. Ed. Christopher Tolkien. London: Unwin Hyman. [HME V]
_____. 1991. *The Lord of the Rings*. One-volume ed. Boston: Houghton Mifflin. [LotR]
_____. 1994. *The War of the Jewels*. Ed. Christopher Tolkien. London: HarperCollins.
_____. 1995. *The Gnomish Lexicon*. Ed. Christopher Gilson, Patrick Wynne, Arden R. Smith, and Carl F. Hostetter. *Parma Eldalamberon* XI, pp. 17–76. [XI]
_____. 1996. *The Peoples of Middle-earth*. Ed. Christopher Tolkien. London: HarperCollins.
_____. 2007. *The Hobbit*. Seventieth Anniversary Edition, with a Preface by Christopher Tolkien. Boston and New York: Houghton Mifflin. [H]

From Nauglath to Durin's Folk
The Hobbit and Tolkien's Dwarves

Gerard Hynes

John D. Rateliff has described Tolkien's reinterpretation of his dwarves in *The Hobbit* as the single most significant departure that the work makes from the earlier "Silmarillion" material (Rateliff 76). In *The Book of Lost Tales* (c.1919), the 1926 *Sketch of the Mythology*, and the 1930 *Quenta* Tolkien presented dwarves as treacherous, avaricious, and prone to evil, if not outright monsters. Their depiction in *The Hobbit* as proud, honorable, and ultimately dependable is a remarkable development. Rateliff compares it to having a company of goblin wolf-riders arrive at Bag-End to recruit Bilbo for their venture (76). The change is sudden but it is not a complete re-write of the earlier dwarves. The mostly evil dwarves of the early "Silmarillion" and the mostly good dwarves of *The Hobbit* share a number of essential characteristics: a reputation for craftsmanship, an intimate relationship with treasure, and a tendency to vengefulness when crossed. These characteristics derive mainly from Germanic mythology. Tolkien was also, however, exposed to depictions of dwarves in several nineteenth-century works: William Morris, Andrew Lang, and the Brothers Grimm. Just as Tolkien's elves were created in dialogue with medieval and modern fairy-lore, in all likelihood so too were Tolkien's dwarves. Writing in a tradition, Tolkien had to address both negative and positive depictions of dwarves, drawing on sources which were often ambivalent about them. *The Hobbit* may mark a point where Tolkien began to engage more critically with his sources, presenting dwarves as honorable rather than merely mercenary. This essay will examine Tolkien's construction of "dwarves" as a category in the early "Silmarillion" and the nature and consequences of his reinterpretation of that category in *The Hobbit*. It will trace Tolkien's engagement with sources which present dwarves as evil as well as those which present dwarves as honorable. *The Hobbit*'s dwarves emerged at a particular moment in Tolkien's literary career. To understand them they must be situated in the context of Tolkien's contemporary writings and academic work. *The Hobbit* did not, however, cause an immediate and complete change in Tolkien's depiction of dwarves in his legendarium, and so his reinterpretation of them must be seen as the beginning of a process which would continue throughout his later writings. While a full treatment of Tolkien's engagement with dwarves over the course of his career would be too large an undertaking for this essay, the nature of the effects of *The Hobbit* on Tolkien's dwarves deserves study.

Dwarves make their first appearance in Tolkien's legendarium as villains, indeed undistinguished from the other monsters of the tales. In the early outlines of *Gilfanon's Tale* Melko's servant Fangli is accompanied by "hosts of Nauglath (or Dwarves)" when he occupies Palisor (*Lost Tales I* 236). In the later outlines Fankil, assisted by dwarves and goblins, breeds estrangement between humans and elves (237). The first dwarf to appear as a character is Mîm "the fatherless," the captain of Glorund's guards (*Lost Tales II* 103, 114). Mîm establishes the characteristics of Tolkien's early dwarves: he is "misshapen," enamoured with gold, and seeks vengeance through curses (113).[1] Mîm's curse upon the treasure of the Rodothlin dominates the narrative where dwarves feature most fully: *The Nauglafring*, The Necklace of the Dwarves. In the outline for this tale Tolkien wrote that the elven king Linwë had a great necklace made "by certain Úvanimor (Nautar or Nauglath)" whom he defrauded, leading to his death and the ruin of his kingdom (136). Úvanimor had already been defined as "monsters, giants and ogres" (*Lost Tales I* 75) and were the same agents of Melko who featured in *Gilfanon's Tale* (236). At this stage the dwarves may have been taking on specific qualities as a race but they were still categorized among the monsters.

In *The Nauglafring* the Nauglath, while still ignoble, moved from the category of monster to a position they would long hold: a third party between the Elves and Melko. They are recorded as being ignorant of Ilúvatar, serving neither Melko nor Manwë, and not caring for either elves or humans (*Lost Tales II* 223). Their great skill in crafts is introduced, as is a scientific knowledge of the substances of the earth, yet these early dwarves are characterized by skill without art, technical brilliance but not aesthetic beauty. The cunning of the Nauglath is contrasted with the beauty of the designs of the Noldoli (225). Such beauty as is in their works is attributed to the influence of renegade Gnomes (224). The events of *The Nauglafring* reveal both the skill of dwarven craft and the darkness of dwarven anger. The treasures the dwarves of Nogord make for king Tinwelint are described as "more wondrous far than the scanty vessels and the ornaments that the Rodothlin wrought of old" and the subtlety of the craftsmanship amazes Tinwelint (226). Yet the skill of the dwarves is quickly overshadowed by their vengefulness, when Tinwelint takes the dwarves and their elvish ally Ufedhin captive until they have finished their labour. Deliberately insulting Tinwelint by demanding an outrageous payment, they leave poor, chastised, and bitter. Here their greed for the gold is equaled if not surpassed by their desire for vengeance. To the anger of the Nauglath is added that of the Indrafangs of Belegost, who have learned of Mîm's death at Úrin's hands and the origin of Tinwelint's gold (230). The ruthlessness of the dwarves is then demonstrated through their hiring of Orcish mercenaries, the sacking of Artanor, and the desecration of Tinwelint's body (230–2). The dwarves are less destructive than the Orcs, departing with the treasure while the Orcs stay to burn what is left of the realm, but the return journey to Nogrod reveals another characteristic of these early dwarves: treachery. Bodruith, lord of Belegost, intended to murder both Naugladur and Ufedhin and take the Nauglafring (235).[2] The ensuing battle between the dwarves of Nogrod and the Indrafangs leads to "the agelong feud between those kindreds of the Dwarves that had spread to many lands and caused many a tale" (235). The sack of Artanor may have severed elves and dwarves in feud ever since (230), but in this version of the story dwarves are similarly divided. As the narrator comments, the curse of Mîm came to rest among his own kin early on (235).

The 1926 *Sketch of the Mythology* and the 1930 *Quenta* repeat and emphasize these negative characteristics of the early dwarves. The dwarves enter the *Sketch* "warring" with the sons of Fëanor in the east (*Shaping* 24) and they "plot treachery" against Thingol even without his misuse of Ufedhin as a motive (32). The description of the dwarves in the *Quenta* echoes statements in *The Book of Lost Tales*, adding "they are in many things more like [Morgoth's] people, and little did they love the Gnomes" (103). Their greed is reinforced by a description of their mercantile spirit: "Trade and barter was their chief delight and the winning of wealth of which they made little use" (104).[3] The dwarves profit from arming Maidros' army, thus acquiring much of the wealth of elves and men, though they themselves stay neutral for pragmatic reasons (116). The treachery of the dwarves is reiterated when the snapping of Celegorm's knife against the crown of Morgoth is attributed to its treacherous dwarvish maker (112–3). One other dwarvish characteristic emphasized by these early texts is their secrecy. The narrator of *The Nauglafring* had commented how dwarven faces seldom show what they think (*Lost Tales II* 227). *The Book of Lost Tales*, the *Quenta*, and the *Earliest Annals of Beleriand* all stress the mystery of dwarven origins (*Lost Tales II* 223, *Shaping* 103, 331) and their aloofness from the affairs of elves and humans. From this early material a coherent, and largely negative, image of the dwarves emerges: they are skilled but inartistic, obsessed with treasure, greedy and opportunistic, possess trading partners rather than friends, are secretive about themselves, and ruthless when crossed. Some of these characteristics would prove lasting in Tolkien's dwarves while others, as we shall see, would be modified or overturned.

Two things must be stressed about the dwarves of *The Hobbit*: they are explicitly the same race as the dwarves of the early "Silmarillion," and they are presented in a very different light. The dwarves of *The Hobbit* are specifically connected to the earlier dwarves in three ways. Thorin is a descendant of Durin "father of the fathers of the eldest race of the Dwarves, the Longbeards" (*H*, iii, 50). "Longbeards" is a translation of Indrafang, the name for the dwarves of Belegost (*Lost Tales II* 344). In Goblin-town we are told that goblins do not especially hate dwarves and "in some parts wicked dwarves had even made alliances with them" (*H*, iv, 59). If not a reference to the dwarf-Orc army which sacked Artanor, it at least demonstrates that certain dwarves in the world of *The Hobbit* were capable of such actions. The third point of contact is the reference to the ancient conflict between the dwarves and the wood-elves, where the elves accused the dwarves of theft and the dwarves claimed the elf-king withheld payment when they shaped his gold and silver (*H*, viii, 152). It is unclear whether this is a reference to the events of *The Nauglafring* or a recapitulation of these events in Mirkwood at some later time (Rateliff 413). In either case, it again establishes that the dwarves of *The Hobbit* are the same race and capable of the same actions as those of the earlier tales.

At the same time *The Hobbit* challenges or reinterprets several of the attributes of the dwarves of the "Silmarillion." The notion dwarves have skill but not artistry is called into question almost immediately. In the first chapter they sing and play instruments, practices which are more artistic than practical. Their song does not make a distinction between the skill of their craft and its beauty. The song allows Bilbo an insight into the hearts of dwarves, specifically "the love of beautiful things made by hands" (*H*, i, 15). Thorin recalls how in the glory days of the Kingdom under the Mountain even the poorest dwarf had "leisure to make beautiful things just for the fun of it" and remembers fondly the toy market of Dale as "the wonder of the North" (*H*, i, 22). Much later when Thorin thinks of the Arkenstone he does not dwell on its value but its beauty: "it shone like silver in the firelight, like water in the sun, like snow under the stars, like rain upon the Moon!" (*H*, xii, 208). Fili and Kili's first thoughts when they see the treasure is to celebrate through music (*H*, xiii, 214). On a related note, though Thorin is aware of the value of the hoard, as he touches the treasure his thoughts are on "the labours and sorrows of his race" rather than its material value (H, xv, 237). The dwarves of *The Hobbit* appear both more artistic and more introspective than their earlier counterparts.

Other traits of the dwarves of the "Silmarillion" are carried over but are reinterpreted in various subtle ways. The vengefulness of the dwarves is certainly retained with the goal of their expedition revenge against Smaug (*H*, i, 14–15).[4] The related notion of dwarven curses is still present, though it plays a much smaller role than it did in *The Nauglafring*. The dwarves sat cursing Smaug while he sacked the Lonely Mountain and now they intend to "bring our curses home to Smaug—if we can" (*H*, i, 23).[5] They had already taken vengeance on the goblins of Moria, though they still remember Moria bitterly at the Battle of Five Armies (*H*, xvii, 253), and Thorin gives thought to vengeance on the Necromancer (*H*, i, 25). When the dwarves depart Lake-town the narrator comments: "there is no knowing what a dwarf will not dare and do for revenge and the recovery of his own" (*H*, x, 180). When Bilbo assures Smaug that they had come for revenge, he may be still riddling but he is telling the truth (*H*, xii, 203). Thorin also promises to avenge himself on anyone who withholds the Arkenstone from him (*H*, xvi, 240), marking a clear parallel with Fëanor and his sons and suggesting the ruthless vengeance he is prepared to carry out. Discovering Bilbo's treachery, he was willing to kill him before Gandalf intervened (*H*, xvii, 247). This however is somewhat unusual, as the vengeance of the dwarves in *The Hobbit* is otherwise always presented as justified. Azog murdered Thror, and furthermore was a goblin, while Smaug had no right to the dwarves' treasure, having seized it after devastating two innocent communities. *The Hobbit*, for the most part, stresses the honorable side of the dwarves' eagerness for revenge.

While there are some references to the opportunism and unreliability of dwarves in *The Hobbit*, they are mostly presented as loyal and dependable. Bilbo states, in a moment of anger, "I have been told that dwarves are sometimes politer in word than in deed" (*H*, xvii, 247). During the siege Thorin considers whether he might with Dain's help recapture the Arkenstone and withhold any treasure from Bard (*H*, xvii, 248). The narrator describes the dwarves as "calculating folk" when they demur from accompanying Bilbo down the tunnel to Smaug's lair (*H*, xii, 192), yet the same passage notes that this was the job for which he was hired. The narrator also notes here that the dwarves had put themselves in danger to rescue Bilbo from the trolls when they had only recently met him and had no particular reason to be grateful to him (*H*, xii, 192). Though one unnamed dwarf counseled abandoning Bilbo in the goblin tunnels, we never learn if the dwarves would have gone back to search for him as he was prepared to do for them (*H*, vi, 85). Unlike the dwarven infighting in *The Nauglafring*, the dwarves of *The Hobbit* stick together. Despite the imminent danger from Smaug, Thorin ensures Bilbo and some of the dwarves are safely in the tunnel before rescuing Bombur and Bofur from the valley below (*H*, xii, 196). When the Mountain is under siege the dwarves present a united front despite their disagreements with Thorin (*H*, xv, 239; xvii, 248). Dain and several hundred of his followers respond immediately to Thorin's call for aid (*H*, xv, 233; xvi, 240). The narrator is careful to distinguish the treacherous dwarves known to exist from Thorin's folk who are "decent enough people" (*H*, xii, 192). The dwarves of *The Hobbit* are not inherently unreliable, are very loyal to each other, and only show duplicity when affected by dragon-infected treasure.

Treasure, and the dwarves' relationship with it, defines both Tolkien's early and later dwarves. This is not simply a relationship founded upon greed, though there are admittedly hints at the greed of dwarves. Elrond does not entirely approve of dwarves and their love of gold (*H*, iii, 49) and while they are on the doorstep the narrator comments that they have "a great idea of the value of money" (*H*, xii, 192). Interestingly, however, Tolkien considered having the dwarven relationship to treasure be intrinsically different to that of other peoples. In his plot notes for the final chapter of *The Hobbit*, Tolkien appears to have considered making the dwarves less susceptible to the draw of gold: "dwarves understood better than all others the power of the greed of gold and fear therefore more certainly to extend it" (Rateliff 570). Several of the sentences which mark the onset of the bewilderment of the dwarves were changes in the fair copy to more positive passages in the original manuscript. The statement "when the fire of the heart of a dwarf is kindled by jewel and gold his courage grows" (580) ultimately became "when the heart of a dwarf, even the most respectable, is wakened by gold and by jewels, he grows suddenly bold, and he may become fierce" (*H*, xiii, 214).[6] The comment about Bilbo keeping his head better than the dwarves was altered to read that he had kept his head "more clear of the bewilderment of the hoard" (Rateliff 590 n.18). The dwarves fingering gems with a sigh also entered in the fair copy (590 n.21). The notion that dwarves may be resilient to dragon-sickness in fact goes back to *The Book of Lost Tales*, where Mîm claimed that the treasure of the Rodothlin would bring no good to elves or humans due to the evil of the dragon upon it, "but I, only I, can ward it" (*Lost Tales II* 114). The susceptibility of the dwarves in *The Hobbit* is an innovation and introduces new complications.

The Nauglafring and *The Hobbit* both reach a crisis point when dwarves encounter a treasure. In each text two forces are invoked. In *The Nauglafring* these are the effect of Glorund upon the treasure and the curse of Mîm (*Lost Tales II* 114, 222), and it is Mîm's curse which is given far more prominence. In *The Hobbit* by contrast the two forces are the effect of Smaug upon the treasure and the nature of dwarvish hearts, with the two working in tandem. This distinction alters the dwarves' relationship with treasure and the nature of the destructive influence of treasure. The hoard of the Rodothlin was both tainted and cursed, while the treasure of the Lonely Mountain was tainted but not explicitly cursed.[7] Mîm's curse and Glorund's evil are essentially external forces operating upon Tinwelint and the dwarves of Nogrod, and in the original drafts of *The Hobbit* greed over the dragon's hoard likewise affected Thorin and company from outside in the form of the threat of the besieging armies. The dwarves themselves did not succumb to dragon-sickness in the Second Phase of writing *The Hobbit* (see Rateliff 595).[8] Tolkien's decision in the Third Phase of composition to make the dwarves particularly susceptible to dragon-sickness changed the nature of the threat they faced from external to internal. As well as giving the final chapters of *The Hobbit* a moral complexity not always credited to Tolkien, this decision makes his depiction of the dwarves similarly complicated. Having presented the love of the dwarves for the works of their hands in a positive light in the first chapter, Tolkien then problematized the dwarves' relationship with their own treasure. This complicated relationship with treasure would continue to colour and add subtlety to Tolkien's dwarves for the rest of his writing career. The dwarves of *The Hobbit* emerge as both similar to and distinct from Tolkien's earlier dwarves: they are skilled and artistic, loyal to friends but implacable to foes, vengeful when wronged but generally honorable in their agreements, with a love of treasure which is both fierce and jealous. They are still recognizably dwarves, but the definition of dwarf has altered somewhat from *The Book of Lost Tales*.

The differences between the dwarves of *The Hobbit* and those of the early "Silmarillion," however, lie not just in the characteristics attributed to them but in the means by which information about them is conveyed. The "Silmarillion," at least in the early stages of its development, is from an elvish perspective, while *The Hobbit* is presented through Bilbo's eyes. This in itself makes a difference to the presentation of dwarves in the respective texts. The elvish perspective and bias of the early "Silmarillion" is readily apparent. The *Gnomish Lexicon* glosses *nauglafel* as "dwarf-natured, i.e. mean, avaricious" (*Lost Tales I* 261). To be called "dwarvish" in Gnomish is an insult. In *The Nauglafring* human and elvish accounts of dwarves are briefly contrasted. Men say that the craft and cunning of dwarves surpasses the Gnomes but, according to the Gnomes, the truth is that the beauty of their works derives from the influence of renegade Gnomes (*Lost Tales II* 224). This privileges elvish knowledge of dwarves above the rumored accounts believed by humans, an irony given that one of the dominant features of elvish commentary on dwarves in the early "Silmarillion" is its admitted ignorance. The same narrative voice which corrects human accounts of dwarves acknowledges, in the same paragraph, how strange the elves find the *nauglath* and how no one knows for certain from whence they came (223). The homes of the dwarves, Nogrod and Belegost, are far from the elvish realms. Tellingly, they are off the edge of the earliest "Silmarillion" map (*Shaping* 232). The dwarves are an unknown quantity, an unaligned third block separate from the wars of Melko and the Gnomes. Though the elves may claim the dwarves are in many things more like Morgoth's people than themselves, they are forced to admit that the dwarves are not friends of the Valar, elves, humans, or Morgoth (103). The strangeness of the dwarves is emphasized in the early "Silmarillion." They are not elves but neither can they be placed among the servants of Melko. The elves trade with the dwarves but do not otherwise have much social or cultural interaction with them. The events of *The Nauglafring*, marked from the beginning by dishonesty and bad-faith, are the most extensive elvish-dwarvish interaction of the early texts, and wars are not conducive to cross-cultural understanding. At this stage in the legendarium dwarves are only seen from an external, and usually hostile, perspective.

Where the early "Silmarillion" keeps dwarves at arms' length, *The Hobbit* brings dwarves into the home of our protagonist. The dwarves of *The Hobbit* are not some barely-known enemy but Bilbo's employers, companions, and friends. The narrative may not be written from a dwarvish point of view, but it allows the reader a glimpse of dwarven society from the inside. The dwarves are present in almost every chapter of the book, and from chapter thirteen onwards we get to see dwarves in their ancestral home, albeit soiled by Smaug's habitation. In one regard we do get direct access to dwarven views of the world: we hear their poetry. The mere existence of this poetry contradicts the notion that dwarves have skill but not artistry. Further, it allows us to see dwarven self-expression without the filter of elvish accounts. The content of the poetry is as important as its existence. "Far over the misty mountains cold," among other things, reveals the love of the dwarves for their craft. The emphasis is not on the wealth of the dwarven hoard but the pride the dwarves took in the making of beautiful objects. Interestingly, the dwarves even remember with pride the hoards they shaped for either Tinwelint or the Elven-king of Mirkwood despite the strife which arose: "For ancient king and elvish lord / There many a gleaming golden hoard / They shaped and wrought" (*H*, i, 14). While the elves may view those interactions as disastrous, the dwarves can separate their feelings about their craftsmanship from those for whom they worked. The song also emphasizes that dwarves have a culture and a tradition of art of which humans and elves are entirely ignorant. They carved goblets "for themselves," they made harps where no man has delved, "and many a song / Was sung unheard by men or elves" (*H*, i, 15). While ignorance of the dwarves in the "Silmarillion" reinforced the elvish sense that dwarves are an unknown "other," here the elvish ignorance is mentioned to stress the existence of a dwarven culture which has not previously been acknowledged. Dwarven songs may have gone unheard by humans and elves but this song is heard by Bilbo, a hobbit, demonstrating the possibility of more open relations with dwarves. Bilbo is permitted a glimpse of the heart of dwarves through the song, and so too for the first time are Tolkien's readers.

Of course this is not the only dwarf poetry to which readers of *The Hobbit* are exposed. There is also "The wind was on the withered heath" in Beorn's hall in chapter seven and "Under the Mountain dark and tall" in the Lonely Mountain in chapter fifteen. These poems have the same meter and rhyme scheme as "Far over the misty mountains" and the third song even repeats stanzas from the first, serving to bind the three songs together. All three songs are performed by the dwarves to raise their spirits in preparation for an approaching challenge: embarking on the quest, crossing Mirkwood, or withstanding a siege of the Mountain. The dwarf songs are not vindictive like the goblins', nor seemingly nonsensical like the elves', and they emphasize a distinctive dwarven culture beyond their physical crafts. If one accepts Corey Olsen's reading of the second song, the dwarves are placing their quest in the larger context of the history and fate of Middle-earth (Olsen 141–6). The wind which speeds them on their way to the Lonely Mountain also fans stars to light (*H*, vii, 117), associating the dwarves, however tentatively, with the stars of Varda and with light and hope. This song also places the dwarves in alliance with the natural world rather than merely as those who exploit it for ore. Even the third song, which deliberately leaves out the verses from the first song which mentioned good relations with humans and elves, calls for dwarven solidarity. "Under the Mountain," by drawing the reader's attention back to the song in Bag-End, reminds us that these are the dwarves we have supported so far. It presents the siege of the Mountain in dwarven terms, stressing the wrongs the dwarves have suffered, the legitimacy of Thorin's position, and their need of help from "friend and kin" (*H*, xv, 235–6). Yet this scene also subtly criticizes the dwarves by having Bilbo react quite differently than he did in Bag-End. Where that song revealed love, this song, despite sharing two stanzas, causes his spirits to fall in reaction to its bellicose tone. This, however, is a judgment on the dwarves by their friend, and allows Tolkien's readers to feel critical towards the dwarves from a position of knowledge and familiarity rather than the ignorance and prejudice of the early "Silmarillion."

These developments in both the characteristics of Tolkien's dwarves and the mode of their presentation, may be compared with the depiction of dwarves in Tolkien's literary forebears. These nineteenth-century predecessors in the fantastic mode were often ambivalent in their depiction of dwarves: at best they were ambiguous figures, at worst utterly malevolent. One of the most negative depictions occurs in William Morris' *The Wood Beyond the World* (1895). There the protagonist Golden Walter is occasionally helped and more often opposed by a dwarf in the service of the Lady, an evil enchantress. The dwarf is presented in monstrous terms: "dark brown of hue and hideous, with long arms and ears exceeding great and dog-teeth that stuck out like the fangs of a wild beast" (Morris 6). Every appearance is accompanied by an unflattering adjective. He is called "hideous," "fearful," "monstrous," and "misshapen" (6, 50, 109, 123) and is repeatedly referred to as "the Evil Thing" (123, 144). The dwarf is depicted in non-human or sub-human terms. He moves like a predatory animal, at times on all fours (53), appearing from and disappearing into the landscape (122–3, 144). Like Gollum, the dwarf rejects cooked food and considers roast or boiled meat to be spoiled, preferring it raw and bloody (51). Perhaps most disquietingly, the dwarf is also predatory in his sexual desire. He gibbers and pounds the grass and begins to laugh horribly at the memory of what is under the Maiden's clothes (52). When the dwarf and Walter fight each other the dwarf wounds the Maiden but does not kill her, saying "I need her body alive, that I may wreck me on her" (145). The "big ungainly sax" (148) the dwarf girds himself with reinforces his sexual menace. The dwarf is however loyal to the Lady, whom he considers his maker (52) and seeks vengeance against Walter and the Maiden on her behalf. Morris's dwarf is admittedly something of an outlier in Tolkien's literary predecessors. Despite being called a dwarf, he has few "dwarvish" traits, having little connection to craft, trade, or treasure. He is loathsome but not in the same way as Tolkien's early dwarves.

Andrew Lang's depictions of dwarves are more varied, perhaps necessarily so given the disparate nature of the tales in his *Coloured Fairy Books*. They range from the thoroughly evil to the generally positive and even sympathetic. One of Lang's most evil dwarves is the titular antagonist of "The Yellow Dwarf." Described as "malicious" and a "little monster" (Lang 1889 36), he allies himself with the malevolent Fairy of the Desert and torments princess Bellissima, whom he seeks to forcibly marry. The dwarf goes so far as to murder the princess' lover (49) and the princess can only escape him through a posthumous Ovidian transformation (50). The dwarf of "Shepherd Paul" is almost as wicked. He steals from and beats Paul's companions but is defeated by Paul (Lang 1903 297). When pursued, the dwarf disappears down a hole and Paul discovers that he and his two brothers had abducted and imprisoned maidens (298–302). The dwarf seeks vengeance for his brothers' deaths but is defeated by Paul and the maidens (301–2). Other dwarves in Lang's collections are much more positively depicted. In "The Headless Dwarfs" Hans the bell-ringer abuses the dwarves but finally spares one and when the headless dwarves have their chance to take revenge on him is spared by the dwarf he earlier spared (Lang 1906 285, 291). The dwarf admonishes him: "perhaps you will learn for the future not to despise any creature, however small" (291). "The History of Dwarf Long Nose" balances sympathy for a character who becomes a dwarf with revulsion at the dwarf's appearance. Jem, the son of a grocer, is transformed into a dwarf by an old woman who is revealed to be a fairy (231–2). Nobody recognizes him, with even his mother calling him a "hideous dwarf" and a "monstrosity" (233). The narrator stresses his physical unattractiveness; his huge nose, pigs' eyes, spindly legs and overgrown arms (237) but also the callousness of the people he once knew and the irony that Jem had once gawked at dwarves (232). His transformation proves temporary and he gains a degree of status through his culinary skills (240–1), but the precarious position of dwarves in human society is emphasized. Curiously, one of the more sympathetic of Lang's dwarves appears in a story Tolkien is known to have read with interest: "The Story of Sigurd." There, the theft of Andvari's gold is prominently mentioned. Andvari is repeatedly called "the poor dwarf" (Lang 1907 359, 365) and the reader is reminded more than once that it was Andvari's last ring (359, 363, 365). While Andvari's curse is invoked it is also described as a prayer (359). The dwarves of Lang's *Coloured Fairy Books* vary greatly not only in their morality but in the degree to which they are separate magical beings or merely stunted humans.

The dwarves of the Brothers Grimm are similarly a mixture of the benign and the malevolent. One feature which applies to many, though not all, of Grimm's dwarves is their reciprocal relationship with humanity. When treated well by humans they repay those humans in kind. Conversely, humans who mistreat dwarves may expect to be punished. Examples include "The Water of Life," "The Three Little Gnomes in the Forest," and "The Golden Goose." In each of these tales a set of siblings interact with a dwarf or dwarves and are rewarded or punished according to their actions. In "The Three Little Gnomes in the Forest" a virtuous girl comes upon three dwarves. She behaves politely, shares her food, and sweeps the snow from their door (Grimm 63–4). Her sister by contrast is rude to the dwarves, refuses them her cake, and will not sweep for them. The dwarves repay the girls with parallel rewards. The virtuous sister will become more beautiful, gold will drop from her mouth when she speaks, and she will marry a king (64). Her wicked sister will grow uglier, toads will drop from her mouth, and she will die a miserable death (65). This reciprocity does not, however, hold universally. Honorable behavior towards dwarves may be met with scorn or even hostility as in "Snow White and Rose Red" and "Strong Hans." In the former, the sisters of the title repeatedly come across a dwarf who needs assistance: his beard is caught in a tree or a fishing line or he is attacked by an eagle (641–3). They help him at the cost of cutting his beard and tearing his coat, but the dwarf offers them only imprecations and when they are faced by a bear the dwarf suggests that the bear should eat them (643–4). The girls are rewarded for their helpfulness, as the bear turns out to be both the bear they earlier helped and a prince under the dwarf's enchantment (644). Reciprocity is still validated but it is unrelated to the dwarf. On the other hand wicked dwarves may still be reciprocal. In "The King of the Golden Mountain" a poor merchant revives his fortunes by making a deal with a black dwarf who keeps to the letter of his agreement even when deprived of the merchant's son whom he had originally desired (414–15). Good dwarves are slightly more common in Grimm than evil dwarves, but reciprocal dwarves are considerably more common than non-reciprocal.[9] This reciprocity may be reflected in Tolkien's dwarves, both good and evil, who respond in kind to their treatment. The dwarves of Morris, Lang, and the Grimms are similar in one interesting aspect: they do not share with Tolkien's dwarves an emphasis on craft, trade, and treasure which might be expected from the information about dwarves in Germanic traditions.[10] The dwarves of these nineteenth-century writers are more concerned with abducting human women and testing human youths than with the hoarded treasure which is their focus in Tolkien's writings.

One nineteenth-century author who connects dwarves to smith-craft and treasure while also having a hostile view of them is Richard Wagner. Attempts to connect Wagner to Tolkien have been controversial as can be seen from Vink (2012, 3–15) and MacLachlan (1–27). At the very least it seems possible to say Tolkien took a disapproving interest in Wagner. The dwarves of *Der Ring des Nibelungen* share many characteristics with the dwarves of *The Nauglafring*. They are great craftsmen. Alberich forges the titular ring from the Rhinegold (*Rhinegold* III, 42) and Mime crafts the Tarnhelm which conveys powers of invisibility and metamorphoses (*Rhinegold* III, 40, 50).[11] They are opportunistic and disloyal, both with outsiders and each other. Alberich steals the Rhinegold and with the power of the ring terrorizes the other Nibelungs (*Rhinegold* I, 16; III, 40–1). Mime plans to use Siegfried, his own foster-son, to win the treasure before murdering him in his sleep (*Siegfried* I, iii, 187). They are driven by resentment and vengefulness. Alberich's motive in seizing the gold is revenge against the Rhinemaidens who have scorned him as much as it is desire for power for its own sake (*Rhinegold* I, 16). Mime attempts to win the gold in part to deprive his brother of it, paying Alberich back for tormenting him and taking the Tarnhelm (*Siegfried* I, iii, 188–9). Mime's desire for power arises from a power to make amends for previous humiliation. Perhaps most of all Wagner's dwarves are greedy: for love, for gold, for power. Alberich and Mime struggle viciously over the gold. When Mime offers a compromise, whether in good faith or not, Alberich refuses him even a nail from the hoard (*Siegfried* II, iii, 210). Alberich claims the gold even at the cost of renouncing love (*Rhinegold* I, 16), and Mime is willing to turn on his relatives in order to win the treasure. Of course Wagner intended the desires of Alberich and Mime to be entangled, with the lust for gold not easily separable from the lust for power. In this regard Wagner's dwarves differ from those of the early "Silmarillion" who may desire gold and vengeance but show no interest in political power. Further, all the traits Wagner's dwarves do share with Tolkien's have a common origin in their shared sources. Wagner's negative view of dwarves may have added to the apparently hostile nineteenth-century view of them, thus coloring Tolkien's early views, but the details of Wagner's dwarves were not original to him. It is to medieval dwarf literature we must now turn for Tolkien's, and Wagner's, ultimate sources for dwarf characteristics.

The existence of cognate forms for "dwarf" in almost all the early Germanic languages strongly suggests dwarves derive from very early Germanic mythology: Old English has *dweorh*, Old High German has *twerg*, Old Norse has *dvergr* (Battles 32).[12] As will be seen, Tolkien took most of his dwarf-lore form Norse sources. One reason for this is that dwarves are much more common in Old Norse than in Old English literature. Unlike "*eotenas ond ylfes ond orcneas*" which appear in *Beowulf* (l.112), dwarves only appear in Old English literature in medical or magico-medical texts, apart from glosses. Old English charms advise how to ward off a *dweorg*, but as Battles points out, do not make it clear whether *dweorg* is the name for the agent of the disease, its symptoms, or the disease itself (Battles 33–4). *Metrical Charm*

3, "Against a Dwarf," represents a dwarf threatening to bridle and mount his victim (Dobbie 121–2), perhaps representing an experience akin to "witch-riding." Needless to say, Tolkien's dwarves show little connection to these dwarves. Instead, Tolkien's dwarves in both the early "Silmarillion" and *The Hobbit* are heavily influenced by Norse sources. Tolkien himself directed G.E. Selby to a Norse origin for *The Hobbit*'s dwarves, referring to them as "this rabble of Eddaic-named dwarves out of Völuspá" (*Shadow* 7).[13] The *Poetic Edda* establishes most of the basic features of Norse dwarves. Unlike Tolkien's early reticence about the origins of dwarves, *Völuspá* gives them a creation myth. The Æsir shaped the first dwarves, Mótsognir and Durin, from Brimir's blood. The rest of the dwarves were then made from the earth (*Völuspá* 9–10).[14] This makes the dwarves a distinct race, created before humanity, something Tolkien would take up when he eventually gave them a creation myth in the 1930s. In Mótsognir and Durin they have founding figures, just as Tolkien would later create the seven fathers of the dwarves. The dwarves of *Völuspá* are associated with stone as well as earth. Dvalin's troop "sought from halls of stone [...] Stony-field" "*sótto frá salar steini* [...] *til Iorovalla*" (*Völuspá* 14).[15] When Ragnarök approaches, the dwarves, "lords of the cliff-wall" "*veggbergs vísir*," groan before their stone doors (*Völuspá* 48). The most readily apparent feature of both Norse and Tolkienian dwarves, their craftsmanship, is also apparent in eddic verse. *Grímnismál* alludes to Skiðblaðnir, "best of ships" "*scipa bezt*," made by Ívaldi's sons (*Grímnismál* 43), whom Snorri identifies as dwarves (*Gylfaginning* 43, 36, 17).[16] *För Skírnis* similarly alludes to the ring Draupnir, which drops eight rings of equal weight every ninth night (*För Skírnis* 21) and which Snorri identifies as of dwarven craft (*Skáldskaparmál* 35, 42, 10). The prose preface to *Reginsmál* describes Sigurd's foster father Regin as "more skillful than any man and a dwarf in height" "*hveriom manni hagari, oc dvergr af vǫxt*" (*Reginsmál* prose 1). Regin forges Gram, which can slice through an anvil but is also sharp enough to cut a hair on water (*Reginsmál* 13–14).

Snorri Sturluson drew upon several of the poems of the *Poetic Edda* for his dwarves while also building on them. According to Snorri the dwarves emerged from the flesh of Ymir of their own accord, but were granted human-like shape and understanding by the Æsir (*Gylfaginning* 14, 15, 34–7). Snorri, interestingly, makes a connection between dwarves and elves, associating dwarves with *svartálfar* "black elves." Odin sends Skírnir to Svartálfaheim, the world of the black elves, to find dwarves to forge the fetter Gleipnir (*Gylfaginning* 34, 28, 2–5). Loki, after cutting off Sif's hair, persuades *svartálfar*, identified as the sons of Ívaldi, to make golden hair as a replacement (*Skáldskaparmál* 35, 41, 29–35). Loki steals the gold of the dwarf Andvari from Svartálfaheim to ransom himself, Odin, and Hœnir from Hreiðmar (*Skáldskaparmál* 39, 45, 21–33). Tolkien attempted to disentangle how the light elves, dark elves, and black elves related to each other (see Shippey 2004), but kept a clear distinction between elves and dwarves from his earliest writings.[17] Regarding the skill of dwarves, however, Tolkien and Snorri were in agreement. As well as Skiðblaðnir and Sif's golden hair, Snorri's dwarves forge Odin's spear Gungnir, Frey's golden boar, the ring Draupnir, and Thor's hammer Mjöllnir (*Skáldskaparmál* 35, 42, 18–35). Snorri may also have influenced Tolkien's notion of the vengefulness of dwarves when an agreement is broken. Having lost his head in a wager with the dwarves Brokk and Eitri, Loki argued that his neck was not included in the terms of the wager and so Brokk took his revenge by sewing Loki's mouth shut (*Skáldskaparmál* 35, 43, 4–10). Snorri also provides an account of dwarven deceitfulness when the dwarves Fjalar and Galar murder Kvasir to create the mead of poetry. They lie about his whereabouts and soon murder the giant Gilling and his wife before finally relinquishing the mead of poetry to Gilling's son in exchange for their lives (*Skáldskaparmál* G57, 3, 17–38). Curiously, their greed is not connected to treasure, and indeed Snorri's dwarves are much more likely to forge and exchange magical objects than to hoard them. Just as Gleipnir was forged from impossible things such as the beard of a woman and the sound of a cat (*Gylfaginning* 34, 28, 2–7), the creation of the mead of poetry shows the dwarves to be capable of creating objects which are not only precious but magical. This episode also serves to connect dwarves with poetry, however disreputably, and provides a number of kennings for poetry which involve dwarves, such as dwarves' drink "*dverga drekku*" or dwarves' vessel "*farskost dverga*" (*Skáldskaparmál* G57, 4, 2–3). While Fjalar and Galar are the only openly deceitful dwarves in the *Prose Edda*, Snorri does allude to Andvari's curse upon his stolen treasure and the sword Dáinsleif, forged by dwarves, which kills every time it is drawn (*Skáldskaparmál* 39, 45, 29–30; 50, 72, 18–20).

Dwarvish craft and dwarvish vengeance also play important roles in several Old Norse sagas, the most relevant of which are *The Saga of King Heidrek the Wise* and *Vǫlsunga Saga*. In the former the sword Tyrfing, forged for king Sigrlami by dwarves, is both an exceptional work of craft, guaranteeing victory to its bearer, but also a dangerous and morally troubling object which when drawn cannot be sheathed without taking a life (*Heiðreks Saga*, ch.1, 2). One version of the saga expands on the sword's origins, telling how Svafrlami, son of Sigrlami, captured two dwarves, Dvalin and Durin, and forced them to forge a great sword for him. When they were done Dvalin cursed the sword so that it would take a life every time it is drawn, making Svafrlami commit shameful deeds, and finally bringing about his death (*Heiðreks Saga*, A, I, 66–8). The parallels with the curses of Mîm and the dwarves of Nogrod are apparent. *Vǫlsunga Saga* was even more important to Tolkien. As early as 1911 he praised it as one of the finest of the sagas (Scull and Hammond, i, 23). In the saga Sigurd finds himself fostered by the smith Regin, here not a dwarf, who tells him the story of the otter's ransom. Having killed Hreidmar's son, the Æsir must ransom their lives from Hreidmar by covering the otter pelt with gold. Loki acquires the gold by extorting it from the dwarf Andvari who curses the gold, promising that it will bring death to whoever possesses it. The treasure immediately leads Hreidmar's son Fafnir to kill his father and depart with the hoard, later becoming a dragon lying upon the treasure (*Vǫlsunga Saga*, ch.14, 26). The gold leads directly and indirectly to the deaths of Fafnir and Regin (ch.28, 32; ch.20, 34), Sigurd (ch.32, 59), and Gunnar and Hogni (ch. 39, 71). The latter deaths are mixed up with the tragic relationship of Sigurd and Brynhild but Andvari's gold is a constant presence. From the Norse sources a number of distinctive dwarven characteristics emerge: their position as a species separate from but interacting with humanity and elves, their extraordinary and at times magical craftsmanship, their association with earth and rock and spaces outside human or divine habitation, their willingness to trade and vengefulness when crossed, extending to the use of devastating curses. These are the characteristics of Tolkien's dwarves but more importantly they are the characteristics of the dwarves of both the early "Silmarillion" and *The Hobbit*. The changes between these two texts cannot be attributed to Tolkien consciously embracing or rejecting Norse tradition when he began to write *The Hobbit* in 1930. The Norse connections are there throughout. As Rateliff has noted, the dwarves of *The Hobbit* are more Norse in their nomenclature (Rateliff 79) but this may merely reflect Tolkien's minimal use of his invented languages in that work. The change to a more positive depiction of the dwarves in *The Hobbit* cannot be attributed to Norse influence: Tolkien was engaging with Norse material all along. Norse dwarves are honorable and cunning, wronged and vindictive. A brief look at the chronology of Tolkien's engagement with Old Norse literature in the academic and personal spheres of his life will bear this out.

Tolkien's attention to Old Norse literature began early and continued throughout the period in which he wrote the early "Silmarillion" and *The Hobbit*. He began to teach himself

Old Norse as early as 1907 so as to read the story of Sigurd in the original (Scull and Hammond, i, 13). Having chosen Scandinavian philology as his special subject from 1913 to 1915, he attended W.A. Craigie's lectures on Scandinavian philology, the *Prose Edda*, and *Vǫlsunga Saga* (41, 46, 50, 54) and kept up his Old Norse while in army training by reading it in his free time (72). At Leeds he set up a Viking Club with E.V. Gordon to read sagas and compose verse in languages including Old Norse (118). In 1926 Tolkien founded the Kolbítar to read and translate the Icelandic sagas and eddic poetry (135). By June 1927 the Kolbítar had read the *Prose Edda* and *Vǫlsunga Saga* and were starting *Laxdæla Saga* (141). As well as this recreational involvement with Old Norse literature, Tolkien also lectured on this material through the period. He lectured on Old Norse philology, poetry, and prose every year from 1924 to 1930 (127, 138, 141, 145, 150, 152). In the late 1920s he appears to have taken a special interest in the Volsung material, reading *Vǫlsunga Saga* with the Kolbítar and lecturing on it in 1928 and 1929 (147–8). As the brief discussion of the Volsung material above indicates, however, this would not have exposed him to a fundamentally different account of dwarves than that he knew when writing *The Nauglafring*. Tolkien was again lecturing on Old Norse poetry and *Vǫlsunga Saga* in 1933 (167–8), which could have strengthened the Volsung themes in the latter chapters of *The Hobbit*, but would be too late to intrinsically alter the dwarves of that work. One other point perhaps worth mentioning is that from 1926 to 1930 a string of Icelandic au pairs lived with the Tolkien family, entertaining the Tolkien children with stories about trolls (135). Their knowledge of Icelandic folklore may have fed into the winter reads out of which *The Hobbit* grew but until more material comes to light this must remain speculation. The dwarves of *The Hobbit* may be more explicitly Norse than the dwarves of the early "Silmarillion," but this did not correspond closely to an exposure to new Norse dwarven material. Tolkien had read the *Prose Edda*, which perhaps contains the most information about dwarves, both in the years before writing *The Nauglafring* and in the years immediately preceding *The Hobbit*. The reinterpretation of dwarves in *The Hobbit* must have its source elsewhere.

That said, Tolkien was engaged in a literary endeavor which involved careful attention to Old Norse literature while writing *The Hobbit*, namely *The New Lay of the Volsungs* and *The New Lay of Gudrún*. Christopher Tolkien tentatively dates these poems to the early 1930s, perhaps shortly after the abandonment of *The Lay of Leithian* in late 1931 (*SG* 5). This would make their composition contemporary to that of *The Hobbit*. Although these poems focus on human interactions, and the intervention of Odin, dwarves play a crucial role in driving the plot. Andvari's gold, and implicitly the curse upon it, is central to the events of both Lays. The curse immediately leads to quarrels and murder over the gold (*SG* 103–4). Fafnir warns Sigurd: "my guarded treasure / gleams with evil, / bale it bringeth" (*SG* 110). Once Fafnir and Regin have been killed, Sigurd takes the treasure regardless of its curse and when he places the *ægishjalmar* on his head a shadow tellingly falls about him (*SG* 115). Brynhild discerns a cloud about Sigurd, with their first meeting accompanied by foreshadowing of strife and storm and an acknowledgement of the strength of fate (*SG* 124). The shadow returns when Sigurd rides through the flames on his disastrous second visit to Brynhild (*SG* 149). Though Gram lay between Sigurd and Brynhild, fate also "lay between" them, dividing them and twisting their relationship (*SG* 151). Sigurd's "fate" may be simply the short life expected of Odin's chosen warriors but it is not entirely separable from Andvari's curse. Strikingly, it is Andvari's ring, "old, enchanted," which Sigurd places on Brynhild's hand, providing the locus of the strife to come (*SG* 152, 156). Andvari's treasure also shapes Sigurd's relationship with the Niflungs. Grímhild thinks of marrying off Gudrún advantageously, but also thinks of the hoard (*SG* 133). When Gunnar talks Högni into a plot against

Sigurd, Gunnar stresses Sigurd's oathbreaking and their own independence but lastly, and perhaps most prominently, mastery of the hoard (*SG* 169). After Sigurd and Brynhild's story has ended strife continues, driven by the hoard. Atli is introduced thinking of the treasure (*SG* 254) and Gudrún's tapestry reminds us of Andvari's gold by beginning its narrative with Odin, Loki, and Andvari rather than the lineage of the Völsungs (*SG* 256–8). "Fate" drives Gunnar and Högni to Hunland but the Hunnish threat arises from Atli's desire for the treasure (*SG* 264, 273). In the end Gunnar will give his and Högni's lives to keep the gold (*SG* 294–6) making Andvari's gold, in one way or another, the cause of the deaths of at least seven main characters, as well as all the followers they bring to war. Just as Sigurd's fate cannot be easily separated from the gold, the curse cannot be completely distinguished from the inherent desirability of the treasure. Yet the repeated allusions to Andvari and the balefulness of the treasure keep Andvari's curse ever present behind the action of the Lays.

Despite the prominence of Andvari, the Lays do not shed much light on Tolkien's reinterpretation of dwarves during the writing of *The Hobbit*. Andvari has more in common with Mîm than Thorin. Some sympathy for Andvari is expressed through Hreidmar who describes him being "dragged and plundere" and forced to surrender all his possessions or his life (*SG* 103). The account of the theft in Section I of the Lay is, however, less sympathetic. Andvari does not curse Loki but the ring itself, even though he knows it will come into Sigurd's possession (*SG* 69). Andvari does not care if he is threatening Odin's hope, and that of the world as a whole. The only other dwarf in the Lays is Regin, who is only called a dwarf long after being introduced as the son of a "demon" (*SG* 66, 112, 114). Further, he is only described as a dwarf in scenes surrounding the killing of his brother Fafnir, connecting dwarvishness to vengefulness and kin-strife. Neither Regin nor Andvari support the more positive depiction of dwarves in *The Hobbit*. Their depiction in the Lays is of course determined by the Norse material Tolkien was attempting to disentangle and clarify, and so depends on the attitude towards dwarves in the original Volsung legends. *The Hobbit* and the Lays share certain motifs, principally the slaying of a dragon and the evil influence of a treasure hoard, but they intersect least in their depiction of dwarves. Again the reinterpretation of the dwarves in *The Hobbit* stands out as strange.

One other possible explanation for Tolkien's reinterpretation of the dwarves should be raised, if only to be shown as inadequate. This is the possibility that Tolkien was already connecting his dwarves with the Jewish people and reinterpreted his dwarves out of sympathy for their plight. There are considerable problems with this reading. Tolkien's comments about his dwarves and Jews are quite late. The first appears to be in a 1947 letter to Jennifer Paxman where Tolkien compares dwarves to Jews, and Gypsies, for having their own secret language (quoted in Rateliff 757). The earliest mention of the secret language of the dwarves occurs in *The Lhammas* which can be imprecisely dated to the mid–1930s, and as such postdate the composition of the first draft of *The Hobbit* (Scull and Hammond, i, 172). As John Rateliff points out, there is no reason to believe the dwarves of *The Hobbit* are not using their real names (79). Despite noting the weakness of the connection between dwarves and Jews, Rateliff still suggests Tolkien partially identified dwarves with Jews while writing *The Hobbit*. He bases this upon their enforced exile and diaspora, habitation in enclaves among other peoples, martial capabilities, reputation for craftsmanship, and involvement in money-lending (Rateliff 80). Renée Vink has critiqued the identification of the dwarves of *The Hobbit* with Jews by pointing to Tolkien's assertion to the German publisher Rütten and Loening that Jewishness had no bearing whatsoever on *The Hobbit* (Vink 2013 135). This may simply reflect Tolkien's angry reaction to the judging of literary works on spurious racial grounds, but it also suggests Tolkien had not intended the dwarves to be Jewish. If they were, it would be surprising he did not mention it in his anger. There are also chronological problems with an identification of *The Hobbit*'s dwarves with Jews. The positive reinterpretation of dwarves dates from the earliest drafts, with "Far over the misty mountains" existing in the Bladorthin typescript, that is 1930–1 (Rateliff 36–7). If Tolkien revised his depiction of dwarves in reaction to Anti-Semitism, he was aware of Jewish suffering at an extremely early date, almost three years before the Nazi party came to power and began legal discrimination against German Jews. It is unlikely *The Hobbit* revisions of the "Silmarillion" dwarves had any connection with this identification. Having ruled out exposure to Norse literature, the composition of the new Lays, or his political environment as causes of Tolkien's reinterpretation of his dwarves in *The Hobbit*, it must be admitted that this author at least cannot find a clear cause.

While the cause of Tolkien's reinterpretation of his dwarves may be unclear, their effect upon his larger legendarium was readily apparent, though complicated. The earliest of these effects may be the specific edits Tolkien made to the 1930 *Quenta*. The account of the sons of Fëanor making war upon the dwarves of Nogrod and Belegost was altered to the statement that they "had converse with" the dwarves (*Shaping* 108 n.4). The claim that dwarves had little love for the Gnomes was also bracketed for exclusion (*Shaping* 108 n.6). Christopher Tolkien considers these edits to be late but could not date them precisely (108). The *Later Annals of Beleriand*, from the mid–1930s and so post–*Hobbit*, show both a traditional hostility towards dwarves but also make positive comments clearly indebted to *The Hobbit*. The entry for the year 104 introduces the story of the making of the dwarves by Aulë (*Lost Road* 129) which both reduces the mystery of the dwarves' origins and connects them to the Valar. It is also, however, a problematic creation story involving the partial rebellion of a Vala against the designs of Ilúvatar. This entry in the *Annals* also claims "Dwarves have no spirit indwelling," unlike the Children of Ilúvatar, and upon death return to the stone from which they were formed (129). Tolkien later altered this passage so the dwarves' lack of souls and return to stone become the belief of the Noldor rather than accepted fact (146 n.16). Like the *Later Annals*, the *Quenta Silmarillion*, written before 1937, has an account of the dwarves which is more positive than the pre–*Hobbit* "Silmarillion" but retains a certain ambivalence about them. Here the story of their creation is attributed to the elf Pengolod. While it stresses the positive aspects of Aulë's actions, his yearning for the Children and desire for pupils, Pengolod is also critical of Aulë. He draws a pointed connection with Melkor: "Wherefore the Dwarfs are like the Orcs in this, that they come of the willfulness of one of the Valar" (273). Like the *Annals* Pengolod also reports dwarves returning to stone upon death (273). The revisions to the *Later Annals*, however, introduce the story, of undefined origin, that Aulë cares for the dwarves after death and that Ilúvatar will accept them as Aule's work so they shall not perish utterly (146 n.16). This is clearly a reaction to Thorin's dying words in *The Hobbit* that he goes "to the halls of waiting to sit beside [his] fathers, until the world is renewed" (*H*, xviii, 258). Just as Tolkien clarified dwarvish origins, he also revised their ultimate fate. The notion that Aulë will care for them and Ilúvatar give them life connects them to the Children of Ilúvatar more strongly even than Aulë's making of them. It also further effaces the elvish claim that dwarves are without souls, which Tolkien had started to edit out of these 1930s "Silmarillion" texts. This is a major reinterpretation of dwarves and one which grew directly from *The Hobbit*, proving Tolkien was revising the "Silmarillion" to bring it into line with *The Hobbit* before he had even begun to write *The Lord of the Rings*.

It is to *The Lord of the Rings* we must turn, however, to see the clearest example of the influence of Tolkien's reinterpretation of dwarves upon his legendarium. The depiction of dwarves in *The Lord of the Rings* is even more positive than in *The Hobbit*. This has led

Rebecca Brackmann to claim the latter work marks a break with the former regarding dwarves (91–103).[18] Instead, *The Lord of the Rings* intensifies the feature of *The Hobbit* which primarily allows for a more positive view of dwarves: exposure to dwarvish perspectives. Gimli serves as the most obvious example of this. Just as "Far over the misty mountains" revealed dwarven culture, Gimli's chant "The world was young, the mountains green" imbues Moria with the same nostalgic love the dwarves of *The Hobbit* felt for the Lonely Mountain. Gimli's poem also hints at a past when relations between elves and dwarves were better by mentioning Nargothrond and Gondolin as examples of the fairness of the world in Durin's day: "In Elder Days before the fall / Of mighty kings in Nargothrond / and Gondolin" (*FR*, II, iv, 316). Further, the song is sung in Moria itself, juxtaposing its former glory with its current gloom and creating the sense of loss and longing which makes Tolkien's locations so attractive for so many readers. Gimli's interactions with elves re-establishes the friendship between the two races recorded in his song and on the doors of Moria. Galadriel deliberately recalls those days of better elven-dwarven relations when she meets Gimli by using the Khuzdul names for Mirrowmere, Celebrant, and Moria (*FR*, II, vii, 356). Further, she quotes the stanza of "The world was young, the mountains green"[19] which mentioned Nargothrond and Gondolin but rewords it to refer to Khazad-dûm: "in Elder Days before the fall of mighty kings beneath the stone" (*FR*, II, vii, 356). Between them Gimli and Galadriel counter the legacy of mistrust and hostility between elf and dwarf by asserting the other side of elf-dwarf history, a memory of cooperation and mutual understanding. This is further than Tolkien went in *The Hobbit*, but it directly builds upon his use of dwarf poetry to reveal dwarf culture and suggest alternatives to the hostile accounts of dwarves in some elvish histories. Gimli's greatest moment as representative of dwarven kind is, however, almost certainly his description of the Glittering Caves of Aglarond (*TT*, III, viii, 547–8). Here we are exposed to the outpouring of dwarven love, not just for precious things or the work of their hands, but for the beauty of the fabric of the earth. It is specifically a love without possessiveness. Gimli stresses how dwarves would disregard the value of the gems and minerals of the caves if only they could behold their beauty. Just as "Far over the misty mountains" revealed the jealous love of the dwarves, this paean to the Glittering Caves reveals the selfless love of which they are capable. It is the dwarven viewpoint introduced in *The Hobbit* taken to its furthest development.

The Lord of the Rings was, however, by no means Tolkien's last engagement with dwarves. As with the 1930s "Silmarillion" material, the post–*Lord of the Rings* "Silmarillion" shows the influence of *The Hobbit* but does not make dwarves uncomplicated or entirely virtuous. One topic in the later "Silmarillion" which must be briefly touched upon here is the Petty-dwarves. The Nibin-Noeg are a relatively late development. The first probable mention of them is the reference in *The Wanderings of Húrin* (c.1958) to Mîm being "of a different race" (*Jewels* 255). In the essay *Quendi and Eldar* (1959–60) we are told the Petty-dwarves were hunted as animals by the elves and despised by the "great Dwarves" who had expelled them for being "deformed or undersized, or slothful or rebellious" (*Jewels* 389). *The Shibboleth of Fëanor* (c.1968) reports how the great dwarves expelled the Petty-dwarves from Nargothrond at the behest of Finrod (*Peoples* 352). The only Petty-dwarf to receive full characterization is Mîm, who had existed since *The Book of Lost Tales* but found his role greatly enlarged in the *Narn i Chîn Húrin* (1950s). Mîm possesses all the worst characteristics associated with dwarves: he is greedy, vengeful, and disloyal. He risks his life rather than part with some of his gold (*UT* 126–7), betrays the location of the outlaws' refuge to Orcs, and attempts to kill Beleg when he finds him wounded (*S* 245). In the fuller account of Mîm's betrayal in *The Children of Húrin* we are told that in one version of the story Mîm deliberately sought out the Orcs, and gloated over Beleg while sharpening his knife (*CH* 148, 150). Yet

Mîm is not without redeeming features. We are shown his grief over his son Khîm and he reacts to Túrin's magnanimity with respect and growing friendship (*UT* 131, 195). His resentment towards all outsiders, especially elves, is the legacy of dispossession and persecution. Mîm may be a villain but he is a developed and complicated villain.

It may be tempting to say Tolkien's "Silmarillion" dwarves bifurcated in the wake of *The Hobbit* into the good "great dwarves," such as Azaghâl lord of Belegost (*S* 229), and the evil Petty-dwarves, represented by Mîm. The reality is more complicated. Tolkien's suggestions that the great dwarves persecuted the Petty-dwarves serve to make his great dwarves more ambiguous and his Petty-dwarves more sympathetic. One could see it as a return to the dwarves of Nogrod and Belegost fighting over the spoils of Artanor but it differs in being more morally ambivalent. Rather than being a struggle over gold it reflects tensions and prejudices within dwarven societies themselves. Even when Tolkien's late dwarves are morally reprehensible they are more complicated than the villains of the early "Silmarillion." However distasteful Mîm is, even he is given a certain tragic nobility as the last of his race, lingering on in the empty halls of his forefathers, mourning his son.

* * *

Tolkien's dwarves retained an essential unity throughout his career: their skill and craft, their love of treasure, their wrath when wronged. *The Hobbit* however marked a noticeable and important change in their presentation. Tolkien's dwarves were originally as villainous as many of the dwarves of his nineteenth-century predecessors but were much closer to the dwarves of Norse mythology in their characteristics. They retained and in some ways strengthened this connection with the dwarves of Norse literature in *The Hobbit*. Yet Tolkien also found innovative ways to make his dwarves relatable and admirable. The causes of this reinterpretation whether personal, academic, or literary remain obscure but the change is noteworthy. Tolkien's reinterpretation of his dwarves began a process that continued throughout his later writings, having lasting effects on *The Lord of the Rings* and the later "Silmarillion." He returned to them in the story of their creation by Aulë, in "Durin's Folk" in Appendix A of *The Lord of the Rings*, in the introduction of Azaghâl's heroism to the "Silmarillion," and in his late essays. Exploring the reinterpretation of dwarves throughout his works sheds light on Tolkien's interests, techniques, and development as a writer.

Notes

1. Compare Tolkien's poem "Iúmonna Gold Galdre Bewunden" (1922), which recapitulates much of the detail of Mîm (Anderson 335–7).
2. Elves, principally Ufedhin, are however equally capable of greed and treachery in this tale. Also the dwarves of Nogrod prove loyal to Ufedhin when Thingol seizes him.
3. Blodrin, a renegade Gnome, who joined Túrin's band in search of plunder, had lived long with the dwarves (*Shaping* 123).
4. Admittedly their focus is equally on their treasure but depriving Smaug of the treasure would be revenge for the wrongs he did them (*H*, i, 23).
5. There is also the dwarven curse inscribed on the great cup visible in the foreground of "Conversations with Smaug" (Rateliff 602–3). Cf. the spells the dwarves place on the troll treasure (*H*, II, 41).
6. See (Rateliff 588 n.14) for the intermediate stages.
7. There is the curse of Thror and Thrain engraved on the cup but this is never invoked.
8. See (Rateliff xx) for the dates of the phases of composition.
9. The numbers are by my count: five good dwarves to four bad dwarves, with six being reciprocal and three non-reciprocal.
10. Wilhelm Grimm edited "Snow White" to connect the dwarves more closely with mining and smithcraft (see Battles 69).

11. References are to act, scene, and page in the Porter edition.
12. The Gothic form would be *dvairgs* (Battles 32 n.8).
13. As John Rateliff has pointed out, Tolkien in fact took the dwarves' names from the *Prose Edda* as well as the *Poetic Edda* (Rateliff 866–8).
14. All references to eddic poems are to the Neckel-Kuhn edition.
15. Save for editions which provide parallel translations, all translations from Old Norse are my own.
16. References are to chapter, page, and line number.
17. The dark elf Eöl is associated with dwarves (*S* 101) and so may gesture towards the confusion in Snorri.
18. Brackmann's claim that Tolkien revised his depiction of the dwarves to counter the Anti-Semitism of *The Hobbit* has been convincingly refuted by Vink (2013).
19. Demonstrating her knowledge of dwarf poetry or possible the song's composite elven-dwarvish authorship.

Works Cited

The Anglo-Saxon Minor Poems. 1942. Dobbie, E.V.K., ed. ASPR 6. New York: Columbia University Press.
Battles, Paul. 2005. "Dwarfs in Germanic Literature: *Deutsche Mythologie* or Grimm's Myths?" In Tom Shippey, ed. *The Shadow-Walkers: Jacob Grimm's Mythology of the Monstrous*. Turnhout: Brepols, 29–82.
Brackmann, Rebecca. 2010. "Dwarves Are Not Heroes: Anti-Semitism and the Dwarves in J.R.R. Tolkien's Writing." *Mythlore* 28:3/4 (Spring-Summer): 85–106.
Edda: Die Lieder Des Codex Regius, rev. Hans Kuhn, 2 vols. 1962. Neckel, Gustav, ed. Heidelberg: Carl Winter, Universitätsverlag.
Grimm, Brothers. 2007. *The Complete Fairy Tales*. Ed. Jack Zipes. London: Vintage.
Klaeber's Beowulf and the Fight at Finnsburgh, 4th ed. 2008. R.D. Fulk, Robert E. Bjork and John D. Niles, eds. Toronto: University of Toronto Press.
Lang, Andrew, ed. 1889. *The Blue Fairy Book*. London: Longmans, Green.
_____. 1903. *The Crimson Fairy Book*. London: Longmans, Green.
_____. 1906. *The Violet Fairy Book*. London: Longmans, Green.
_____. 1907. *The Red Fairy Book*. London: Longmans, Green.
MacLachlan, Christopher. 2012. *Tolkien and Wagner: The Ring and Der Ring*. Zurich and Jena: Walking Tree.
Morris, William. 1969. *The Wood Beyond the World*. New York: Ballantine.
Olsen, Corey. 2012. *Exploring J.R.R. Tolkien's* The Hobbit. Boston: Houghton Mifflin.
Rateliff, John D. 2007. *The History of* The Hobbit*: Part One, Mr. Baggins*. London: HarperCollins.
_____. 2007. *The History of* The Hobbit*: Part Two, Return to Bag-End*. London: HarperCollins.
Saga Heiðreks Konungs ins Vitra: The Saga of Kind Heidrek the Wise. 1960. Christopher Tolkien, ed. London: Nelson.
The Saga of the Volsungs. 1965. R.G. Finch, ed. London: Nelson.
Scull, Christina, and Wayne G. Hammond. 2006. *The J.R.R. Tolkien Companion and Guide, Vol. 1: Chronology; Vol. 2: Reader's Guide*. London: HarperCollins.
Shippey, Tom. 2004. "Light-elves, Dark-elves, and Others: Tolkien's Elvish Problem." *Tolkien Studies* 1: 1–15.
Snorri Sturluson. 2005. *Edda: Prologue and Gylfaginning*. Ed. Anthony Faulkes, 2nd ed. London: Viking Society for Northern Research.
_____. 1998. *Skáldskaparmál*. Ed. Anthony Faulkes, 2 vols. London: Viking Society for Northern Research.
Tolkien, J.R.R. 1997. *The Hobbit: Or There and Back Again*. Boston: Houghton Mifflin.
_____. 1998. *Unfinished Tales of Númenor and Middle-earth*. Ed. Christopher Tolkien. London: HarperCollins.
_____. 1999. *The Silmarillion*. Ed. Christopher Tolkien. London: HarperCollins.
_____. 2002. *The Annotated Hobbit*, rev. ed. Ed. Douglas A. Anderson. London: HarperCollins.
_____. 2002. *The Book of Lost Tales, Part One*. Ed. Christopher Tolkien. London: HarperCollins.
_____. 2002. *The Book of Lost Tales, Part Two*. Ed. Christopher Tolkien. London: HarperCollins.
_____. 2002. *The Lost Road and Other Writings*. Ed. Christopher Tolkien. London: HarperCollins.
_____. 2002. *The Peoples of Middle-earth*. Ed. Christopher Tolkien. London: HarperCollins.
_____. 2002. *The Return of the Shadow*. Ed. Christopher Tolkien. London: HarperCollins.
_____. 2002. *The Shaping of Middle-earth*. Ed. Christopher Tolkien. London: HarperCollins.
_____. 2002. *The War of the Jewels*. Ed. Christopher Tolkien. London: HarperCollins.
_____. 2004. *The Lord of the Rings*. 50th Anniversary Ed. London: HarperCollins.

_____. 2007. *Narn i Chîn Húrin: The Tale of the Children of Húrin*. Ed. Christopher Tolkien. London: HarperCollins.
_____. 2009. *The Legend of Sigurd and Gudrún*. Ed. Christopher Tolkien. London: HarperCollins.
Vink, Renée. 2013. "'Jewish Dwarves': Tolkien and Anti-Semitic Stereotyping." *Tolkien Studies* 10: 123–45.
_____. 2012. *Wagner and Tolkien: Mythmakers*. Zurich and Jena: Walking Tree.
Wagner, Richard. 1977. *The Ring of the Nibelung*. Ed. and trans. Andrew Porter. London: Faber, 1977.

Part II
Durin's Day

"It passes our skill in these days"
Primary World Influences on the Evolution of Durin's Day

KRISTINE LARSEN

Introduction

It is well known that J.R.R. Tolkien incorporates a great deal of astronomy into his Middle-Earth novels. From inventing constellations to utilizing a detailed lunar chronology to coordinate the parallel adventures of the main characters in *The Lord of the Rings*, Tolkien displays his astronomical knowledge throughout his writings, and expects a reasonable astronomical literacy from his readers in return. The astronomy of *The Hobbit* focuses on the moon's phases, more particularly the observation and cycles of such phases. On Midsummer's Eve, the elvish Lord Elrond of Rivendell holds up the dwarf lord Thorin Oakenshield's heirloom map, and when the light of a "broad silver crescent" moon (several days after new moon) passes through it, once-invisible letters are seen (Tolkien, 2007, 2). These "moon-letters" are special runes that can only be seen when the light of a moon of the same phase and time of year as the moment of their writing passes through them (Tolkien, 2007, 3). The runes reveal that a secret keyhole will be revealed in the side of the Lonely Mountain if the map's reader stands by a "grey stone when the thrush knocks" at the exact moment that the penultimate ray of the setting sun on Durin's Day shines upon the rock (Tolkien, 2007, 4). Thorin is alarmed that he and his companions will fail in their quest to enter Erebor, because he admits that "it passes beyond our skill in these days" to calculate the timing of Durin's Day, as the dwarves' New Year is termed when it is not merely the "first day of the last moon of Autumn," but in addition the sun and moon are visible together in the sky (Tolkien, 2007, 4).

Both Tolkien scholars and astronomers have shown considerable interest in various aspects of Durin's Day, including attempts to determine a definitive primary world calendar date for the opening of the secret door to Erebor[1] and lesson plans that use *The Hobbit* to interest children (and teachers) in observing a very young crescent moon (Larsen, 2012). This essay posits that the evolution of Durin's Day in the drafting of *The Hobbit* reflects in part Tolkien's interest in and knowledge of basic astronomical principles, cultural astronomy, and (conjecturally) astronomical references and debates of the time in British scientific and literary circles as well as in the academic culture of Oxford.

Tolkien, Astronomy, and Scientific Debate

As noted in his famous essay "On Fairy-stories," Tolkien's childhood interests include "history, astronomy, botany, grammar, and etymology" (Flieger and Anderson, 2002, 56).

Tolkien clearly draws upon all of these interests in his role of subcreator, and is one of the reasons that it is possible for readers to become so deeply immersed in his secondary world. Quiñonez and Raggett report that Priscilla Tolkien confirmed that her father had "a great interest in astronomy" and that he "had enough interest in and knowledge of astronomy to use it convincingly and to lend believability to his stories" (Quiñonez and Raggett, 1990, 5). It is therefore no wonder that numerous scholars have written about Tolkien's use of diverse astronomical concepts in his writings, and have found that many of these astronomical references to the night sky are fairly accurate. For example, in the chapter "Three Is Company" of *The Fellowship of the Ring*, Tolkien gives an accurate, detailed description of the rising of the constellations Taurus and Orion on a late evening in September (Tolkien, 1993a, 91), while in his unfinished poem "The Lay of Leithian" he uses the seasonal appearance of the Big Dipper in the sky in an equally masterful manner (Larsen, 2013). In *The Silmarillion* the planet Venus is depicted as Eärendil sailing the heavens in his Valar-enhanced ship with a silmaril on his brow, instead of an earth-sized rock and iron planet. However, the apparent motions of Venus as Morning Star and Evening Star are faithfully represented by Tolkien, despite the mythological flourish (Tolkien, 2001, 250).

Tolkien's ability to take astronomical observations and turn them into beautiful astromythology is one of the hallmarks of his legendarium. In doing so, Tolkien remains faithful to the appearance of the night sky while simultaneously crafting a romantic mythology to explain both ordinary (e.g., the constellations and lunar phases) and extraordinary (such as aurora and eclipses) events seen in the heavens (Larsen, 2008). Perhaps the best known example is the tale of how the sun and moon are created from the final fruit and flower of the Two Trees of Valinor. While this creation myth clearly takes serious poetic license with astronomical fact, it does provide a reasonable mythological explanation for a number of observables, such as the relative motions of the sun and moon, lunar phases, and eclipses (Tolkien, 2001, 100–2). In the end, Tolkien himself was troubled with the license he had taken in the creation mythology scattered throughout *The Silmarillion*, especially what he calls the "astronomically absurd business of the making of the Sun and Moon" and in the 1940s and 1950s experiments with alternative mythologies that are more clearly aligned with the known universe (Tolkien, 1993b, 370). The timing of these attempted revisions is important, being concurrent with the writing and completion of *The Lord of the Rings*. During this period, Tolkien was concerned with aligning his earlier writings with the universe of *The Lord of the Rings*, and as Christopher Tolkien explains, was faced with the increasing realization that the "cosmos of the old myth was no longer valid"(Tolkien, 1993b, 369). His first foray into rewriting the old mythology is an alternate creation myth written in the mid–1940s and denoted as "Ainulindalë C*" by Christopher Tolkien (Tolkien, 1993b, 39–44). In this revised myth, as well as other uncompleted experiments published in the "Myths Transformed" section of *Morgoth's Ring*, Tolkien has the sun as coeval with the earth, and attempts to find an explanation for the creation of the moon that fits within the struggles between Melkor and the other Valar (Tolkien, 1993b, 375–385).

While Tolkien never incorporates any of these new mythologies into the legendarium—what his son refers to as a "radical—one might say a devastating—change in the cosmology (Tolkien 1993b, 3)—it is interesting to note that these experimental astromyths align quite closely with the main scientific hypotheses for the creation of the moon that were popular in Tolkien's day (Larsen, 2008a). This is not the only example of Tolkien appearing to integrate the astronomical debate and hypotheses of his time into his tales. Elsewhere I argue that Tolkien's inclusion of a meteoritic origin for the cursed sword Anglachel in revisions to the tale dating to circa 1930 may have been motivated by a series of well-publicized discoveries and observations concerning meteorite impacts in the late 1920s (Larsen, 2006). Scull and Hammond note an incident in the December 21, 1927, Father Christmas letter in which the moon is seen "going out" when the Man in the Moon falls asleep during a visit to Father Christmas (Tolkien 2004, 22). They argue that this is "surely a reference to the lunar eclipse that occurred on 8 December" (Scull and Hammond, 2006, 143). A NASA map of the event demonstrates that the moon was nearly totally in eclipse when the moon rose that night, certainly a sight that would have impressed Tolkien and his children (Espanek, 2009).

In the same letter, Father Christmas explains that the North Pole is quite dark due to an absence of the Northern Lights (aurora). To compensate, Father Christmas notes that he has "hired a comet to do my packing by"(Tolkien, 2004, 21). Comets were certainly in the press in 1927, with nine discovered and announced between January and November of that year (Van Biesbroek, 1927, 586). One of these, Comet Skellerup-Maristany, had been discovered with the unaided eye in November and actually became so bright that it was seen during broad daylight (Bortle, 1998). While the comet was mainly a Southern Hemisphere object, it was widely publicized across the globe. Another 1927 comet, Pons-Winnecke, "aroused considerable scientific and popular interest" (Leuschner, 1927, 275) when it passed three and a half million miles from earth, making it the seventh closest recorded passage by a comet, at the time the sixth closest ("Closest Approaches, n.d.). Father Christmas hired the comet due to a lack of aurora; in the previous year's letter, Father Christmas explains that North Polar Bear has mischievously set off two years' worth of aurora in one display, and hence they will have no aurora until 1928 (Tolkien, 2004, 16). Tolkien's reference to uncharacteristically high aurora activity in 1926 may very well be a reference to the unusually high solar activity in 1926 that resulted in numerous wire service interruptions and spectacular auroral displays (Odenwald, n.d.). For example, on March 9 a red aurora seen in Salzburg, Austria, was so vivid that the fire department was summoned to put out what residents believed to be flames engulfing the city ("Salzburg Calls," 1926, 1). The same display was visible in London, and dubbed "The Great Crimson Aurora" (1926, 373).

Astronomy is also not the only science whose hypotheses and public debates find their way into Middle-earth. For example, Gerald Hynes (2012) explores Tolkien's understanding and use of geological concepts in his writings circa the 1930s and earlier, and finds evidence that Tolkien was influenced by the then new and somewhat controversial continental drift hypothesis. Therefore considerable evidence exists to suggest that it is normal for Tolkien to incorporate current day astronomical observations and scientific debates into his writings, including circa 1930, the year he began work on *The Hobbit*.

The Evolution of Durin's Day

John Rateliff makes the case in *The History of* The Hobbit that the work was written between the summer of 1930 and January 1933, and was primarily worked on during vacations between Oxford terms. Rateliff (2007a, viii–xx) names the various periods of prepublication writing the First, Second, and Third Phases. Hunnewell (1999, 6) refers to the evolution of the concept of Durin's Day in the work as "Tolkienesque as he starts with a simple idea and makes it more complex with each draft." In the first section of the First Phase, called the "Pryftan Fragment," the moon-letters on Thorin's map refer to the keyhole being illuminated by the "rising sun [will] at the moment of dawn on Durin's Day" (Rateliff, 2007a, 22). This is later crossed out and replaced with the "setting sun on the last light of Durin's Day"(Rateliff, 2007a, 23), a change that is necessitated, as Hunnewell (1999, 7) points out, because the secret entrance is on the west side of Erebor from the earliest drafts. In the Second Phase, the moon-letters say that the keyhole will be illuminated by "the [rising] setting sun on the last light of Durin's Day." It is explained for the first time exactly what Durin's Day is; Gandalf notes that the dwarves' New Year is "the day of the first moon of autumn," and that Durin's Day is the "day when the first moon of autumn and the sun are in the sky together"(Rateliff, 2007a, 116). There is no suggestion in this first iteration that this event is difficult to predict. The Third Phase begins with Tolkien producing the so-called First Typescript, starting with the first twelve chapters of the work, and therefore including all the references to Durin's Day (in Chapters III and XI). At some point during this period Tolkien shifts Durin's Day from the first to last moon of autumn, which introduced a series of difficulties in the chronology of the tale by compressing the timeline of the last few chapters. That Tolkien decides on this change by December 1932–January 1933 is clear because this winter timeline is referred to in the later chapters (which are first written in this Third Phase).[2] Along with the change of the timing of Durin's Day from the beginning to end of autumn, there is another significant addition that appears in the work as published, the declaration from Thorin that "it passes our skill in these days to guess when such a time will come again" (Tolkien, 2007, 51).

While the drafts provide an interesting behind-the-scenes view of the changes Tolkien makes in the story, in the case of Durin's Day we initially appear to be left with more questions than answers. These include:

1. Why did Tolkien include an observation of the moon in his definition of Durin's Day?
2. Why was the Dwarves' New Year initially in early autumn?
3. Why was it changed to late autumn?
4. Why did he feel the need to specifically add that it was so difficult to calculate that the exiles from Erebor were no longer able to do so?
5. Is Durin's Day as literally described in the text even astronomically possible?

As will be shown, several of these questions are closely related, and while a number of these questions have logical answers, in at least one case (question 3) there may be insufficient evidence to do more than openly speculate.

Lunar and Luni-Solar Calendars

In the published *Hobbit* (Tolkien, 2007, 51) we are told that the dwarves' New Year falls on "the first day of the last moon of Autumn." This fact tells us that the dwarves' calendar is based on the phases of the moon, specifically on observing the newborn crescent moon (the first day of the moon's cycle). The use of the moon's phases to keep track of the passage of time is perhaps the oldest system used by humans, possibly dating back to the Paleolithic (McCluskey, 2000, 17). These changes in the moon's appearance are obvious to the unaided eye, and follow a relatively regular pattern of (on average) about 29.5 days. There are, however, a number of problems with using a strictly lunar calendar. Firstly, this period is not a whole number of 24 hours days, so the length of a lunar month needs to vary between 29 and 30 days. Secondly, the length of the period of the moon's phases (the synodic period) does fluctuate slightly, between about 29.3 to 29.8 days (McCluskey, 2000, 17). Thirdly, there are not a whole number of lunar months in a solar (tropical) year of 365.24 days. In order to compensate, a culture has two choices. In the first, a lunar "year" of 12 lunar months is strictly used, leaving a year of 354 days, which is clearly too short. As a result, that culture's holidays will process forward during the seasons. Imagine, if you will, Christmas starting in winter, then slowly sliding earlier and earlier each year, eventually falling in the summer and then continuing its forward march and ending up back in winter after a total of about 32 to 33 years. This is what happens today with Islamic holidays, such as the holy month of Ramadan, as the Islamic calendar is the only major calendar used today that is strictly lunar. If a culture wishes its holidays to remain within a single season, it needs to occasionally add additional lunar months, called intercalary months. Different cultures develop their own specific rules in deciding when to add these months. This is one reason why the Chinese and Tibetan New Years sometimes fall on the same date and are sometimes (for example in 2012) one lunar cycle apart.[3] Such calendars are more accurately termed *luni-solar* calendars, as they rely on both cycles of the sun (the tropical year) and moon (the lunar month). A well-known example is the Jewish calendar, in which holidays such as Hanukkah shift slightly forward within a single season for a few years, and are then reset backwards by the insertion of an intercalary year.

The beginning of the lunar cycle can be calculated with relative precision, as the moment of the astronomical new moon depends on the relative position of the sun, earth, and moon. This is the reason why your desk calendar has the dates (and sometimes even times) of the important lunar phases (new, first quarter, full, and third quarter) despite the fact that it was printed well before the start of the year in question. This allows for the dates of Jewish holidays to also be determined and publicized well in advance of the actual celebration. However, these holidays were once determined by eyewitness observations of the moon, and today are still determined in this manner by the Karaite sect of Judaism.[4] Since it is not possible to actually see a new moon, a sighting of the youngest possible waxing crescent (usually within 24 hours of new) is used. This is also the method used by Muslims to determine the start of their lunar months and holidays. In the case of Muslim holidays, there is an added complication that most regard the sighting of the new moon in the holy city of Mecca to be the definitive word on when the lunar month begins. This is an issue, because different locations around the world will be able to first see a particular newborn moon either before Mecca or afterwards, both due to the relative position of that location on the earth (in longitude as well as latitude) and local weather conditions. For this reason, some mosques (especially in North America) will use local observations rather than Mecca observations to time their celebrations (especially Ramadan). This leads to considerable confusion, with groups of Muslims celebrating their holidays on different dates. Islamic scientists have tried to encourage the use of predictions of the potential visibility of the newborn moon rather than an actual sighting in order to standardize the celebrations around the world, but there is considerable resistance to the idea (Cartlidge, 2011, 513).

The original alignment of the dwarves' New Year with the first new moon of autumn suggests that Tolkien took the Jewish New Year—Rosh Hashanah[5]—as his inspiration (Hunnewell, 1999, 10; Rateliff, 2007a, 123). It is known that Tolkien did consider his dwarves to have much in common with Jewish culture. For example, in a 1955 letter to Naomi Mitchison he offers "I do think of the 'Dwarves' like Jews: at once native and alien in their habitations, speaking the languages of the country, but with an accent due to their own private language"(Carpenter, 2000, 229). In a 1965 BBC interview with Denys Gueroult Tolkien goes further, explaining that his dwarves are "quite obviously a—wouldn't you say that in many ways they remind you of the Jews?" Tolkien lists their language, "tremendous love of the artifact" and "immense warlike passion" as evidence of the connection (Rateliff, 2007a, 86). John Rateliff uses a previously unpublished letter from 1947 (in which he connects the dwarves' use of a "secret language" to that of Jews and Gypsies) as evidence that this connection between the dwarves and Jews is in Tolkien's mind during the Second Phase of the writing of *The Hobbit*, the time during which the initial definition of the dwarves' New Year is written (Rateliff, 2007b, 757; Rateliff, 2007a, 79).

While the date of the dwarves' New Year is eventually shifted to the last new moon of autumn, it remains a holiday determined by the direct observation of the young crescent moon within 24 hours of new (the "first day"). Perhaps the original impetus for the construction of Durin's Tower on the peak of Zirakzigil above Moria is precisely such an observation (Tolkien, 1993c, 105). What are we to make of the published description of Durin's Day, as being a special case of the New Year when this moon and sun are "in the sky together," and why would it be beyond the ability of Thorin and his company to calculate the next occurrence of such an event? For the moment we will take a page from astronomer Bradley Schaefer and conflate the two events (the dwarves' New Year and Durin's Day)[6] and explore the difficulties in (and importance of) being able to predict the visibility of an extremely young crescent moon.

Observing the Young Moon

Famed amateur astronomer and author Phil Harrington (2001, 67) notes that one of the "greatest challenges posed to naked-eye observers is trying to spot the crescent Moon less than 24 hours after the instant of the New Moon." An individual's likelihood of seeing a particular newborn moon depends on a variety of factors, including the location of the moon relative to the sun and the horizon (itself dependent on factors such as the time of year, the time since actual new moon, distance between the earth and moon, and the observer's latitude, longitude, and altitude), weather and other atmospheric conditions, and the individual's experience and visual acuity.[7] A generally accurate rule of thumb is the so-called Danjon limit, a calculation that the crescent moon is invisible when it is closer than 7 degrees[8] from the sun (Danjon, 1936).. For reference, the record for a confirmed observation of a young moon with the unaided eye is about 15.5 hours after new (Doggett and Schaefer, 1994, 402).

At the time of Tolkien's youth, this record would have been enviable by amateur astronomers in Britain. In an April 1909 letter published in the *Journal of the British Astronomical Association* French astronomer M.E.J. Gheury (1909, 219) explains that he has been able to see a moon that was 31.5 hours old, the youngest he has ever seen, and asks readers of the journal to share their personal records for youngest viewed moon. There are at least six replies published in the journal over the next few months, including famed meteor observer W.F. Denning's statement that the youngest claim he has heard of is of a moon that was only 18 hours 22 minutes old in 1889, and that he himself saw a moon in 1881 that was 20 hours 28 minutes old. (Denning, 1909, 242). Clearly amateur astronomers of the time feel that a gauntlet had been thrown and a number of them are eager to take up the challenge.

A letter by meteorologist and amateur astronomer Charles J.P. Cave (121) in the March 1911 edition of *The Observatory* (a magazine founded at the Royal Greenwich Observatory that was widely read by both professional and amateur astronomers) reignites the competition by asking for information on the current record for observing a young moon (and offering his personal best of 31 hours 40 minutes as a "short interval for this country"). His inquiry garners a number of replies over the next six months, with D.W. Horner, another meteorologist and amateur astronomer, claiming that he and three friends have achieved "a 'record' for England" of seeing a moon only 17 hours old while trying to observe a comet, a claim that draws scrutiny from others in the British amateur astronomy community (Horner, 1911, 162–3). An editorial note to Horner's letter draws attention to "a valuable article" in the *Monthly Notices of the Royal Astronomical Society* written by J.K. Fotheringham that uses successful and unsuccessful observations of young moons to devise "an approximate law" for the visibility of a particular young moon, based primarily on the altitude (height in degrees) of the moon at sunset (Horner, 1911, 162–3). A third flurry of interest in observations of the young crescent moon plays out in 1920–1, between the aforementioned J.K. Fotheringham and Caesar scholar T. Rice Holmes. The debate centers around the dating of events in the life of Julius Caesar and the construction of the Julian calendar, through references to the visibility of the moon's phases. Holmes' original paper (1920a), Fotheringham's critique (1920a), and Holmes' rebuttal (1920b) all appear in *The Classical Quarterly*, as does a final piece by Fotheringham's collaborator, actuary and amateur astronomer Carl Schoch, who pointedly addresses Holmes's rebuttal query as to whether any "trustworthy observer has ever seen with the naked eye a moon not more than 27 hours old in an atmosphere no clearer than that of Geneva"(Schoch, 1920, 194). After enumerating a number of such observations he has personally done, Schoch notes a "sensational observation" then recently published in the *JBAA* of claims of an observation of a 14.50 hour old moon by two English housemaids in 1916 (1920, 194).[9]

With an apparent plethora of both ancient and current observations (and nonobservations) of extremely young crescent moons at their disposal, one would expect astronomers to have an algorithm that can accurately predict the probability of a particular individual seeing a specific young crescent moon (and hence able to weed out false claims). For example, the ancient Babylonians did such computations over 2000 years ago, and medieval Muslim astronomers developed tables for such predictions (Doggett and Schaefer, 1994, 388). However, these methodologies have limited reliability. In his aforementioned 1910 article in the *Monthly Notices of the Royal Astronomical Society*, J.K. Fotheringham publishes his own mathematical equation for predicting the visibility of a newborn moon, based on a set of successful and unsuccessful observations made between 1859 and 1880 by observers in Troy, Athens, and Corinth. Fotheringham finds that the primary indicator as to whether the moon can be seen is the altitude of the moon above the horizon, and he fits the data set to an empirically devised equation:

$$\text{Minimum Altitude} = 12° - 0.008° \, Z^2$$

where Z is the number of degrees of azimuth (distance along the horizon) between the positions of the moon and the sun. Fotheringham argues that the atmospheric effects are secondary (so long as the sky was clear), so that this formula should apply to any location (so long as the resulting azimuth difference for that location, time of year, and position of the moon in its orbit) is properly calculated (Fotheringham, J.K., 1910b, 530–1).

As noted above, Fotheringham's paper is well-received by the astronomical community and garners considerable attention, but it is not seen to be without faults. For example, esteemed Royal Greenwich Observatory astronomer and founder of the British Astronomical Society E. Walter Maunder (1911, 355) called Fotheringham's paper "important" but took issue with the claim that local atmospheric effects are unimportant, citing observations by specific observers that appear to contradict Fotheringham's line of delineation. In fact, Holmes's comment questioning the visibility of the moon in Geneva is a direct attack on Fotheringham's insistence that local atmospheric effects are of nominal importance, as he is questioning whether Greek observations should be used to develop a law that can be equally applied outside the Mediterranean region. Fotheringham himself publishes a follow-up study in *The Observatory* in 1921 to address these doubts (which are in essence the same as those posed earlier by Maunder), using 15 observations from across Europe and the United States. The only results that seem at odds with Fotheringham's prediction are the aforementioned controversial 14.5 day old moon May 2, 1916, observations by the housemaids in Scarborough and two similar observations (14.75 days) by a mother and daughter on that same date in Heighington (Fotheringham, J.K., 1921b, 310).

While not perfect, Fotheringham's methodology stands as the sole widely used modern methodology to estimate the visibility of the newborn moon until the 1970s and 1980s (Doggett and Schaefer, 1994, 388). After several methods are proposed that are no better at calculating the observation probabilities, and because of the importance in estimating the visibility of the newborn moon to those in the Muslim community (and for other reasons germane other religious traditions, as will explained later in this essay), in the late 1980s a series of coordinated "Moonwatch" sessions are advertised through the U.S. Naval Observatory and *Sky and Telescope* magazine, resulting in the collection of over 1500 observations done between 1987 and 1990 (Doggett and Schaefer, 1994, 401).These observations are then used to test previous algorithms, including Fotheringham's (which is judged "reasonably accurate"), but the most accurate algorithm is deemed to be that developed by one of the study's authors, astronomer Bradley Schaefer (Doggett and Schaefer, 1994, 402). Today the Nautical Almanac Office in England (HMNAO) continues to collect observations of the newborn moon (both successful and unsuccessful) in order to make further adjustments to computer algorithms. The Office also publishes monthly maps and tables of the predicted earliest visibility of the young crescent moon as a service to those interested in observing the young moon for both religious and scientific reasons.[10]

What connections can be drawn to Tolkien thus far? At the time of the first flurries of interest in viewing the newborn moon in England, Tolkien is a college student at Oxford. While he may have heard of this debate through some peripheral connection, there is no evidence to corroborate this. At the time of the debate between Holmes and Fotheringham, Tolkien holds a readership in English Language at the University of Leeds.[11] While it is possible that Tolkien knows about *The Observatory*, it is certainly more likely that he peruses issues of *The Classical Quarterly*. Yet there is no evidence that he reads any of the relevant articles described here. At this point the evidence for a real-world influence on the evolution of Durin's Day (outside of the dating of the Jewish New Year) seems weakly circumstantial at best. Fortunately there is much more to the story, namely J.K. Fotheringham himself.

Fotheringham and the Oxford Observatory

John Knight Fotheringham (1874–1936) was the second of three sons born to Presbyterian minister David Fotheringham and his wife Jane (née Ross).[12] A "delicate child" who suffered from health problems his entire life (Stephenson, 2004), Fotheringham was trained in the Classics at Merton College, Oxford, earning a first (honors) in the Oxford "Greats" (Classics) curriculum (1896) and Modern History (1897). His first position was as a senior demy (half-fellow) at Magdalen College from 1898 to 1902. During this time he began to research ancient chronology and in 1903 published two articles on this topic in *The Journal of Philology*. In 1905 he published an edition of The Bodleian Manuscript of Jerome's version of *The Chronicle of Eusebius* and in 1906 published a completed and revised volume of *Longman's Political History of England* (covering 1801 to 1837). In recognition of his work on Eusubius he received a DLitt from Oxford in 1908 (Stephenson, 2004).

In 1904 he was appointed a Lecturer in Classical Literature at King's College, London, and was promoted to Reader of Ancient History in 1912 (a post he held until the start of World War I). At the same time he continued to work at Magdalen as a Research Fellow (1909–1916), necessitating commutes between London and Oxford. Fotheringham became interested in astronomy in the late 1890s, and began studying both that subject and mathematics (with the help of Oxford Astronomer Herbert Hall Turner, Professor J.B. Dale of King's College, and Superintendent of the Nautical Almanac Office Philip Herbert Cowell) and applied his knowledge to the intersections between ancient chronology and astronomy (such as ancient calendars, the dating of eclipses and ancient observations of the phases of the moon). Although he published widely in both astronomical and Classics journals, World War I and his poor health interrupted his work. By 1918 his academic posts lapsed and he eagerly accepted an assistantship offered to him by Turner at the Oxford Observatory. Although it was barely enough to support him and his wife Mary, he flourished in his academic work under Turner's mentorship, although his work was not without controversy (for example, as seen in the exchange between he and Holmes previously cited). In 1925 Fotheringham was finally offered a Readership in Ancient Astronomy and Chronology (a position created for him) and a commensurate raise, as well as an honorary assistantship at the University Observatory, positions he kept until his death in 1936.

Over his career, Fotheringham became known as "one of the leading authorities in his field of work ("Recent Deaths," 1937, 50). Unfortunately, the interdisciplinary nature of this work made it not only a narrow specialization, but one whose value was not always obviously apparent to strict disciplinarians. Much of his work is dedicated to using careful interpretations of ancient astronomical observations to correctly date historical events and texts. Fotheringham was also interested in using modern observations to understand ancient ones, such as his work on an empirical law for the visibility of newborn crescent moons, and a 1925 project in which the Astronomer Royal Sir Frank Dyson issued a public appeal for observations of the January 25 solar eclipse, not of the eclipse itself, but rather whether bright stars could be seen in the sky during the eclipse (Fotheringham, J.K. 1925, 509). Fotheringham understood that his work was only possible through uniting his background in Classics with his newfound studies in mathematics and astronomy, noting that "very few astronomers have sufficient knowledge of ancient astronomy or of ancient literature to understand the problems" and very few classicists "have sufficient knowledge of the astronomical literature which would enable them to solve these problems" (Fotheringham, J.K., 1929, 306). In his 1921 Halley Lecture at Oxford entitled "Historical Eclipses," Fotheringham warned that "Injury has been done both to astronomy and to history by a too eager enthusiasm on the part of votaries of either science to obtain exact and reliable data from the other.... We must weigh our evidence with caution." He believed that "Each science has need of the other, but neither has a right to force from the other more than it is able to give" (1921a, 32).

In addition to his well-known work on the visibility of the crescent moon,[13] his most important contribution to modern astronomy came with his "definitive evaluation" of the secular acceleration of the moon and sun (Schlesinger and Brouwer, 1939, 249). In the eighteenth century it was discovered through a comparison of modern and ancient eclipse records that the moon's orbital velocity changes, and in order for the earth-moon system to conserve angular momentum the moon's distance from the earth is slowly receding and the earth's rate of rotation is slowing. This "secular acceleration" was explained by George H. Darwin, son of Charles Darwin as a tidal effect, and is part of his larger fission model of lunar formation. As this author argued in a previous paper (Larsen, 2008a), Tolkien was not only aware of this work by Darwin, but incorporated it into his experimental revisions to the cosmology, right down to having the Melkor-created moon ripped from the earth and then moved farther from the earth (by the Valar).

Through a careful study of ancient observations of eclipses, occultations (the moon passing in front of bright stars and planets), and the precession of the equinoxes, Fotheringham was able to precisely determine the rate of this secular acceleration as well as the values of additional shifts in the apparent motions of the sun, Mercury, and Venus (Fotheringham and Longbottom, 1915; Fotheringham, J.K., 1920b). These additional "accelerations" were already known to astronomers, but Fotheringham's detailed observations allowed for the testing of various hypotheses put forward to explain them. Fotheringham proposed the term "trepidation" as a blanket term for these accelerations (a term that had traditionally been used in ancient and medieval texts to refer to oscillations in the motion of the equinoxes) and eschewed the most widely held hypothesis that they are caused by changes in the rate of rotation of the earth (Fotheringham, J.K., 1926, 166). Instead, he cited a 1914 address to the British Association for the Advancement of Science by Yale University Astronomy Professor Ernest W. Brown (who had studied under George Darwin) in which Brown suggested it might be due to a magnetic "surge spreading through the solar system" (Fotheringham, J.K., 1926, 143). Unfortunately for Fotheringham, Brown had since come to accept irregularities in the rotation of the earth as the cause for these observed effects, and had published several papers to this effect the same year as Fotheringham's massive two-part paper on "Trepidation," leading the influential Brown to openly criticize Fotheringham's work. According to his brother, Fotheringham was also not a believer in the expansion of the universe, instead preferring a "Retardation of Light"[14] to explain the observed red shifts of other galaxies (Fotheringham, D.R. 1937, 327).

In 1930 Fotheringham caught a glimmer of hope that he would realize his long-held dream of attaining a professorship. H.H. Turner, his long-time mentor and sponsor, unexpectedly died of a brain hemorrhage in August 1930 while attending a conference of the International Geophysical Union in Stockholm (Cannon, 1931, 59). Upon Turner's sudden death, the prestigious position of Savilian Professor of Astronomy (a chair once held by Edmund Halley) became open. Fotheringham applied for the position in 1931, and amassed a 34 page dossier of testimonials from astronomers to support his application.[15] Fotheringham's bid was ultimately unsuccessful, and solar astronomer Harry Plaskett was elected to the chair in 1932.

It is my hypothesis that Tolkien's addition of an observation of the young crescent moon that is difficult to predict is quite possibly due, in part, to the work of J.K. Fotheringham. Tolkien certainly knew of Fotheringham, either through his writings on ancient chronologies or observing the newborn crescent moon, or as a fellow Oxford academic. Tolkien may even have known about Fotheringham's work on the secular acceleration, given his later incorporation of that concept into his experimental cosmologies. Possibly as part of his campaign to become Savilian Professor, Fotheringham wrote a rather self-serving article in *The Oxford Magazine* in October 1930 in which he not only detailed the importance of his research in "Ancient Astronomy and Cosmology" in general, but described the connection of his work to the broader university, and listed a number of specific problems he had been asked to tackle by fellow Oxford academics and individuals in America and Germany in the past month alone (Fotheringham, J.K., 1930). Certainly Tolkien would have seen this article, as he was familiar with the magazine, having published in it himself in the previous term (Tolkien, 1930). Finally, as Tolkien was an elected member of the General Board of the Faculties at Oxford (the equivalent of the Faculty Senate) from 1929–1932 (Scull and Hammond, 2006, 150), he would have certainly been aware of Fotheringham's 1931 application as an internal candidate to succeed Turner as Savilian Professor of Astronomy, if only through the grapevine. But if this evidence is not sufficient, we turn next to another relevant application of Fotheringham's work, one that more closely links to the question of Durin's Day, namely the timing of two of the most important Christian holidays, Good Friday and Easter.

Complicated Holidays: Easter

Bradley Schaefer (1990, 53) notes that the "exact date of the crucifixion of Jesus Christ has long held a fascination for scholars. Part of the reason lies in the fundamental importance of the crucifixion in Christian theology and part in the fact that sufficient information may be available to yield a specific date for the event." According to the Gospels and historical evidence, the crucifixion occurs on a Friday that falls on the fourteenth or fifteenth day of the month of Nisan in the Jewish luni-solar calendar somewhere between CE 28 and 33 (Schaefer, 1990, 53). Since the ancient Jewish calendar relies on observations of the newly born moon to mark the beginning of each lunar month, in order to establish a historical date for the crucifixion a scholar would ideally have an understanding of ancient chronology and history as well as lunar phases. John Knight Fotheringham certainly fits the bill. It is therefore not surprising that Fotheringham's first two publications are back-to-back related articles in *The Journal of Philology* in 1903, the first on the astronomy and the Julian Calendar, the second on astronomical evidence that could aid in the determination of the date of the crucifixion (Fotheringham, J.K., 1903b; 1903a). In the second paper, Fotheringham examines the astronomical evidence for a number of possible years for the crucifixion, and settles on the year CE 33 as the most likely.

After the publication of his empirical formula for crescent moon visibility in 1910, Fotheringham revisits the date of the crucifixion in a paper he publishes in *The Journal of Theological Studies*, and, while he maintains that CE 33 is still, in his opinion the most likely year, he confirms a suggestion by Yale Professor B.W. Bacon that April 7, 30 CE is also a possibility (Fotheringham, J.K. 1910a). Fotheringham's older brother, David, a Presbyterian minister and amateur astronomer in his own right, takes great interest in his brother's work on the crucifixion and in an April 1911 article in *The Churchman* claims that his brother's work "not only narrows the uncertainty of the year, but also definitely decides once and for ever the still more engrossing question as to the exact date of the Crucifixion" on the Jewish calendar (Maunder, 1911, 362). It is partly in response to these sweeping claims that E.W. Maunder writes his 1911 article in the *Journal of the British Astronomical Association* questioning Fotheringham's claim that local atmospheric effects are of little consequence in determining whether a newborn crescent will be visible. In Maunder's words, Fotheringham's equation "supplies a simple and efficient criterion of the probability of the visibility of the new Moon; it is not sufficient to determine its possibility. In the general case it may be trusted; in any exceptional case, it is clear that reliance cannot be placed upon it" (Maunder, 1911, 362).

Just as the date of the original crucifixion, and therefore the original Easter Sunday, depends on the ancient Jewish lunar calendar, so too does all subsequent celebrations of the holidays. A major problem for the early Christians is that because the Jewish calendar is lunar in nature, the fourteenth day of the lunar month of Nisan will not always fall on the same day of the week. Therefore what becomes known as "Good Friday" will not always fall on a Friday, and therefore Easter will not always be on a Sunday. In response, there arise two rival camps, one that holds to a strict dating of the crucifixion by the Jewish calendar, and the other that believes that it is more important for Easter to fall on a Sunday. Another difficulty is that by utilizing the Jewish calendar to determine Easter, Christians are seemingly forever tied to Judaism. Also, since the Jewish calendar is, at that time, still determined using actual observations of the newborn moon, and the visibility of the newborn moon depends on the location of the observer, Easter can potentially fall on different dates in the Holy Roman Empire. A decision is made to use an "ecclesiastical" or theoretical moon and a fixed date for the vernal equinox of March 21 (regardless of the actual date of the equinox in a given year, which is determined in part by the cycle of leap years). This leads to the need for a complex set of calculations to determine Easter (even after the Gregorian calendar reform of the sixteenth century). It does not simply fall on the first Sunday after the first Full Moon after the Vernal Equinox, as is often stated (Richards, 1999, 346–52). The result is that Easter can fall anywhere within a window of March 22 and April 25, in stark contrast to the other major celebration of the Christian calendar, Christmas, which always falls on December 25.

In a widely disseminated, slender volume entitled *The Date of Easter and Other Christian Festivals*, David Fotheringham not only utilizes his brother's work to argue for a date for the crucifixion of April 7, 30 CE (ironically in contrast to his brother's preference for 33 CE) but puts forth the argument that a standardized date should be internationally adopted for Easter, the Sunday in April closest to the original April 9 (Fotheringham, D.R., 1928, 52). The preface to Fotheringham's book is written by Lord Desborough (William Grenfell), who had introduced a bill into the House of Lords in 1921 to establish the second Sunday in April as Easter. A similar bill is introduced into the House of Commons in 1927, and in 1928 the Easter Act is passed, establishing a fixed Easter, The law has never been enforced, partially because a consensus has not been reached by all major Christian churches (as stipulated in the legislation).[16] The law is widely discussed in English churches and newspapers at the time, and it is impossible for Tolkien to not know about the debate.

J.K. Fotheringham's final paper on the date of the crucifixion is published in 1934, based on a lecture he gives at Oxford on December 4, 1930, presumably during the time he is or is preparing to lobby for the job of Savilian Professor. In the lecture he admits that what he is presenting is not new, but is rather a review of his previous work as well as the work of others (Fotheringham, J.K., 1934). Referring to his work on the visibility of the moon and his understanding of general calculations of the rising and setting of the moon (using data tables developed by his friend Carl Schoch), Fotheringham not only argues for April 3, 33 CE as the best date but estimates that nineteen minutes of a lunar eclipse would be visible from the historical location of the crucifixion (Fotheringham, J.K., 161). Using his own algorithms for moon motions and visibility, Schaefer argues in 1990 that the moon would have not risen until after the umbral portion of the eclipse had ended, and only a subtle effect due to the penumbral shadow would be visible (53). While Tolkien certainly does not need a scientist to date the crucifixion in order to bolster his faith, he would find such work at least interesting if not uplifting. For as he notes in a 1944 letter to son Christopher, "the Resurrection was the greatest 'eucatastrophe' possible in the greatest Fairy Story" (Carpenter, 2000, 100), and in "On Fairy-stories," he muses about the "peculiar excitement and joy that one would feel, if any specially beautiful fairy-story were found to be 'primarily' true, its narrative to be history" (Flieger and Anderson, 2002, 78). While he affirms that the Resurrection is certainly "true" and in it "Legend and History have met and fused," the addition of science to the mix would be the proverbial icing on the cake (Flieger and Anderson, 2002, 78).

Looking at the evidence, it seems likely that Tolkien may have been influenced by a confluence of primary world traditions, laws, hypotheses, and speculations in his decision to make the dwarves' most important holiday based on observations of the moon, and difficult to predict observations at that. Two lingering questions remain, the first being why Tolkien shifted the date of the dwarves' New Year from the beginning to end of autumn. Here we must rely on sheer speculation, as John Rateliff (2007b, 831) recounts that he has located "no explicit statement from Tolkien about any decision regarding shifting Durin's Day." Perhaps in the end, despite the fact that the dwarves have much in common with the Jews, Tolkien does not wish to make their culture a carbon copy of that religious tradition. Both Rateliff (2007a, 123–24) and Hunnewell (1999, 3) point out that in shifting the Dwarves' New Year to the end of autumn it is more closely aligned with Celtic (i.e. pagan) holidays. Nothing more will be said here about this possibility, as it is beyond the purview of the current analysis. Instead, we finally will turn our attention to a more decidedly astronomical question, whether or not Durin's Day, as described by Tolkien, is astronomically possible.

Is Durin's Day Astronomically Possible?

As noted above, Bradley Schaefer (1994, 12) equates Durin's Day with the Dwarves' New Year, apparently taking this from a misquote of Robert Foster's *The Guide to Middle-earth*. Hunnewell (1999, 8–10) appears to be the only author to attempt to tackle the thorny issue of how the detailed description of Durin's Day in the published *Hobbit*—as a special case of the New Year in which the newborn crescent moon is seen in the sky together with the setting sun—might possibly refer to an actual astronomical observation. The scene at The Lonely Mountain clearly describes a slender crescent moon being visible at the same time as the setting sun. After the last sunbeam illuminates the secret keyhole, "the sun sank, the moon was gone, and evening sprang into the sky" (Tolkien, 2007, 194). The observations of a newborn moon described in the above sections (and the algorithms determining its potential visibility) refer only to the visibility of the moon *after* sunset (but during early twilight). Hunnewell (1999, 8–10) notes this distinction and attempts to explain this by using personal observations trying to sight the new moon and the sun together in the sky the day after New Moon (when the moon is more than 24 hours old). While his efforts are laudable, this Tolkienist and astronomer has a simpler explanation: Tolkien is not trying to be *completely* scientific in this case, but rather mixing poetic license with actual astronomical observation to create a desired dramatic effect for the sake of the story.

Such a claim might sound strange coming from a scholar who has made a cottage industry of writing about how correctly Tolkien utilizes astronomy in his legendarium. It is especially unexpected given the well-known care Tolkien takes with his lunar chronology of *The Lord of the Rings*, timing the parallel journeys of the main characters to the phases of the moon.[17] Tolkien requires a rigid, consistent chronology for his characters to follow because their journeys across Mordor, Rohan, and Gondor are separated in space but follow a parallel timeline. Utilizing the moon's phases not only gives Tolkien a convenient calendar to follow, but one that the astute reader can follow without it being intrusive into the story itself. Christopher Tolkien explains how his father first aligns the lunar chronology to the actual moon phases of 1941–2 during the drafting of the post–Moria adventures,[18] while John Rateliff (2007b, 827–9) describes how the final novel-wide consistency is only achieved through the construction of "many-columned sheets listing where each character was on each day of the story," a "cheat-sheet" that is now housed in the Tolkien archive at Marquette. There is no corresponding chart for *The Hobbit*, as the main characters stay in close proximity for most of the tale, with the exception of Gandalf (Rateliff, 2007b, 827–9).

Without a real-world calendar or careful lunar chronology chart to follow, how does Tolkien manage to keep his timeline in *The Hobbit* consistent? The answer is, he does not. As John Rateliff describes in detail in *The History of* The Hobbit, not only does the change in Durin's Day from the first to last new moon of autumn pose serious problems in compressing the timeline of the later action in the novel, but the travel times between various events in the novel do not match those for similar journeys in *The Lord of the Rings*. There are also a number of serious errors in his moon phases, errors made all the more glaring because of the centrality of moon phases to two important scenes in the tale, namely the reading of Thorin's map in Rivendell, and the opening of the secret keyhole at Erebor. In the decades after the publication of *The Hobbit*, Tolkien attempts to make corrections to the text, including the chronology and moon phases,[19] successfully fixing some, while leaving others as is, either because the changes will create other difficulties in the text (a chain reaction of sorts) or because the changes will remove important dramatic elements from the text.

An example of the former deals with the phase of the moon in the scene with Bilbo and the three trolls. Working backwards from the moon-letters scene in Rivendell, it is impossible for the phase of the moon to be waning (after full), nor to be visible in the sky before sunset. In later editions Tolkien changes the reference to a "wandering" rather than "waning" moon, a curious description, but one that at least is not explicitly incorrect (Rateliff, 2007b, 829). An example of the latter is the famous scene at Laketown where Bard is able to see the gap in Smaug's jewel-encrusted armor by the light of a rising moon in the east late at night (similar to a moon after full). Unfortunately, since the death of Smaug takes place soon after Durin's Day, the moon must be a waxing crescent, setting in the west within a few hours of sunset. Tolkien is unable to correct this mistake without ruining the dramatic plot point, and so it remains part of the text to this day (Tolkien, 2007, 228).

The inconsistencies in Tolkien's chronology and use of moon phases pose a difficulty for those who attempt to determine when exactly Durin's Day occurs in the novel in terms of the primary world (Gregorian) calendar, although a number of authors have made valiant attempts to do so.[20] However, there is an additional problem with *The Hobbit*'s lunar chronology that this author was the first to point out to John Rateliff,[21] namely that according to Tolkien's notes (as published in *The History of* The Hobbit), even as late as the 1960 edits to the tale,[22] he is using a 28 day cycle for the moon's phases rather than the correct 29.5 days.[23] Therefore a strictly 'correct' lunar chronology, including a definitive identification the date of Durin's Day in the novel in terms of the Gregorian calendar is not possible (although a "consistently wrong" identification using a 28 day lunar cycle is possible, and might prove to be an interesting exercise, although not one that this author is willing to undertake).

Returning to Durin's Day itself in light of the recognition that lunar errors *do* occur in *The Hobbit*, it is instructional to examine all the available evidence Tolkien has left us. First, recall that the addition of the crescent moon to the mix comes only with the Second Phase in the writing. In the First Phase, only the sun is mentioned (initially the rising sun, changed to the setting sun). The crescent moon is probably added partly for effect, partly in response to its importance to real world calendars and ancient chronologies (specifically the Jewish calendar and perhaps the crucifixion), and partly due to the added mystique of its appearance being difficult to predict (as described in the literature of the day). Hammond and Scull (2000, 148) also connect the "'magical' conjunction" of the sun and moon with the tale of the Two Trees in *The Silmarillion*. While it is certainly possible that this may have played some role in the inclusion of the moon, especially because a mythological explanation for the phases of the moon is included in the creation myth of the sun and moon (the waywardness of Tilion due to his attraction to the brilliant Arien and the resulting burning of the moon), this author has not found any relevant mystical or symbolic references to the crescent moon in *The Silmarillion* texts. In the scene at Erebor we have important information concerning the relative position of the sun and moon in the sky: the sun sinks, then the moon disappears (sinks as well) and then darkness arrives. This suggests that the moon is slightly higher in the sky than the moon (but only slightly so); the crescent after new has to be above the sun, so this is consistent with astronomical observations.

In the first extant sketch for the dust jacket[24] the moon is pictured on the left side (back) of the jacket, against a dark (nighttime) sky, with the half-set sun on the right (front) against a daylight sky. The moon is set slightly above the sun in the sky. The horns of the crescent moon point away from the sun, also astronomically correct, but the moon is depicted as half the diameter of the sun, an astronomical error, as the apparent angular size of the sun and moon in the sky are approximately equally (otherwise total solar eclipses would be an impossibility). One caveat is required in this criticism of Tolkien's astronomy; the image of the sun shows a circle drawn within the solar disk, the inner circle being the same angular size as the moon. This suggests that Tolkien's drawing of the sun is stylized, and does include some acknowledgment of the true relative sizes of the sun and moon. In the dust jacket of the published volume[25] the sun and moon are the same angular size and the sun has not yet begun to set. Again, the horns of the moon are approximately correct in their angle, and the moon is slightly higher in the sky than the sun (but the relative difference in altitude between the sun and moon is less than in the original sketch because the sun is set higher in the sky).

This relative positioning of the sun and moon is interesting; recalling that in the original version (as written in the Second Phase), the Dwarves' New Year falls at the first new moon of autumn, or closer to the Autumnal Equinox than the Winter Solstice. Interestingly, the first crescent moon of autumn is the lowest in the sky, and hence the most difficult to view. As depicted on Tolkien's dust jackets, the difference in azimuth (the angle along the horizon) between the sun and moon is large at this time, and as can be seen from Fotheringham's equation cited above, the altitude of the moon above the sun is at a minimum. This is due to the tilt of the earth and the resulting angle between the horizon and the ecliptic, the plane of the earth's orbit around the sun that defines the apparent path that the sun, moon, and planets appear to take across the sky.[26]

The actual difference in azimuth (and hence altitude) depends on the observer's latitude. The higher (more northerly) the observer's latitude, the greater the azimuth and the lower the resulting altitude of the moon above the sun.[27] The author used the Spitz 512 planetarium projector of the Copernican Planetarium at Central Connecticut State University to recreate the moon/sun angle at sunset at various times of the year as seen from Oxford (latitude 51.75°), and the low angle of the moon on the Autumnal Equinox in September is quite striking, mimicking very well Tolkien's original dust jacket sketch. It is possible that Tolkien once saw a growing crescent moon low in the September or early October sky (but more than one day after new) and either consciously or unconsciously included it within the mythos of Durin's Day. Unfortunately, in moving Durin's Day to the last new moon of autumn the angle is not as low and striking, but it is still far lower than during the majority of the year. Therefore while Durin's Day as written—with the sun and newborn moon visible in the sky at the same time—is not strictly astronomically possible, Tolkien may have witnessed a reasonable approximation for himself during one Oxford autumn, and for this and reasons detailed above, adds it to his description of the magical event at Erebor.

Conclusion

Tolkien's use of astronomy in crafting Middle-earth ranges from sublimely accurate to agonizingly incorrect. The many instances of the former make the latter that much more frustrating to scholars, especially when connected to as major a plot point as Durin's Day is in *The Hobbit*. The inconsistencies and outright errors are all the more striking when set in contrast with the care Tolkien takes in crafting the lunar chronology of *The Lord of the Rings*. John Rateliff warns us that we risk such frustration whenever we try to use the same rigid scholarly lens to view *The Hobbit* as we are used to using on *The Lord of the Rings*. For in the end, as Rateliff admonishes, *The Hobbit* is a story told using the "tradition of long ago and far away, where details are only included when dramatically relevant or aesthetically effective.... Bilbo's is a world where the moon only just past new can rise after the sun sets ... because that's how Tolkien envisioned the scene" (Rateliff, 2007b, 836–7). The tale is, even more so that its later and far longer brother, just a tale, not "pseudo-history or pseudoscience" Rateliff, 2007a, 18). But we even see a hint of this use of the impossible (because it is "aesthetically effective") in *The Lord of the Rings*, despite Tolkien's boast that he didn't think "the moons rise or are in the wrong place at any point" (Rateliff, 207b, 827). Christopher Tolkien describes in *The Treason of Isegard* how his father had too many references to the moon from the scene at the Gate of Moria because he initially writes it as a waxing crescent phase (which is visible in the west after sunset) rather than the waning gibbous that the chronology demands—a phase that *rises* in the *east* a few hours after sunset (Tolkien, 2000, 179). Despite his understanding that the moon cannot be visible, he retains the reference to the ithildin of the door being illuminated by moonlight and starlight in the final version, and the impossible configuration of moonlight shining upon the west-facing gate, because it is "aesthetically effective." Another famous example is found in *The Silmarillion*. Despite Tolkien's obvious understanding of the proper visibility of the planet Venus as the Evening Star and Morning Star (in the west after sunset in the first case, and the east before sunrise in the second), in "Akallabêth" astronomical reality is openly flaunted as Eärendil and his silmaril are seen continually in the west, "even at morning," a sign set by the Valar to guide the Edain to their new home, Numenór (Tolkien, 2001, 260). The visual is beautiful, powerful, symbolic, and utterly impossible in the primary world.

Stephen McCluskey (2000, 14) sagely notes that if we "describe a culture's astronomy from the outside using modern astronomy as the norm, we will paint a false picture of what they are doing." Rather than view the moon of *The Hobbit* as a photograph or a digital image from which we can identify individual craters, rilles, or maria, we should instead enjoy it as we would an impressionistic painting, and turn our analysis from the placement of individual pixels to the overall effect and the possible real world motivations of the artist. This is where we will find the true meaning of the art. And if it inspires us to go out and catch a fleeting glimpse of a slender crescent moon under cold, crisp autumn skies with our own eager eyes, have we not paid Tolkien's work a compliment without measure?

Notes

1. See, for example, Karen Wynn Fonstad, *The Atlas of Middle-earth*, rev. ed. (Boston: Houghton Mifflin, 1991); Bradley E. Schaefer, "*The Hobbit* and Durin's Day," *The Griffith Observer* 58, no. 11 (1994): 12–17; Sumner Gary Hunnewell, "Durin's Day," *Ravenhill*, August 1, 1999, 1–14; Andreas Moehn, "The Moon and Durin's Day, 2941 TA," Lailaith's Middle-earth Science Pages, last modified September 25, 2002, http://lalaith.vpsurf.de/Tolkien/Durin%27s_Day.html; Douglas Wilhelm Harder, "Timeline/Chronology for 'The Hobbit,'" personal webpage, nd, https://ece.uwaterloo.ca/~dwharder/Personal/Hobbit/.

2. Rateliff details this change and the difficulties that resulted from it. See, for example, *Return to Bag-End*, 481 and 652.

3. For more information on lunar calendars, see McCluskey, "The Inconstant Moon."

4. For information on the Karaites, see http://www.karaites.org.

5. It should be noted that the determination of the date of Rosh Hashanah is more complicated than just the date of the first new moon of autumn, as it cannot fall on a Sunday, Wednesday, or Friday. For more information, see Solomon Gartenhaus and Arnold Tubis, "The Jewish Calendar—A Mix of Astronomy and Theology," *Shofar* 25, no. 2 (2007): 104–24.

6. In the second installment of Peter Jackson's film adaptation of *The Hobbit*, this conflation is taken a step further, as the exact timing of Durin's Day is apparently trivial to ascertain ahead of time. In addition, Jackson makes, in my opinion, an unacceptable alteration to the definition of Durin's Day and the moon runes, by having it be the light from the moon that illuminate the keyhole after the sun has already set. The change may have been motivated by Jackson's desire to tie his vision of *The Hobbit* closely to his previous adaptation of *The Lord of the Rings*, in particular to set up the scene at the Gates of Moria where moonlight exposes the ithildin-traced doorway. Jackson makes an extreme astronomical error, in having what appears to me to be a broad, approximately 4 day old moon in this scene (rather than a slender newborn crescent). In addition, Thorin is apparently able to read the moon runes by the light of dusk rather than having to be read by moonlight. There is a small, related error in the first film as well, as Elrond is able to read the runes when the moonlight shines *upon* them, rather than *through* them.

7. For more information, see http://aa.usno.navy.mil/faq/docs/crescent.php.

8. A recent revisiting of this limit puts it closer to 5 degrees (Amir Hasanzadeh, Study of Danjon Limit in Moon Crescent Sighting," *Astrophysics and Space Science* 339 (2012): 211–221).

9. This claim is doubted by astronomers. See, for example, http://earthsky.org/space/young-moon-visibility.

10. See http://astro.ukho.gov.uk/moonwatch/ for more information.

11. For information on Tolkien's timeline, see Scull and Hammond, *The JRRT Companion and Guide: Chronology*.

12. Unless otherwise noted, biographical information on Fotheringham was synthesized from F. R. Stephenson, "Fotheringham, John Knight (1874–1936)," *Oxford Dictionary of National Biography*, Oxford University Press, 2004, http://www.oxforddnb.com/view/article/33220; W.M.H. Greaves, "John Knight Fotheringham," *Monthly Notices of the Royal Astronomical Society* 97 (1937): 270–2; and Stephen Langdon, "Dr. J.K. Fotheringham, F.B.A.," *Nature* 139 (1937): 788–90.

13. A complete listing of Fotheringham's 130 publications can be found by combining R.A. Sampson, "John Knight Fotheringham (1874–1936)," *Isis* 27 (1937): 485–92; and A. Pogo, "The Writings of J.K. Fotheringham," *Isis* 29 (1938): 58–68.

14. This is a possible reference to the work of astronomer Fritz Zwicky ("On the Red Shift of Spectral Lines Through Interstellar Space," *Proceedings of the National Academy of Sciences of the United States of America*, 15 (1929):773–779).

15. These letters and Fotheringham's letter of application are housed in the archive of Magdalen College, according to its online catalog (http://www.magd.ox.ac.uk/libraries-and-archives/archives/online-catalogues/fotheringham-papers/).

16. The legislation can be read at http://www.legislation.gov.uk/ukpga/Geo5/18-19/35.

17. See, for example, Carpenter, Letters, 74, 80, 97.

18. Actually five days off the moon phases of 1941–2; see J.R.R. Tolkien, *The Treason of Isengard* (Boston: Houghton Mifflin, 2000), 367–9.

19. See Rateliff, *Return to Bag-end*, 731–838 for details of this "Fourth Phase" and "Fifth Phase."

20. See note 1.

21. See http://www.sacnothscriptorium.com/works/errata2.html.

22. For example, see Rateliff, *Return to Bag-end*, 830–2.

23. See Kristine Larsen, "The Lunacy of *The Hobbit*," *Amon Hen* no. 230 (2011): 20–1, for more details.

24. See Ibid., 149, or the dust jackets for the two volumes of Rateliff, *The History of The Hobbit*.

25. See Hammond and Scull, *Artist and Illustrator*, 151, or the edition of Tolkien, *The Hobbit* included in the box set with Rateliff, *The History of* The Hobbit.

26. See Harrington, *Cosmic Challenges*, 68 for more details and illustrations.

27. For a detailed animation of the seasonal variations in this angle as seen from Madison, WI (at a latitude of 43° N) see https://planetariumweb.madison.k12.wi.us/mooncal/crescent-tilt/Crescent.html.

Works Cited

Cannon, Annie J. 1931. "Herbert Hall Turner." *Popular Astronomy* 39: 59–66.
Cartlidge, Edwin. 2011. "When Is Ramadan? An Arab Astronomer Has Answers." *Science* 33: 513.
Cave, Charles J.P. 1911. "Early Visibility of the New Moon." *The Observatory* 34: 121.
"Closest Approaches to the Earth by Comets." Minor Planet Center. N.d. http://minorplanetcenter.net/iau/lists/ClosestComets.html.
Danjon, A.1936. "Le Croissant Lunaire." *L'Astronomie* 50: 57–65.
Deming, W.F. 1909. "Visibility of the New Moon and the Pleiades." *Journal of the British Astronomical Association* 19: 242–3.
Doggett, LeRoy E., and Bradley E. Schaefer. 1994. "Lunar Crescent Visibility." *Icarus* 107: 388–403.
Espanek, Fred. 2009. "Total Lunar Eclipse of 1927 Dec 08." NASA Eclipse Website. Last modified April 29. http://eclipse.gsfc.nasa.gov/LEplot/LEplot1901/LE1927Dec08T.pdf.
Fonstad, Karen Wynn. 1991. *The Atlas of Middle-earth*, rev. ed. Boston: Houghton Mifflin.
Fotheringham, David Ross. 1928. *The Date of Easter and Other Christian Festivals*. London: Society for Promoting Christian Knowledge.
_____. "J.K Fotheringham." 1937. *Astronomische Nachrichten* 261: 327.
Fotheringham, J.K. 1903a. "The Date of the Crucifixion." *The Journal of Philology* 29: 100–18.
_____. 1903b. "The Formation of the Julian Calendar, with Reference to the Astronomical Year." *The Journal of Philology* 29: 87–99.
_____. 1910a. "Astronomical Evidence for the Date of the Crucifixion." *The Journal of Theological Studies* 12: 120–7.
_____. 1910b. "On the Smallest Visible Phase of the Moon." *Monthly Notices of the Royal Astronomical Society* 70: 527–31.
_____. 1920a. "Astronomical Comments on Dr. Holmes's Note on the Julian Calendar." *The Classical Quarterly* 14, no. 2: 97–9.
_____. 1920b. "Note on the Secular Accelerations of the Sun and Moon as Determined From the Ancient Lunar and Solar Eclipses, Occultations, and Equinox Observations." *Monthly Notices of the Royal Astronomical Society* 80: 578–81.
_____. 1921a. *Historical Eclipses*. Oxford: Clarendon Press.
_____. 1921b. "The Visibility of the Lunar Crescent." *The Observatory* 44: 308–11.
_____. 1925. "Visibility of Stars in Great Britain During the Solar Eclipse of 1925 January 24." *Monthly Notices of the Royal Astronomical Society* 85: 509–10.
_____. 1926. "Trepidation." *Monthly Notices of the Royal Astronomical Society* 87: 142–67; 182–196.
_____. 1929. "Astronomical Chronology." *The Observatory* 52: 305–8.
_____. 1930. "Ancient Astronomy and Chronology." *The Oxford Magazine* 49: 48–50.
_____. 1934. "The Evidence of Astronomy and Technical Chronology for the Date of the Crucifixion." *The Journal of Theological Studies* 35: 146–62.
_____. and Gertrude Longbottom. 1915. "The Secular Acceleration of the Moon's Mean Motion as Determined from the Occultations in the Almagest." *Monthly Notices of the Royal Astronomical Society* 57: 377–94
Gartenhaus, Solomon, and Arnold Tubis. 2007. "The Jewish Calendar—A Mix of Astronomy and Theology." *Shofar* 25, no. 2: 104–24.
Gheury, M.E.J. 1909. "Early Visibility of the Crescent Moon." *Journal of the British Astronomical Association* 19: 219.
"The Great Crimson Aurora of March 9, as Seen Over the City of London." 1926. *Scientific American* 134, no.6: 373.
Greaves, W.M.H. 1937. "John Knight Fotheringham." *Monthly Notices of the Royal Astronomical Society* 97: 270–2.
Hammond, Wayne G., and Christina Scull. 2000. *J.R.R. Tolkien, Artist and Illustrator*. Boston: Houghton Mifflin.
Harder, Douglas Wilhelm. N.d. "Timeline/Chronology for 'The Hobbit.'" Personal webpage, https://ece.uwaterloo.ca/~dwharder/Personal/Hobbit/.
Harrington, Philip S. 2001. *Cosmic Challenges*. Cambridge: Cambridge University Press.
Hasanzadeh, Amir. 2012. "Study of Danjon Limit in Moon Crescent Sighting." *Astrophysics and Space Science* 339: 211–221.
Holmes, T. Rice. 1920a. "The Earliest Visible Phase of the Moon." *The Classical Quarterly* 14, no. 3/4: 172.
_____. 1920b. "A Supplementary Note on the Julian Calendar." *The Classical Quarterly* 14, no. 1: 46–7.
Horner, D.W. 1911. "Early Visibility of the New Moon." *The Observatory* 34: 162–3.

Hunnewell, Sumner Gary. 1999. "Durin's Day." *Ravenhill*, August 1: 1–14.
Hynes, Gerald. 2012. "'Beneath the Earth's Dark Keel': Tolkien and Geology." *Tolkien Studies* 9: 21–36.
Langdon, Stephen. 1937. "Dr. J.K. Fotheringham, F.B.A.," *Nature* 139: 788–90.
Larsen, Kristine. 2006. "Swords and Sky Stones: Meteoric Iron in *The Silmarillion*." *Mallorn* no. 44: 22–6.
_____. 2008. "A Little Earth of His Own: Tolkien's Lunar Creation Myths." In *The Ring Goes Ever On: Proceedings of the Tolkien 2005 Conference, Vol. 2*, edited by Sarah Wells, 394–403. Coventry: Tolkien Society.
_____. 2008. "Shadow and Flame: Myth, Monsters, and Mother Nature in Middle-earth." In *The Mirror Crack'd: Fear and Horror in J.R.R. Tolkien's The Lord of the Rings and Its Sources*, edited by Lynn Forest-Hill, 169–96. Newcastle: Cambridge Scholars.
_____. 2011. "The Lunacy of *The Hobbit*." *Amon Hen* 230: 20–1.
_____. 2012. "Durin's Day and Moonlit Maps—Astronomy of the Moon Taught by *The Hobbit*." *The Classroom Astronomer* 13: 8–10, 24.
_____. 2013. "'That Sickle of the Heavenly Field': Celestial Motifs in 'The Lay of Leithian.'" *Mallorn* no. 54: 38–40.
Leuschner, A.O. 1927. "The Pons-Winnecke Comet." *Publications of the Astronomical Society of the Pacific* 39: 275–94.
Maunder, E. Walter. 1911. "On the Smallest Visible Phase of the Moon." *Journal of the British Astronomical Association* 21: 355–62.
McCluskey, Stephen. 2000. "The Inconstant Moon: Lunar Astronomies in Different Cultures." *Archaeoastronomy* 15: 14–31.
Moehn, Andreas. 2002. "The Moon and Durin's Day, 2941 TA." Lailaith's Middle-earth Science Pages. http://lalaith.vpsurf.de/Tolkien/Durin%27s_Day.html.
Pogo, A. 1938. "The Writings of J.K. Fotheringham." *Isis* 29: 58–68.
Quiñonez, Jorge, and Ned Raggett. 1990. "Nólë I Meneldilo: Lore of the Astronomer." *Vinyar Tengwar* no. 12: 5–15.
Rateliff, John D. 2007a. *The History of The Hobbit, Part One: Mr. Baggins*. Boston: Houghton Mifflin.
_____. 2007b. *The History of The Hobbit, Part Two: Return to Bag-End*. Boston: Houghton Mifflin.
"Recent Deaths." 1937. *Publications of the Astronomical Society of the Pacific* 49: 50.
Richards, E.G. 1999. *Mapping Time: The Calendar and Its History*. Oxford: Oxford University Press. EBSCO Host eBook.
"Salzburg Calls Fire Brigade to Put Out Aurora Borealis." 1926. *New York Times,* March 11, 1, ProQuest Historical Newspapers.
Sampson, R.A. 1937. "John Knight Fotheringham (1874–1936)." *Isis* 27: 485–92.
Schaefer, Bradley E. 1990. "Lunar Visibility and the Crucifixion." *Quarterly Journal of the Royal Astronomical Society* 31: 53–67.
_____. 1994. "*The Hobbit* and Durin's Day." *The Griffith Observer* 58, no. 11: 12–17.
Schlesinger, Frank, and Dirk Brouwer. 1939. "Biographical Memoir of Ernest William Brown (1866–1938)." *National Academy of Sciences Biographical Memoirs* 21, no. 6: 243–73.
Schoch, Carl. 1921. "The Earliest Visible Phase of the Moon." *The Classical Quarterly* 15, no. 3/4: 194.
Scull, Christina, and Wayne G. Hammond. 2006. *The J.R.R. Tolkien Companion and Guide: Chronology*. Boston: Houghton Mifflin.
Stephenson, F. R. 2004."Fotheringham, John Knight (1874–1936)." *Oxford Dictionary of National Biography*, Oxford University Press. http://www.oxforddnb.com/view/article/33220.
Tolkien, J.R.R. 1930. "The Oxford English School." *The Oxford Magazine* 48: 778–82.
_____. 1993a. *The Fellowship of the Ring*. Boston: Houghton Mifflin.
_____. 1993b. *Morgoth's Ring*. Boston: Houghton Mifflin.
_____. 1993c. *The Two Towers*. Boston: Houghton Mifflin.
_____. 2000. *The Letters of J.R.R. Tolkien*. Ed. Humphrey Carpenter. Boston: Houghton Mifflin.
_____. 2000. *The Treason of Isengard*. Boston: Houghton Mifflin.
_____. 2001. *The Silmarillion*, 2d ed. Boston: Houghton Mifflin.
_____. 2004. *Letters from Father Christmas*. Boston: Houghton Mifflin.
_____. 2007. *The Hobbit*. Boston: Houghton Mifflin.
Tolkien on Fairy-stories. 2002. Eds. Verlyn Flieger and Douglas A. Anderson. London: HarperCollins.
Van Biesbroeck, G. 1927. "Comet Notes." *Popular Astronomy* 35: 586–88.
Zwicky, Fritz. 1929. "On the Red Shift of Spectral Lines Through Interstellar Space." *Proceedings of the National Academy of Sciences of the United States of America*, 15:773–779.

A Scientific Examination of Durin's Day

Sumner Gary Hunnewell

What Is Durin's Day?

One of the keys to the story of *The Hobbit* is Thror's Map. It is described in the first chapter, has secrets hidden away until Rivendell, and is brought forth for the last time during the dangerous search for the Secret Door on the Lonely Mountain. This map, it is revealed by Elrond, holds the answer of how Thorin & Co. will be able to enter the mountain after which Bilbo must ply his new found trade. Elrond reads Moon-letters on the map "Stand by the grey stone when the thrush knocks and the setting sun with the last light of Durin's Day will shine upon the key-hole" (Tolkien, 1966, 62).

This is indeed a cryptic message to Elrond, especially *Durin's Day*, but Thorin, due to his lineage, knows its meaning full well.

> "Durin, Durin!" said Thorin. "He was the father of the fathers of the eldest race of Dwarves, the Longbeards, and my first ancestor: I am his heir."
> "Then what is Durin's Day?" asked Elrond.
> "The first day of the dwarves' New Year," said Thorin, "is as all should know the first day of the last moon of Autumn on the threshold of Winter. We still call it Durin's Day when the last moon of Autumn and the sun are in the sky together. But this will not help much, I fear, for it passes our skill in these days to guess when such a time will come again" [Tolkien, 1966, 62–63].

Other than Gandalf's premonition ("That remains to be seen") this fact is carefully tucked away but soon forgotten by the dwarves.

It might be useful to have the dwarves' New Year and Durin's Day explained more thoroughly than the haughty Thorin Oakenshield has done. Confusion comes from the unfortunate way that Tolkien describes it in the text. It is easier to understand if you read Thorin's comments in two complete sentences, the description provided by the second relying on the first. "The first day of the dwarves' New Year ... is ... the first day of the last moon of Autumn on the threshold of Winter" (Tolkien, 1966, 62–63).

Here Thorin states that the New Year occurs with the new moon ("first day") *and* the moon must be the last moon of autumn. In this way, there is a dwarvish New Year every year. Thorin goes on to answer Elrond's question "We still call it Durin's Day when the last moon of Autumn and the sun are in the sky together" (Tolkien, 1966, 63).

A dwarvish New Year happens *every* year but Durin's Day has an additional caveat: the sun and moon *must* be seen in the sky together during the time of the first moon. Further evidence of the distinction between the dwarvish New Year and Durin's Day can be found when Thorin & Co. are in the Misty Mountains. The dwarves "thought of coming to the secret door in the Lonely Mountain, perhaps that very next first moon of Autumn—'and perhaps it will be Durin's Day' they had said"[1] (Tolkien, 1966, 65). So, it must be an unusual (but not impossible) event indeed to be able to see the sun and first moon both in the sky together.

What Tolkien Meant by "Autumn" and "Winter"

With this knowledge, there seems to be a discrepancy in *The Hobbit*, as we know that Winter would start on 21 or 22 December, the time of the solstice—well after the Battle of the Five Armies. We are told that

> by mid-winter Gandalf and Bilbo had come all the way back, along both edges of the Forest, to the doors of Beorn's house; and there for a while they both stayed. Yuletide was warm and merry there; and men came from far and wide to feast at Beorn's bidding [Tolkien, 1966, 278].

If we understand Yuletide to be 25 December, there is no possible way for Bilbo and Gandalf to return to Beorn's house unless they take over a year to do so from Durin's Day to Yuletide. We know this is not true because Bilbo returns home in June, a little over one year from when his adventure started[2] (Tolkien, 1966, 282–84).

So, why the discrepancy? The problem lies in the assumption that Tolkien is using *the astronomical definition* for the basis of when winter starts.[3] This leads one to the question, what definition was Tolkien using? The answer is that Tolkien used the Celtic calendar to define the seasons.

Early northern European calendars used a different way of determining a year. They did not have months but rather a "week-year" system of 52 weeks to one year, lacking 1 1/4 days per solar year. On occasion these days were gathered and an extra week was added. The calendar year was split into two seasons of 26 weeks each, winter and summer. Each season was split by the solstice, with 13 weeks occurring before and after the solstice. The Celts improved the calendar by dividing the year into four parts and like its predecessor, a solstice or equinox split each season. Seven weeks before the solstice and equinox and six weeks after made for a 13-week season (Parise, 1982, 293).

The winter solstice falls either on 21 or 22 December; seven weeks before these dates are 2 and 3 November, respectively. The modern Celtic calendar, however, starts on *Samhain*, 1 November. This date is also called *Calan Gaeaf* in Welsh, *Calan Gwaf* in Cornish, and *Kala-Goañv* in Breton, which means "The First Day of Winter" (Anon., 1991, n.p.). The first of November is not exactly seven weeks before the winter solstice, but it is generally considered the first of winter, so I have accepted our current calendar as a proper guide.

If we assume Tolkien uses this seasonal calendar system, then this puts the *opportunity* for Durin's Day in October of every year. In this way, Thorin & Co. can be at Erebor at the end of autumn and the beginning of winter and still give Gandalf, Bilbo and Beorn plenty of time to return to Beorn's house by mid-winter and Yuletide. In this case Tolkien uses "mid-winter" in the same sense as he uses "mid-summer": the time of the solstice. It is not a coincidence that earlier Tolkien has Bilbo and Gandalf arriving at Elrond's house on 1 May, the date of *Bealtaine*, the Celtic festival celebrating the first of summer (Anon., 1991, n.p.).

Tolkien's Illustrations Provide a Key

Back to our story: Bilbo waits until all of the signs on Thror's Map come to life. It is the last week of autumn, the Thrush knocks snails against a stone, and then Bilbo sitting on the doorstep

> could see a glimpse of the distant forest. As the sun turned west there was a gleam of yellow upon its far roof, as if the light caught the last pale leaves. Soon he saw the orange ball of the sun sinking towards the level of his eyes. He went to the opening and there pale and faint was a thin new moon above the rim of Earth [Tolkien, 1966, 200].

The position of the moon is not given,[4] although it must be in the western sky and near to the sun to be a "new moon."

How providential! Not only do Thorin & Co. stumble onto the moon-letters but also they happened to pick a year which has a seemingly unusual astronomical event![5]

What may be (or may not be) surprising is that Tolkien was very particular about depicting this scene. In letter number 12 to Allen & Unwin, he discusses the draft for the dust jacket.

> There are too many colours: blue, green, red, black. (The 2 reds are an accident; the 2 greens inessential.) This could be met, with possible improvement, by substituting *white* for *red*; and omitting the sun, or drawing a line round it. The presence of the sun and moon in the sky together refers to the magic attaching to the door [Carpenter, 1981, 16].

If one looks at the dust jacket of *The Hobbit*, it is obvious that he has drawn Durin's Day (Hammond and Scull, 1995, 151). The sun and moon are in the sky together and, other than just artistic balance of providing a celestial feature on the front and the back of the dust jacket, it provides a nice tie-in with the story.[6] An earlier example of the dust jacket shows a much thinner crescent moon, which is more representative of Durin's Day (Hammond and Scull, 1995, 151). Both illustrations show a moon in a thin crescent, which is astronomically correct in relationship to the sun (in other words, the lit part of the moon is at the correct angle to the position of the sun). Two other examples are Tolkien's sketches and final book binding of *The Hobbit* (Hammond and Scull, 1995, 147, 148). There should not be any doubt that Tolkien depicts Durin's Day.[7]

A Mistake in the Phase of the Moon

Dr. Bradley E. Schaeffer correctly states that

> *The Hobbit* must have a scribal error of some sort, since on the day after Durin's Day the moon is said to rise in the evening and was used by Bard to sight the chink in Smaug's armor. This is inconsistent with the moon having set just after sunset on the previous evening[8] [Schaeffer, 1994, 14].

An explanation may lie with Tolkien's unfinished sketch "Death of Smaug" which first appeared on the Unwin Books paperback edition of *The Hobbit*. The colored pencil sketch shows Smaug, shot with the Black Arrow, ready to fall upon Esgaroth. A crescent moon is seen in the upper left-hand corner of the illustration. It is marked with an "x" to show a relationship with a caption written in the border of the drawing. The note reads "The moon should be a *crescent*: it was only a few nights after the *New Moon* on Durin's Day" (Hammond and Scull, 1995, 144).

Even if Tolkien had planned on having Smaug attack Esgaroth "a few nights after," it would have to be nearly two weeks before a moon would rise full, but there is no doubt in the published story that the attack took place the next day [Tolkien, 1966, 234].

The Evolution of Durin's Day

Tolkien's evolution of Durin's Day during his writing of *The Hobbit* is Tolkienesque as he starts with a simple idea and makes it more complex with each draft. The earliest surviving manuscript containing the moon-runes reads:

> Stand by the grey stone when the crow knocks and the rising sun [will] at the moment of dawn on Durin's Day will shine upon the keyhole." Soon it was replaced by "Stand by the grey stone where the thrush knocks. Then the setting sun on the last light of Durin's Day will shine on the key hole [Rateliff, 2007, 22–23].

This is an obvious change needed due to Tolkien's placement of the secret door, which was on the *western* side of Erebor, even on Tolkien's oldest map of the mountain (Hammond and Scull, 1995, 92).

The first extensive manuscript reads:

> Stand by the grey stone where the thrush knocks. Then the [rising>] setting sun on the last light of Durin's Day will shine upon the key hole.
>
> * * *
>
> "The first day of the dwarves' New Year" said Gandalf "and that is, as everyone knows, the day of the first moon of autumn. And Durin's day is that [*penciled in:* first] day when the first moon of autumn and the sun are in the sky together" [Rateliff, 2007, 116].

This first typescript was reworked into a second (unpublished) typescript and then the final published concept of the dwarvish New Year became "the last moon of Autumn on the threshold of Winter." Also, the event of Durin's Day "when that last moon of Autumn and the sun are in the sky together" (Rateliff, 2007, 116, 123–24; Tolkien, 1966, 62–63). Changes in the timing of these dwarvish events demand alterations later in the story as Thorin & Co. sit on the doorstep. For example, in the first manuscript Thorin the dwarf states "Autumn will be in tomorrow," which is altered to "Tomorrow begins the last month [>week] of Autumn" (Rateliff, 2007, 475, 480–81).

Date of Durin's Day in The Hobbit

It might be worthwhile at this point to calculate when Durin's Day actually occurred in *The Hobbit*. Although this has been attempted elsewhere, the calculations have been based on counting back from the return to Beorn's house. Since the Shire Calendar was not conceived at this time, Tolkien uses our current calendar, so using other stated dates should be easy to determine.

Actually dating Durin's Day as it appears in *The Hobbit* has stumped the fan and scholar for many years, but the clue may be in the text when Thorin says "Tomorrow begins the last week of Autumn" (Tolkien, 1966, 200). The next day Durin's Day occurs. We might be able to place Durin's Day, if we take for granted that Gandalf is telling us the truth about Thrain's disappearance "on the twenty-first of April, a hundred years ago last Thursday," then we can extrapolate the last week of October. The twenty-first of April only appears on a Thursday once (excluding a leap year) and the last week of October starts on Sunday, 30 October. This is where I would place Durin's Day.[9]

In 1960 Tolkien attempted to synchronize the storyline in *The Hobbit* within the construct of his legendarium. As a part of this effort, he endeavored to reconcile the moon phases as he had done extensively in *The Lord of the Rings*. The touch points were the encounter with the trolls ("waning moon"), the reading of the moon runes ("broad silver crescent"), and Durin's Day ("this new moon"). Rather than change the phases of the moon, he attempted to adjust the travel time to make the moons fit. Tolkien decided to use the newly introduced Shire Calendar system, which brought about its own problems. With some effort, Tolkien set Durin's Day to his satisfaction on 17 October (Winterfilth) Shire Reckoning (Tolkien, 1966, 43, 62, 200; Rateliff, 2007, 825–36).[10]

A Critical Point: The Distance of the New Moon from the Sun

After solving the calendar riddle, one must ask about the first moon riddle. But, first it might be useful to explain simply the motion of the sun and moon in relation to the observer on (Middle-)earth. The moon revolves around the earth in 29.53 days and this is known as a *lunation*. Astronomically speaking, a new moon occurs when the earth, moon and sun are in conjunction—the moon lies between the earth and sun. The moon and sun look to us to travel daily east to west. The sun (relative to the stars in the sky) moves along a path, called the *ecliptic*, at roughly 1 degree per day, while the moon travels about 13 degrees per day, with its path slightly off-kilter to the sun (at times about 5 degrees above or below the ecliptic). This would put the approximate 24-hour distance between the sun and the moon at 12 degrees. So, we arrive at a question: can the sun and the thin crescent of the moon both be seen in the sky together when the moon and sun are a scant 12 degrees away?

Thin crescent moon visibility has been very important to many religious cultures, especially the ancient Jews and Muslims, but it has not been until the last three decades when there has been a concerted secular effort to find the youngest thin crescent. Due to the mechanics of the sun and moon, one has a limited time in which to identify the youngest moon. In 1936 André Danjon, a French astronomer and director of the Strasbourg Observatory, calculated that the moon must be at least 7 degrees away from the sun to be visible (due to the shadow of the mountains of the moon). Early and current scientific observations have been to identify the youngest moon relative to the time of the astronomical new moon. The current record is between a fourteen and fifteen hour moon (as seen by the naked eye) which upholds Danjon's 7-degree limit; however, the observations have been when the sun has set long before in order to cut down on the background brightness of the sky and glare of the sun (Ashbrook, 1984, 200–9).

Other than my empirical and far from scientific work, there has been very little written on the visibility of a waxing thin crescent new moon while the sun is still in the sky. Dr. Bradley Schaeffer suggests that in full daylight a distance of at least 35 degrees is necessary (Schaeffer, 1995). Perhaps it would be helpful to present three of my personal observations.

On 6 October 1994, more than a day after the new moon, I located the moon in some hazy clouds some five to seven minutes after the sun went below the horizon. Jupiter was very bright in the sky and helped point out the way to the moon. Had there not been the haze, I would imagine that I would have seen the sun and moon in the sky together. The distance between the moon and sun was approximately 21 degrees.

On 1 December 1994, more than a day *before* the new moon, I was able to observe the *oldest* moon and the sun in the sky together at sunrise. Venus provided direction during this observation. The moon was visible but only for a few minutes. The distance between the sun and moon at this time was a little more than 24 degrees.

The distances between the sun and moon with these two observations are very far from the needed 24-hour period to make this a "first day" but these observations are useful as will be seen later.

I attempted to again see the oldest moon on 23 September 1995. This time the moon would be 18 degrees away from the sun, but a good fifteen minutes before sunrise the moon, which had been very visible a half hour before, winked out—the light of the sky overwhelming it.

With the failure of my last observation, I felt that Durin's Day as Tolkien described it was not possible. In order to make Durin's Day "work" suggested that my thinking about the new moon, the first day of the moon, was incorrect and this led me after many conversations to use a different paradigm: if Tolkien is not using an astronomical definition of winter then why should he use an astronomical definition of a new moon? This started my search for clues to discover exactly what Thorin (and, therefore, Tolkien) meant by "the *first day* of the last moon of Autumn."

The "First Day" of the Moon and the Jews

"The Towneley Play of Noah" can be found in Sisam's *Fourteenth Century Verse and Prose*. It retells the story of the Flood and during the play the Noah character says to his wife, "*For this is the fyrst day of the tent moyne*" ("For this is the first day of the tenth moon"). Tolkien in his *Middle-English Vocabulary* describes this word (*moyne*) under the entry of *mone* (ME for moon) as a "lunar month" (Sisam, 1975, 201, 384). This passage from the play is taken from *Genesis 8:5*. A survey of four English language Bibles (including an interlinear Hebrew/English edition) does not contain the word "moon" but "month" in its stead. What would cause the discrepancy between a fourteenth-century playwright's reading of this passage in *Genesis* and the current interpretation?

It is important at this point when talking about the first book of *The Bible* to understand the reckoning of months in the *ancient* Hebrew calendar. The Hebrew calendar was a lunar-solar calendar, meaning that it depended on lunation to reckon months, but the solar cycle was used as well to maintain agricultural and religious customs during the same season of the year.[11] Originally the Hebrew month started with the first sighting of the new moon (*Rosh Hodesh*). Witnesses would testify before the Sanhedrin in Jerusalem, the court would confirm the sighting with calculations, and declare (if the observation was valid) the start of the new month. Signal fires would be lit on mountains or messengers would be deployed to spread the news. During the fourth century, the patriarch Hillel II, due to external pressures on the Sanhedrin, created the modern Hebrew calendar. Doing so, he realized that the standardization would lead to common dates (which could differ due to the day of the sighting of the new moon) for the Jews of Palestine and the Diaspora. Also at this time, the secret calculations for discerning the earliest new moon were revealed (Speir, 1952).

There are four different Hebrew words used in the *Old Testament* for moon. One, *lebanah* (le ban áh), is used as a metaphor for the pallor of the moon. The other remaining three—*jerah* (yér ach), *jarah* (ye ráy ach), and *hodesh* (hó desh)—have very similar senses and are used interchangeably for "month"/"new moon" or "the new moon"/"The first day of the month" (Green, 1979; Green, 1987; Strang, n.d.; Waldstein, 1967). Knowing all of this helps solves our problem with our fourteenth century playwright: either word was acceptable and understood by the people of that time, and it was understood by Tolkien as well when creating his *Middle English Vocabulary*.

On at least three occasions Tolkien had suggested that the dwarves were similar to Jews in some respects. In a 1947 letter he states, "Now the Dwarves have their own secret language, but like Jews and Gypsies use the language of the country" (Rateliff, 2007, 757). In Letter 176 he states "I do think of the 'Dwarves' like Jews: at once native and alien in their habitations, speaking the languages of the country, but with an accent due to their own private tongue" (Carpenter, 1981, 228–29). Also, more extensively in an interview with Basil Bunting, he states:

> ...And the dwarves, of course, it's quite obviously—couldn't you in many ways say they remind you of the Jews? All their words are Semitic, obviously, and could expect to be Semitic. There is a tremendous love of the artifact and, of course, the immense warlike past of the Jews, too, which we tend to forget nowadays[12] [Tolkien and Bunting, 1980].

Would these quotes also suggest that the dwarves used a similar lunar calendar to the Jews? I would say, yes, Tolkien is drawing from the Jewish tradition. So, if we assume that these are Tolkien's intentions, what does this tell us about the "first day" in Thorin's quote?

A Story and Another Dwarvish Concern

Let us assume that we have a very sharp eyed group of dwarves waiting on the slopes of the Lonely Mountain at the end of autumn. The sun has set some time ago and a pale crescent moon, a new moon, a first moon, can be seen westwards above the horizon. The day is proclaimed as the Dwarvish New Year. A year passes and the dwarves await the first moon, but the moon is too close to the sun to be seen. The dwarves leave and come back the following day. The moon has traveled away from the sun in this time. They look above and to the left of the sun trying to spot the crescent. It *is* spotted and it grows in brightness as the sun sinks below the horizon. This is the dwarvish New Year *and* Durin's Day.

This takes us down a different and final path with regards to the visibility of the new moon. As you may remember, the Jews of Jerusalem had lit fires upon the confirmation of the first of the month as a signal to other Jewish communities. Later, a structured calendar was created in part to synchronize the calendars for all Jews. They understood the concept of the visibility of the new moon depending on the viewer's location on earth. This idea was explored by B.D. Yallop, M. Ilyas and later refined by B. Schaeffer and is called the Lunar Date Line, an imaginary line which helps determine whether a new crescent can be seen or not (Doggett and Schaeffer, 1994, 388–403). Relating this to our dwarves—it might very well be Durin's Day at the secret door but not perhaps at Moria or the Ered Luin. This leads one to wonder how or if dwarves reckoned their own months and how they might be able to clear up discrepancies. It is no wonder that Thorin when explaining Durin's Day laments "it passes our skill in these days to guess when such a time will come again" (Tolkien, 1966, 63).

Acknowledgments

Thanks go to Christopher Gilson who patiently showed enough interest to make me want to find the answer; to David Bigwood, who looked over this manuscript for glaring astronomical errors; to Pat Wynne who supplied me with the Celtic Calendars with his marvelously illustrated work; to Dr. Bradley Schaeffer for clues about the moon's visibility and review of this revised paper; to John Rateliff for help with the original manuscripts; to Steven Massey, who opened my eyes to a different way of looking at things; and, special thanks go to John Houghton and Sylvia and Tristan Hunnewell, who heard me rant on the subject for over a year until the answer became clear.

Notes

1. Tolkien meant the *last* moon of autumn. This mistake survived until identified by John D. Rateliff and then corrected in the 1995 fourth edition (Rateliff, 1995; Anderson, 2002, 102–3).

2. Karen Wynn Fonstad in *The Atlas to Middle-earth* extrapolates back from the Yuletide quote above and decided to make Durin's Day fall upon 30 October 2941, Third Age or our 8 November based on "our New Year's Day corresponded more or less to the Shire January 9." J.R.R. Tolkien, *The Return of the King*, Appendix D (Tolkien, 1965, 483). Still, this is nowhere near the solstice.

3. I believe Rateliff mistakenly believes Tolkien use the solstice to determine the set the start of winter in the text, especially as Tolkien continues to use "mid-summer" and "mid-winter." Even Tolkien's 1960 revision places Durin's Day in October (Rateliff, 2007, 480–81, 592, 828).

4. It is curious to note that of all of the illustrations depicting this scene, which the author has seen, have left the moon out entirely, except for two drawings. The first is found in the 1989 Russian illustrated edition of *The Hobbit* (Tolkien, 1989, 224 facing). The second is the English Folio edition of *The Hobbit*. Fraser's illustration places the moon above and to the right of the sun (Tolkien, 1979, 164).

5. So intent were the dwarves to find the Secret Door, they forgot entirely about the dwarves' New Year. Also, Bilbo's urgency is not understated. In order to get the key into the lock, they have a handful of minutes between Bilbo's epiphany and the sun setting below the horizon.

6. The dust jacket is not representative of the story at a certain moment in time. Other than the occurrence of the Durin's Day scene, the Eagles, Mirkwood, Smaug, the Lonely Mountain, Esgaroth, etc., appear together.

7. It might also be of interest to note that Tolkien's illustration found on the dust jacket of *The Hobbit* shows a star, the Moon, and Sun. If we take the star to be Venus (Eärendil) then a similar configuration of the night sky appeared on 23 October 1930, the year Tolkien started writing *The Hobbit*. Of course this comparison is pure speculation as Tolkien's draft of the dust jacket does not have a star and Venus is farther from the moon on that day in October. However, Tolkien's size of the Moon and Sun as seen on the published dust jacket is exaggerated.

8. Roäc also states Smaug died "at the rising of the moon" (Tolkien, 1966, 245).

9. A timeline constructed based on an early account by Roäc of Smaug's death "Tuesday night" would put Durin's Day on a Monday. However, the day of Smaug's death does not survive to the published text (Rateliff, 2007, 619, 622; Tolkien, 1966, 245).

10. 17 October is equivalent to our 9 October based on Appendix D.

11. With a month equal to a lunation and twelve lunations equaling year, it can be seen that this falls short of a 365 day year by around eleven days. In order to synchronize the lunar calendar to the solar one, the Jews introduced an additional month and/or an extra day in a regular fashion.

12. "love for the artifact" is echoed in Tolkien's notes for his 1960 revision of *The Hobbit*. "But they [Thorin's folk] had the notion that hobbits were a slow stupid folk, with few artefacts, and simpleminded" (Rateliff, 2007, 816).

Works Cited

Anderson, Douglas A. 2002. *The Annotated Hobbit*. 2d ed. Boston: Houghton Mifflin.
Ashbrook, Joseph. 1984. *The Astronomical Scrapbook: Skywatchers, Pioneers, and Seekers in Astronomy*. Cambridge, MA: Cambridge University Press and Sky Publishing Corp.
Carpenter, Humphrey, ed. 1981. *The Letters of J.R.R. Tolkien*. Boston: Houghton Mifflin.
Celtic Calendar 1992. 1991. Bronx: Celtic League American Branch.
Doggett, LeRoy E., and Bradley E. Schaefer. 1994. "Lunar Crescent Visibility." *Icarus* 107:2 (February): 388–403.
Fonstad, Karen Wynn. 1981. *The Atlas to Middle-earth*. Boston: Houghton Mifflin.
Green, Jay. 1979. *The Interlinear Hebrew/Greek English Bible*. Lafayette, IN: Associated Publishers and Authors.
_____, ed. 1987. *A Concise Lexicon to the Biblical Languages*. Peabody, MA: Hendrickson.
Parise, Frank, ed. 1982. *The Book of Calendars*. New York: Facts on File.
Rateliff, John D. 1995. Personal correspondence to Gary Hunnewell, 1 March.
_____. 2007. *The History of* The Hobbit. 2 vols. London: HarperCollins.

Schaefer, Dr. Bradley E. 1994. "*The Hobbit* and Durin's Day." *The Griffith Observer* 58:11 (November): 12–17.
_____. 1995. Personal correspondence to Gary Hunnewell, 16 June.
Sisam, Kenneth, ed. 1975. *Fourteenth Century Verse and Prose*. Oxford: Oxford University Press.
Spier, Arthur. 1952. *The Comprehensive Hebrew Calendar*. New York: Behrman House.
Strang, James. n.d. *Comprehensive Concordance of the Bible*. Iowa Falls, IA: World Bible.
Tolkien, J.R.R. 1965. *The Return of the King*. New York: Ballantine.
_____. 1966. *The Hobbit*. Rev. ed. New York: Ballantine.
_____. 1979. *The Hobbit*. London: Folio Society.
_____. 1989. *Хоббит, или туда и обратно*. Novosibirsk.
Tolkien and Basil Bunting. 1980. BBC Cassettes ECN 117. Guilford, CT: Jeffrey Norton.
Waldstein, A.S. 1967. *Hebrew English/English Hebrew Dictionary*. Brooklyn: P. Shalom.

Part III
Themes

Tolkien's French Connection

VERLYN FLIEGER

It may surprise some of you (and it would certainly have surprised him) to learn that Bilbo Baggins, the original hobbit, fat, bumbling, suburban in outlook and slightly compared by Gloin to a grocer, should actually be more respectfully compared to a knight in the tradition of medieval French romance. There's a reason for this surprise. Ever since the publication of Humphrey Carpenter's biography, conventional wisdom has held that J.R.R. Tolkien was averse to all things French. He unequivocally stated his distaste for the French language, saying flat out "I dislike French" (Tolkien, 2000, 288); and for French cuisine, Carpenter refers to "tiresome French cooking" (119) and its "pernicious influence" in England (129). He deplored the Norman Conquest (Carpenter, 1977, 129), and promoted a return to "English goodliness of speechcraft," by which, says biographer John Garth, he meant "a language purged of ... French derivatives" (Garth, 2003, 52). And then there is his sniffy comment in "On Fairy-stories" that in France the fairy tale "went to court and put on powder and diamonds" (Tolkien, 1983, 111). Although this is not a scathing criticism, it is certainly not a compliment, while in an early draft he goes further, declaring that French fairy-stories are "not to [his] taste" and that he "never had much affection" for "these French things" (Tolkien, 2008, 214). Carpenter lumped all this together as Tolkien's "Gallophobia," and conventional wisdom has embraced the term ever since.

But dislike does not preclude influence—indeed it can sometimes foster it—and an author is not always the most reliable authority on his own work. Neither conventional wisdom nor Carpenter, let alone Tolkien himself, should be taken as the last word on his relationship to France and things French. Two of his early poems," The Lay of Leithian" and the "Lay of Aotrou and Itroun," derive from France. *Lay* itself is a loan-word from Old French *lai*, a long narrative in verse. And while *leithian* is Tolkien's own Elvish, meaning "release" (*LR* 368), the words *aotrou* and *itroun,* meaning "lord" and "lady," are Breton, as is the poem on which Tolkien modeled his own, "Aotrou Nann Hag Ar Gorrigan." It can be argued that these last terms and Tolkien's source for them are Celtic, and thus not strictly French, and while this is correct, it is not the whole picture. "Aotrou Nann Hag Ar Gorrigan" was first published in France in a dual-language French and Breton anthology of folklore, an edition of which was bought and inscribed by Tolkien in 1922. The anthology was the work of a French folklorist of Breton descent, and ties in well with Tolkien's interest in the mythic and folkloric substrates of European cultures. All of which brings it a lot closer to France than to Tolkien's more recognized influences in Germany and Scandinavia and Anglo-Saxon England.

And if we turn from poetry to prose, we will find some important and notably French-derived terms in Tolkien's essay "On Fairy-stories (Tolkien, 2000, 118). In one memorable sentence he used two such terms, declaring that fairy-stories are about "the *aventures* of men in the Perilous Realm" which he called *Faërie* (Tolkien, 1983, 113). Thus the same essay that showed him looking down his nose at French powder and diamonds shows him turning to French vocabulary when he needs the precise word to convey a particular meaning. Moreover, these words are not merely precise and apt, they are essential to his critical and creative vocabulary, recurring significantly, as we shall see.

Nevertheless, *aventures* is so unlikely a word for a presumed Gallophobe to use that the copy editor for *The Tolkien Reader* thought it was a typo and inserted a "d," correcting it to *adventures*. In fact, *adventures* is the typo, and *aventures* is Tolkien's correct spelling and usage. The editorial mistake is pardonable, however, as *aventure* is not a word in common parlance—not, at least, in English. It is part of the specialized vocabulary of French romance, where it denotes the exploits of knights errant in a magical otherworld often called "the forest of *aventure*." The Celtic equivalent is Old Irish *echtra, echtrae, ectra, echtrai*, usually translated "adventure," an Irish tale type involving the hero's journey to the Otherworld, of which there are numerous examples (MacKillop, 1998, 148), and to which the medieval French stories clearly have some relationship. There is an equivalent Welsh tale type exemplified in the *Mabinogion* by the adventure of Pwyll prince of Dyfed in Annwuyn (from *an* "in, inside" + *dwuyn* "deep" (*Pwyll*, 1957, 26). The Modern Breton equivalent of the word is *Anaon*, the world of the dead. I have been unable to find an equivalent Welsh or Breton term for the tale type *echtrae*, but the tales themselves certainly exist. Tolkien would have been aware of all these examples (he made his own translation of *Pwyll Pendeuic Dyuet*) and their relationship through shared Celtic heritage with the medieval French romances, but the closest parallels to Bilbo's adventures are in the French rather than the more strictly Celtic stories.

Adventure comes from the French into Middle English as *auentur(e)/aunter*, which Tolkien's *Middle English Vocabulary* glosses as "chance (notable) occurrence, feat, risk." But even here it means more than just escapade. It implies the kind of danger embodied in the *echtrae*, implying entry into the Otherworld, encounter with the unexpected, the unexplained, even the supernatural, as in the Middle English *The Awnters off Arthure at the Terne Wathelyne*, in which Arthur encounters a ghost at a haunted tarn or lake. In the French romances the word was sometimes spelled *avanture*, linking it to *avant*, "forward," and connoting "what's coming," meaning the unknown and by implication the mysterious future. When Tolkien talked about "the *aventures* of men in the Perilous Realm" he meant all of this.

The same is true of his other notable French derivative, *Faërie*, the Perilous Realm. *Faërie*, like *aventure*, means more than its modern counterpart. It does not refer to fairies, but to *faërie*, described by Tolkien as "the realm or state in which fairies have their being" (Tolkien, 1983, 113). The agentive suffix *erie* denotes both a process and a condition, as in *cook-ery, witch-ery, slave-ery*. Thus *faë-erie* is both the process of enchantment and the condition of being enchanted, the altered state produced by fairy-stories. The word derives from Old French *fae* or *fée* from Latin *fata/fatum*, "Fate," the past participle of *fari*, "to speak," hence a word spoken, a spell cast, or a story told. The connection to *Fate* as that which is spoken suggests the reason Tolkien called *Faërie* the Perilous Realm and French romance called it "the forest of *aventure*." "Small wonder," said Tolkien in the essay, "that *spell* means both a story told, and a formula of power over living men" (Tolkien, 1947, 56; Tolkien, 1983, 128).

But what has this to do with *The Hobbit*? Or to put it more bluntly, "so what?" French words in a poem and an essay do not necessarily translate to French influence in a children's story. Moreover, *The Hobbit* has been getting on very well for seventy years without recourse to French influence. I suggest a couple of answers. First, recognition of French influence expands *The Hobbit* from children's fairy tale to the more "literary" genre of romance. With one notable anomaly, which I'll address in due course, the narrative structure of the first half of *The Hobbit* replicates the narrative structure of medieval French romance. (The change of mode in the latter half of *The Hobbit* from romance to saga has been recognized ever since C.S. Lewis commented in "On Stories" that "it is if ... Badger had begun to talk like Njal.") The romance structure goes like this. A hero—usually a knight—leaves home—usually King Arthur's court—on errantry (from Fr. *errer* "to wander"). He undergoes trials in battles against extraordinary opponents, after which he returns to home base.

The pattern is a recognizable sub-set of the Hero Path, the master paradigm described by Joseph Campbell as Separation, Initiation and Return. But instead of Campbell's one decisive encounter with a single foe, medieval romance gives its heroes a series of random encounters with a succession of foes—other knights, giants, robbers, lions, wild men, serpents. It is easy to see Bilbo's path in *The Hobbit*—leaving Bag End to wander from trolls to wolves to goblins to Gollum to wood-elves—as a clear parallel. His comically-named sword Sting has an ancestor in Arthur's Excalibur and Roland's Durendal. Even in the story's second half, Thorin Oakenshield's exhortation in the dragon's cave that Bilbo "Cast off [his] old coat and put on" the *mithril* mail-coat, belt, and helmet (*H* 203) carries out the dictum that "clothes make the man" (or the hobbit) and effectively transforms Bilbo from amateur burglar to medieval knight, and Bard the Bowman's comment that he is "worthy to wear the armour of elf-princes" (*H* 230) confirms his new status.

Second and more specifically, the French Connection invites a re-reading of the opening conversation between Gandalf and Bilbo that directly counters conventional wisdom regarding French influence, Carpenter's "Gallophobic" appellation, and Tolkien's own statements about taste. In the first five pages of *The Hobbit* the word *adventure* occurs a total of twelve times—a little more than twice on every page. That's a pretty high average, and it is conscious repetition, not careless writing. I hope to persuade you that when Tolkien said *adventure* in *The Hobbit* he meant *aventure* as in the essay. Here are the relevant sentences.

> Page 11, the narrator: (1) The Bagginses "never had any *adventures*"; (2) "This is a story about how a Baggins had an *adventure*." Page 12 (1) "once in a while members of the Took-clan would go and have *adventures*"; (2) "not that Belladonna Took ever had any *adventures*." Page 13 (1) "tales and *adventures* sprouted up all over the place wherever [Gandalf] went"; (2) Gandalf to Bilbo: "I am looking for someone to share in an *adventure*"; (3) Bilbo to Gandalf: "I have no use for *adventures* ....!" Page 14, Bilbo to Gandalf: (1) "We don't want any *adventures* here"; (2) Bilbo to Gandalf: "Not the Gandalf who was responsible for so many quiet lads and lasses going off into the Blue for mad *adventures*." Page 15 (1) Gandalf to Bilbo: "I will ... send you on this *adventure*"; Bilbo to Gandalf: (2) "I don't want any *adventures*"; the narrator: (3) "Bilbo ... was beginning to think he had escaped *adventures* very well."

Like a leit-motif in music, this recurrence is cumulative, echoing and re-echoing until the word spoken becomes "a spell cast, a formula of power" and finally "a story told." I do not suggest that the copy-editor of *The Tolkien Reader* emended *The Hobbit*, but I do suggest that Tolkien's intention is best served if we remove that 'd'. I also suggest that when he said "into the Blue" in *The Hobbit* he meant *Faërie* as in the essay.

But even if the words and the concepts behind them are French-derived, does that necessarily make *The Hobbit* a French romance? Not by itself, no; but it helps. Supporting evidence comes from actual French romances. If we look at *The Hobbit* in the context of three actual romances, two by the French poet Chrétien de Troyes, and one adapted from the French by Sir Thomas Malory in *Le Morte D'Arthur*, we will see sufficient similarity to support my argument. I want to emphasize that I am not analyzing plot here, merely tallying *aventures* as they occur in the episodic world of French romance. I also want to emphasize that like *The Hobbit* the humor of these stories undermines their subject matter. All three are spoofs, seeming to extol *aventure* while actually poking sly fun at it, as when Chrétien's hero Yvain, asked to fight some giants, hopes they will be on time so he won't be late for his date to rescue a maiden from burning at the stake. Malory, too, plays for laughs, having that paragon of knighthood, Launcelot, so lost in a dream of Guinevere that he forgets where he is and falls ingloriously off his horse. Tolkien's burglarious hobbit hero starts out as equally incompetent, trying to steal a talking purse whose unexpected vocal ability betrays him to the Trolls. Like the knight in *Monty Python*, he gets better, but it takes time.

In Chrétien's *Erec and Enide*, the young knight Erec gets lost in the *"forest of aventure,"* where he is insulted by an arrogant knight. He pursues him through the forest, defeats him in a tournament, and brings home the beautiful Enide as a bride. When after their wedding he overhears her incautious lament that spending too much time with her has damaged his knightly reputation, he forces her to go on errantry with him so that he can prove his prowess. The satire here is edged and cutting. One of Arthur's knights puts his lady at risk by using her as sexual bait to attract highway thugs, predatory seducers, and potential rapists, yet when she tries to warn him what's coming commanding her to keep her mouth shut. Unlike Bilbo and Launcelot, Erec is not incompetent; he is just bullying and tyrannical and criminally irresponsible. His *aventures*, which he intends to present him in a heroic role, are cumulatively ironic as he is wounded by one attacker, knocked unconscious by another, and finally apparently killed by a third. While in each of these episodes it is Erec who seeks *aventure*, it is the long-suffering Enide who finds it, repeatedly having to save him from her attackers. The final episode, "The Joy of the Court" (explicitly called an *aventure*), occurs in an orchard (not quite a *forêt*, but close enough) and has Erec defeat another knight, Maboagrain, who is also fighting to impress his sweetheart. Both pairs of lovers are reconciled by means of this senseless mayhem, and all four live happy ever after.

In Chrétien's next romance, *Yvain*, the eponymous hero leaves Arthur's court to go "adventuring" (Troyes, 1975, *Yvain* l. 167) in *la forêt aventureuse* of Broceliande, a notoriously Otherworld locality. Here he encounters a Wild Man, unwittingly provokes a tempest, kills the magical Knight of the Storm, marries his widow but leaves her for a year to fight in tournaments, after which he defends a lady from attack by a wicked seneschal, saves a lion from a serpent, kills the aforementioned giants—who fortunately show up on time to be killed—and rescues the maiden. It is important to note that in each of these episodes, the *aventure* is simply there for its own sake, with no larger unifying purpose or plot. Like Erec, Yvain is looking for *aventure* and he finds it. After fighting incognito as "the knight with the lion" (compare the epithets Bilbo assumes with the dragon) he returns to his abandoned wife and they live happily ever after.

I hope you have seen some parallels with *The Hobbit* here, but I hope you have also noticed the glaring difference I mentioned in my first paragraph. Unlike the romances it parodies, Tolkien's story has no love interest. It strains imagination to picture Bilbo Baggins as a lover or a husband. Indeed, Tolkien himself, planning the sequel that became *The Lord of the Rings*, considered but dismissed as unworkable the notion that Bilbo could marry and have children. However, while a love interest is a standard trope in medieval romance, it is not a requirement, and Bilbo's other attributes qualify him. Malory's "Noble Tale of Sir Launcelot Du Lake," adapted from the French Prose *Lancelot*, plays down the love interest while otherwise following the pattern. Like Erec and Yvain, Launcelot rides away from Arthur's court to "preve" himself in "straunge [that is, 'marvelous'] adventures." He tells his nephew, Sir Lyonel that "we must go seke adventures" (Malory, 1979, 149). Why "must" they? Because that is what knights do, and Malory provides plenty of comedic *aventures* to keep his knight errant busy. Launcelot is kidnapped for illicit purpose by Morgan le Fay, hit on by two women (he turns them both down out of love for Guinevere), climbs a tree in his underwear to rescue a hawk, defends himself with a tree branch against a fully armed knight, and fails to prevent another knight from beheading his own wife. Launcelot finally gets his payback by trading armor with the biggest wimp in Arthur's court, Sir Kay, making Kay unattackable, while beating the pants off all the knights who think he's an easy mark. At the end of his *aventures* Launcelot returns to Arthur's court with "the grettyste name of ony knight of the world" (173). Makes you wonder just what "greatest" means in this upside down romance world.

All three of these figures trace a narrative arc that we can see also in *The Hobbit*. Departure from home and entry into *Faërie*, followed by an escalating series of *aventures*, culminating in a final battle and a return to home base and happy ever after. The word used for Erec's and Yvain's and Launcelot's deeds—*aventure*—is deliberately echoed in Bilbo's opening conversation with Gandalf. Tolkien's hero is a parodic romance knight, a bumbling, suburban householder pitched without warning into a series of knightly *aventures* for which he seems ludicrously unfitted. Bilbo does not "seke" a "grete name." He does not kill a giant, win a wife, rescue a maiden, or make friends with a lion. But he does get captured by trolls, ambushed by goblins, surrounded by wolves, rescued by eagles, lost in Mirkwood (a *forêt aventureuse* if there ever was one), attacked by spiders, and detained by elves. In his final encounter, the Battle of Five Armies, he like Erec is knocked unconscious.

As is the case with Erec and Yvain and Launcelot, no plot connects Bilbo's *aventures* to one another. They are episodic, unrelated, each *aventure* self-contained and discrete. In *Master of Middle-earth*, Paul Kocher points out that unlike Frodo, "Bilbo's enemies are serial, not united under any paragon of evil as is to happen [in *The Lord of the Rings*]. *The Hobbit*'s trolls, goblins (orcs), spiders, and dragon know nothing of one another, and all are acting on their own" (Kocher, 1972, 30). At the end of his adventure Bilbo returns home, leaving in his wake peace and prosperity, and bringing with him treasure, plus the comment of Gandalf that he is "not the hobbit" that he was when he set out (*H* 253). Like Erec and Yvain, he has been changed by his *aventures*, although (also like Erec and Yvain) that was not his reason for seeking them. Retrospective references in *The Fellowship of the Ring* to his journey in *The Hobbit* deliberately repeat the key word, and tend to support the idea of adventure for its own sake, as was the case in *Erec* and *Yvain*. In Chapter One of *The Lord of the Rings* Bilbo, like Erec and Yvain and Launcelot, leaves Bag End as he did in *The Hobbit* with no goal in mind but the need for a "holiday" (*FR* 40). At the Council of Elrond, he whispers to Frodo, "I almost wish that my adventures were not over" (*FR* II, ii, 261), and the narrative points out that Frodo's fiftieth birthday marks the age at which "adventure had suddenly befallen Bilbo" (*FR* 52). I believe we may safely confer a French pronunciation on this apparently English word.

Comparison of *The Hobbit* with *The Lord of the Rings* is inevitable, but reveals more differences than similarities. In the most general sense, both follow the traditional romance trajectory—a hero's journey and return. Within that, however, are substantial sub-genre distinctions, what Paul Kocher calls "polarities in tone and scope between *The Hobbit* and its successor" (Kocher, 1972, 30) that make *The Hobbit* and *The Lord of the Rings* "so unalike fundamentally as to be different in kind" (Kocher, 1972, 19). In spite of surface similarities—journey plots, hobbit heroes, multi-cultural elves, dwarves, orcs and wizards—the two are not just different books, they are, as Kocher says, different *kinds* of books. One is a fairy tale romance for children, the other a bigger and darker story closer to epic than romance.

Each kind is signaled by its key word: *aventure* for *The Hobbit*, *quest* for *The Lord of the Rings*.

Like *aventure* and *faërie*, *quest* is French in origin, coming into Middle English through Old French *queste* "to seek or search for," from Latin *quaerere* "pursuit or search" from earlier Latin *quaerere*, "to seek." The nature of Frodo's quest, in contrast to Bilbo's adventure, imposes a more unified structure on his story. That Tolkien was well aware of the distinction is shown by his post–*Lord of the Rings* re-casting of the events of *The Hobbit* from Gandalf's perspective as "The Quest of Erebor," which takes all the *aventure* out of the story, and takes out all of the fun as well.

In the second chapter of *The Lord of the Rings* Frodo—and Tolkien—make a clear distinction between Bilbo's journey as "a series of *adventures* ... ending in peace" (*FR* I, ii, 72) and Frodo's journey with the Ring as a "perilous *quest*" (*FR* I, 11, 70). Elrond twice refers to a quest, telling the Council that "the quest may be attempted by the weak with as much hope as the strong" (*FR* II, ii, 283) and when the Company sets out, actually giving it a title, the "Quest of Mount Doom" (*FR* II, ii, 294). Galadriel, also, refers to the "quest," telling Frodo that "Your quest is known to us," and warning that "your Quest stands upon the edge of a knife" (*FR* II, vii, 372), as does Celeborn, who tells the Company that the time has come when "those who wish to continue the Quest must harden their hearts to leave this land (*FR* II, viii, 383). At Mount Doom Frodo tells Sam that but for Gollum "the Quest would have been in vain. "So let us forgive him," he councils, "For the Quest is achieved" (*RK* VI, iii, 225).

Frodo's journey is in a different key from Bilbo's, and not only because Tolkien spent more time and care on developing *The Lord of the Rings* than he did *The Hobbit*, but also because he was conscious of a different authorial purpose. Bilbo had *aventures*—dangerous escapades exciting for their own sake, ending in peace and prosperity for Elves, Men, Dwarves, and Bilbo himself. Frodo goes on a *quest*—a journey as perilous for soul as for body—with a fixed purpose, a goal beyond itself. And while Frodo's quest, like Bilbo's adventure, ends in peace, the peace will not include him, for his quest has left him unable to enjoy it. Unlike Erec, Yvain, and Bilbo, Frodo gets no happy ever after.

In its emphasis on quest *The Lord of the Rings* has less relationship to *The Hobbit* and romance than to the spiritual and psychological "Tale of the Sankgreal" from *Le Morte D'Arthur*. We might say that *The Lord of the Rings* is to the "Tale of the Sankgreal" as *The Hobbit* is to "The Tale of Launcelot." Built on a century's worth of literature about the Quest for the Holy Grail, Malory's "Sankgreal" is the apogee of the quest narrative, whose goal is the highest in Christian European literature—the Cup symbolizing Christ's sacrifice for humanity. Frodo's quest likewise involves sacrifice, but here the values are reversed, for his goal is not achievement but destruction, and the sacrifice is the result of the quest, not its highest vision. Yet each object stands in its particular work as a test of the major characters. Malory's portrayal of the various effects of the Quest on a selection of Arthur's knights— Gawain, Bors, Lyonel, Perceval, and Launcelot—is designed to show the levels of spirituality from lowest to highest at Arthur's court. Consider the following quote about Gawain:

> Whan sir Gawayne was departed from his felyship he rode longe withoute ony adventure, for he founde nat the tenth parte of aventures as they were wont to have. For sir Gawayne rode from Whytsuntyde tylle Mychaelllmasse, and found never adventure that pleased him [Malory, 1971, 558].

Malory's repetition of the word is not unlike Tolkien's in the opening of *The Hobbit*, but here it is a sure sign that Gawain is on the wrong track. He has no spiritual goal. He doesn't want *quest*, he wants *aventure*. He's just looking for fun. The fact that he does not find it suggests that he's not only on the wrong track, he doesn't even know it.

The contrast to Gawain is his close friend, Launcelot, who is on the right track but like Gawain, though for different reasons, also will not find what he seeks. On his return to Arthur's court, Launcelot tells Guinevere, "I was but late in the quest of the Sankgreall, and ... I saw in that my queste as much as ever saw ony synfull man lyvynge" (Malory, 1971, 611). The difference in the two men's terminology will not have escaped your notice. Like the difference between *The Hobbit* and *The Lord of the Rings*, the difference between *aventure* and *quest* is the measure of the difference between Bilbo and Frodo, Gawain and Launcelot, and in the outcome for each.

As the Grail is a test, so is the Ring. In Launcelot's struggle between God and Guinevere we can see a parallel with the struggle of Frodo to resist the Ring. There is no comedy here, as there is in the romances, only irony. Both Frodo and Launcelot fail in their struggle and consequently in their quest. Both are irrevocably marked by their failure, and come to painful self-knowledge as a result. In both cases the drama and irony of the stories rely on the paradox that although the heroes fail, it is through their failures that the quests are achieved. Where Launcelot fails, his son Galahad achieves the quest and the Grail. But without Launcelot there would have been no Galahad. When Frodo fails by putting on the Ring instead of throwing it into the fire, he makes it possible for Gollum to take the Ring and himself fall into the fire. Without Frodo's failure the quest would not have succeeded.

Both heroes have to live with the knowledge of their failures. Returned to court, Launcelot tells Guinevere, "if that I had nat had my prevy thoughts to return to youre love agayne as I do, I had sene as grete mysteryes as ever saw my sunne Sir Galahad" (Malory, 1971, 611). Returned to Bag End, Frodo cannot re-integrate into the community he left behind. Tolkien commented that after his return to the Shire Frodo was afflicted by "unreasoning self-reproach: he saw himself and all that he had done as a broken failure. 'Though I may come to the Shire, it will not seem the same, for I shall not be the same'" (Tolkien, 2000, 328). And this is the final, fundamental difference between Bilbo and Frodo and *adventure* and *quest*; not just that one succeeds where the other fails, but that such success or failure is built into the nature of each journey and thus the nature of each book.

Adventure for its own sake is self-contained, with rewards in keeping with the consequences of the adventure. This is not to suggest that Bilbo is Tolkien's Sir Gawain, for the comparison won't hold either in the writing or the reading. Bilbo is a much better person than Malory's Gawain, and unlike Gawain he knows the difference between an adventure and a quest. But I will suggest that Frodo comes close to being Tolkien's Launcelot, the honest, honorable, flawed hero of a quest in which he is doomed to fail and in failing show the pathos and poignance of the human condition as Tolkien saw it. "I am a Christian, and indeed a Roman Catholic," he wrote in 1956, "so that I do not expect 'history' to be anything but a long defeat" (Tolkien, 2000, 255). This is not a hopeful vision. But it fits Frodo's situation. It does not fit Bilbo's, and that is the chief difference between the two books.

Nevertheless, both heroes, each on a different journey but both operating within separate aspects of a well-recognized tradition, show clearly what Carpenter misconstrued, what conventional wisdom has ignored, and what Tolkien tried to downplay, that the vocabulary and mechanisms of French romance left their Gallic stamp on the "English goodliness of speechecraft" in Tolkien's narratives, and on their shape and content as well. Tolkien's French connection was stronger and its influence more formative than either he or the many scholars of his work have wanted to admit.

Works Cited

The Awntyrs off Arthure at the Terne Wathelyn: An Edition Based on Bodleian Library MS. Douce 324. 1974. ed. Ralph Hanna, III. Manchester: Manchester University Press.
Carpenter, Humphrey. 1977. *J.R.R. Tolkien: A Biography*. London: George Allen and Unwin.
de Troyes, Chrétien. *Yvain or The Knight With the Lion*. 1975. Trans. Ruth Harwood Cline. Athens, GA: University of Georgia Press.
_____. 1992. *Erec and Enide*. Trans. Dorothy Gilbert. Berkeley: University of California Press.
_____. 2000. *Erec and Enide*. Trans. Ruth Harwood Cline. Athens: University of Georgia Press.
Garth, John. 2003. *Tolkien and the Great War: The Threshold of Middle-earth*. London: HarperCollins.
Kocher, Paul. 1972. *Master of Middle-earth*. Boston: Houghton Mifflin.
Lewis, C.S. 1947. "On Stories." In *Essays Presented to Charles Williams*. London: Oxford University Press.
MacKillop, James. 1998. *Dictionary of Celtic Mythology*. Oxford and New York: Oxford University Press.
Malory, Sir Thomas. 1971. *Works* [*Le Morte D'Arthur*]. ed. Eugene Vinaver. London: Oxford University Press.
Pwyll Pendeuic Dyuet: The First of the Four Branches of the Mabinogi. 1957. Ed. from the White Book of Rhydderch with variants from the Red Book of Hergest by R.L. Thomson. Medieval and Modern Welsh Series Vol. I. Dublin: Dublin Institute for Advanced Studies.
Tolkien, J.R.R. 1925. *A Middle English Vocabulary*. Oxford: Clarendon Press.
_____. 1947. "On Fairy-stories." In *Essays Presented to Charles Williams*. London: Oxford University Press.
_____. 1965. *The Fellowship of the Ring*, 2nd ed. Boston: Houghton Mifflin Co.
_____. 1965. *The Lord of the Rings*, 2nd ed. 3 vols. Boston: Houghton Mifflin Co.
_____. 1983. "On Fairy-stories" in *Tolkien: The Monsters and the Critics and Other Essays*, ed. Christopher Tolkien. London: George Allen and Unwin.
_____. 1987. *The Hobbit*, 50th anniversary ed. London: Unwin Hyman.
_____. 1988. *The Return of the Shadow:* The History of *The Lord of the Rings* Part One, ed. Christopher Tolkien. Boston: Houghton Mifflin.
_____. 2000. *The Letters of J.R.R. Tolkien*. Ed. Humphrey Carpenter. Boston: Houghton Mifflin.
_____. 2008. *Tolkien On Fairy-Stories*, Expanded Edition ed. Verlyn Flieger and Douglas A. Anderson. London: HarperCollins Publishers.
Villemarqué, Théodore Hersart de la. 1846. *Barzaz Breiz: Chants Populaire de la Bretagne*. 2 vols. Paris: A. Franck.
The Welsh Review. 1945. ed. Gwyn Jones. Vol. IV, No. 4, December.

Tolkien's Hybrid Mythology
The Hobbit as Old Norse "Fairy-Story"

Jane Chance

The Hobbit (1937) has often been dismissed as a simple children's story. However, given its final publication after a period when Tolkien had worked on his Old Norse poem *Legend of Sigurd and Gudrún,* his seminal lecture "On Fairy-Stories," and what became *The Silmarillion*, I argue in this essay that the work constitutes a pivot on which his medievalized mythology of magic is balanced. As an example of his favorite genre, the "fairy-story," *The Hobbit* borrows and transforms magical elements from his beloved fairy-story of Andrew Lang's Old Norse Sigurd to help create a "mythology for England" by means of the filter of his own "Silmarillion" An examination of early drafts of "On Fairy-Stories," used as a gloss on *The Hobbit*, provides a taxonomy for the Hobbit anti-hero Bilbo, the Elves (Fairies), and humankind and stamps it as both "epic" and "fairy-story" in his hybrid mythology.

Tolkien's Andrew Lang lecture "On Fairy-Stories" (8 March 1939) has been acknowledged as a "watershed in his development as a writer" by its editors, Verlyn Flieger and Douglas A. Anderson: "although this was ancillary to the defence of fairy-stories, he was able to look both backwards and forwards at the practice of his craft" (Tolkien, 2005, 16). In it, they also muse, somewhat astonishingly, that "we can find between the lines his recognition of the flaws in his own fairy-story, *The Hobbit*," flaws such as jokes without real humor, marvels such as talking purses, and other inconsistencies (Tolkien, 2008, 16). I say "astonishingly," because, whatever its imagined flaws and despite its early critical neglect as a "children's story" and its modern critical interpretation as Jungian or Freudian psychoanalytic narrative (Helms, 1974, 41–55; Matthews, 1975, 29–42; and O'Neill, 1979), *The Hobbit* (1937) actually exemplifies the kind of legend that Tolkien proclaims was his intention to create in dedication to his country, England, in the much-discussed letter 131 in 1951 addressed to his potential new publisher Milton Waldman of Collins Press.

After his old publisher, Allen and Unwin, having professed a desire to publish a "second *Hobbit*," had declined to publish both *The Lord of the Rings* along with the much earlier manuscript of what would become *The Silmarillion*, Tolkien writes in this letter, in past tense, "I had in mind to make *a body of more or less connected legend*, ranging from the *large and cosmogonic* to the level of *romantic fairy-story*—the larger founded on the lesser in contact with the earth, the lesser drawing splendour from the vast backcloths—which I could dedicate simply: to England, to my country" (Tolkien, 1981, 144; my emphasis). Certainly Tolkien meant this statement to refer to what later became *The Lord of the Rings* (1954–55) and the posthumously published *The Silmarillion* (1976), *Unfinished Tales of Númenor and Middle-earth* (1979), and the twelve volumes of *The History of Middle-earth* (1983–96), that is, the mythology of Middle-earth that he had begun after World War I, in 1918, written and revised without completion throughout his life. But, as Flieger and Anderson also note, even earlier,

The Hobbit already combines the mythological doubleness of the cosmogonic with romantic fairy-story, "hobbit earthiness" with "fairy tale, the tentative beginnings of a Faërie Otherworld" (Tolkien, 2005, 16).

Scholars and readers have for some time tried to interpret what Tolkien's biographer had described as his desire to create, this "mythology for England" (Carpenter, 1977, 89–90).[1] Long recognized is the Oxford professor's incorporation into his own fiction of aspects of earlier literature, mainly in Old and Middle English[2] or in Old Norse,[3] whether the genre is epic, saga, or romance, although scholars have only begun to explore Tolkien's interest in the late-nineteenth century fairy-tale compilations of Jacob and Wilhelm Grimm and other Victorian storytellers (Shippey, 2005; and Fimi, 2009, esp. chaps. 2–5), as well as the mythmaking of Elias Lönnrot in his epic collection of tales, the *Kalevala* (Shippey, 2000, 79–96; Flieger, 2002, 26–35; and Flieger, 2004, 277–83). The concept of a double-genred fiction, one that implies a reading of the work as both Northern epic and romantic fairy-story, and imbued by Tolkien's mythology, has been mostly ignored, to the detriment of the second component, the fairy-story.

Yet fairy tales have played an important social and political role since the eighteenth century, as vehicles for ideology, subversion, and the shaping of manners and mores, despite their later Victorian role as entertainment for children (Zipes, 1979; rev. ed. 2002; Zipes, 1988; rev. ed. 2011). Tolkien himself asserts in his essay "On Fairy-Stories" that much of his own fiction serves primarily as "fairy-stories" and, on that basis he considers himself as a mythmaker. In terms of the stages of his development as mythmaker, according to Dimitra Fimi, who in her study of Tolkien's early interest in fairies in children's stories has helpfully chronologized the writing of his fiction during his lifetime (one that includes the variations to *The Lord of the Rings* and *The Silmarillion* in *The History of Middle-earth*), "Tolkien's route from fairies to hobbits shows the evolution of his creative imagination" (Fimi, 2009, 196–97).

What was involved in this transition from fairies to Hobbits, and why should that transition matter? Tolkien notes, circa 1958, that "the cosmogonic myths are Númenórean, blending Elven-lore with human myth and imagination" (Tolkien, 1990, 374n2), by which, he means "Mannish" (Tolkien, 1996, 357n17). Basically, "The Silmarillion" in its earliest form comprises four lays of the Atani (Quenya; in Sindarin, Edain, or Second People), beginning with the story of Fëanor's making of the Silmarils. By around 1926 Tolkien had worked out "The Earliest 'Silmarillion'" of twenty-eight pages, which he continued revising until 1930.[4]

Apparently his "hybrid story" of *The Hobbit*, when it was finally published in 1937, must have been, as Fimi has hinted, also "inseparably linked with Tolkien's mythology" (Fimi, 2009, 118). As Tolkien's first published long narrative, it derived from stories told to his children (as early as the mid-twenties, perhaps 1926–27, according to an interview with his oldest son, Father John Tolkien [1917–2003], in a film documentary on a DVD video, *Tolkien Remembered*, 2005); John, Michael, and Christopher Tolkien recollect dates from the mid- to the late twenties, although Tolkien himself thought no earlier than 1930 (Scull and Hammond, 2006, 386–87; Rateliff, 2007–08,1:xiv). As a result of this hybridity, "rifts created in Tolkien's ever-evolving legendarium by the publication of *The Hobbit*" emerged, namely, Tolkien's fairies had metamorphosed into Elves, even though, for Tolkien, "Hobbits became the 'mediators' to Middle-earth" (Fimi, 2009, 197). While Fimi does not actually focus on interpretation of *The Hobbit*, clearly the Elves themselves, as the mythological heirs to Victorian fairies, remained "still the agents of Tolkien's spiritual concerns" in *The Lord of the Rings* and the body of unpublished work of the Silmarilliad, even as they reflect a signal transformation in his mythmaking. Nevertheless, *The Hobbit*, during his composition of *The Lord of the Rings*, became a problem text in terms of incongruities between the two works, specifically involving the nature and origin of the Ring and the role of Gollum in *The Hobbit* chapter titled "Riddles in the Dark," which necessitated a second edition of *The Hobbit* in 1951.[5]

It is not surprising, then, given Tolkien's dual interest in cosmogonic mythology and the romantic fairy-story—which seem to merge and blend throughout his writings, including *The Hobbit*—what he considers the "fairy-story" to be. In the earliest manuscript of "On Fairy-stories," known as Manuscript A Proper (written between December 1938 and March 1939, in advance of the Andrew Lang Lecture on 8 March 1939),[6] the Oxford medievalist confesses that a Victorian version of an Old Norse saga was his favorite "fairy-story": "The adaptation of the Story of Sigurd (done by Andrew Lang himself from [William] Morris's transl. of *The Volsunga Saga*) was my *favourite without rival*. Even as it stands in the *Red Book* it is no Conte des Fées. It is strong meat for nurseries" (Tolkien, 2005, 188–89; my emphasis).

Not only was Lang's 1890 redaction Tolkien's favorite fairy-story, the medievalist himself also wrote an English version of the *Völsunga Saga* in the late 1920s to early 30s (Scull and Hammond, 2006, 654) that he subsequently dismissed in a 29 March 1967 letter to the English poet W[ystan] H. Auden as "a thing I did many years ago when trying to learn the art of writing alliterative poetry: an attempt to unify the lays about the Völsungs from the Elder Edda, written in the old eight-line fornyrðislag stanza." The term *fornyrðislag*, according to Humphrey Carpenter, editor of Tolkien's letters, refers to the Old Norse term for the stanzaic meter in which the Eddic narrative poems were written, which closely resembled the alliterative meter of Old English poetry) (Tolkien, 1981, 452n3). Tolkien scholar Tom Shippey assumed that this poem was intended to fill an eight-page gap in the Sigurðr cycle in the Codex Regius manuscript of the Poetic *Edda* (2007, 187–202); however, Tolkien's poem was much longer than eight manuscript pages. Tolkien titled his long poem of 339 stanzas "Völsungakviða en nýja" (or "New Lay of the Volsungs"), adding to it the 166 stanzas of "Guðrúnarkviða en nýja," or what has now been printed together as his *Legend of Sigurd and Gudrún* (2009), which centers on "material dealing with Sigurd and Gunnar," according to another Tolkien letter to Auden, dated 29 January 1968 (Tolkien, 1981, 379).

Certainly Tolkien had long been attracted to the epic *Völsunga Saga*, as far back as his days at the King Edward's School in Birmingham, when he had attempted to read it in the original Old Norse; he had also purchased a copy of William Morris's 1870 translation (from which Lang had redacted his own version) while a student at Exeter College, Oxford, with money he had received for the Skeat Prize for English (Scull and Hammond, 2006, 599). That William Morris provided a powerful northern influence on Tolkien's writing has been argued convincingly (Burns, 2005, 75–92). Especially important here, however, was Tolkien's preference, "without rival," for Lang's *Red Fairy Book* tale of the dragon-slayer and king's son Sigurd, "The Story of Sigurd" (1890; rpt. 1966, 357–67). Anglo-Saxonist Professor Tolkien must have noticed that Lang's headnote to his redaction indicates that details of this unhappy tale were apparently carved into rock by the Danes who did battle with King Alfred and the Anglo-Saxons in tenth-century England. His groundbreaking essay, "Beowulf: The Monsters and the Critics," had been initially presented as the Sir Israel Gollancz Lecture in 1936 (Tolkien, 1936, 245 95, rprt. Donoghue, 2002, 103–29), a year before the publication of *The Hobbit* and three years before the delivery of the Lang Lecture, "On Fairy-Stories."

When Tolkien himself was questioned about *The Hobbit*'s sources, he replied, in a letter published in the *Observer* on 20 February 1938, that the work derived from "epic, mythology, and fairy story" (Tolkien, 1938, 9). Further, in that same letter Tolkien identified as its "most valued" source the Anglo-Saxon epic *Beowulf*, an epic poem on he was writing a lecture and an article in the early thirties, "though it was not consciously present to the mind in the process of writing, in which the episode of the theft [from the Dragon's lair] arose naturally (almost inevitably) from the circumstances." Finally, Tolkien also acknowledged, seemingly without contradiction if one accepts his interest in the cosmogonic, that "[m]y tale is not consciously based on any other book—save one, and that is unpublished: the 'Silmarillion,' a history of the Elves, to which frequent allusion is made."

Thus, it seems clear that in *The Hobbit*, however Tolkien may have reshaped the Old Norse story of Sigurd in his own *Legend of Sigurd and Gudrún*, he borrows some magical elements from Lang's tale while transforming and inverting others to stamp it as a "fairy-story" in his hybrid mythology—but always guided at least implicitly by his overarching and developing legendarium, for it is fairies and the magic associated with them that provide the key to his mythology throughout much of his fiction. *The Hobbit*, as this essay will argue, represents *both* a legendary epic, or the "lesser in contact with the earth," *and*, appearing to "draw splendor" from the "large and cosmogonic," the "romantic fairy-story."

The Three Faces of the Fairy-Story, Mystical, Magical, and Mirroring

Even in the earliest manuscripts of Tolkien's seminal essay on Faërie, "On Fairy-Stories," he contextualized his general concept of magic within a definition of the fairy-story that includes a cosmogonic hierarchy of representation. Only one early manuscript, Oxford Bodleian Library, Manuscript A Proper, served as the forerunner to the Andrew Lang Lecture he was invited to deliver at St. Andrews University on 8 March 1939—about which he had begun thinking about a year after he had published *The Hobbit* (1937), likely between December 1938 and March 1939. Another manuscript represents a later stage in the evolution of the essay as published in 1947. In Oxford Bodleian Library Manuscript B (written during 1943), as in his final published version of the essay, he emphasizes that "[e]ven fairy-stories as a whole have three faces: the Mystical towards the Supernatural; *the Magical towards Nature*; and the Mirror of scorn and pity towards Man. The essential face of Faërie is the middle one, *the Magical*" (Tolkien, 2005, p. 226; my emphasis).

Just as Tolkien here cautions that the fairy-story's crucial element is the magical, he also acknowledges in this same passage in Manuscript B that "The mystical may be embodied in the magical and the fairy-tale." This line he replaces in the final published version with an ascription to George MacDonald's accomplishment in his fairy-tale *The Golden Key*: "The Magical, the fairy-story, may be used as a *Miroir de l'Omme*; and it may (but not so easily) be made a vehicle of Mystery" (Tolkien, 1947; rpt. 1966; rev. ed., 1988, 1989, p. 44). Apparently for Tolkien the fairy-story is equivocal with the magical but can exist as a hybrid incorporating all three facets, even if the mystical represents the most difficult. What exactly Tolkien means by these three faces is not entirely clear, either in his theorizing or in its applicability to his own fairy-stories; the line in Manuscript B, rephrased in the published version, suggests the problem in merging all three modes.

Some clues to Tolkien's intentions surface in the earliest extant version of "On Fairy-Stories," known as Draft A, the closest in time to the actual Andrew Lang Lecture (of which no copy remains). Details of this lecture did appear a few days after its delivery in contemporary reviews in the local newspapers, one of which, an anonymous review that appeared in *The Scotsman* (8 March 1939, 9 col. 2), remarks that Tolkien views fairies as "natural," not supernatural; the fact that they die is "their doom" (that is, their fate, or destiny), according to another review in *The St. Andrews Citizen* (March 1939, 4, cols. 3–5; rpt. in Tolkien, 2005, 165). "Doom," a word drawn from Old English *dōm*, "judgment," "decree," or "law," according to Bosworth-Toller's *Anglo-Saxon Dictionary* (1898; rpt. 1976, *s.v.*), can also denote "free will" or "choice," as in *Beowulf*, line 894, in reference to "þæt hē beāh-hordes brūcan mōste/ selfes *dōme*" (that he might enjoy the ring-hoard by his own *free will*) (my emphasis). Interestingly, this line refers to Sigemund, son of Wæls and uncle (and father) of Fitela, who, in the tale recited by Hrothgar's *scop* in celebration of Beowulf's victory over Grendel, valorously kills a dragon and, thereby, wins his treasure-hoard. In fact, Sigemund is the Norse hero Sigmundr (Lang's and Tolkien's Sigurd) who was given a magical sword by a god in the *Völsungasaga* (Klaeber, 1950, rpt. 1968, 162n). "Doom" is also a word Tolkien uses to describe the final outcome of the Elves' journey in *The Silmarillion*, in particular, the unhappy history of the Noldor and the story of Túrin Turambar. And as "free will," doom is a concept that recurs throughout Tolkien's legendarium, logically connected in Roman Catholicism with the consequence of actions that might result in a judgment, but a surprising one to consider in relation to Tolkien's fairies—or Elves.

For Tolkien to use this odd word "doom" for fairies, given its connection with *Beowulf*, suggests the mix of ideas he was working through in the same time period. Natural fairies are, in his mind, the same as Elves: and the fairies of "On Fairy-stories" are actually the Elves of *The Silmarillion*. Both are earthly, for one thing: according to another news reporter in *The St. Andrews Citizen* reviewing Tolkien's Lang Lecture in March 1939, Professor Tolkien defined "stories about Faërie" as "stories concerning *all that realm* which contains many things besides fauns (great or small), besides elves or fairies, dwarfs, witches, giants, or dragons; it holds the sea, and the sun; the moon, the sky, the earth, and they themselves, when they are enchanted" (4, cols. 3–5; rpt. in Tolkien, 2005, 166; my emphasis).

Various accounts of what Tolkien means here by "Faërie" have been offered by critics, usually paraphrases of his complex text in the final publication of his Lang Lecture as "On Fairy-stories," or attempts to analyze his own children's stories (that is, generally, short stories in which fairies appear), often approached theologically: notably, *Roverandum*, "Leaf by Niggle," *Farmer Giles of Ham*, and *Smith of Wootton Major*. Although these stories are often termed "shorter works," they are usually treated as fairy-stories or children's stories (see, for example, the collection edited by Hiley and Weinreich, 2008). Tolkien scholars R.J. Reilly (1968; rpt. 2004, 2005) and J. S. Ryan (1981; rpt. 2004, 2005) first attempted, separately, to position "On Fairy-stories" as a Coleridgian explanation of the use of the imagination in constructing the Christianized fantasy of *The Lord of the Rings*, given Tolkien's emphasis in his essay on the eucatastrophe of the Gospel as the fairy-story's ultimate fantasy, escape, recovery, and consolation; Ryan added a discussion of Tolkien's *Beowulf* essay and G. K. Chesterton on the fairy-story and folk-tale.

Yet no scholar has yet examined Tolkien's *Hobbit* as a fairy-story in the light of his Andrew Lang lecture, in terms of Lang's own *Red Fairy Book* story of Sigurd. A comparison of the major aspects of Tolkien's northern elven / fairy-story, *The Hobbit*, as borrowed from Lang's redaction of the Sigurd legend will demonstrate Tolkien's understanding of the relationship among fairies/Elves, magic, and men in the three faces of the fairy-story. After beginning with the most essential element of the fairy-story, the Magical, in relation to the dragon and the ring in each work, the argument will turn to each fairy-story as a *Miroir de l'Omme*, or Mirror of Scorn and pity towards Man, in their development of the roles of the heroes Bilbo and Sigurd. The conclusion will focus on the fairy-story's "Mystical towards the Supernatural," with the magician Gandalf the Istar taking the place of Regin the Smith and Odin, to show how luck, chance, and providence coincide to offer the escape, hope, and consolation of the eucatastrophe, the happy ending, in *The Hobbit*, fulfilling the fairy-story's nature as a "vehicle of Mystery."

"The Magical Towards Nature": The Ring and the Dragon

The Hobbit may well be considered a fairy-story because many magical creatures and mythical beings appear in it naturally—that is, in "Nature—including trolls, goblins, giant spiders, Beorn the Shape-changer, and most especially, the Elves (or fairies). But we would need to turn for help to the influential Andrew Lang *Red Book* fairy-story for a smith/magician's use of a magical ring and his connection with a dragon, a tale that represents the other two faces of the Tolkienian fairy story: as a mirror of pity towards man and as the mystical towards the supernatural. The key magical device in both the "Story of Sigurd" and, as we shall see, *The Hobbit* is the ring borne by the hero, and the key magical adversary in both is the stingy and homicidal dragon, Fafnir in one and Smaug in the other, although, along the way, various apparently avaricious dwarves do figure in the narrative, including Andvari in Lang's tale of Sigurd and Thorin in *The Hobbit*. In the "Story of Sigurd" the adversary is Regin the smith, whose magic is turned towards selfish, avaricious ends; in *The Hobbit* the equivalent magician is good Gandalf, whose role allows him to connect the natural world of faërie with the "mystical tending towards the supernatural": the mythology of the *Silmarillion*, which will be examined later.

In the "Story of Sigurd," the magic ring and the dragon are both connected with Sigurd's tutor, Regin, apparently supplied by the Danish king who had captured his mother (a queen in her own right). This smith, a sword-maker and magician, helps to arm Sigurd but also plans on betraying him to retrieve his own lost treasure. Regin does tell Sigurd to ask the king for a magical horse—Grani, "swift as the wind"—whom the hero in fact obtains from an old man in the forest, likely Odin, the god of the north, because Grani comes from the same breed as Sleipnir, Odin's horse. After some unsuccessful attempts at crafting a sword on his own for Sigurd, Regin at the hero's request next forges together the broken sword of Sigurd's father for the hero to use in killing the dragon, who guards a gold treasure that used to belong to the dwarf Andvari. At this point the story becomes complex in its identification of why the dragon must be killed by Sigurd. The smith does explain to him that the dragon Fafnir is actually Regin's metamorphosed brother, who had murdered their father for the gold that the slayer of Regin's second brother, Otter, had provided as legal recompense for his death when Otter had unfortunately assumed this animal's shape to swim and lie in the sun. Because Otherr's killer had also murdered the dwarf Andvari for this gold, the dwarf before he died had cursed both gold and his last ring.

Sigurd apparently misses the real point of the magician's tale—the curse of the gold and its role in the story of the downfall of the brothers—for after he defeats the dragon Fafnir, ill fortune in magical form dogs him throughout the tale. This paradigmatic fairytale presents both a mirror of human weakness in the hero, Sigurd, and others and also manifests "the Mystical towards the Supernatural" in the incomplete aid extended to Sigurd by divine mentors. The manifestation of the divine is made to others who also come into contact with the magical ring; additional magic transforms Regin's avaricious brother into an adversarial (and avaricious) dragon. For example, when Sigurd roasts Fafnir's heart for Regin to eat, he accidentally tastes it and discovers he can magically understand the woodpeckers' prophecy, that Regin will betray him, and is thus encouraged to take the gold and kill Regin. However, the birds also prophesy that Sigurd will find an enchanted sleeping maiden whom he will awaken from her long sleep on a pile of treasure. Sigurd accomplishes this awakening by seizing from the treasure a magical gold helmet, the Helm of Dread, which makes its wearer invisible and, with his magical horse, Grani, leaps over the flames to rescue her: the warrior maid Brynhild. Enchanted for displeasing the god Odin, Brynhild has vowed to marry a fearless man, who turns out to be Sigurd. Unfortunately, without thinking Sigurd gives her the magic ring cursed by the dwarf.

Whether treasure or ring, gold leads to death in the story of Sigurd. And so Brynhild is similarly cursed, for, after Sigurd rides away, he meets and marries Gudrun, a king's daughter who falls in love with him and, with the aid of her mother's magical cup of drugs, induces him to forget Brynhild. Worse, when Gudrun's brother Gunnar magically exchanges shapes with Sigurd to leap over the flames and thereby win Brynhild's hand in marriage, Brynhild, thinking Sigurd has forgotten her, returns to Sigurd the ring of Andvari for his wife, Gudrun. Unfortunately, when Brynhild irritates Gudrun by bragging about the superiority she has gained by means of Gunnar's alleged act of heroism, Gudrun reveals to her the truth about Gunnar's ruse. Mourning the loss of the true hero Sigurd, Brynhild then tells Gunnar she knows the truth about his deceit and feeds Gunnar's younger brother a magical dish that maddens him to the point that he tries to kill Sigurd with a sword—although Sigurd, before he dies, also kills him. In grief over his death, both Sigurd's horse, Grani, and Brynhild die.

In *The Hobbit* a similar magic ring that the hero acquires plays a role in two major episodes, one by chance, involving Gollum, and one by intention, the latter involving the dragon, Smaug (there is no Gudrun-equivalent in *The Hobbit*). The first episode occurs in chapter 5, "Riddles in the Dark," when Bilbo finds a ring—"a turning point in his career, but he did not know it" (Tolkien, 1937, 1966; 64) —and, while he engages in a riddling contest with Gollum whose outcome will determine whether Bilbo will live or die, at a significant juncture the ring accidentally slips upon his finger to render him invisible. Bilbo escapes from Gollum, but not before Gollum happens to ask what has "it got in its pocketses?" And Bilbo also asks himself, "What have I, I *wonder?*," an important word perhaps chosen by Tolkien to emphasize the magic involved in the providential answer to the question, for, at the moment that Bilbo puts his hand in his pocket, "The ring felt very cold as it *quietly slipped on* to his groping finger" (77; my emphases).

The second narrative event that involves a magic ring used against an unusual adversary is split into two related ventures in chapter 12. In the first venture, "Inside Information," Bilbo slips it on to sneak into the dragon's lair at night to conceal himself by means of magical invisibility from the sleeping Smaug and then steals a cup as proof of his success. In the second venture, in the same chapter, after the ire of Smaug about the theft has become apparent and the dwarves are trapped in the mountain recesses without escape, he puts it on to become invisible and see what Smaug is up to. Ironically, the magic ring is unnecessary on both visits, in the first, because Smaug is gone, and in the second, because visual concealment does not in fact matter to the dragon, whose olfactory sense is exceedingly acute: he smells the Hobbit. Nor does the magic ring matter to clever Bilbo: it is during this second visit that he tricks Smaug into revealing the bare spot on his left breast—a "treasure" that will lead to the dragon's later downfall.

Interestingly, in contrast to the "Story of Sigurd," and to underscore the nature of "the Mystical tending towards the Supernatural" in *The Hobbit,* the magic ring does not even matter on Bilbo's third visit to the dragon's lair, in chapter 13, "Not at Home." When, after the desperate dwarves have been locked within for many days and Smaug has blocked the upper door to the tunnel, Bilbo offers to finish his job and "burgle" dwarf treasure stolen by Smaug if they will accompany him to help carry it. However, because the dragon is absent this time and invisibility does not matter, Bilbo's blindness in the dark–literal and figurative—means that he has to depend on the dwarves instead of himself to retrieve a light and then to guide them all out through the palace into the open air at the opposite end from the tunnel: a providential if ironic light. But in the moment, Bilbo's magical invisibility becomes symbolically necessary as subterfuge for his deceit, to conceal from the dwarves the theft of the precious Arkenstone, part of the treasure he has promised them. Bilbo, now truly a burglar, knows that "trouble would yet come of it," for this "payment" that the dwarves did not and would not ever choose to make for his services far exceeds what the dwarves had meant to pay him (Tolkien, 1937, 213).

Surely Tolkien does not intend for the Arkenstone to be equivalent symbolically to the ring of Sigurd in Lang's fairy-story, even though Sigurd's ring originally stolen from the dwarf Andvari— like the Arkenstone that the dragon wrongfully stole previously from the dwarves—is part of stolen treasure. Representing what Bilbo considers payment for his services as a burglar, it eventually provides a solution to the man-dwarf enmity when he chooses to give it away to Bard, man of Dale, primarily because it signifies the sovereignty that Thorin believes has been stolen from him and, therefore, comes to represent a bargaining chip. The dwarves' apparent avarice poses a problem only for Bard, not, ultimately, for Bilbo, because at the end the Hobbit keeps only two small treasure chests. Yet at this moment it is Bilbo who seems to resemble the cursed hero Sigurd.

"The Mirror of Sorrow and Pity Towards Man": Heroes Bilbo and Sigurd

For the flawed (or abject) hero Bilbo in *The Hobbit* Tolkien borrows from Lang's fairy-tale protagonist Sigurd, a type who also plays a major role in *The Silmarillion* in the Noldo Fëanor (Arul, 2009), as does Kullervo, the orphan hero of the Finnish epic *Kalevala* (Chance, 2002; West, 2004, 285–94). As heroes, Lang's Sigurd and Bilbo share an ancestry that includes the possibility of nobility, by blood or by heroism, definitely, in Sigurd's case, less so, in Bilbo's, but, while heedless Sigurd may be guilty of avarice and pride in continuing on to kill Fafnir even after Regin warns him of the curse on the dwarf's treasure, Bilbo ultimately is not, nor is he heroic in any conventionally recognizable way. However, Sigurd's mother not only descended from kings, she also possessed an inner nobility signified by her own magic ring, different from the ring Sigurd obtains from the dragon's hoard. Her magic ring set her apart from her maid, with whom she switched clothing as a disguise before their capture by a king; despite her subterfuge, by means of her ring the king recognized her as an aristocrat.

Somewhat similarly to Sigurd and his noble mother, Bilbo has inherited his "nobility"–the nobility of the Fallohide Hobbits—from his Took mother, as did his distant cousin Frodo later on from his Took grandmother. Bilbo's mother and Frodo's grandmother as Took sisters descended from the Took line founded by Took of Great Smials, with Isengrim II representing the tenth Thain of that line. Further, Bilbo's mother, Belladonna Took, was the fourth daughter of Gerontius (the "Old") Took (son of the nobly-named Fortinbras I and grandson to Ferumbras II, himself the lone brother of the heroic "Bullroarer," or Bandobras,

Took). Finally, Frodo's mother, Primula Brandybuck, was herself mothered by the youngest daughter of Old Took, who had married a Brandybuck, which makes Bilbo Frodo's cousin. But, of course, both Frodo and Bilbo are Bagginses,[7] their paternal surname reflective of their ancestors' bourgeois (and materialistic) natures (Shippey, 1982, rev. ed., 1992, 51–86, especially his comment that Bilbo is "admittedly a *bourgeois*," 66–67, my emphasis).

Gandalf thought of Bilbo for an adventure, then, because of the wizard's familiarity with and knowledge of the Fallohide branch of the Hobbits and because of his previous experiences with Bilbo's heroic ancestor, "Bullroarer" Took. But, at the beginning of *The Hobbit*, Bilbo is neither an established hero nor the burglar for whom the dwarves have been searching, despite the potential suggested by his ancestry. Indeed, Bilbo likes to stay at home and smoke tobacco and he loathes adventures: "Nasty disturbing uncomfortable things!" Bilbo says; "Makes you late for dinner! I can't think what anybody sees in them" (6). Yet Gandalf correctly suspects that Bilbo will be a good adventurer (contrary to the Hobbit's own low opinion of adventures) because the Hobbit's curiosity about the world outside derives from his grandfather on his mother's side. The "Old Took" was a Hobbit leader, like the other Tooks in this family (their Thainship was hereditary), and adventuresome, unlike most Hobbits. The Tooks, with their Fallohide Hobbit blood, belonged to the smaller strain of Hobbits that originated in the north, in the upper Anduin, lived in trees and loved forests, traveled and had adventures, and were taller, thinner, and more fair and more artistic than the less noble Hobbit strains, the Harfoots and the least noble of all, the Stoors; the Tooks also associated with the Elves (a typology later described by Tolkien in the prologue to *The Lord of the Rings*) (1954–55, 2nd ed., 1994, 3–4). In contrast to the Fallohide Hobbits, the Harfoots, the most common branch of the three and the most typically "Hobbitish," representing a middle strain, were darker and smaller, browner, and friendlier with dwarves; they also liked hills. The least of the Hobbits, the Stoors—Gollum is a Stoor—came from the south, were heavier and often bearded, occasionally wore boots, liked boating and fishing, and were friends with men.

So it is through his gifted ancestry that Bilbo relates positively to heroic Sigurd. Graced with the horse of the Norse god Odin who reforges the broken sword of Sigurd's dead father, Sigurd slays Fafnir the dragon in an act that, in effect, reaffirms the hero's noble ancestry. Sigurd kills Fafnir by hiding underneath the dragon and thrusting that very reforged paternal sword into the dragon's vulnerable underbelly. But how do Bilbo's two major feats—overcoming Gollum and the dragon Smaug—despite his lack of a welded broken sword or magical horse of Odin—illustrate Sigurd-like (magical) virtues or powers?

If we focus on these two major monstrous adversaries whom Bilbo confronts during his adventure, it will be clear how magic works, ultimately, as a force for goodness. Chapter 5, "Riddles in the Dark," is the focal point for Bilbo's meeting with what might be called the "Dark Hobbit"—Gollum—(later described by Tolkien as representative of the Stoor strain of Hobbit-kind), just as chapters 12 and 13, "Inside Information" and "Not at Home," function as the equivalent for Bilbo's signal adventure with the dragon (and dwarves). In each confrontation, a magical ring figures; in each, Bilbo succeeds partly because of his own individual skills and his own Hobbitness and partly because of what appears to be luck; in each, it is some goodness in him and in the universe that is ultimately responsible for the mystical overturning of its opposite.

Further, the "monstrous adversary" in *The Hobbit* may be understood as in "The Story of Sigurd," as representing the "magical towards Nature." Gollum (as we learn later in *The Lord of the Rings*) killed his cousin Deägol to gain his ring, which works magically through the power that Sauron the Maia (the Necromancer in *The Hobbit*, presumably) invested in it to master the bearer's will and to distort his judgment (Gollum was also tortured while imprisoned by Sauron, which presumably distorted his physical as well as his spiritual being). Bilbo's second major adversary, the dragon Smaug guarding his stolen dwarf treasure at the Lonely Mountain, is not a mythical creature, nor were the dragons in medieval and modern texts with which Tolkien was familiar from boyhood on. Like the avaricious Gollum and the dwarves, and like the dragon of *Beowulf* and Fáfnir of the *Volsunga Saga*, the treasure-hoarding Smaug also represents a natural creation; conquering these monsters, in a more figurative way, symbolizes the quelling of those monstrous equivalents in the hero. In his most famous, much reprinted essay, "Beowulf: The Monsters and the Critics," Tolkien argues that the two monsters of *Beowulf*—the oversized man-like Grendel and the avaricious Dragon—and the hero's encounters with them explain the epic's two major parts, which correspond to the early and late life of Beowulf as a man as he copes with his own conflicts and failures (1936; also Donoghue, 2002, 103–29), although later scholars have pointed out there are in fact three major monsters in *Beowulf*, including Grendel's Mother, and, therefore, three parts, relating to Beowulf's three battles, (see Chance [Nitzsche] (1980), 287–303; rpt. in Donoghue, 2002, 152–67). In the light of Tolkien's two-part/two-adversary argument, the Gollum of *The Hobbit* has been likened to Grendel in *Beowulf* as Smaug has to the Dragon (Christiansen, 1970; 1972–73, 16–20; Chance, 1979, 1980, rev. ed. 2001).

In this respect of monstrous opponents reflecting internal flaws, the protagonists of both *The Hobbit* and "The Story of Sigurd" seem (at least initially) more antiheroic than heroic—and also like Beowulf, the son of the exiled homicide Ecþeow who has something to prove. Bilbo mirrors Sigurd as an abject (or ignoble and flawed) hero in keeping Gollum's ring, when he knows that Gollum has lost just such an object (in Roman Catholic terms, a sin of omission), and in stealing the Arkenstone from the dragon's treasure that he is supposed to be retrieving for the dwarves (a sin of commission). Thematically, in both fairy-stories it is envy, avarice, and wrath (three of the deadly sins) as well as the chief deadly sin, pride, that lead to the downfall of Gollum, or the "Dark Hobbit," the dragon Smaug, and Thorin the dwarf-king. But one might say these same sins—especially avarice and pride of life—initially seduce Bilbo: in the tunnel Bilbo does not tell Gollum he has found his ring, even though he has heard Gollum mourning its loss, because he fears for his life. Further, in the confrontation with the dragon, when Smaug questions him how he plans to carry a fourteenth of the treasure back to Hobbiton, what works upon Bilbo to convince him to steal the easily-portable Arkenstone is a paranoid fear that he is a laughingstock: "Now a nasty suspicion began to grow in his mind—had the dwarves forgotten this important point too, or were they laughing at him all the time?" (202).

Of course, during that same conversation with Smaug, perceptive Bilbo had enough presence of mind to notice how proud Smaug is, particularly of his strength, which leads him to ask the dragon, timorously, about the legendary soft underbelly dragons are reputed to have (a feature also key to Fáfnir's defeat by Sigurthr in the *Edda*). While Smaug arrogantly denied having any such underbelly, when he responded to Bilbo's flattery he inadvertently showed off the bare hollow of his left breast exposed to view (204). Fortunate Bilbo, as a true hero—someone who acts nobly and is not merely semi-divine or descended from noble ancestors—finds the ring of invisibility that Gollum believes has been "stolen" from him, but which twice saves Bilbo's life, and Bilbo retrieves the treasure stolen from the dwarves by the dragon Smaug (and, more figuratively, from Bilbo by the dwarves).

Thus, *The Hobbit* splits into two parts Sigurd's adventure involving a cursed ring and treasure: what in one story is cursed and unfortunate in Tolkien's version becomes lucky, magical, and providential. In *The Hobbit*, instead of the Old Norse concept of fate or an eye-for-an-eye tribal code of vengeance that governs events, as it does in the Old Testament and in "The Story of Sigurd," it is luck (or chance), along with Bilbo's own free will, coupled with a lively intelligence and a developing valor as hero, plus a form of Middle-earth providence—universal goodness—that works most benevolently for Bilbo. Whatever luck this Hobbit has—despite his minor flaws as a hero—ultimately works to aid the diverse and divided communities of Middle-earth.

"The Mystical Towards the Supernatural": Magician Gandalf as Istar, Agent of Manwë, and Regin the Smith

The role of Gandalf as a magician who appears to engineer the adventure for Bilbo in response to righting a moral and legal injustice to the community and the cosmos—the theft of the dwarves' treasure by Smaug—explains specifically how providence works through luck or chance and fate. If Lang's smith Regin metamorphoses in *The Hobbit* into the important figure of Gandalf the magician, Gandalf is, nevertheless, in no way evil or treacherous towards Bilbo. More like Odin, as Marjorie Burns as argued (Burns, 2000, 19–32), the wizard represents in many ways the agent of divine forces that Tolkien believes derives from the gods, or God—enabling this fairy-story, both as a mirror of nature but, also, as a narrative that delineates the workings of the loftier "Mystical towards the Supernatural." The power that Gandalf exerts to help Bilbo eventually broadens to include all the dwarves and then the forces of good—men, dwarves, Elves—as they fight the Goblins in the Battle of Five Armies, settled by the arrival of the Eagles.

It is true that, from the very beginning, events of *The Hobbit* seem to happen by chance, luck, or accident. Although Gandalf has told the dwarves that they are likely to find a good burglar at the Hobbit-hole of Bilbo Baggins in the Shire, whose door Gandalf has marked with a sign, in fact, Gandalf does not know Bilbo at all and has not visited Hobbiton since the Old Took (Bilbo's grandfather) died (5). The narrator even tells us that this first meeting between Gandalf and Bilbo occurs "By some curious *chance* one morning long ago in the quiet of the world, when there was less noise and more green, and the Hobbits were still numerous and prosperous" (5; my emphasis). And yet, the meeting does *not* occur by chance: Gandalf the wizard is instrumental in intervening here at this moment: he confesses that "I am looking for someone to share in an adventure that I am arranging, and it's very difficult to find anyone" (6). His initial intervention, significantly, happens "in the quiet of the world"—what is described as a "first moment," or point of origin, not like any later time, especially given the fact that Gandalf actually does not reappear in the second half of the story for some time.

From the moment Bilbo meets Gandalf and, thereafter, as Bilbo recalls, Gandalf possesses considerable magical skills—given his nature as a wizard—as exercised in Bilbo's various adventures up to his meeting with Beorn the shape-changer in chapter 7, "Queer Lodgings." Early on Bilbo remembers that Gandalf had given Old Took two "magic diamond studs that fastened themselves and never came undone till ordered," had told "wonderful tales ... about dragons and goblins and giants and the rescue of princesses and the unexpected luck of widows' sons" and devised marvelous pyrotechnics for the Hobbits (7). Bilbo also recalls that Gandalf had been responsible for "many quiet lads and lasses going off into the Blue for mad adventures" (7). Not only will Gandalf help awaken the love of the unknown in Bilbo merely by bringing into his life the thirteen song-singing dwarves who knock on his door in response to Gandalf's "queer sign" (8), but Gandalf also uses his authority with the dwarves to convince them that this "excitable little fellow" is "one of the best" in his ferocity—"as fierce as a dragon" (17). Further, during the first seven chapters, Gandalf "rescues" Bilbo when his training as a hero is jeopardized by some fearsome magical adversary—for example, in chapter 2, "Roast Mutton," when the Trolls threaten to eat him *and* the dwarves—Gandalf throws his voice to sound like a Troll and divert them into a quarrel until the sun rises and they turn to stone. Gandalf with his sword and wand also rescues them from the Goblins (Orcs) in chapter 4, "Over Hill and Under Hill," and he lights pine-cones in chapter 6, "Out of the Frying-Pan into the Fire," to ward off the Wargs of the Misty Mountains, with the resultant fires catching the notice of the Eagles, who rescue them all from the Goblins who have joined the Wargs. After the sojourn at Beorn's "queer lodgings," Gandalf departs so that Bilbo can hone his newly-acquired valor as a thief until the wizard returns after the Battle of Five Armies, in chapter 18, "The Return Journey."

Gandalf is, in fact, an Istar, Quenya for "wizard," according to "The Istari," which Tolkien wrote in 1954 while compiling an unfinished index for *The Lord of the Rings* published later in *Unfinished Tales* (Tolkien, 1979, 388–402; also Scull and Hammond, 2006, 432–34). Five chiefs of this order with knowledge of the history of the world and its nature functioned as emissaries from the Valar, the Lords of the West, incarnated in men's bodies that aged but did not die. These five included the head wizard, the White Messenger, Curunír (Saruman), or "The Man of Craft," who was skilled in "works of hand" and adept at uncovering secrets; two in sea-blue who went into the East and never returned; one in earth-brown, Radagast, "tender of beasts," who lived among the birds and beasts; and one in gray, the wisest of all but also bearing a staff, Gandalf, or Mithrandír the Gray Pilgrim, Enemy of Sauron. To Círdan, Elven master of the Grey Havens, Gandalf had entrusted the Third Elven ring, Narya the Red (Tolkien, 1979, 389–90). A wanderer, Gandalf had neither wealth nor followers and helped all those in need. Known also as "Olórin" to the Valar, this lover of the Eldar was sent to Middle-earth by the Vala Manwë, just as Vala Yavanna, wife of Aulë, had asked Curumo (Saruman) to take there Aiwendil (Radagast) (Tolkien, 1979, 390–91, 393). Appearing in the Third Age in "shapes weak and humble," the Istari were told to "advise and persuade men and Elves to good, and to seek to unite in love and understanding all those whom Sauron, should he come again, would endeavor to dominate and corrupt" (Tolkien, 1979, 389).

Each of the chief wizards in "The Istari" corresponds to a Vala or Valar: "Olórin" (Gandalf), to Manwë and his wife Varda; Curumo (Saruman), to Aulë; Aiwendil (Radagast), to Yavanna; and Alatar (a blue wizard) to Oromë, as well as to Pallando (the second blue wizard), but—as Christopher Tolkien acknowledges, this latter "replaces Pallando to Mandos and Nienna" (Christopher Tolkien, Notes to "The Istari," in *Tolkien,* 1979, 393n). These wizards, elsewhere in Tolkien's notes in "The Istari," are identified as Maiar, like the godlike Valar in the hierarchy of being on Middle-earth, "persons of the 'angelic' order, though not necessarily of the same rank. The Maiar were 'spirits,' but capable of self-incarnation, and could take 'humane' (especially Elvish) forms.... Now these Maiar were sent by the Valar at a crucial moment in the history of Middle-earth to enhance the resistance of the Elves of the West, greatly outnumbered by those of the East and South (Christopher Tolkien, Notes to "The Istari," in *Tolkien,* 1979, 393n). Tolkien also adds in "The Istari" that many of the "Faithful" in later days believed that Gandalf "was the last appearance of Manwë himself, before his final withdrawal to the watchtower of Taniquetil" (Tolkien, 1979, 412).

What Tolkien means by the "magical" face of Faërie in his created world, then, results from the power of the gods—the Valar and the Maiar. This definition of the divine becomes clearer when he distinguishes between magical and scientific operations—the latter, called "mechanisms"—in a passage found in the Manuscript B Miscellaneous Pages of the variorum edition of "On Fairy-stories" (MS. 6, Oxford, Bodleian Library, fols. 6–8, in Tolkien, 2005, 253). Magical power derives from the created world, but its operations differ from scientific operations, despite their often similar appearance: "Magic [sic] does not come from outside the world. Magic is the special use (real, imagined, or pretended) of powers that, though they must derive ultimately from God, are inherent in the created world, exterior to God" (Tolkien, 2005, 253–54). An example of this phenomenon occurs in *The Hobbit* when the thrush knocks a snail against the secret stone door barring the entrance to the Lonely Mountain at the exact moment the sun sets and sends a ray of light pinpointing the keyhole, allowing Bilbo to open it magically with the key brought by the Dwarves so they may enter the tunnel (190). This magical incident forms an exact parallel to the fateful incident in the "Story of Sigurd" when he accidentally eats the heart of the dragon and magically understands the woodpeckers' prophecy that reveals Regin's perfidious intentions toward him.

In the *Silmarillion* Tolkien fantastically historicizes his discussion of faërie as a "perilous realm" in which magic is natural and derives from God, namely, Eru the One, or Ilúvatar, in Middle-earth. In the first chapter of Tolkien's *Silmarillion*, "Ainulindäle," a hierarchy of beings derives from the one God, as part of him, a figure whose nature has been described as Neoplatonic (Flieger, 1986, 127–33). Ilúvatar offers a vision, a new World in which the Music contains each Ainur's being and, as well, Ilúvatar's own: "no theme may be played that hath not its uttermost source in me, nor can any alter the music in my despite. For he that attempteth this shall prove but mine instrument in the devising of things more wonderful, which he himself hath not imagined" (Tolkien, 1976; 2d ed., 1999; rpt. 2001, 17). As part of the third theme, in extension of himself and all earlier beings as his thoughts, Ilúvatar creates the Children of the World (the Elves and Men) to people his cosmos of Arda, the Earth (Tolkien, 1976; 2d ed., 1999; rpt. 200,1, 17). To each part of Arda—air, water, earth—Ilúvatar sends the Imperishable Flame, so that the world might exist as Eä, and along with the Flame, any Ainur who wish to go there. Those Ainur who go become the Valar, the Powers of the World, otherwise known as "gods," Tolkien declares (Tolkien, 1976, 20). These gods and their queens, the Valier, are fourteen in number and hierarchize different powers of the Earth and its regions and inhabitants (Tolkien, 1976, 25–32).

The four elements of Middle-earth, fire, air, water, and earth, are neatly linked with the hierarchy in his chain of being, beginning with the Valar and continuing with the two kinds of Elves, the Quendi, with its three races; and the Avari. Highest on earth are the Valar and the Maiar associated with Manwë (the winds and the air) and Varda (the stars), while below are the Valar, Maiar, and other beings—including Sauron—associated with Aulë and the earth from which Aulë harvests gems (the realm of the dwarves and the Noldor). Like the Ainur, the Elves may choose to make a journey; also like them, they are divided by their choices into groups of greater and lesser being. During the First Age, the Firstborn, or Quendi, initially mean all the Elves, "Those who speak with voices" (Christopher Tolkien, "Index of Names," in Tolkien, 1976, s.v.). Later on, the name refers just to the first group of Elves, the Eldar, "The People of the Stars," who accept Manwë's summons to make the Great Journey to Aman and, as a result, benefit by their life there. Those who do not, the second group of Elves, the Avari ("The Unwilling; the Refusers"), refuse the summons in order to stay where they are in Cuiviénen (where the first awakening of the Elves occurred). Once these Elves are killed or die of grief, they retreat to the halls of Manos (not to return to Middle-earth). Later still there exists a group of the Avari known as the Moriquendi, "Elves of the Darkness," because of their refusal to journey to Aman during the days of the Two

Trees. For this reason of never having seen the Light of the Trees, they are known as the "Dark Elves" (Shippey, 2004, 1–15).

Among the first group of the Elves, that is, of the Eldar, a hierarchy of three kindreds exists, depending on how quickly these Elves elect to travel: (1) the Vanyar, first in time on the Great Journey to Aman; (2) the Noldor next, and (3), after, the Teleri, whose name means "Last." All three kindreds who journey are known later as the Calaquendi, "Elves of the Light," or High Elves. The golden-haired Vanyar are linked with the chief Vala, Manwë (the wind), and love the light of the Trees; they wander in Valinor and live at Taniquetl. The second group of Eldar, the Noldor, dark-haired and grey-eyed, are identified with the Vala Aulë (earth). Known for their crafts and learning, they are associated with the dwarves because of their craftsmanship and their love of material creation and objects. Because of this earthly link, the Noldor are more easily seduced by the lies of the fallen Vala Melkor, later "Morgoth," who is jealous of their creations. The third group of the Eldar, the Teleri, who love music, are linked with the Vala Ulmo (water). The Teleri lag behind on the great journey, one group, called Nandor, moving south; some stay behind in Falas and are called Sindar (and speak Sindarin). Most of the sea-loving Teleri go west.

Tolkien's Elves paradoxically appear human in hands, face, voice, and language but are neither human nor spirits of the dead, according to Manuscript B of "On Fairy-stories" (Tolkien, 2005, 254). Yet the Elves are capable of evil because they have a choice, a free will. Tolkien calls them a "'separate creation,' 'spirits, daemons'; inherent powers of the created world, deriving more directly and 'earlier' (in terrestrial history) from the creating will of God, but nonetheless created, subject to Moral Law, capable of good and evil, and possibly (in this fallen world) actually sometimes evil. They are in fact non-incarnate minds (or souls) of a stature and even nature more near to that of Man (in some cases possibly less, in many maybe greater) than any other rational creatures, known or guessed by us. They can take form at will, or they could do so: they have or had a choice" (Tolkien, 2005, 254–55). The free will of Elves is a concept that Tolkien may have borrowed from Christianity, but in his construction of the Elven history in *The Silmarillion* he is emphatic that it derives from Ilúvatar's act of Thought at the beginning of creation in which Melkor, one of the "offspring of [Eru's] thought," or the Ainur, is free to create his own discordant music, an act that endlessly cycles back into the universe as good by means of Ilúvatar's three musical themes.

Once the essential being of the Elves as the Children of God, capable of choice, is clarified in *The Silmarillion*, we may also be able to see their link with the Elves in *The Hobbit*. These Elves transcend the negative connotations of both the smith Regin and the dwarf Andvari in "The Story of Sigurd" through their knowledge and wise counsel and rescue and restoration of others, primarily Bilbo, but also *The Hobbit*'s dwarves, at several key points in their journey. For example, the (Noldor) Elves the company first encounters after the episode with the trolls, in chapter 3, "A Short Rest," sing songs about the dwarves and Hobbit that reveal the Elven understanding of what has happened to them and the Elves provide counsel to them about the happenings of the current day. And when the travelers meet Half-Elven Elrond at the Last Homely House, he teaches them about the High Elven origin of the old swords they have won from the Trolls' lair and about the meaning of their map's rune-letters, particularly a magic spell that will aid Bilbo in opening the door to the Lonely Mountain on the dwarves' New Year, the day on which the "last moon of Autumn and the sun are in the sky together" (50). Even the (Sindarin) Wood-Elves who capture Bilbo and the dwarves close to the end, in chapter 9, "Barrels out of Bond," although lesser in nature than the other Elves whom the company meets, inadvertently provide the means for their rescue—the wine barrels.

The Hobbit, then, includes a mythological back-story linked to Tolkien's legendarium with its providential network of Maiar and Ainur and the Children of God, Elves, and dwarves that transcends the fate-driven Old Norse "Story of Sigurd" of Andrew Lang from which Tolkien's fairy-story derives. Key to answering the question posed at the beginning of this section—whether magic has any connection with God, if not with religion—are two framing dialogues between Bilbo and Gandalf at the beginning and end of *The Hobbit*. Bilbo initiates the first dialogue by means of his initial "Good morning!" (5) to Gandalf, to which simple greeting Gandalf responds rather scholastically and literally with an interrogation into the meaning of "good": "What do you mean? ... Do you wish me a good morning, or mean that it is a good morning whether I want it or not; or that you feel good this morning; or that it is a morning to be good on?" (5). Bilbo's more philosophical and essential reply is important: "All of them at once" (6). Bilbo means, in truth, that there is goodness in nature (the morning, part of that cosmic good, whether Gandalf wants it or not), goodness in Bilbo the hero-to-be (he feels "good"—well—this morning and he wishes a similarly beneficial, "good," morning to Gandalf), and "goodness" in wizard Gandalf (a morning on which he can do "good," that is, perform his mystical role as a Maia and Istar). All three goodnesses reflect the impact of nature, magic, and mysticism in the end result of this fairy-story.

And at the end, when Bilbo notes that the prophetic old songs of the Elves have been proven to be true, Gandalf sums up the reason that Bilbo has succeeded in his adventure. It is not that the Hobbit did not disprove the prophecies and not that he succeeded because of "mere luck," or "just for [Bilbo's] sole benefit" (272). Bilbo succeeds because of the combination of his intelligence and valor and lack of pride, along with the aid of wizard Gandalf within a much greater, if providential, universe: "You are a very fine person, Mr. Baggins," says Gandalf, "and I am very fond of you; but you are only quite a little fellow in a wide world after all!" (272), meaning that he is only one part of a greater whole that providence oversees. Thus, Bilbo can humbly but profoundly reply, "Thank goodness!" with a laugh and a charitable pass of the tobacco jar to the wizard. In his humility the unSigurdlike Bilbo recognizes that a larger goodness in him—a universal Good, or God—has facilitated his success, namely, the remedial retrieval of the dwarves' lost treasure from the dragon Smaug by means of a found magical ring and the restoration of peace between the men of Dale and the dwarves by means of the gift of the Arkenstone, for which he is grateful.

Tolkien thus emphasizes throughout *The Hobbit*, *The Silmarillion*, and "On Fairy-stories" that the essential power of Faërie is magical, natural, and derived from the gods, or God. Providence is a paramount force in Middle-earth, meaning, not the specifically Christian concept of Providence, but an analogous force of goodness inherent in the visual materialization of the harmonious music of Tolkien's Ainur that first fills the void and continues throughout the Three Ages and the coming Fourth, of Man, at the end of *The Lord of the Rings*. If Elves and fairies and their magical powers seem to have disappeared in the Fourth Age, of Man, Tolkien reminds that, whatever this diminution of essential being, the goodness of Ilúvatar lives on in it.

The Hobbit exists, then, not as a muddle of various ideas that impacted negatively on the construction of Tolkien's later works, or as a simple children's story that we might well ignore, but as the pivot on which his medievalized mythology of magic and his favorite genre, the fairy-story, with its transcendental and even mystical tendencies, is balanced, and by means of which his other works may be interpreted. Epic, fairy-story, and mythology: an understanding of the interrelationship of all three sources—whether Old English and Old Norse epic, Lang's fairy-story of Sigurd, or Tolkien's own mythological "Silmarillion" for the works he generated during the same period of time as *The Hobbit*, and, in particular, the essential critical statement of "On Fairy-stories"—may provide yet another answer to Tolkien's own professed desire to create a "mythology for England."

Notes

This article grew out of a Rice University Alumni College Faculty lecture, "Tolkien's Magical Mystery Tour," delivered in Houston, Texas, on March 14, 2009; it became "The Mythology of Magic: Tolkien's *Hobbit* and Andrew Lang's *Red Fairy Book* 'Story of Sigurd,'" in a session on *The Hobbit* organized by Brad Eden and moderated by Douglas A. Anderson, in Tolkien at Kalamazoo, at the Forty-Seventh International Congress on the Middle Ages, Western Michigan University, Kalamazoo, MIichigan, May 10, 2012.

1. See, for example, Chance, 1978, 1979, rev. ed., 2001; Hostetter and Smith, 1996, in Reynolds and Goodknight, 281–90; and Stenström, 1996, in Reynolds and Goodknight, 310–14.

2. For Tolkien's reworking of Old and Middle English literature and language, see, in chronological order, esp. on *Beowulf*, Chance [Nitzsche], 179; rev. ed., 2001;on Germanic philology and Tolkien, Shippey, 1982; rev. ed. 1992; on medieval bibliography on Tolkien, Chance and Day, 1991, 375–88; on the *Gawain*-Poet, Shippey, 1992 and 1996, pp. 213–20; on *Beowulf* and Old English studies, Mitchell, 1996, 206–11; and Orchard, 1992, 73–84; on Old English and Old Norse traditions of dragon-lore, Evans, 2000, 21–38; on the true hero, Clark, 2000, 39–52; on exile in *The Seafarer* and *The Lord of the Rings*, Wilcox, 2002, 133–54; on Tolkien's Anglo-Saxon mythology, Drout, 2004, 229–47; on Old English oaths and their breaking in Tolkien's myth, Holmes, 2004, 249–61; on the past in Beowulf and *The Lord of the Rings*, Bolintineau, 2004, 263–73; on race, the Old English *Sigelwara*, and Tolkien's Swertings, McFadden, 2005, 155–69; and on race and gender in the Old English *Exodus* and other poems and in Tolkien, Chance, 2005, 171–86.

3. On Old Norse literature and language, for the names of the Dwarves derived in part from the *Eddas*, see Callahan, 1972, 20; for the antecedents of Gandalf, the Dwarves, the Elves, the Ring, and other elements in Norse mythology, see Brunsdale, 1983, 49–50; and Bryce, 1983, 113–19. Shippey has focused on Old Norse philology and literature as the core of Tolkien's fiction, 1982; rev. ed. 1992; and also 1995, 145–61; see also Burns on Gandalf and Odin, 2000, 219–32; on Norse and Christian Gods in Tolkien, 2004, 163–78; and on Celtic and Norse in Tolkien, 2005; on the Old Norse Valkyries and Tolkien's women characters in *The Lord of the Rings*, Donovan, 2002, 106–32; and on the end of the world in Norse mythology and in Tolkien, Dimond, 2004, 179–89.

4. See Tolkien's unfinished "Sketch of the Mythology with Especial Reference to the 'Children of Húrin,'" in *The Shaping of Middle Earth*, 1986, 11–75. Scull and Hammond, 2006, 901–04, provides a helpful but brief summary of the stages in the making of "The Silmarillion."

5. *The Hobbit*, first published in in Great Britain in 1937, appeared in a second edition in 1951, in which the problematic chapter 5, on the riddle game with Gollum, in when Bilbo uses the ring he has found, was revised (this rewriting actually occurred in 1947) to provide a transition to *The Lord of the Rings*; *The Hobbit* was again revised for the third edition, of 1966. See the discussion of how Tolkien revised *The Hobbit* in Christiansen, 1975, 9–28; and Anderson, 1988; rev. 2003.

6. See Flieger and Anderson, in Tolkien, 2005, 122; the history of the making of "On Fairy-Stories," an essay that was not published until 1947, is detailed on pp. 122–28. This edition contains all variants from the two major manuscripts of Tolkien's Andrew Lang Lecture (1939), including its final published version as edited by Christopher Tolkien in Tolkien's *The Monsters and the Critics and Other Essays* (1983).

7. In Tolkien's *Lord of the Rings*, Bilbo and Frodo were also linked as distant cousins because their fathers were members of the less noble—in fact, bourgeois—Baggins family, probably to be identified as members of the more conventional, mid-level Hobbit strain, the Harfoots. Bilbo's mother, Belladonna Took, married Bungo Baggins (son of Bungo and brother of Longo), who, in marrying Camelia Sackville, took on her hyphenated name because of its social distinction and fathered the pretentious Otho Sackville-Baggins (who later married the avaricious Lobelia Bracegirdle). Frodo's father was Drogo Baggins, son of Fosco (who was himself first cousin to Bilbo's father, Bungo). See Tolkien, 1954–55, 2d ed., 1994, 22–23 (chap. 1); and the genealogical table of the Baggins of Hobbiton and the Tooks of Great Smials in Appendix C, "Family Trees," 1074–75.

Works Cited

Anderson, Douglas A., ed. 1988. Rev. 2003. *The Annotated Hobbit*. London: HarperCollins.

Arul, Melissa Ruth. 2009. "A Critical Study of the Self and the Other in Selected Texts of Tolkien." M.A. thesis. U of Malaya-Kuala Lumpur.

Bolintineau, Alexandra. 2004. "On the Borders of Old Stories: Enacting the Past in *Beowulf* and *The Lord of the Rings*." In *Tolkien and the Invention of Myth*. Ed. Chance. 263–73.

Bosworth, Joseph. 1898; rpt. 1976. *An Anglo-Saxon Dictionary*. Ed. T. Northcote Toller. Oxford: Oxford University Press.

Brunsdale, Mitzi M. 1983. "Norse Mythological Elements in *The Hobbit*." *Mythlore* 9 (1983): 49–50.

Bryce, Lynn. 1983. "The Influence of Scandinavian Mythology in the Works of J.R.R. Tolkien." *Edda* 7 (1983): 113–19.

Burns, Marjorie J. 2000. "Gandalf and Odin." In *Tolkien's 'Legendarium': Essays on The History of Middle-earth*. Eds. Flieger and Hostetter. 219–32.

_____. 2004. "Norse and Christian Gods: The Integrative Theology of J.R.R. Tolkien." In *Tolkien and the Invention of Myth*. Ed. Chance. 163–78.

_____. 2005. *Perilous Realms: Celtic and Norse in Tolkien's Middle-earth*. Toronto: University of Toronto Press.

Callahan, Patrick J. "Tolkien's Dwarfs and the Eddas." *Tolkien Journal* 15 (1972): 20.

Carpenter, Humphrey. 1977. *Tolkien: A Biography*. London: Allen and Unwin; New York: Houghton Mifflin.

Chance [Nitzsche], Jane. 1979; 1980; rev. ed. 2001. *Tolkien's Art: A "Mythology for England."* London, Macmillan; New York: St. Martin's, rpt. Papermac. Rev. ed. Lexington: University of Kentucky Press.

_____. 1980; rpt. various. 2002. "The Problem of Grendel's Mother: The Structural Unity of *Beowulf*." *Texas Studies in Literature and Language* 22 (Fall): 287–303; rpt. in *Beowulf*. Ed. Donoghue. 152–66.

_____. 2002. Interview. *National Geographic: Beyond the Movie "The Lord of the Rings."* National Geographic TV DVD, directed by Lisa Kors.

_____. 2002, 2003. Ed. *Tolkien the Medievalist*. Routledge Studies in Medieval Culture and Religion, vol. 3. London: Routledge; New York: Routledge.

_____. 2004. Ed. *Tolkien and the Invention of Myth: A Reader*. Lexington: University of Kentucky Press.

_____. 2005. "Tolkien and the Other: Race and Gender in Middle-earth." In *Tolkien's Modern Middle Ages*. Eds. Jane Chance and Alfred Siewers. New York and London: Palgrave Macmillan. 171–86.

_____ and David Day, 1991. "Medievalism in Tolkien: Two Decades of Criticism in Review." *Medievalism: Inklings and Others* (special issue). Guest ed. Jane Chance. *Studies in Medievalism* 3:3 (1991): 375–88.

_____, and Alfred Siewers. 2005. Eds. *Tolkien's Modern Middle Ages*. New Middle Ages Series. New York and London: Palgrave Macmillan.

Christiansen, Bonniejean. 1970. "*Beowulf* and *The Hobbit*: Elegy into Fantasy in J.R.R. Tolkien's Creative Technique." Ph.D. diss. University of Southern California.

_____. 1972–73. "Tolkien's Creative Technique: *Beowulf* and *The Hobbit*." *Orcrist* 7: 16–20.

_____. 1980. "Gollum's Character Transformation in *The Hobbit*." In *A Tolkien Compass*. Ed. Jared Lobdell. Lasalle, IL: Open Court, rpt. New York: Ballantine. 9–28.

Clark, George. 2000. "J.R.R. Tolkien and the True Hero." In *J.R.R. Tolkien and His Literary Resonances*. Eds. Clark and Timmons. 39–52.

_____, and Daniel Timmons. 2000. Eds. *J.R.R. Tolkien and His Literary Resonances: Views of Middle-earth*. Westport, CT, and London: Greenwood.

Dimond, Andy. 2004. "The Twilight of the Elves: Ragnarök and the End of the Third Age." In *Tolkien and the Invention of Myth*. Ed. Chance, 179–89.

Donoghue, Daniel. 2002. Ed *Beowulf: A Verse Translation: Authoritative Text, Contexts, Criticism*. Trans. Seamus Heaney. Norton Critical Edition. New York: W.W. Norton.

Donovan, Leslie A. 2002. "The Valkyrie Reflex in J.R.R. Tolkien's *The Lord of the Rings*: Galadriel, Shelob, Éowyn, and Arwen." In *Tolkien the Medievalist*. Ed. Chance. 106–32.

Drout, Michael D. C. 2004. "A Mythology for Anglo-Saxon England." In *Tolkien and the Invention of Myth*. Ed. Chance. 2004. 229–47.

Evans, Jonathan. 2000. "The Dragon-Lore of Middle-earth: Tolkien and Old English and Old Norse Tradition." In *J.R.R. Tolkien and His Literary Resonances*. Eds. Clark and Timmons. 21–38.

Fimi, Dimitra. 2009. *Tolkien, Race, and Cultural History: From Fairies to Hobbits*. London: Palgrave Macmillan.

Flieger, Verlyn. 1983; rev. 2002. *Splintered Light: Logos and Language in Tolkien's World*. Grand Rapids, MI.: Wm. B. Eerdmans. Rev. ed. Kent, OH: Kent State University Press.

_____. 1986. "Naming the Unnamable: The Neoplatonic 'One' in Tolkien's *Silmarillion*." In *Diakonia: Studies in Honor of Robert T. Meyer*. Eds. Thomas Halton and Joseph P. Williman. Washington, D.C.: Catholic University of America Press. 127–33.

_____. 2002. "'There Would Always Be a Fairy-Tale': J.R.R. Tolkien and the Folklore Controversy." In *Tolkien the Medievalist*. Ed. Chance, 26–35.

_____. 2004. "A Mythology for Finland: Tolkien and Lönnrot as Mythmakers." In *Tolkien and the Invention of Myth*. Ed. Chance. 277–83.

_____, and Carl F. Hostetter. 2000. Eds. *Tolkien's* Legendarium: *Essays on the History of Middle-earth*. Westport, CT, and London: Greenwood.

Gay, David Elton. 2005. "J.R.R. Tolkien and the *Kalevala*: Some Thoughts on the Finnish Origins of Tom Bombadil and Treebeard." *Tolkien and the Invention of Myth*. Ed. Chance. 295–304.

Hiley, Margaret, and Frank Weinreich. 2008. Eds. *Tolkien's Shorter Works: Essays of the Jena Conference 2007*. Conmarë Series 17. Zurich, Switzerland, and Jena, Germany: Walking Tree.

Holmes, John R. 2004. "Oaths and Oath-Breaking: Analogues of the Old English Comitatus in Tolkien's Myth." *Tolkien and the Invention of Myth*. Ed. Chance. 249–61.

Hostetter, Carl J., and Arden R. Smith. 1996. "A Mythology for England." In Reynolds and Goodknight, 281–90.

Isaacs, Neil D., and Rose A. Zimbardo. 1968. Eds. *Tolkien and the Critics: Essays on J.R.R. Tolkien's Lord of the Rings*. Notre Dame and London: University of Notre Dame Press.

_____. 1981. *Tolkien: New Critical Perspectives*. Lexington: University of Kentucky Press.

_____. 2004; 2005. *Understanding "The Lord of the Rings": The Best of Tolkien Criticism*. Boston: Houghton Mifflin; rpt. pb. Mariner.

Klaeber, Fr. 1950; rpt. 1968. Ed. *Beowulf and the Fight at Finnsburg*. 3d ed. Boston: D.C. Heath.

Lang, Andrew. 1890; rpt. 1966. "The Story of Sigurd." *The Red Fairy Book*. New York: Dover. 357–67.

Lönnrot, Elias, comp. 1849. *Kalevala: The Land of Heroes*. 1907. Trans. W. F. Kirby. London: J. M. Dent.

Matthews, Dorothy. 1975; rpt. 1980. "The Psychological Journey of Bilbo Baggins." *A Tolkien Compass*. Ed. Jared Lobdell. Lasalle, IL: Open Court. Rpt. New York: Ballantine. 29–42.

McFadden, Brian. 2005. "Fear of Difference, Fear of Death: The *Sigelwara*, Tolkien's Swertings, and Racial Difference." *Tolkien's Modern Middle Ages*. Eds. Chance and Siewers. 155–69.

Mitchell, Bruce. 1996. "J.R.R. Tolkien and Old English Studies." In Reynolds and Goodknight, *Proceedings of the J.R.R. Centenary Conference*, 206–11.

Morris, William. 1870; 1962. Trans. *Volsunga Saga: The Story of the Volsungs and the Niblungs*. Rpt. with an intro. and glossary by Robert W. Gutman. New York: Collier.

Nitzsche, Jane Chance. *See* Jane Chance.

Orchard, Andy. 1992. "Tolkien, the Monsters, and the Critics: Back to Beowulf." In K.J. Battarbee, ed. *Scholarship and Fantasy: Proceedings of the Tolkien Phenomenon, May, 1992, Turku, Finland*, Anglicana Turkuensia no. 12. Turku: University of Turku. 73–84.

Rateliff, John D. 2007–08. *The History of* The Hobbit: Part 1, *Mr. Baggins*; Part 2: *Return to Bag-End*. 2 vols. London: HarperCollins.

Rearick III, Anderson. 2004. "Why Is the Only Good Orc a Dead Orc? The Dark Face of Racism Examined in Tolkien's World." *Modern Fiction Studies* 50: 861–75.

Reilly, R. J. 1968; rpt. 2004. "Tolkien and the Fairy-Story." *Tolkien and the Critics*. Eds. Isaacs and Zimbardo. 128–50. Rpt. *Understanding "The Lord of the Rings."* Eds. Isaacs and Zimbardo. 93–105.

Reynolds, Patricia, and Glen H. Goodknight. 1996. Eds *Proceedings of the J.R.R. Tolkien Centenary Conference, Keble College, Oxford, 1992*. Mythlore 80/Mallorn 30 (Winter, 1996).

Ripley, William Z. 1899. *The Races of Europe*. London: Kegan Paul.

Ryan, J. S. 1981; rpt. 2004. "Folktale, Fairy-Tale, and the Creation of a Story." In *Tolkien: New Critical Perspectives*. Eds. Isaacs and Zimbardo. 19–39. Rpt. *Understanding "The Lord of the Rings."* Eds. Isaacs and Zimbardo. 106–21.

Scull, Christina, and Wayne G. Hammond. 2006. *The J.R.R. Tolkien Companion & Guide: Reader's Guide*. London: HarperCollins.

Shippey, T[om] A. 1982; Rev. ed. 1992. *The Road to Middle-earth*. Rev. ed. London: Allen and Unwin.

_____. 1996. "Tolkien and the Gawain-Poet." In *Proceedings of the J.R.R. Centenary Conference*. Ed. Reynolds and Goodknight. 213–20.

_____. 2000; 2007. "Grimm, Grundtvig, Tolkien: Nationalisms and the Invention of Mythologies." *The Ways of Creative Mythologies: Imagined Worlds and Their Makers*. Ed. Maria Kateeva. 2 vols. Telford: Tolkien Society. 1:1–17. Rpt. *Roots and Branches*. By Shippey. 79–96.

_____. 2004. "Light-elves, Dark-elves, and Others: Tolkien's Elvish Problem." *Tolkien Studies* 1: 1–15.

_____. 2004. "Tolkien and the Appeal of the Pagan: *Edda* and *Kalevala*." In *Tolkien and the Invention of Myth*. Ed. Chance. 145–61.

_____, 2005. Ed. *The Shadow-Walkers: Jacob Grimm's Mythology of the Monstrous*. Tempe, AZ: Arizona Center for the Study of Medieval and Renaissance Studies/Brepols.

_____. 2007. *Roots and Branches: Selected Papers on Tolkien by Tom Shippey*. Zollikofen, Switzerland: Walking Tree.

———.2007. "Tolkien and Iceland: The Philology of Envy." *Roots and Branches*. By Shippey. 187–202.

Stenström, Anders. 1996. "A Mythology? For England?" In Reynolds and Goodknight, *Proceedings of the J.R.R. Tolkien Centenary Conference,* 310–14.

Tolkien, J.R.R. 1936; rpt. various, 2002. "Beowulf: The Monsters and the Critics." *Proceedings of the British Academy* 22 (1936): 245–95. In Donoghue, 103–29.

———. 1937, 1938; 3d ed. 1966, 1967; rpt. 1997. *The Hobbit; or There and Back Again*. London: Allen and Unwin, Boston: Houghton Mifflin, 1938, 1967; rpt. Boston: Houghton Mifflin.

———. 1938. Letter to *The Observer*, 20 February, p. 9.

———. 1947; rpt. 1966; rev. ed., rpt. 1988, 1989. "On Fairy-stories." *Essays Presented to Charles Williams*. Ed. C. S. Lewis. London: Oxford University Press. 38–89. Rpt. Grand Rapids, MI: William B. Eerdmans. Rev. ed., rpt. in *Tree and Leaf* and in *The Tolkien Reader*, and in *Tree and Leaf, Including the Poem "Mythopoeia,"* with intro. by Christopher Tolkien. London: Allen and Unwin.

———. 1954–55, 2nd ed., 1994. *The Lord of the Rings* with Note on the Text by Douglas A. Anderson. Boston: Houghton Mifflin.

———. 1976; 2d ed. 1999; rpt. 2001. *The Silmarillion*. Ed. Christopher Tolkien.London: HarperCollins; Boston: Houghton Mifflin.

———. 1979; rpt. 1980. "The Istari." In *Unfinished Tales of Númenor and Middle-earth*. Ed. Christopher Tolkien. London: Allen and Unwin; Boston: Houghton Mifflin. 388–402.

———. 1981. *The Letters of J.R.R. Tolkien*. Ed. Humphrey Carpenter with the assistance of Christopher Tolkien. Boston: Houghton Mifflin.

———. 1983; rpt. 1984. *The Monsters and the Critics and Other Essays*. Edited by Christopher Tolkien. London: Allen and Unwin; Boston: Houghton Mifflin.

———. 1986. "Sketch of the Mythology with Especial Reference to the 'Children of Húrin.'" In *The Shaping of Middle Earth*. Ed. Christopher Tolkien. *The History of Middle-earth*. Vol. 4. London: HarperCollins. 11–75.

———. 1988; rpt. 1989. *Tree and Leaf, Including the Poem "Mythopoeia."* Intro. Christopher Tolkien. Rev. ed. London: Allen and Unwin; Boston: Houghton Mifflin.

———. 1989. *The Tolkien Reader*. 2d ed. New York: Ballantine.

———. 1990. *Morgoth's Ring*. Ed. Christopher Tolkien. *The History of Middle-earth*. Vol. 10. Harper-Collins.

———. 1996. *The Peoples of Middle-earth*. Ed. Christopher Tolkien. *The History of Middle-earth*. Vol. 10. London: HarperCollins.

———. 2008. *Tolkien on Fairy-stories: Expanded Edition, with Commentary and Notes*. Ed. Verlyn Flieger and Douglas A. Anderson. London: HarperCollins.

———. 2009. *The Legend of Sigurd and Gudrún*. Ed. Christopher Tolkien. London: HarperCollins.

Tolkien Remembered. 2005. DVD video. Princeton, NJ: Films for the Humanities and Sciences.

West, Richard C. 2000. "Turin's Ofermod: An Old English Theme in the Development of the Story of Túrin." *Tolkien's* Legendarium. Eds. Flieger and Hostetter. 233–45.

———. 2004. "Setting the Rocket Off in Story: The *Kalevala* as the Germ of Tolkien's Legendarium." In *Tolkien and the Invention of Myth*. Ed. Chance. 285–94.

Wilcox, Miranda. 2002. "Exilic Imagining in *The Seafarer* and *The Lord of the Rings*." In *Tolkien the Medievalist*. Ed. Chance. 133–54.

Zipes, Jack. 1979; rev. ed., 2002. *Breaking the Magic Spell: Radical Themes of Folk and Fairy Tales*. Lexington: University of Kentucky Press.

———. 1988; rev. ed. 2011. *Fairy Tales and the Art of Subversion: The Classical Genre for Children and the Forces of Civilization*. London: Methuen.

From "The Silmarillion" to The Hobbit *and Back Again*
An Onomastic Foray

Damien Bador

Introduction: "the mythology on the outskirts" of The Hobbit

In several letters, J.R.R. Tolkien tried to explain *a posteriori* the links between the redaction of *The Hobbit* and his invented mythology, which he often referred to as his "legendarium." In a famous letter from 1951, written to Milton Waldman, editor with the London publisher Collins, Tolkien claimed that *The Hobbit* was "quite independently conceived" (Tolkien, 1995b, 145) from his existing body of legends known as "The Silmarillion."[1] He also drew a comparison between the redaction of *The Hobbit* and two of his shorter tales: *Leaf by Niggle* and *The Farmer Giles of Ham*. These two works had already been printed at the time of this letter and were admittedly well outside the scope of Middle-earth. The previous year, Tolkien had already said to his current editor, Sir Stanley Unwin, that *The Lord of the Rings* was "not really a sequel to *The Hobbit,* but to *The Silmarillion*" (Tolkien, 1995b, 136), this time opposing his yet unpublished masterwork to *Farmer Giles of Ham*. These clear opinions have frequently been taken as face value by critics of Tolkien's works, although Tolkien's comments on the relations between *The Hobbit* and "The Silmarillion" are in fact more contrasted than these excerpts suggest.[2] Yet the statements quoted proved very popular with commentators, as they provided a convenient framework to explain the significant differences of tone between the high mythological style of *The Silmarillion* and the facetious, patronizing narration of *The Hobbit*. But before examining in more details Tolkien's claims above, one needs to take into account their context.

Shortly after *The Hobbit* was released, Tolkien had already proposed the manuscripts of "The Silmarillion," together with some of his narrative poems on the same theme; however, they had been rejected by George Allen & Unwin as unsuitable for publication (Carpenter, 2000, 187–189; Scull and Hammond, 2006, 205–209, 357–358, 379–380, 789). Aware that his work on the Elder Days of Middle-earth strayed quite far from the conventions of modern novels, a fact that had clearly perplexed his reviewer (Tolkien, 1995b, 25–26), Tolkien was very anxious to find a way to have it published. As soon as he had completed *The Lord of the Rings*, he started looking for a publisher who would accept to simultaneously publish it with "The Silmarillion." Yet, as he recognized several times, such a release would have been a risky endeavor, with little prospects at the time to ever cover the costs of publication, especially in the context of post–Second World War shortage of printing paper. Hence, Tolkien needed to stress the strong links between the two works in order to make them inseparable in the minds of his correspondents.

Looking back at these claims, it is now possible to see that they fail to account for the long and intricate evolution of the three Middle-earth works, an evolution that did not stop with the release *The Lord of the Rings*, but went on for most of Tolkien's life.[3] When Christopher Tolkien completed the publication of *The History of Middle-earth* series in 1996, it was finally possible to access most of Tolkien's drafts for *The Lord of the Rings* as well as various manuscripts that had been used as the basis for the posthumous *Silmarillion* compilation in 1977. These texts show that *The Silmarillion*'s tone significantly evolved over the years. Tolkien's first stories known as "The Book of Lost Tales" (Tolkien, 1991; Tolkien, 1995a), written at the end of the Great War, have a very different scope and style than the later narratives of "The Annals of Aman" and "The Grey Annals" (Tolkien, 1994a; Tolkien, 1995c), post-dating the publication of *The Lord of the Rings* and constituting the majority of the contents of the published *Silmarillion*. Further, the successive drafts of the first chapters of *The Lord of the Rings* feature stories in the straight line of the ending of *The Hobbit*. In fact, Tolkien long hesitated to make Bilbo the main hero of what he had dubbed "the new *Hobbit*," only dismissing the idea for good after he had completed the whole of Book I of the new tale (Tolkien, 1994c, 370). More recently, the edition of the drafts of *The Hobbit* by John D. Rateliff under the name *The History of The Hobbit* has shown that Tolkien's intention to relate his hobbit adventures to the epic romances of the First Age of Middle-earth existed from the start, as testified by many allusions to the Elder Days, some of which were dropped before publication. Indeed, one of the main characters of "The Silmarillion," the great Elf-king Elu Thingol of Doriath, was at some point considered as a suitable protagonist in *The Hobbit*, where he would have taken the part of the Elvenking of Mirkwood. Why Tolkien renounced this particular link is unclear, but might be linked to his reluctance to change the story of the death of Thingol in "The Silmarillion" and to the absence of a powerful feminine figure such as Melian, Thingol's wife, in Bilbo's narrative (Rateliff, 2011, 408–416).

As a consequence, a deeper exploration of the links between *The Hobbit* and "The Silmarillion" is worthwhile in order to assess the place of *The Hobbit* in the larger legendarium and the evolution of the narratives linked to Middle-earth in the mid–1930s, a time when Tolkien started expanding them beyond the end of the war against Morgoth.[4] Rateliff investigates these relationships from the narrative standpoint in his commentary on the drafts of *The Hobbit*. He also analyses several names in the wider context of the legendarium; however, a complete linguistic analysis is still lacking. As testified in Tolkien's conference "A Secret Vice" (Tolkien, 1997b, 198–223), language and language-making truly fascinated him.[5] Shortly after the release of *The Lord of the Rings*, Tolkien mentioned in a paper prepared for journalists: "The invention of languages is the foundation. The 'stories' were made rather to provide a world for the languages than the reverse. To me a name comes first and the story follows" (Tolkien, 1995b, 219).

At first sight, however, it would seem that very few linguistic concepts are embedded in *The Hobbit*. Tolkien even pointed out that the only "philological remark" in the book was an obscure allusion to Owen Barfield's theories about the progressive fragmentation of language and meaning, as exposed in his book *Poetic Diction*. However, this remark is integral to Tolkien's conception of the stories about the Elder Days, which deal with the gradual scattering of light and language since the origins of the world, as Verlyn Flieger pointed out in *Splintered Light* (Flieger, 2002). In "The Silmarillion," the destructive actions of Melkor Morgoth, the fallen Vala, cause the original Lamps illuminating the world to be broken. Later, he poisons the Two Trees shining on Valinor, and finally attempts but fails to extinguish the light of the Sun and Moon. While Tolkien's description of these events evolved as he rewrote his stories, each destruction causes the world to be more and more submitted to the law of Time, reducing the influence of the Valar upon Middle-earth. In the end, the main remaining sources of light are polluted by the actions of Melkor and preserve only a fraction of their former divine power. This process is paralleled by the splintering of the Elvish languages in various groups, whose members later fight against each other. The two disintegrating processes are tightly linked to Tolkien's concept of Arda Marred, the world fallen from its former glory. As noted by Flieger, this decay occurs faster and to a greater extent in Middle-earth than in Valinor, better protected by the blessed influence of the Valar.

But the use of Barfield's theory for artistic purposes is not the only linguistic link between "The Silmarillion" and *The Hobbit*. The main purpose of this chapter is to investigate the onomastic content of proper names appearing in *The Hobbit*. It will be seen that Tolkien not only reused the names of races already present in his legendarium, but specific names of places and peoples as well. Nouns such as *Elrond*, *Gondolin* or *Dorwinion* enabled Tolkien to firmly place his new story in the geography and history of the Elder Days as they were conceived at this stage of elaboration. Some names original to *The Hobbit* were used as a tool to develop the legendarium in previously unforeseen directions. This appears to be the case with the Norse Dwarf-names of Thorin & Co, which introduced a new view on the Dwarvish race, thrown in a much more positive view than in the stories recounted in "The Book of Lost Tales." Finally, the most original character of *The Hobbit*, Bilbo himself, proved to be the linchpin to the whole legendarium. Not only did he provide the means by which Tolkien reached a satisfying conclusion to his cycle of stories, but his very Englishness proved useful in a surprising fashion. His anachronistic name and behavior required additional explanations to fit in a world of Elves, wizards and dragons. This forced Tolkien to invent a consistent background for the Hobbits, including a language: the Common Speech. As a consequence, Tolkien was able to build a linguistic tie between most of the peoples of the North-West of Middle-earth, relating them to the history of the previous Ages through the tales of the colonization of Middle-earth by the Dúnedain. Hobbits thus became a key feature in the evolution of stories and lands developed during the writing of *The Lord of the Rings*. In addition, their naïve perspective on the world surrounding their little land was also a lever to introduce readers to a world filled with magic and wonder. Hence, they proved the best possible narrators for the legends in which they intruded, and provided Tolkien with the most adequate frame for his whole legendarium.

Of place-names

The various maps Tolkien drew during the redaction of *The Hobbit* are a good place to start this investigation. Though the geography of the two tales may now seem wholly different, this was not necessarily the case when Tolkien started writing the adventures of Bilbo Baggins. While the first "Silmarillion" map was begun around 1926–1930, before Tolkien started telling the story of Bilbo, the geography of the tales of the Elder Days was still in a state of flux and this "Silmarillion" map was significantly changed as the stories evolved over the years (Tolkien, 1993, 269). The first version of the map of the Mountain drawn for the first draft of *The Hobbit* is known as Fimbulfambi's Map. As conclusively demonstrated by Rateliff, it can be superposed with the Northern part of the first "Silmarillion" map. Each of the main elements of the first layer of Fimbulfambi's Map has exact counterparts in the geography of Beleriand. The Wild Wood (original name of Mirkwood in *The Hobbit* drafts) can be equated with the forest of Deadly Nightshade (*Taur-na-Fuin*) in Northern Beleriand. The Black Mountain (initial name of the Lonely Mountain) would correspond to a mountaintop of the highlands south of *Taur-na-Fuin*. Finally, the Withered Heath, "where the Great Dragons used to live" seems equivalent to the Plain of Thirst (*Dor-na-Fauglith*), the blasted expanse at the feet of Thangorodrim (Rateliff, 2011, 20–22, 487–489). Two elements reinforce these similarities. First, the name *Taur-na-Fuin* is translated as *Mirkwood* in a draft of "The Silmarillion" (Tolkien, 1992, 282), while the name *Mirkwood* already appears in the second layer of Fimbulfambi's Map.[6] Second, the compass rose of Fimbulfambi's Map represents the Gates of Morn to the East and the mountain of Taniquetil to the West, two important features of the legends of the Elder Days as Tolkien conceived them at this stage.

Despite these equivalences, it is worth noticing that Tolkien avoided reusing the exact names appearing in his body of legends of the Elder Days and preferred approximating terms such as Plain of Thirst/Withered Heath or Taur-na-Fuin/Mirkwood/Wild Wood. It is highly possible that he foresaw that either story could still be modified and preferred avoiding the task of matching changes in both texts, especially since "The Silmarillion" materials were already dispersed in a great numbers of drafts and manuscripts. This did not prevent both stories to be co-located in the same imaginary world: as shown by some chronological elements in the drafts of *The Hobbit*, such as the Wizard's allusion to the story of Beren and Tinuviel (Rateliff, 2011, 73), the events of "The Silmarillion" were then supposed to have taken place in a more or less recent past. Hence, Tolkien probably considered believable that new names be given to the old locations of "The Silmarillion." Such a renaming would have been likely enough in the aftermath of the Great Battle that saw the overthrown of Morgoth and the reshaping of the lands of Beleriand.

Revisions to Bilbo's tale, however, soon differentiated the geography of the region around the Lonely Mountain from Beleriand. Yet many reminiscences remained, such as a tentative use of Tolkien's invented Noldorin language for the messages on Thror's map (Hammond and Scull, 2011, 49, 51, 55–56). It seems highly probable that the first Map of Wilderland (Rateliff, 2011, Plate I) was Tolkien's first attempt to draw the lands East of the Blue Mountains marking the borders of Beleriand in "The Silmarillion." The Grey Mountains and the Iron Hills in this map are in the location expected for the eastern spurs of Morgoth's Iron Mountains as depicted in the first "Silmarillion" map and in the *Ambarkanta* (Tolkien, 1993, Map IV, V). In fact, the name of the Iron Hills appears to be a direct allusion to the Iron Mountains, the *Ered Engrin* of the Elder Days, which are also named Iron Hills (*Eiglir Engrin* or *Aiglir-angrin*), in "The Lay of the Children of Húrin" (Tolkien, 1994b, 33, 49). The similarity between the Blue Mountains in "The Silmarillion" and the Misty Mountains in *The Hobbit* is also striking: both mountain ranges could easily be superposed. In this case, Tolkien does not explicitly equate the Blue and the Misty Mountains, but one can propose a similar approximation as in Fimbulfambi's Map above. In addition, the Old Forest Road crossing Mirkwood and ending on the Eastern eaves of the forest may well be a reminder of the Dwarf-road to Belegost and Nogrod, whose Western end reaches Menegroth, the capital dwelling of Thingol (Tolkien, 1993, 271). Indeed, Tolkien later referred to the Mirkwood road as the "ancient Dwarf-road," or *Men-i-Naugrim*, in a later story published in *Unfinished Tales* (Tolkien, 1998, 363), although by that time the geography had further been changed by the introduction of the land of Eriador between Wilderland and the former location of Beleriand.

In addition to these geographical similarities, a number of names from "The Silmarillion" also appear in *The Hobbit*. The most obvious is certainly Elrond's mention of *Gondolin* "stone of song" (Gilson and Wynne, 2004, 26), the famous Elven-city of Turgon, which was the last to resist to Morgoth during the wars of Beleriand. This name entered Bilbo's narrative from the first draft of chapter 3 (Rateliff, 2011, 115). Placed in a distant past, the Fall of Gondolin provides an added depth to the story, and increases the value of the two swords Glamdring and Orcrist found in the Trolls' lair.[7] Also mentioned in two different "Silmarillion" traditions are the "great gardens of Dorwinion," whence a potent wine comes. In "The Lay of the Children of Húrin," this region, named *Dor-Winion*, is located in "the burning South" of Middle-earth. Its wine is brought to the Elves of Beleriand by the Dwarves of Nogrod (Tolkien, 1994b, 111–112). In the conclusion of the "Quenta Silmarillion," the "undying flowers in the meads of Dorwinion" are located on Tol Eressëa, in the Undying Lands (Tolkien, 1992, 334). It is however unclear whether this was a change of conception, or simply a case of two regions bearing the same name—as would later happen with the garden of Lórien in Valinor and Galadriel's domain in Middle-earth. In *The Hobbit*, the wine of Dorwinion is one of the most prized wines of the Elvenking's cave, rare enough to be reserved to the king's table. After the publication of *The Lord of the Rings*, Tolkien explained the name of *Dorwinion* as meaning "Young-land country" or "Land of *Gwinion*," the name *Gwinion* being left unexplained.[8] He located it "far south down the River Running" (Gilson, 2007, 54), thus probably obsolescing the occurrence in "The Lay of the Children of Húrin." Interestingly, this name is used exactly in the same way in the three different occurrences, although it apparently referred to three different locations. It is a way to bring geographical depth to the narratives by stressing that other locations exist beyond the boundaries of the known maps, where a civilisation is advanced enough to produce wines appreciated by the Elves.

Another noun is particularly interesting, since it draws a link between Noldorin Elvish and English names in *The Hobbit*. Tolkien says that the city of Lake-town upon the Long Lake had been known as *Esgaroth* in Smaug's young days (Anderson, 2002, 281), though in the later part of the text the town is indifferently referred to by either name, and a preliminary drawing also uses its Noldorin name (Hammond and Scull, 2011, 96–97). This place-name is also found in two places of the "Etymologies," a major linguistic essay explaining most of the terms found in "The Silmarillion" as it stood in the late 1930s. The first mention translates the name as "Reedlake," a gloss explained by the presence of reed-banks on the western shore (Tolkien, 1992, 356), yet this translation cannot really explain the city-name, unless one supposes it was named after the lake. This is probably why Tolkien elaborated the alternate translation "strand-burg," from an Elvish word *esgar* "shore" (Tolkien, 2004, 14).[9] But after the publication of *The Lord of the Rings*, Tolkien realized his Elvish languages had evolved to such an extent that *Esgaroth* no longer fitted the new conception, and he now contended that the name was "perhaps 'Sindarized' in shape" but not pure Sindarin (Gilson, 2007, 54). One needs also mention the "mines of Moria," another Elvish name first mentioned in a draft of *The Hobbit* (Rateliff, 2011, 73, 80). Again, it was afterwards inserted in the "Etymologies," where it is translated as "Black Gulf," derived from the Noldorin *ia* "gulf" (Tolkien, 1992, 400). It appears there are two early attempts by Tolkien to insert new Elvish names into his existing mythology, distinguishing the locations of both stories, but co-locating them in the same imaginary world. This is all the more interesting because these two names respectively occur near either end of *The Hobbit*: linking both strands of stories had clearly been a constant concern for Tolkien.

Several English names in *The Hobbit* also seem to contain allusions to the stories of "The Silmarillion." The Eagle's Eyrie where Thorin & Co. are brought by the Eagles after being saved from the Goblins can remind the reader of the eyries of Thorndor (later renamed Thorondor), King of Eagles in the Elder Days. Thorndor's most famous eyries were located in the mountains surrounding Gondolin, mentioned in various narratives of "The Silmarillion." Indeed, the unnamed Lord of the Eagles in *The Hobbit* might be seen as Thorndor/Thorondor himself, who receives the title "Lord of Eagles" both in "The Book of Lost Tales" (Tolkien, 1995a, 251) and in the published *Silmarillion* (Tolkien, 2007, 221). In a similar way, the Enchanted River of Mirkwood can be a remainder of the river Esgalduin in Doriath, which is several times nicknamed "the enchanted river" in *The Lord of the Rings* and *The Silmarillion*, although *Esgalduin* means "river under shade" (Gilson, 2007, 15, 184). Here, place-names in *The Hobbit* work as distant echoes of places and events in "The Silmarillion." The Eagle's Eyrie may evoke the Encircling Mountains, but also the battle where the Eagles saved the refugees of Gondolin from the Orcs, much as the Eagles save the lives of Thorin & Co. in *The Hobbit*. The Enchanted River is indeed under the shade of Mirkwood, but also the boundary of the Wood-elves' kingdom. Its sedative power is a reminder of the enchantments of the Girdle of Melian as well as a forerunner of the sleep charm affecting Bilbo Baggins and Thorin when they try to get some food from the Wood-elves.

Two other names, already mentioned, are even more tightly linked to the stories of the Elder Days. The *Withered Heath*, whence came Smaug, is mentioned in "The Book of Lost Tales" as the new name for the Heath of the Sky-roof (*Ladwen-na-Dhaideloth*), a plain located one league from the Elvish town of Tavrobel, after a great battle was fought between Men, causing the Elves to flee (Tolkien, 1995a, 284, 287, 344). As pointed out, the name *Mirkwood* was also used in "The Silmarillion." Interestingly, the forest in *The Hobbit* is also designated as the *greenwood* (without capital) in the farewell speech of the wizard Gandalf to the Elvenking (Anderson, 2002, 352). This word had already been used in "The Book of Lost Tales," apparently with a geographical value and in relation to the Elves (Tolkien, 1995a, 72). In *The Lord of the Rings*, Tolkien built upon this conception and decided that the original name of the forest was Greenwood the Great, a name he later translated in Sindarin as *Eryn Galen* (Tolkien, 1998, 363). *Taur e-Ndaedelos* "forest of the great fear" is another Sindarin name Tolkien invented for the forest in the Appendices to *The Lord of the Rings*, apparently as an equivalent of Common Speech *Mirkwood*. From an external standpoint, this name may have been intended to distinguish the Wilderland forest from the one in Beleriand, which was renamed *Taur-nu-Fuin* "Forest under Night" in the later versions of "The Silmarillion." Finally, Tolkien decided in *The Lord of the Rings* that the Wilderland forest would be given a new name by the Elves after the final defeat of Sauron, becoming *Eryn Lasgalen* "Wood of Greenleaves"—yet another allusion to "The Silmarillion," since *Lasgalen* is given as one of the names of the Golden Tree Laurelin (Tolkien, 1994a, 155; see also Tolkien, 1992, 210, 367 for an earlier version of this name).

Indeed, the ties between the Elvish tales of "The Silmarillion" and the adventure of Bilbo are further reinforced through *The Lord of the Rings*, where Tolkien introduces new Noldorin/Sindarin translations for many place-names of *The Hobbit*. This is particularly true for the mountains: looking at the maps of *The Lord of the Rings*, one can find *Hithaeglir* for the Misty Mountains, *Ered Mithrin* for the Grey Mountains, *Rhovanion* for Wilderland, and *Erebor* for the Lonely Mountain. The Mountains of Mirkwood did not get an Elvish name in *The Lord of the Rings*, but a later manuscript explains that they were initially named *Emyn Duir* "Dark Mountains," and renamed *Emyn-nu-Fuin* when the Forest became known as *Mirkwood* (Tolkien, 1998, 363–364). Another late essay says that *Mount Gundabad* was originally a Khuzdul name, tying its origin to the line of Durin (Tolkien, 1997a, 301). Two rivers also receive a Sindarin translation in *The Lord of the Rings*: *Anduin* for the Great River of Wilderland, and *Celduin* for the Running River. This is neither the case for the Forest River nor the Long Lake. This retrofitting process appears more exceptional for constructions or dwellings: the only attested example in *The Lord of the Rings* is Elrond's house, which receives the Sindarin name of *Imladris*, henceforth supposed to be the original name of the place, *Rivendell* being a translation.[10] A last example can be taken from the drafts of *The*

Lord of the Rings, where the Goblin Gate is twice referred to by a Noldorin name: *Annerchin/Arad Dain* (Tolkien, 1994c, 416, 432), later changed to *Annerchion* (Tolkien, 1993c, 114). Although it is not a geographical name *per se*, one should also mention here the *mithril*, a metal Tolkien invented in the course of writing *The Lord of the Rings* (Tolkien, 1994c, 465), which was inserted back into the story of *The Hobbit* in the 1966 revisions (Anderson, 2002, 295).

As one can see, the geography of *The Hobbit* was always linked to "The Silmarillion," first as being set in a region of Beleriand at a later age, then as a different country, still sufficiently close to the settings of the wars against Morgoth for Elvish blades of Gondolin to be found by Thorin & Co. in a Troll-lair. Numerous allusions reinforced the links between the two stories, which were further strengthened during the redaction of *The Lord of the Rings*, when Tolkien worked out the final version of the shape of the Western Lands of Middle-earth. In fact, very few names from *The Hobbit* were left without an Elvish connection. Of these, the most obvious is the High Pass above Rivendell, which is however named the Pass of Imladris in a late manuscript (Tolkien, 1998, 364). More surprising perhaps is the absence of Elvish names for the Forest Gate, the Forest Elf-path, and the Elvenking's Halls, although it might be due to the fact that these locations play no part in *The Lord of the Rings* and Tolkien did not have the opportunity to review the names. On the other hand, the names of Dale, the Old Ford, the Carrock, and Mount Gram were later seen by Tolkien as an opportunity to elaborate a detailed background history for the Men who lived in Wilderland.[11] The same can be said for the Hobbitish names of Hobbiton-across-the-Water, Bywater, The Water, The Hill, Under-hill, Bag-End, and the Green Dragon Inn. In this case, the expected absence of link between The Shire and the stories of the Elder Days is the starting point of the Prologue of *The Lord of the Rings*, where Tolkien sets out to present the Hobbits at the time when they finally become "both important and renowned" in the eyes of the other peoples.

Of races and creatures

Another important aspect that links *The Hobbit* to "The Silmarillion" is the reuse of the names of Tolkien's imaginary races in the legendarium: Elves, Dwarves, Goblins, Trolls, Giants, dragons, giant spiders and talking eagles. Of course, this alone would not be sufficient to ascertain that *The Hobbit* belongs to the legendarium: both Elves and Goblins are also found in *The Letters from Father Christmas*, which uses the admittedly traditional image of Elves as helping-hands of Father Christmas and strays far from Tolkien's writings on Middle-earth. Dragons also play a significant part in *Roverandom* and *Farmer Giles of Ham*, and a giant is Giles's first adversary in the later tale.[12] Yet, such a choice is significant, especially since most of the races mentioned in *The Hobbit* are explicitly linked to events from the wars against Morgoth. Elrond is said to descend from Elves and Men who illustrated themselves in the wars against the Goblins "before the beginning of History" (Anderson, 2002, 93–94). The Goblins recognize the Elvish swords Glamdring and Orcrist. The Elves of Rivendell come from the High Elves of the West, and are contrasted to the Wood-elves of Mirkwood. The three tribes of the Eldar are even mentioned: Light-elves, Deep-elves and Sea-elves, which correspond at that time to the *Lindar*, the *Noldor* and the *Teleri* of "The Later Annals of Valinor" (Tolkien, 1992, 112) — the *Lindar* would later be renamed *Vanyar*, the name found in the published *Silmarillion*.[13] On the other hand, Raft-elves are never mentioned outside of *The Hobbit*, but they seem to form a craft guild in charge of traffic on the Forest River, rather than an independent tribe. Finally, it seems the Wargs are the only new race introduced in *The Hobbit*, although wolf-riding Orcs are mentioned as early as "The Tale of Tinúviel" (Tolkien, 1995a, 44). It is only in the drafts of *The Lord of the Rings* that the magical nature of Wargs is first introduced, thus linking them to the werewolves of "The Silmarillion" (Tolkien, 1993c, 178).

Only two Elves are named in *The Hobbit*: *Elrond* and the Elvenking's butler, *Galion*. The name of Elrond is of prime interest. This character first appears in the "Sketch of the Mythology," composed in 1926–1930, already as the son of Eärendel and Elwing, and is soon nicknamed "Half-elfin." His decision to stay in Middle-earth after the defeat of Morgoth is immediately introduced. From the start, his role in transmitting a strand of Elvish blood to Men is highlighted (Tolkien, 1993b, 43, 182). Yet the story of his life after the end of the Elder Days remains unclear. In "The Earliest Annals of Beleriand," Tolkien mentions that Elrond "remained and ruled in the West of the world" (Tolkien, 1993b, 371). In the first version of "The Fall of Númenor," he helps the Elf-king Amroth of Beleriand in overcoming the wizard Thû, who was already considered as a necromancer in "The Lay of Leithian" (Tolkien, 1994b, 228) and would ultimately be renamed *Sauron*. But in the second version of the story, Elrond becomes the founding king of Númenor (Tolkien, 1992, 18, 25). It seems this was still his status when *The Hobbit* was written, since Elrond's brother *Elros* is not mentioned in the "Etymologies," whereas *Elrond* is already glossed as "starry-dome" or "vault of heaven" (Tolkien, 1992, 355, 360, 384). The Elrond of *The Hobbit* is immediately presented as a character linked to the heroes of the Elder Days, and Tolkien's drawing of Smaug's death introduces his full lineage: "Elrond Earendel's son Tuor's son of the house of Hador" (Hammond and Scull, 2011, 112–114). Hence, Bilbo's adventures are instrumental in setting up the new dwelling of Elrond in Rivendell and in introducing his role as a Loremaster and an advisor, which is later expanded in *The Lord of the Rings*. This in turn required a revision of the story of the founding of Númenor, and the introduction of Elros as a twin brother of Elrond (Tolkien, 1993b, 186).

The name *Galion*, though obviously supposed to be Elvish, makes its first appearance in *The Hobbit*. It was probably conceived as a Noldorin name, perhaps from *galw* "prosperous, rich, blessed" and *-ion* "son" (Tolkien, 1992, 357, 400). This name is later reused in "The Grey Annals," where it becomes the name of Húrin's father, in replacement of *Gumlin*, but is later superseded by *Galdor*, the name used in *The Silmarillion* published (Tolkien, 1995c, 123). After Tolkien published *The Lord of the Rings*, he tried to explain some of the Elvish names from *The Hobbit*, but in this case had to conclude that *Galion*, much as *Esgaroth*, might have a Sindarized phonology, but was not a Sindarin name (Gilson, 2007, 54). Though remaining unnamed in *The Hobbit*, the Elvenking also played a large part in shaping Tolkien's conception of Wood-elves, which was later developed in *The Lord of the Rings* and in the manuscripts published in *Unfinished Tales*. In these later tales, Tolkien introduced his real name, *Thranduil*, as well as his lineage.

Two additional Elvish-sounding names appear in *The Hobbit*, although they were ultimately attributed to Men: *Girion* and *Bladorthin*.[14] Both are only mentioned in *The Hobbit* and related writings. *Girion* does not seem to have any bearing on the wider legendarium, except in the abandoned story of the Gem of Girion, which ultimately became the Arkenstone, and was at some point conceived as a Silmaril found again (Rateliff, 2011, 603–609). Yet there is little doubt that Girion's name was originally conceived as Elvish. It should probably be linked to Gnomish *gîr* "yesterday" and *-ion*, a plural genitive, an appropriate name for a king whose days are long past at the time of Bilbo's story (Gilson *et al.*, 1995, 10, 38). *Bladorthin* however is far more interesting, even if the story of the "great King Bladorthin" does not seem to have been developed by Tolkien. Indeed, this name was originally given to the Wizard (later renamed Gandalf) in the drafts of Bilbo's story, and remained so for a long time. Rateliff signals that this name could be interpreted as "grey wanderer," which would make it a forerunner of *Mithrandir*, Gandalf's Elvish name in *The Lord of the Rings* (Rateliff, 2011, 48–53). Even more significantly, the Wizard is still named thus when he introduces himself to Medwed (the original name of Beorn) by referring to his "good cousin Radagast." Interestingly enough, Medwed's original reply does not suggest that Tolkien already considered Radagast as a Wizard at that stage (Rateliff, 2011, 233, 248). Thus "cousin" was probably intended in its primary meaning. Even if this suggestion that Bladorthin/Gandalf had a real physical family disappeared before *The Hobbit* was published, it had far-reaching implications, as *Radagast* cannot easily be analyzed as an Elvish name. Indeed, as Rateliff points out, Tolkien changed his mind several times about this name after the publication of *The Lord of the Rings* (Rateliff, 2011, 268–280). The presence of this name was probably instrumental in making Tolkien change the Wizard's name to the non–Elvish *Gandalf*. Later on, the revision of Radagast's status making him another Wizard introduced still more changes, as it was the first hint of an order of Wizards, later developed as the *Istari*, the Valar's messengers in Middle-earth, in charge of marshalling the Free People against Sauron's return.

Back in the first drafts of *The Hobbit*, *Gandalf* had been the name of the chief Dwarf of the expedition, later named *Thorin*. Both names have long been analyzed as Norse Dwarf-names from the *Völuspá*, as is the case with most of the other Dwarf-names mentioned in *The Hobbit*, except for *Balin*, whose origins are uncertain (Allan, 1978, 220–226).[15] This was a double departure from Tolkien's previous writings about the Dwarves, who had previously been given Gnomish names (Bador, 2014, 88–89) and described as unfaithful creatures, often allied with the Goblins.[16] This change, however, was a deliberate reframing of the existing story, rather than a separate strand of imagination, as Tolkien's picture "Conversation with Smaug" testifies. This drawing features a pot of gold with the initials of *Thror* and *Thrain* written in Anglo-Saxon runes beneath a text written in *tengwar*, one of Tolkien's invented alphabets, whose invention in the frame of the legendarium was later attributed to the Elf Fëanor (Hammond and Scull, 2011, 104–105).[17] In the first edition of *The Hobbit*, the Dwarf *Durin*, already described as the first ancestor of Thorin, was "the father of the fathers of one of the two races of dwarves, the Longbeards" (Anderson, 2002, 98). As a consequence, Thorin was linked to the Dwarves of Belegost, called *Indrafangs* "long beards" in "The Book of Lost Tales" (Tolkien, 1995a, 230, 234–235; cf. Gilson *et al.*, 1995, 34, 51). Since the narrator of *The Hobbit* later mentioned that Thorin's kin "had nothing to do with the old quarrel" between Dwarves and Elves (Anderson, 2002, 220), this marked the first departure from Tolkien's original story, where both the Dwarf-cities of Nogrod and Belegost were involved in the sack of Doriath, although the original offence had been done solely against the Dwarves of Nogrod. Tolkien later definitively adopted the idea that the Dwarves of Belegost did not participate in the sack of Doriath, though the Dwarves' origin had been altered in the meantime to include seven kindreds, of which Durin's line was the eldest and originated in the Misty Mountains rather than in the Blue Mountains (Anderson, 2002, 98).[18] The confrontation of Thorin and the Elvenking in *The Hobbit* is also the first place where the narrator includes an allusion to the Dwarves' remembrance of the incident that led to the sack of Doriath, insisting on the fact that they told a different story than the Elves. While made in passing, this remark also had far-reaching consequences: it was the first allusion to Dwarvish chronicles, thus being the nucleus of the idea of the Book of Mazarbul in *The Lord of the Rings*. In addition, it was one of the first points where Tolkien suggested that the stories of the Elder Days might be recounted by people who were not students of the Elves. As we will see, this new conception later completely changed the frame Tolkien envisioned for the stories in his legendarium.

The Dwarves are not the only peoples to receive Norse names in *The Hobbit*. This is also the case for *Bard the Bowman*, whose name means "beard," for *Smaug*, which—despite the pun with "smog"—is a declination of the verb *smjúga* "to creep through an opening" (Zoëga, 1967, 42, 391), an apt name for the creature, and possibly for *Golfimbul*, whose name is discussed below. Old English also contributed the name of *Beorn* "man, chief, warrior" (Bosworth, 1898, 86). Taking names from various Germanic languages seems to run counter to the tales of the Elder Days, with their well-ordered nomenclature based on Tolkien's invented languages. Yet these names are already one step toward a standardized nomenclature. The drafts of *The Hobbit* show that the original name of Smaug was *Pryftan*, a clearly Welsh name (Stocker, 2009), while Beorn was initially named *Medwed*, from Slavic *medved* "honey-eater" (Miklošič, 1865, 365). It seems Tolkien felt at first freer to use whatever name seemed phonetically fit in Bilbo's adventure. But he probably realised that taking seemingly random excerpts of foreign languages reduced the coherence of the story and proceeded to bring most non–Elvish names into a tightly-related set of Germanic languages, a solution that would also heighten parallels with the Northern medieval tales he loved so much. After the publication of *The Hobbit*, seeing that he now had a better chance of publishing stories linked to his "Silmarillion," Tolkien would become dissatisfied with "this rabble of Eddaic-named dwarves" (Tolkien, 1994c, 7) out of tone with the rest of his legendarium. It forced him to invent the whole concept of translation from the Common Speech into English and from languages related to the Common Speech to other Germanic languages outlined in Appendix F of *The Lord of the Rings*, a concept he came to exploit to great effect with the Hobbits, the Rohirrim and their ancestors the Northmen.

A few names escaped such a dramatic reconsideration. Some had good reasons to be left alone, for instance the onomatopoeic bird-names *Carc* and *Roäc*. *Gollum* was in the same case, but when Tolkien investigated the origin of the creature, a question that had a great importance for the story of the One Ring, he finally decided that his original Hobbit-name was *Sméagol*. The first Goblin mentioned in Bilbo's adventure is the Goblin-chief killed by Bullroarer Took, first named *Fingolfin* in the drafts of *The Hobbit*. It is in fact the first name of the legendarium borrowed by Tolkien for his Hobbit-story, and as Rateliff pointed out, it was clearly imported without concern for the original use of the name, and only for the applicability of the joke about the invention of golf (Rateliff, 2011, 8, 15).[19] Yet Tolkien soon ordered his new tale to fit with his existing stories of the Elder Days. This was particularly critical in this case, because the Noldo king Fingolfin was a distant relative of Elrond, and it would have been quite unlikely for the servants of Morgoth to take the name of one of their bitterest enemies. The new Goblin-name he invented as a replacement, *Golfimbul*, does not seem to be mentioned outside of *The Hobbit*. It might have been designed as a Norse name, from *gól* "howl, scream" and *fimbul* "mighty, monstrous" (Zoëga, 1967, 136, 175). The *fimbul* element is attested in the Eddaic poem *Vafþrúðnismál*, where *Fimbulvetr* is the terrible winter that will announce the Ragnarök: it is then quite appropriate for the only Goblin who invaded The Shire; however, this name did not properly fit with Tolkien's translation theory developed in *The Lord of the Ring*, and it is probably significant it was not mentioned in the later story. In fact, the author knows from Tolkien's manuscripts that he envisioned altering this name to *Gulfimbul* in a revision of *The Hobbit* never carried out (Rateliff, 2011, 776). The second Goblin, *Bolg*, is first mentioned by the Wizard just before the battle of Five Armies begins. This name means "strong" in Mago or Magol, a language Tolkien invented. Magol was at some point envisioned to be the Orkish language, but Tolkien apparently rejected the idea when he invented instead the Black Speech in the course of writing *The Lord of the Rings* (Rateliff, 2011, 670, 710). *Bolg* was however not changed: Tolkien might have reconsidered it as part of one of the many Orkish dialects he alluded to. On the other hand, the Goblin who killed Thror is not named in the first edition of *The Hobbit*. The name *Azog* only entered the legendarium in the drafts of *The Lord of the Rings* Appendices (Tolkien, 1997a, 284) and was later incorporated to revisions of Bilbo's adventure. Though it is clearly conceived to fit with the phonology of *Bolg*, there is no indication regarding the origin of the name.

The three Trolls' names, Tom, Bert, and Bill (William) Huggins probably remain one of the most obvious anomalies in the nomenclature of *The Hobbit*, even if Tolkien later tried to correct it: Appendix F of *The Lord of the Rings* mentions that the Stone-trolls of the Westlands only spoke a "debased form of the Common Speech," explaining how they could have names so similar to the Hobbits. Yet the naming of the Trolls remains significant, as they are the first enemy creatures whose daily behavior is described by Tolkien. Indeed, apart from a few famous Orc-chieftains, Balrogs, or extraordinary monsters like the wolf Carcharoth, they seem to be the first creatures of Morgoth to receive a name in Tolkien's stories. Through their arguing and display of free will (however debased), they seem in fact to be the forerunners of the Orcs of Minas Morgul and Cirith Ungol who are later spied upon by Sam and Frodo. The Trolls' bickering is quite similar to the intestine quarrels of the Orcs of *The Lord of the Rings*, which helps humanize them, while showing the internally destructive effects of Evil.

The "newfangled hobbits" Tolkien invented had of course no antecedent in his legendarium and did not fit with his existing "consistent nomenclature," as he deplored in a letter from December 1937 (Tolkien, 1994c, 7). Yet Tolkien would soon come to reverse his negative judgement on Hobbits, as proved by the amount of writing he devoted to their daily lives and habits. There are comparatively few Hobbit-names mentioned in Bilbo's adventures, compared to what appears in *The Lord of the Rings*. Apart from Bilbo Baggins himself, a few of his relatives are named: Bullroarer Took, the Old Took, and the Sackville-Bagginses. In addition, the lawyers "Grubb, Grubb, and Burrowes" are mentioned in the last chapter of the book. In all cases, these Hobbits are only known by their family name: the first names of Bilbo's relatives, Bandobras, Gerontius, Otho and Lobelia, only appear in *The Lord of the Rings*. Yet this was already the seed of numerous Hobbit family trees, replete with cousins more or less distantly related to Bilbo, a large number of which made an onstage appearance in his farewell party. Unlike what Tolkien did for later additions to his legendarium, such as the Rohirrim or the Púkel-men, he resisted the temptation of providing a detailed account of the ancestors of the Hobbits. Tolkien does not extend their history much beyond their settlement in Bree and in The Shire. From an internal perspective, the first allusion to Hobbits is dated from T.A. 1015, a comparatively late date in the legendarium. This discretion is necessary to explain why Hobbits had been overlooked by other races and were not mentioned in "The Silmarillion."

Of translation

Not only did the Hobbits direct the legendarium toward a new conclusion, but they even played a major role in reshaping Tolkien's stories of the Elder Days. Before introducing Hobbits to his invented Middle-earth, Tolkien had struggled to explain how the tales he wrote could conceivably be handed down to his modern readers. He firmly believed such a story-frame was required to ensure secondary belief in the stories, and explored various solutions in this respect: an old book surviving from the time of the Elves, a navigator arriving to Tol Eressëa and bringing back the history of the Elder Days, dreams recalling an ancestral memory, etc. Most of these solutions made use of a character named "Elf-friend," serving as intermediary between the Elves and the reader. In many successive versions of the story, this role was taken by the medieval mariner Eriol, or Ælfwine, who reached the island of the Elves and either participated in their struggles or learned from their Loremasters the stories of their past feats.[20] At first, *The Hobbit* did not provide for such an elaborate story-frame, as the reader is immediately drawn into Bilbo's adventures, presented by an omniscient and self-conscious narrator. Only at the end, with the evocation of Bilbo's memoirs, the attentive reader can guess that he is somehow reading them. In this respect, *The Hobbit* was indeed distinct from Tolkien's previous Elvish stories. In the course of writing *The Lord of the Rings*, Tolkien reconsidered the issue and proceeded to compose the Foreword, Prologue and various Appendices framing the main story. This was not a straightforward process, and in 1944 Tolkien also attempted to write an entirely new version of the Ælfwine story, "The Notion Club Papers," where Ælfwine's adventure was itself framed into a fantastic tale involving a number of Oxford dons.[21] But Tolkien finally abandoned this new tale and proceeded to complete *The Lord of the Rings*.

In 1951, a few years before the publication of *The Lord of the Rings*, the second edition of *The Hobbit* included a first note on the text explaining why the encounter between Bilbo and Gollum had been rewritten. This note was the first published allusion to the Red Book of Westmarch, which was already conceived, but not yet disclosed, as encompassing Bilbo's diary (Anderson, 2002, 28). Indeed, Tolkien certainly noticed that introducing Hobbits in his legendarium had generated a number of issues, which could not be solved by the existing Ælfwine story-frame. First, Hobbits were not supposed to reach the Elvish island of Tol Eressëa, and as a consequence their own stories could hardly be taught by the Elves to Ælfwine. More importantly perhaps, the whole onomastic matter of *The Hobbit* had now to be explained: since Tolkien's stories were now supposed to take place in immensely remote times, probably before the Ice Age (Tolkien, 1992, 76), his characters could not bear Germanic names, even less modern English ones. The story itself, if it was supposed to have been handled down since that time, could not have been written in English. Hence, Tolkien's published story had to be a translation. This allowed the names featured in the story to be considered as translations as well. From this kernel, the central idea of the translation theory proposed in Appendix F of *The Lord of the Rings* was developed. Most peoples of North-Western Middle-earth were said to speak Westron, the Common Speech of the newly invented Third Age, in which the entire story of *The Hobbit* and *The Lord of the Rings* was now supposed to have been written. Tolkien then explained that he had translated the story into English and did the same for all understandable Westron names. Since several peoples, such as the Rohirrim or the Lake-men spoke different, but related languages, these had to be translated as well into tongues related to English, such as Old English and Norse. The origin of the Westron language family had then to be explained: hence the invention of Adûnaic, the language of Númenor, which found its origin in the speech of some of the Edain of the Elder Days. This in turn modified the Mannish aspect of the linguistic story in "The Silmarillion," since now most Edain were supposed to have kept their ancestral language, whereas in pre–*Lord of the Rings* versions they had abandoned it for the Elvish languages (Tolkien, 1992, 179, 191, 194).

Having now a credible way to present the linguistic matter of the Hobbits, Tolkien had solved at the same time the whole issue of transmitting the stories to the readers. Since the language in which the story was set corresponded to the Common Speech, it could not have been directly composed or taught by the Elves. Here, Tolkien's mention of Bilbo's diary at the end of *The Hobbit* provided him with a direct and obvious solution: the story of Thorin & Co. and of the destruction of the Ring had been set down by Hobbits. This explained in a satisfactory manner why both tales were written from the Hobbits' point of view. In addition, Tolkien's decision to have Bilbo retire in Rivendell after his farewell party created an opportunity for him to learn the antique lore of the Elves and join it to the relation of his travels. Hence the very late addition of the passage mentioning Bilbo's *Translations from the Elvish* at the end of the new story (Tolkien, 1993a, 72), which finally created a link back to the narratives of the Elder Days. By generating a nomenclature at odds with his existing stories of "The Silmarillion," the introduction of Bilbo Baggins ultimately reduced the role of Eriol-Ælfwine as primary mediator with the Elvish peoples to a mere shadow. Thus Bilbo's diary ensured that the Hobbits and the house of Elrond became the essential link to the Elder Days, together with the archives of Minas Tirith.[22] This in turn helped Tolkien to provide a credible explanation of his supposed role as translator and adaptor of a fictive history of times long past. And so was created the framework he thought to be essential in ensuring the reader's secondary belief in his subcreated world.

Conclusion

Can the nomenclature of *The Hobbit* then help in determining the links between this story and "The Silmarillion?" It is quite obvious both stories were from the beginning supposed to take place in the same imaginary world; however, the relation between the two works evolved in the course of the writing of *The Hobbit*, as testified by its geographical changes. Initially conceived as a story located in Beleriand after the fall of Morgoth, Bilbo's adventures then took the more important role of expanding both the existing timeframe and geography of Tolkien's legendarium. By strictly limiting the reuse of existing *dramatis personae* from "The Silmarillion" to the minor character of Elrond, Tolkien both gained more freedom for his children-story and created opportunities for further enrichment of his imaginary world. This freedom allowed Tolkien to try many new conceptions that did not fit with his existing and highly coherent tales of "The Silmarillion," such as good Dwarves, mysterious Wizards, or Germanic nomenclature. Far from creating a self-contained story, as Tolkien claimed (Tolkien, 1999, 24), *The Hobbit* proved to be a door to the wider story of the War of the Ring, further enriching the legendarium and strengthening links between the Elder Days and what became known as the Third Age.

Indeed, some of the freedom taken in the writing of *The Hobbit* proved quite complex to explain when Tolkien had the opportunity to shed further light on his "Silmarillion" tales in the Appendices of *The Lord of the Rings*. This can explain the numerous occurrences where Tolkien expressed his growing distaste for the inconsistencies of Bilbo's adventures with the older parts of his legendarium. Yet *The Hobbit* was instrumental in reshaping Tolkien's older conceptions, introducing new Elvish and Mannish peoples, and changing the existing story of the founding of Númenor (as well as the language supposed to be spoken there). Finally, the greatest change of all was introduced in passing, right at the end the new story. With the mention of Bilbo's memoirs was introduced the first seed of the Red Book of Westmarch, which later became the principal mean through which the stories of the Elder Days could reach modern readers in a believable way. As Gandalf concluded at the end of

The Hobbit, Bilbo's adventures clearly did not occur for his sole benefit, but for the greater good of a much wider world.

Notes

1. As customary, I will designate the body of texts constituting the legends of the Elder Days of Middle-earth as "The Silmarillion" and the book posthumously published by Christopher Tolkien as *The Silmarillion*.
2. See Rateliff, 2012, for a detailed analysis of Tolkien discourse on links between *The Hobbit* and "The Silmarillion."
3. This is particularly true for "The Silmarillion," of course, but also applies to *The Hobbit*, revised in 1947 and in 1965–1966, and to *The Lord of the Rings*, also revised in 1966.
4. A different attempt to bridge the gap between the Elder Days and the modern area is presented by Christopher Tolkien in *The Lost Road*. Most of the material first developed there by Tolkien was ultimately integrated in the history of Númenor as presented in *Unfinished Tales* and *The Silmarillion*.
5. An in-depth analysis of the importance of philology in Tolkien's fiction can be found in Shippey, 2003. Gilliver *et al.*, 2006, also provide interesting insights on Tolkien's philological interplay between academic study and fiction.
6. It would pass the scope of this essay to trace all occurrences of the name *Mirkwood* in Tolkien's works. As Tolkien pointed out, this name is deeply connected with a number of Germanic legends, and he apparently found it very appealing indeed, since he reused it both in *The Legend of Sigurd and Gudrún* and in *The Fall of Arthur*, in addition to its dual use in Middle-earth.
7. Interestingly enough, these two swords were not named in the first version of the story and only entered the narrative in a much later revision (Rateliff, 2011, 122). They remain a puzzling point in "The Silmarillion" tradition, as Tolkien never named the sword of Turgon in his stories of the Elder Days, nor mentioned the initial owner of Orcrist. Still, naming their origin in *The Hobbit* and having them recognized (and dreaded) by the Goblins reinforce the ties with the famous swords mentioned in "The Silmarillion," such as *Gurtholfin* "Wand of Death" (renamed *Gurthang* in the later versions of Túrin's story) or *Ringil* "Cold Star," the sword of Fingolfin. Thus Tolkien evokes a heroic past in keeping with the tone of the wars against Morgoth. He later reused the motive of ancient swords in *The Lord of the Rings* to heighten the prestige of Aragorn and place the Hobbits in the footsteps of Bilbo. See Whetter and McDonald, 2006, for a fuller analysis of sword-lore in Tolkien.
8. But see the analysis in Rateliff, 2011, 417–420. In addition to the rejected Gnomish term *gwinwen* "youth, freshness" Rateliff mentions, which is clearly akin to a rejected Noldorin word *Gwin* related to the root GWIN—"new, fresh" (Hostetter and Wynne, 2003, 16), one can also suggest some other possibly related words, such as *gwindod* "elder tree, elderberry" (Gilson *et al.*, 1995a, 45), *Gwinnian*, a rejected name for "Elfinesse" (Gilson *et al.*, 2005, 155), and the Noldorin adjective *gwind* "pale blue" (Tolkien, 1992, 399).
9. This last gloss is overlooked by Rateliff in his analysis of the name (Rateliff, 2011, 561–562).
10. Tolkien also gave the name *Mar Vanwa Tyaliéva* "House of Past (*or* Departed) Mirth" to Rivendell, reusing one of his oldest concepts from "The Book of Lost Tales" (Smith, 2012, 80; cf. Tolkien, 1991, 14, 21, 260). On the other hand, the name of *Last Homely House* does not seem to have been translated by Tolkien. In the post–*Lord of the Rings* context, it would appear as a purely Mannish name, probably given to Elrond's house by the Dúnedain of the North.
11. For an analysis of the bearing of the name *Carrock* on the writing of *The Lord of the Rings*, see Bador, in press. If Mount Gram is only mentioned *The Hobbit*, it is also the name of the eighth king of the Rohirrim, thus making it likely that is was located in the vicinity of the lands of the Éothéod in the North.
12. While giants do not appear in *The Lord of the Rings* and seem to disappear from the later versions of the legendarium, they were mentioned in "The Book of Lost Tales," where the "neck of Gilim the giant" was among the "tallest and longest things upon Earth" (Tolkien, 1995a, 19, 46). Other giants are alluded to in "The Lay of Leithian" (Tolkien, 1994b, 205, 227). A list of "Earthlings," among which are listed giants, dwarves and pygmies, also appears in a text titled "The Creatures of the Earth" (Wynne and Gilson, 2010, 9). See Mallet, 2001, and Stenström, 1993, for a fuller account of giants in Tolkien's legendarium.
13. Providing the names of the Elvish tribes in English could also be considered as an allusion to the various kinds of *Alfar* of Norse mythology. See Shippey, 2004, for an analysis of the relations between the Elves in the *Edda* and in Tolkien's legendarium.
14. It should also be noted that the Goblin chief *Golfimbul* was initially named *Fingolfin* in the first surviving manuscript of *The Hobbit*, reusing a name already given to a most famous of king of the Noldor. This name is discussed together with the other Goblin-names.

15. Some Dwarf-names mentioned only in the drafts of *The Hobbit* or in superseded versions of the story, such as *Fimbulfambi* or *Thrym Thistlebeard* also relate to Scandinavian mythology, though they might be taken from other texts than the *Völuspá*. See Bador, 2014, for a complete analysis of Dwarf-names attested in Tolkien's fiction.

16. See Rateliff, 2011, 76–80, for a summary.

17. A number of Tolkien's pictures related to stories outside of the legendarium, such as "Lunar Landscape," describing a scene from *Roverandom* (Hammond and Scull, 2000, 78), have titles written in one of Tolkien's invented alphabets; however, the only example of Elvish writing set *inside* a story not belonging to the legendarium is in the *Letters from Father Christmas*. One of the Christmas messages from the Elf Ilbereth to Christopher and Priscilla features an English sentence written in an early version of *tengwar* (Tolkien, 1999, 120). It may be considered significant that Tolkien never intended to publish these letters, unlike other children-stories such as *Roverandom* or *Mr. Bliss*, which he sent for consideration to Allen & Unwin.

18. The original dwelling of the Longbeards apparently caused troubles to Tolkien, who had to correct both *The Hobbit* and *The Lord of the Rings* in the course of the 1966 revisions to reach a satisfying solution. See Christopher Tolkien's comments in Tolkien, 1995c, 207–208.

19. In the same way, Mount Gundabad was at first named *Gondobad*, a name clearly demarked from Gondolin. It was later changed to *Gundobad* before reaching the orthography adopted in the published story (Rateliff, 2011, 670, 675, Plate I).

20. Flieger, 2000, provides an in-depth analysis of the Elf-friend figure in Tolkien's legendarium.

21. See Flieger, 2004, for a detailed account of the various avatars of Ælfwine in "The Notion Club Papers."

22. See Bador, 2012, for a fuller analysis of this evolution.

Works Cited

Allan, Jim, ed. 1978. *An Introduction to Elvish and to Other Tongues and Proper Names and Writing Systems of the Third Age of the Western Lands of Middle-earth as Set Forth in the Published Writings of Professor John Ronald Reuel Tolkien*. Hayes: Bran's Head.

Anderson, Douglas A., ed. 2002. *The Annotated Hobbit*. Rev. ed. Boston: Houghton Mifflin.

Bador, Damien. 2012. "Transmettre la tradition : Númenor ou la route retrouvée » [Transmitting the tradition: Númenor or the regained road]. *L'Arc et le Heaume* 3: 76–92.

_____. 2014. "Un peuple secret : les noms des Nains dans l'œuvre de J.R.R. Tolkien" [A secret people: Dwarf-names in the works of J.R.R. Tolkien]. *L'Arc et le Heaume* 4: 82–109.

_____. In press. "Des deux Carroc à la Pierre d'Erech" [From the two Carrocks to the Stone of Erech]. *Tolkien, le façonnement d'un monde, vol. 2: Astronomie & Géographie*. Didier Willis, ed. Toulouse: Le Dragon de Brume.

Bosworth, Joseph. 1898. *An Anglo-Saxon Dictionary*. 2d ed. T. Northcote Toller, ed. Oxford: Clarendon Press.

Carpenter, Humphrey. 2000 [1977]. *J.R.R. Tolkien: A Biography*. Boston: Houghton Mifflin.

Flieger, Verlyn. 2000. "The Footsteps of Ælfwine." In *Tolkien's Legendarium: Essays on The History of Middle-earth*. Verlyn Flieger and Carl F. Hostetter, eds. Pp. 183–198. Westport, CT: Greenwood.

_____. 2002. *Splintered Light: Logos and Language in Tolkien's World*. 2d ed. Kent, OH: Kent State University Press.

_____. 2004. "Do the Atlantis Story and Abandon Eriol-Saga." *Tolkien Studies* 1: 43–68.

Gilliver, Peter, with Jeremy Marshall and Edmund Weiner. 2006. *The Ring of Words: Tolkien and the Oxford English Dictionary*. Oxford: Oxford University Press.

Gilson, Christopher, ed. 2007. "Words, Phrases and Passages in various tongues in *The Lord of the Rings*." *Parma Eldalamberon* 17: 11–191.

_____, with Bill Welden, Carl F. Hostetter, and Patrick H. Wynne, eds. 2005[2001]. "Early Noldorin Fragments." *Parma Eldalamberon* 13: 91–165.

_____, and Patrick H. Wynne, eds. 2004. "Name-list to *The Fall of Gondolin*." *Parma Eldalamberon* 15: 19–29.

_____, with Patrick H. Wynne, Arden R. Smith, and Carl F. Hostetter, eds. 1995. "i·Lam na·Ngoldathon." *Parma Eldalamberon* 11: 7–75.

Hammond, Wayne G., and Christina Scull, eds. 2000 [1995]. *J.R.R. Tolkien: Artist & Illustrator*. Boston: Houghton Mifflin.

_____, eds. 2004. "Addenda and Corrigenda to the *Etymologies*—Part Two." *Vinyar Tengwar* 46: 3–34.

_____, eds. 2011. *The Art of The Hobbit by J.R.R. Tolkien*. Hammersmith, London: HarperCollins.

Hostetter Carl F., and Patrick H. Wynne, eds. 2003 "Addenda and Corrigenda to the *Etymologies*—Part One." *Vinyar Tengwar* 45: 3–38.

Mallet, Sébastien. 2001. "La disparition des Géants" [The Giants' disappearance]. *La Feuille de la Compagnie: Cahiers d'études tolkieniennes*, vol. 1. Michael Devaux, ed. Pp. 65–88. Paris: L'Œil du Sphinx.
Miklošič, Franz von. 1865. *Lexicon palaeoslovenico-graeco-latinum*. Vienna: Wilhelm Braumüller.
Rateliff, John D., ed. 2011. *The History of* The Hobbit. 2d ed. Hammersmith, London: HarperCollins.
———. 2012. "Un Fragment, détaché : Bilbo le Hobbit et le Silmarillion" [A Fragment, Detached: The Hobbit and The Silmarillion]. Vivien Stocker, trans. *L'Arc et le Heaume* HS1: 45–57.
Scull, Christina, and Wayne G. Hammond. 2006. *The J.R.R. Tolkien Companion and Guide: Chronology*. Boston: Houghton Mifflin.
Shippey, Tom. 2003. *The Road to Middle-earth: How J.R.R. Tolkien Created a New Mythology*. 3d ed. Boston: Houghton Mifflin.
———. 2004. "Light-elves, Dark-elves and Others: Tolkien's Elvish Problem." *Tolkien Studies* 1: 1–15.
Smith, Arden R., ed. 2012. "The Qenya Alphabet." *Parma Eldalamberon* 20: 17–159.
Stenström, Anders. 1993. "Some Notes on Giants in Tolkien's Writings." In *Scholarship & Fantasy: Proceedings of the Tolkien Phenomenon*. Katja J. Battarbee, ed. Anglicana Turkuensia, 12. Pp. 53–71. Turku: University of Turku.
Stocker, Vivien. 2009. "Les Fragments de Pryftan" [The Pryftan Fragments]. Tolkiendil. http://www.tolkiendil.com/langues/textes/fragments_pryftan, accessed December 4, 2013.
Tolkien, J.R.R. 1991 [1983]. *The History of Middle-earth*, vol. 1: *The Book of Lost Tales, Part I*. Christopher Tolkien, ed. Hammersmith, London: HarperCollins.
———. 1992 [1987]. *The History of Middle-earth*, vol. 5: *The Lost Road and Other Writings*. Christopher Tolkien, ed. Hammersmith, London: HarperCollins.
———. 1993a [1992]. *The History of Middle-earth*, vol. 9: *Sauron Defeated*. Christopher Tolkien, ed. Hammersmith, London: HarperCollins.
———. 1993b [1986]. *The History of Middle-earth*, vol. 4: *The Shaping of Middle-earth*. Christopher Tolkien, ed. Hammersmith, London: HarperCollins.
———. 1993c [1989]. *The History of Middle-earth*, vol. 7: *The Treason of Isengard*. Christopher Tolkien, ed. Hammersmith, London: HarperCollins.
———. 1994a [1993]. *The History of Middle-earth*, vol. 10: *Morgoth's Ring*. Christopher Tolkien, ed. Hammersmith, London: HarperCollins.
———. 1994b [1985]. *The History of Middle-earth*, vol. 3: *The Lays of Beleriand*. Christopher Tolkien, ed. Hammersmith, London: HarperCollins.
———. 1994c [1988]. *The History of Middle-earth*, vol. 6: *The Return of the Shadow*. Christopher Tolkien, ed. Hammersmith, London: HarperCollins.
———. 1995a [1984]. *The History of Middle-earth*, vol. 2: *The Book of Lost Tales, Part II*. Christopher Tolkien, ed. Hammersmith, London: HarperCollins.
———. 1995b [1981]. *The Letters of J.R.R. Tolkien*. Humphrey Carpenter, with the assistance of Christopher Tolkien, eds. Hammersmith, London: HarperCollins.
———. 1995c [1994]. *The History of Middle-earth*, vol. 11: *The War of the Jewels*. Christopher Tolkien, ed. Hammersmith, London: HarperCollins.
———. 1997a [1996]. *The History of Middle-earth*, vol. 12: *The Peoples of Middle-earth*. Christopher Tolkien, ed. Hammersmith, London: HarperCollins.
———. 1997b [1983]. *The Monsters and the Critics and Other Essays*. Christopher Tolkien, ed. Hammersmith, London: HarperCollins.
———. 1998 [1980]. *Unfinished Tales of Númenor and Middle-earth*. Christopher Tolkien, ed. Hammersmith, London: HarperCollins.
———. 1999. *Letters from Father Christmas*. 2d ed. Baillie Tolkien, ed. Hammersmith, London: HarperCollins.
———. 2004. *The Lord of the Rings*. 50th Anniversary Edition. Hammersmith, London: HarperCollins.
———. 2007 [1999]. *The Silmarillion*. 2nd ed. Christopher Tolkien, ed. Hammersmith, London: HarperCollins.
Whetter, K. S., and R. Andrew McDonald. 2006. "'In the Hilt Is Fame': Resonances of Medieval Swords and Sword-lore in J.R.R. Tolkien's *The Hobbit* and *The Lord of the Rings*." *Mythlore* 25(1/2): 5–28.
Wynne, Patrick H., and Christopher Gilson. 2010 [2003]. "Early Qenya Fragments." *Parma Eldalamberon* 14: 3–34.
Zoëga, Geir T. 1967 [1910]. *A Concise Dictionary of Old Icelandic*. Oxford: Oxford University Press.

Civilized Goblins and Talking Animals
How *The Hobbit* Created Problems of Sentience for Tolkien

Gregory Hartley

> What of talking beasts and birds with reasoning and speech? These have been rather lightly adopted from less "serious" mythologies, but play a part which cannot now be excised.
>
> —*Morgoth's Ring* 409

Introduction

In *The Hobbit*, trolls, orcs, and even the dragon operate simply within the fairy tale register. The trolls behave like the trolls of Scandinavian literature; the goblins are remarkably similar to George MacDonald's goblins, and Smaug is much like Fáfnir—archetypal, stereotypical—all basking in unexamined sentience. As *The Lord of the Rings* and *The Silmarillion* took shape, however, Tolkien took on the difficult task of melding a fairy tale with epic, which was in turn bonded with a Christian myth. Characters and creatures began functioning on a multiplicity of registers. The fairy tale hobbit became an epic hero as well as a Christian pilgrim. Many of these elements carried the extra weight quite well—Gandalf, the Ring, and Gollum were easily augmented—but despite his master storytelling ability and years of rewriting, Tolkien never could quite fit all of his creatures within the new paradigm without creating inconsistencies.

Metaphysically speaking, J.R.R. Tolkien caused trouble for himself when he published *The Hobbit*. By creating a fairy-tale version of Middle-earth, he effectively side-tracked important mythological elements that he was developing simultaneously; however, once he returned to more serious mythological tropes, the light-hearted informality of *The Hobbit* frequently came back to haunt him as he struggled to synchronize a previously published fairy tale with the much more intricately structured epic of *The Lord of the Rings*. Christopher Tolkien provides both a rationale and synopsis of this tension in his introduction to the "Myths Transformed" section of *Morgoth's Ring*:

> In these writings can be read the record of a prolonged interior debate. Years before this time, the first signs have been seen of emerging ideas that if pursued would cause massive disturbances in *The Silmarillion*.... [My father] had come to believe that such a vast upheaval was a necessity, that the cosmos of the old myth was no longer valid; and at the same time he was impelled to try to

construct a more secure "theoretical" or "systematic" basis for elements for the Legendarium that were not to be dislodged. With their questionings, their certainties giving way to doubt, their contradictory resolutions, these writings are to be read with a sense of intellectual and imaginative stress in the face of such a dismantling and reconstitution, believed to be an inescapable necessity, but never to be achieved [Tolkien, 1993, 369].

As Tolkien himself admitted, the more complex his legendarium became, the more aware he was of its theological foundations (Tolkien, 2000, 172). In *The Hobbit*, then, Tolkien made decisions that were not consciously concerned with theological matters, whereas the late drafts of *The Silmarillion* reveal an author very much focused on establishing a kind of orthodoxy. This chapter will argue that the publication of *The Hobbit*, prior to the publication of any other works in the legendarium, created a series of continuity challenges for Tolkien regarding the spiritual state of his non-human characters. The Cockney trolls, boulder-tossing giants, socialized goblins, and anthropomorphized beasts found within *The Hobbit* all run contrary to Tolkien's later ideals of how Ilúvatar structured the lives and moralities of the races of Middle-earth. Unlike the more bestial trolls and orcs of *The Lord of the Rings*, *The Hobbit* incorporates a "civilized" race of goblins, replete with an apparently independent king, a developed culture, and autonomous self-awareness. Similarly, a fairly diverse cast of talking animal characters lends *The Hobbit* an almost Narnian feel, a tone very distinct from the rest of Tolkien's works (Tolkien, 2000, 42). The Lord of the Eagles wears an incongruous golden crown, and the spiders of Mirkwood banter humorously while taking offense at bad poetry, all in sharp contrast to the lordly eagles and fearful spiders of the other published works. This chapter will argue that Tolkien struggled to coordinate these contrasts into a consistent whole in the years after *The Hobbit* was published. Tolkien's three races of sentient, created beings (Elves, Men, and Dwarves) each have their own cosmology and eschatology, designed by Tolkien as distinct threads in the fabric of Arda. Talking animals and civilized orcs simply did not fit Tolkien's theological hierarchy, a fact that required existing myths to be re-written and the foundations of Middle-earth to be completely re-imagined. At the heart of this matter, and therefore the chief topic of this study, is the theology of soul giving.

Tolkien was not keenly interested in debating the nature of the soul. He addresses quite plainly what a soul *is* and then moves on: it is a rational spirit (or *fëa*) indwelling within a body (*hröa*), and it is almost always placed there by Eru Ilúvatar—the One God of the legendarium (Tolkien, 1993, 330, 428). Instead, he spent an inordinately large amount of time concerned with *who* gets a soul. Early drafts of the legendarium originally conceived of only two races "rational incarnate" creatures, or "Children of Ilúvatar," the Elves and the Humans (Tolkien, 2000, 189). The Dwarves were a third race added shortly after. Hobbits and Ents were the last to be invented, and each of the five "Freeborn Peoples," as Treebeard calls them, received distinct origin stories (or cosmologies), were granted souls by Eru Ilúvatar, and have an afterlife provided within the mythology. Vala and Maiar as well, being essentially pure spirits, were *fëar* who could assume a *hröa* at will (Tolkien, 1993, 218). No other creatures in Middle-earth share in these unique spiritual distinctions. Hence, this raises the question of how readers are to conceive of creatures who do not fall into these divisions but still bear the signs of sapience.

Melkor's lust for creative power complicates matters greatly. In early drafts, Melkor's minions—or *uvanimor*—are crafted from inanimate objects and given locomotion by Morgoth himself.[1] The orcs, for example, are originally said to have been made of granite in *The Shaping of Middle Earth*, yet later drafts of *The Silmarillion* show Tolkien considering numerous origin stories, and it took Christopher Tolkien, working after his father's death, to settle on the "authorized" explanation that the orcs were originally elves twisted by Morgoth (Tolkien, 1995, 100).

Orthodox Doctrine

To untangle the complicated web of what to think regarding creatures which behave like rationale incarnates but should not be, one must examine two aspects of Tolkien's work. The first is *The Hobbit*, which is where much of the complexity has its origins. The second is the criteria given above for what it means to *possess* a soul. This criteria ultimately stems from Roman Catholic Orthodoxy, so one will need to examine that as well.

There can be no question that Tolkien believed in the dichotomy of human existence as taught by the Catholic Church. He believed that the substance of the human creature can be separated into body and soul. The medievals and ancients did not distinguish between the concept of soul and life itself. All living things had souls; only differences in kind separated humans from plants and animals. Plato hypothesized three parts of the soul: "the intellect (*nous*), the nobler affections (*thumos*), and the appetites or passions (*epithumetikon*)" (Dubray 1909). From there, Thomas Aquinas distinguished three levels of biological existence: the vegetative soul, source of reproductive energy and found in all living creatures, especially plants; the passionate soul, or animal soul, which is the seat of emotions; and the intellectual soul, exclusive only to mankind. It is the intellectual soul that grants humans their self-awareness, and only the intellectual soul is eternal. Hence, to be fully human means to possess an intellect. Tolkien's doctrine of soul-giving mirrors this Platonic-Thomist progression. His three degrees of existence, expressed in elvish as *olvar* for plants, *kelvar* for animals, and *fëar* for rational souls, correspond rather precisely to the three categories of soul presented by Aquinas and Plato. One distinction, however, is that the Children of Ilúvatar who possess *fëar* do not also possess an animal soul (*kelvar*) and a vegetative soul (*olvar*).

To fully understand Tolkien's work with souls, one also must explore soul cosmology— answering the questions of both where the soul comes from and who gives it. The first question may be answered directly. Plato's "Timaeus" imagines a world-soul created by the demiurge to transmit life to all other living things and is therefore a *primuum mobile* (Plato, 1989, 30a-f).[2] Similarly, Tolkien's Ilúvatar functions as the demiurge who divests the Secret Fire—or Flame Imperishable—with prime mover capabilities. Both the *Ainulindale* and the *Valaquenta* describe the Secret Fire/Flame Imperishable as "burning in the heart of the world" much as Plato imagines the World Soul pantheistically possessing all of the Universe (Tolkien, 1977, 20, 25). But Tolkien is not a pantheist, so Eru, Tolkien's one God, kindles the Flame Imperishable within the Ainur and grants them a limited ability to create life; this seems to be closer to what he means by "burning in the heart of the world" (Tolkien, 1977, 15).

This brings one to the second question: who gives souls? At this point, one must return to the Thomist model of soul and make some distinctions. Whereas to Aquinas, "soul" means simply "life," several of the Ainur are granted permission to proliferate life-giving energy. This encompasses the Thomist categories of vegetative and passionate souls. Such power was certainly granted to Manwë, Ulmo, Yavanna and Vanya to generate birds, fish, plants, and flowers respectively (Tolkien, 1977, 26–28). Ilúvatar alone, however, retains the ability to grant the gift of Intellect, which requires the generation of a completely new *fëa* incarnated within a body—or *hröa*. None of the Ainur possess this power, although Melkor, Aule, and Yavanna eventually come to desire it, thus creating confusion as to how *fëar* may be conferred.

As one moves forward from these foundational components, it will be helpful to note that for the remainder of this essay, the word "soul" shall be used to refer to this intellectual soul—or *fëa*¬.

Tolkien's utilization of *fëar* aligns quite closely with Aquinas' teaching. Aquinas said that the soul was created (Aquinas, 1990, I.90.2). The soul must be *breathed* into Adam by God just as the Flame Imperishable must be kindled within a *hröa* (Genesis 2:7; Aquinas, 1990, I.90.2; Tolkien, 1977, 15). Souls can exist without a body ("incorporeal and subsistent"), and they possess intellect (Aquinas, 1990, I.75.2). Three criteria provide evidence of intellect: autonomy—both in terms of will and responsibility, self-awareness, and awareness of the infinite (Aquinas 1990, I.76.2, I.87.3, I.86.2; Hardon, 1975, 103). Aquinas also notes that animal souls are *not* subsistent because they possess only sense and not intellect, hence Tolkien's differentiation between Children of Ilúvatar and *kelvar*. Perhaps most importantly, Aquinas says that the presence of speech is the prime distinction of intellect; therefore, the presence of speech effectively indicates the presence of a rational soul.

The power of speech emerges as a significant point of contrast between *The Hobbit* and *The Lord of the Rings*. In the former, nearly everything alive which Thorin and company encounter has a voice: trolls, birds, wolves, spiders, and dragons. Not so in *The Lord of the Rings*. The trolls clam up, spiders go silent, and dragons vacate the premises entirely. The chief conundrum Tolkien created for himself with the Trolls, Goblins, Ravens, and Eagles of *The Hobbit* is speech, for in the Middle Ages speech was the central distinction between human and beast and signified the possession of a rational soul. Once a character speaks, however, the Catholic Tolkien well understood what that implied, and it had to be addressed, as evidenced in the following comment regarding the trolls of *The Hobbit*, "Of course ... when you make Trolls *speak* you are giving them a power, which in our world (probably) connotes the possession of a 'soul'" (Tolkien, 2000, 191). In the late texts for *The Silmarillion*, Tolkien planned to compose a sort of elvish catechism that would include "questions ... asked concerning the fate and death of Men. [Also] concerning other 'speaking,' and therefore 'reasonable,' kinds: Ents, Dwarves, Trolls, Orcs—and the speaking of beasts such as Huan, or the Great Eagles" (Tolkien, 1993, 251). Since Tolkien, the philologist and maker of languages, knew the metaphysical implications of speech and gave every indicator that the abundance of speaking creatures in *The Hobbit* was a concern to him, it stands to reason that one may examine his texts for his attempts to work out the problems created by them.

In spite of the grand diversity of life within Middle-earth, metaphysically speaking, Tolkien had only three options as to which tier of existence to assign any new creation: beast; sentient Children of Ilúvatar, who natively possessed both *fëa* and *hröa*; and sentient spiritual beings, limited to the Valar and Maiar, who may take on bodies at will but do not natively possess them. Quite plainly speaking, *The Hobbit* muddies these distinctions. This fact poses only small problems within the story itself, but as the legendarium expanded into *The Lord of the Rings* and as Tolkien resumed work on *The Silmarillion*, the complexities of the muddy pool of life swirling within the pages of *The Hobbit* became cumbersome. Nevertheless, as Tolkien wrote, he attempted to redact the histories of each of the incongruent creatures from *The Hobbit* to make them fit better into the great work.

The Fate of The Hobbit's *Sentient Bestiary*

In folklore, monsters come in two general categories: altered humanoid and oversized animals (Evans, 2007b, 433). Tolkien uses these categories, and each must be treated somewhat differently. Humanoid monsters share characteristics with humans, so may display greater autonomy and intellect than the oversized animals. Hence, Trolls, Orcs, and Giants will be discussed together as twisted humanoids, and the great eagles, giant spiders, Smaug, wargs, ravens, and thrush will be grouped as oversized animals. These categories will be helpful beyond mere organization since, as Jonathan Evans says, the monsters from neither category seem to possess "personhood, and none are included in Treebeard's list of Living Creatures," but do share certain similarities with the Freeborns (Evans, 2007b, 433). Since by Tolkien's own definitions, these creatures should not be in possession of rational souls, the discussion of each will center on whether or not the metaphysical nature of the creatures allows it to have a soul and, if so, what category of spirit in Tolkien's mythology best fits the creature. The author will also examine how Tolkien rectified the challenges created by each by redacting his existing stories with explanations and origin stories.

Humanoid Monsters: Trolls

The trolls are the first humanoid monsters which Thorin and Co. encounter on the path, and they are one of the more problematic for their famously incongruous cockney behavior. As this author has previously expressed, the purpose here is not to examine the origins of the trolls within the legendarium, for that task has been performed with expertise and abundance elsewhere. Instead, this author wants to examine the metaphysical wake left in the path of Tolkien's inception of such Trolls.

Most assuredly, these trolls pose a problem for any student of Tolkien's metaphysics. For starters, they are almost entirely *unlike* any other creature of darkness which Tolkien portrays anywhere else, and certainly most dissimilar to the trolls the Fellowship meets in Moria or again at the battle before the Morannon (Tolkien, 1982a, 187). Their humorous, cockney-inspired banter aside, the fact that they talk at all—and at such great length—causes them to stand out from the legions of Orcs, Balrogs, and even the great Sauron himself, all of whom possess certain sentience and superior intellect. Signs of civilization linger closely around the trolls' fireside: they carry coin purses, they have a developed culinary aesthetic which makes cooking methodology a debatable topic, they use tools, and collect treasure (Tolkien, 1997, 35–36). These signs point to human sapience rather than bestial evil. Their British names (e.g. "Bill Huggins") and Cockney accents indicate that Tolkien was more focused on spoofing the stereotypical "lower-class Londoners" of his day than making metaphysical claims about evil creatures (Rateliff, 2007a, 102). Lastly, William's apparent pity for Bilbo, expressed in his "Poor little blighter! Let him go!" hints that these creatures might even have latent goodness, which immediately suggest the possibility of redemption (Tolkien, 1997, 37). In short, William, Bert, and Tom behave like Children of Ilúvatar, contrary to everything else Tolkien wrote about trolls.

So problematic was the behavior of these creatures that Tolkien was pressured to address the obvious contrast once *The Lord of the Rings* was published. In a 1954 letter, Catholic bookshop manager Peter Hastings called Tolkien out on—among other issues—allowing evil characters like the trolls to possess "a tendency to good" (Carpenter, 1979, 187). Tolkien's answer is at once an orthodox apology for his subcreation and a guarded confession of the trouble the cockney Trolls caused. So thorough is Tolkien's response to this criticism, effectively touching on numerous relevant points, that it shall form the framework for the remainder of the discussion regarding trolls.

Tolkien begins his response by admitting that he is "not sure about Trolls," saying, "I think they are mere 'counterfeits,' and hence (though here I am of course only using elements of old barbarous mythmaking that had no 'aware' metaphysic) they return to mere stone images when not in the dark" (Tolkien, 2000, 191). Here Tolkien admits that the Trolls at this point are drawn directly from Teutonic myth. Numerous scholars have examined the mythical roots of Tolkien's trolls (Anderson, 2002, 80; Hammond and Scull, 2005, 189; Rateliff, 2007a, 102–3). The trolls of *The Hobbit* align much more collectively with trolls of the Norse Eddas, which talk, wear clothes, and essentially function as large, dimwitted dwarves. This is certainly where Tolkien comes to see Trolls as evil creatures. Jakob Grimm shows that superstitions regarding giants, woodsprites, and trolls became grafted to the more metaphysical conception of the Devil once Scandinavia became Christianized, but it would not have been discussed at all whether the creatures were self-aware (Grimm, 2004, 1004).

In fact, metaphysically, Tolkien admits here that the Trolls are a dead-end. They are mere "counterfeits" of true creations, an explanation corroborated by Treebeard (Tolkien, 1982c, 105). The fact that they turn to stone when they "die" indicates that they are only an elaborate sort of *golem* of Jewish folklore.[3] Tolkien was the first English author to employ the motif of trolls turning to stone in the sunshine (Rateliff, 2007a, 102–3).[4] The device makes for an exceedingly simple eschatology paired with the likewise simple Judeo-Christian image of darkness (sin) being chased away by light (God).[5] More importantly, petrification of the trolls strongly indicates that neither troll culture (whatever that may be) nor troll metaphysics allow for the existence of a troll soul. This literal light-dark sensitivity aligns with the moral-allegorical application which allows us to compare trolls with demons: beings who know all too well the truth of Christ and shudder at it, but still embody evil (James 2:19).

As for Hastings' charge that Tolkien had made his evil Trolls capable of benevolent emotion, Tolkien explains:

> But I do not agree (if you admit that fairy-story element) that my trolls show any sign of 'good,' strictly and unsentimentally viewed. I do not say William felt *pity*—a word to me of moral and imaginative worth: it is the Pity of Bilbo and later Frodo that ultimately allows the Quest to be achieved—and I do not think [William] showed Pity. I might not (if *The Hobbit* had been more carefully written, and my world so much thought about 20 years ago) have used the expression 'poor little blighter,' just as I should not have called the troll *William*. But I discerned no pity even then, and put in a plain caveat [Tolkien, 2000, 191].

Tolkien all but concedes that a post–*Lord of the Rings* version of *The Hobbit* would not have included Trolls of this kind at all. In short, he admits that William, Tom, and Bert do not align to the vision for Trolls cast in the later legendarium. This brings us to the final concern regarding the Trolls of *The Hobbit*: how did Tolkien choose to address their peculiar inconsistency?

Trolls do not figure prominently in the final version of *The Lord of the Rings* at all. In earlier drafts, Tolkien may be seen grappling with the problem of the trolls. He decided early to have the Fellowship pay a nostalgic visit to the petrified trio both as a touch of humor and as a means of uniting the plots of the previous work with the present one. As they approach the Trollshaws, Bingo notices ruined towers and asks Trotter if trolls made them. Trotter responds "No, trolls do not build," suggesting that Tolkien had begun to back away from the tool-using trolls of *The Hobbit* (Tolkien, 1988, 192).

From here all that becomes clear is Tolkien's uncertainty. They seem to receive two simultaneous, and contradictory, developments after *The Hobbit*. The first relates to their origin. Both Treebeard's exposition and the appendices of *Return of the King* agree that Morgoth "made" the trolls, but neither mention who or what they were made from. Stone seems the most likely candidate. J. E. A. Tyler manifests what Tolkien only hints at: that since Trolls revert to stone at their destruction, they must originate from that material (Tyler, 1976, 487). This means they are analogous to stone the way Ents are analogous to wood, which explains how their existence is a "mockery of ents" as Treebeard suggests (Tolkien, 1982c, 105). If the trolls are manufactured of stone, then they would have neither *fëa* nor animal life and could not be classified as *kelvar* or truly alive at all. So in these ways, the trolls may be thought of as *golem*, animated stone that only mimics life so long as the evil will that conjured it holds it together. The spirit animating them is therefore a shadow or particle of the spirit of their controller—either Morgoth or Sauron, depending on the Age— and the troll itself possesses no autonomous life. This certainly makes sense when one examines the final appearance of trolls in *Return of the King*, in which the hill-trolls come "roaring as beasts" out of the Black Gate but then after the fall of Sauron run "hither and thither mindless" as things "spell enslaved" (Tolkien, 1982b, 252).

Competing with this understanding, however, is the second development Trolls receive in *The Lord of the Rings*. Tolkien simply could neither ignore nor delete the talking Trolls from *The Hobbit*, so in spite of having decided that the creatures were born of stone in the First Age, these particular talking specimens must be explained. Allusions to Tolkien's solution can be found in the *Return of the Shadow*. A telling passage in the draft chapter "Ancient History" (the precursor to "The Shadow of the Past" in the published version) ambiguously hints at the proliferation of trolls and other evil creatures: "Goblins were multiplying again and reappearing. Trolls of a new and most malevolent kind were abroad; giants were spoken of, a Big Folk only far bigger and stronger than Men the [?ordinary] Big Folk, and no stupider, indeed often full of cunning and wizardry" (Tolkien, 1988, 253). Tolkien seems to be subtly attempting to explain the unique phenomenon of talking Trolls. This may be the passage to which Tolkien alludes in his letter to Peter Hastings: "But there are other sorts of Trolls beside these rather ridiculous, if brutal, Stone-trolls, for which other origins are suggested" (Tolkien, 2000, 191). By "other origins" it seems Tolkien is hinting that Sauron is once again engineering new species just as Morgoth once did long ago. Perhaps Tolkien was tinkering with the idea of developing a sentient troll. This seems likely when one sees a few pages later that in the first draft of "The Mines of Moria," the goblins assailing the chamber of Mazarbul are led by a troll (Tolkien, 1988, 443). Eventually, however, Tolkien transfers this leadership to a Black Rider and then to the Balrog, after which trolls fade into the brutish battlefield scenery found in the latter volumes (Tolkien, 1988, 443).

One does hear of various kinds of trolls throughout LOTR, however. "Cave trolls" are present in Moria on the bridge of Khazad-dûm, and "mountain trolls" wield the massive battering ram Grond during the siege of Gondor (Tolkien, 1982b, 112). "Hill-trolls" from Gorgoroth assail the Captains of the West during the battle before the Morannon of Mordor (Tolkien, 1982b, 187). These last are the *olog-hai* referenced in Appendix F of *Return of the King*. The reader receives no hint at how they were made, just that "Sauron bred" them, but it is important to remember that the primary purpose of Appendix F is to discuss "The *Languages* of the Peoples of the Third Age." That trolls are included in the Appendix at all suggests that Tolkien is still trying to explain Bert, Tom, and William's chattiness. The first paragraph of the entry confirms that early trolls had "no more language than beasts," but once Sauron began to meddle, "the Stone-trolls spoke a debased form of the Common Speech" (Tolkien, 1982b, 473). This last phrase alludes directly to the trolls in *The Hobbit* as an attempt to sanction the cockney accents. There, as clearly as ever Tolkien is willing to make it, is our solution. The reader must conclude that William, Bert, and Tom are escaped experiments. Still trolls; still originally stone, as their demise confirms, but nevertheless an enhanced breed of trolls evidently engineered by the Necromancer—Sauron in hiding—who had somehow run off and "come down from the mountains and settled in the woods," as Gandalf explains (Tolkien, 1997, 44). Of course some may find this explanation unsatisfactory, even forced, and understandably so, for as has been seen, depending on one's perspective, Trolls can be viewed as stone *golem* and not properly alive at all, beast-like *kelvar* tortured into their evil ways, or sapient persons capable of crude civilization. The reader need not be much surprised at confusion since all are in good company; Tolkien, too, was "not sure about Trolls."

Humanoid Monsters: Giants

From stone trolls the author will now move on to the stone Giants of the Misty Mountains, creatures much more mysterious than their Cockney cousins but much more simple to explain. Only mentioned twice in *The Hobbit* and nowhere explicitly in *The Lord of the Rings* or *The Silmarillion*, giants display much less evidence of developed sapience than the trolls or the goblins, but are still representatives of the monstrous humanoid category. They can play games, as they do with the boulders dodged by Thorin and company, and while no speeches are recorded they do "guffaw and shout," vocalizations not generally attributed to animals (Tolkien, 1997, 57). It is also unclear whether they are good or evil, for although they certainly hinder the company's progress, they do not appear to do so purposefully. The most compelling evidence for giant sentience comes after the company escapes the goblins, when Gandalf vows to "find a more or less decent giant to block" up the new entrance to the goblin city, although this statement likewise confuses their moral alignment (Tolkien, 1997, 94). More cannot be said from the published works, since the word "giant" does not appear in either *The Silmarillion* or *The Lord of the Rings*. In fact, one can only assume that Tolkien pictured these giants in humanoid shape at all, for even that detail is withheld, and only the collective stock of giant folklore informs the general reader of their dimensions or temperament.

One author who does seem to have read *The Hobbit* with great interest and viewed the giants as not only sentient but conceivably civilized is Tolkien's friend C. S. Lewis. Lewis was friends with Tolkien while he was composing and reading out loud *The Hobbit* during meetings of The Inklings, and was even given one of the earliest drafts to read on his own (Carpenter, 1979, 57, 67). Years later, Lewis included giants in one of his Narnian tales and incorporates a scene in which travelers passing through mountains come across a row of creatures that look like rocks but are boulder-tossing giants: "It was a horrible time. There seemed no end to the line of giants, and they never ceased hurling stones, some of which fell extremely close. Quite apart from the real danger, the very sight and sound of their faces and voices were enough to scare anyone" (Lewis, 1981, 83). Later in the story, the adventurers must escape the House of Harfang, a castle of man-eating giants who talk, wear clothes, and write cookbooks.

Lewis's Harfang certainly draws from the wellspring of Jack the Giant Killer folklore, but the earlier episode sounds suspiciously like it has been borrowed—at least partially—from Tolkien. So at least one of Tolkien's close friends seems to have read Bilbo's ordeal in the Misty Mountains and interpreted the giants as sapient and evil, regardless of the fact that the actual text treats the giants more as elementals: creatures who merely personify the hardships of storm and stone for Bilbo and the dwarves (Rateliff, 2007a, 145). This indicates how likely it is that readers of *The Hobbit* will make the same intuitive leap, and predicts that Tolkien most likely knew that his readers would do just that. While assuming that Tolkien's giants are autonomous persons may not be solidly grounded by textual data, it is nevertheless a safe assumption.

As with the trolls, one can see Tolkien struggling to successfully integrate pseudo-sentient creatures into a larger myth with a highly exclusive list of sentient races. As John Rateliff points out, giants play almost no role at all in the early drafts of the Legendarium (Rateliff, 2007a, 143). They are mentioned along with ogres and monsters as comprising the *uvanimor*, creatures made by Melkor and therefore inherently evil (Tolkien, 1983, 75; Tolkien, 1986, 136; Tolkien, 1993, 79). This at once solves the mystery of whether Tolkien viewed the giants as good or evil, but as with trolls, once Tolkien included details about them in *The Hobbit*, they must be explained in greater depth. He certainly planned to make room for a race of giant creatures. By early 1939, only a year after the publication of *The Hobbit*, Tolkien was already at work on *The Lord of the Rings* and told his publisher that "although there is no dragon (so far)" in the new book, "there is going to be a Giant" (Tolkien, 2000, 42). The outward pressure to appease "readers young and old who clamored for more" was competing with Tolkien's inner desire to create an internally consistent world.

But even casual readers of *The Lord of the Rings* will quickly notice that nothing like the giants of *The Hobbit* appear in any of the volumes. If only comparing the two published texts, Tolkien apparently abandoned the giants of the Misty Mountain, but in fact, he was far more successful at integrating a sentient race of giants than with any of the other pseudo-sentient creatures in *The Hobbit*. The giants, as it turns out, gradually transformed into the ents.

The transformation may be observed in *The Return of the Shadow*, the earliest draft of *The Lord of the Rings*. The first draft of the Hobbits' conversation at the Green Dragon has Sam Gamgee saying, "But what about these what do you call 'em—giants? They do say as one nigh as big as a tower or leastaways a tree was seen up away beyond the North Moors not long back" (Tolkien, 1988, 254). The quote shows that Tolkien was waffling between stone (the stuff of towers) and of wood (the stuff of trees) for the giants' natural element. The giants of *The Hobbit* were called "stone-giants," but the trolls were likewise "stone-trolls," and Tolkien perhaps saw an overlap which he wished to rectify, since no creature associated with wood yet existed. Still clinging to these new giants is the idea that they were evil *uvanimor*, creatures of Morgoth. Thus the name "Treebeard" first emerges in the text as the identity of a particularly evil giant who prowls Fangorn Forest and imprisons Gandalf on his way to visit Frodo. Christopher Tolkien transcribes a scrap of narrative written on the back of a letter dated July 27–29 1939 in which Treebeard and Frodo have a brief conversation. Already the giant has taken a decidedly tree-like shape, but his speech patterns are kindly rather than evil: "If you don't let me know where you are, you can't blame me for treading on you" (Tolkien, 1988, 382). Despite Tolkien's intent that Treebeard only "pretends to be friendly, but is really in league with the Enemy," the warmth of Treebeard's first actual speech seems to solidify his latent goodness, and Tolkien eventually gave in and Treebeard became an Ent (Tolkien, 1988, 410; Rateliff, 2007a, 144).

Etymologically, no great gap exists between ents and giants, for the word "ent" literally means "giant" in Old English (Dickerson, 2007, 163). Existentially, however, good giants required a good deal of redaction to the legendarium. They could not be considered one of Morgoth's fabrications, and they must be added to the Children of Ilúvatar, and while in the myth they are one of the oldest creatures, they were the last Tolkien admitted to that narrow fellowship. As "free born" peoples, they must accordingly possess *fëar*. Tolkien never got around to explaining an afterlife for the Entish *fëar* but he did invent its origin. The second chapter of the *Quenta Silmarillion* tells how the Vala Aulë, in his passion for forging and making, crafts the dwarves whose existence is eventually ratified by Ilúvatar. But in a much more subtle follow-up, Yavanna, Vala over all plant life, becomes distressed that the forthcoming Children of Ilúvatar will not respect the trees she loves (Tolkien, 1977, 45). She appears to Manwë and bemoans her plight. In response, Ilúvatar speaks directly through Manwë that "When the Children awake, then the thought of Yavanna will awake also, and it will summon spirits from afar, and they will go among the *kelvar* [animals] and the *olvar* [plants], and some will dwell therein, and be held in reverence, and their just anger shall be feared" (Tolkien, 1977, 46). Thus Yavanna is appeased that the forests shall be protected by "Shepherds of the Trees." While not named directly, these lines certainly refer explicitly to Ents and were written with the events of *The Two Towers* clearly in mind. The phrase "spirits from afar" refers to Maiar entering Arda and "going among" the plants and animals and suggests that these spirits formed an incarnational indwelling.[6] The *fëar* of Ents, then, must be *Maiar* who have taken on trees as their *hröa*, or physical bodies (Dickerson, 2007, 162).

Humanoid Monsters: Goblins

Turning from Giants to the spiritual nature of Goblins and Orcs, one may make an easy claim that no other malevolent creation of Tolkien's has been so widely debated and pondered. Even Tolkien himself struggled at great length to make these creatures fit consistently within the metaphysical boundaries of Middle-Earth, and one may argue that the real trouble began when the Goblins start singing as they drag Thorin and company down their tunnels. Prior to that moment, aside from raucous laughter, the goblins behave as any other pack-hunting predator. The portrait Tolkien paints after that moment is of an autonomous peoples having a rudimentary artistic aesthetic (expressed through singing), a political hierarchy (through the Great Goblin and other Goblin kings), and rather well-developed technology (Tolkien, 1997, 62–3). The narrator pauses from the story long enough to elaborate the latter, explaining that goblins "make very well" certain construction tools and implements of torture and guesses that "they invented the machines that have since troubled the world, especially the ingenious devices for killing large numbers of people at once" (Tolkien, 1997, 62). Other more subtle statements declare the autonomous sapience of the goblin race. The Great Goblin seems to possess a moral compass, and although the goblins are certainly not aligned with a Judeo-Christian morality, Tom Shippey argues that the only difference between orc morality and Christian morality is in how it is followed (Shippey, 2002, 133). The Great Goblin declares that the dwarves are "up to no good," that they are "spying," and urges Thorin to stop lying: "Let's have the truth, or I will prepare something particularly uncomfortable for you" (Tolkien, 1997, 63). Web author Emily Cotlier points out that the underground conversation between Thorin and the Great Goblin is the only time in Tolkien's works that a good character treats an orc as an intellectual peer (Cotlier, 2004, 5).

This broad collection of facts leads to only one conclusion: that the Goblins are "fundamentally a race of 'rational incarnate' creatures" as Tolkien rather plainly tells Peter Hastings in 1954 (Tolkien, 2000, 190). And of course the accepted cosmology for orcs and goblins—that they were originally elves or men who became corrupted by Morgoth—seems to reasonably address both Goblin civilization in *The Hobbit* and other independent exploits of orcs in the greater legendarium. Nevertheless, this accepted "official" story becomes increasingly troublesome when examined from a theological perspective. If orcs are "rational incarnates" they must possess *fëar*, and if so, their spirits must be provided for upon their death, as are the other Freeborn Peoples, opening the possibility for some sort of "orcish" redemption. Tolkien developed neither of these concepts, not because he did not think to but because both completely contradict the narrative fact of the orcs themselves. In other words, orcish cosmology is permanently incompatible with orcish existence.

Tolkien understood these implications and realized rather quickly that the situation would not do at all. The goblins of *The Hobbit* created much greater difficulties than of mere origin stories. In his earliest vision for the orcs, they were created from stone by Morgoth just as the trolls had been (Tolkien, 1986, 159; Tolkien, 1993, 123). Unlike the trolls, however, instead of a few escaped "experiments" to sweep under the rug, Tolkien has overrun the Misty Mountains with an entire civilization of talking, building, and singing goblins. Plus, trolls *are* "provided for" in a sense. They turn to stone because they possess no *fëar*. Orcs— especially with their redacted cosmology in place—cannot be similarly accounted for.

To help address this conundrum, one must turn to the essay in which Tolkien himself wrestles with the issue. In the late 1950s and early '60s, when Tolkien once again began to seriously work on *The Silmarillion* after the publication of *The Lord of the Rings*, he became, as Christopher Tolkien puts it, "absorbed in analytic speculation concerning its underlying postulates" and was driven to "satisfy the requirements of a coherent theological and metaphysical system" made all the more difficult by "obscure and conflicting elements in its roots and its tradition" (Tolkien, 1993, viii). This included *The Hobbit* and its goblin civilization. Tolkien in fact conceptualized numerous origin stories for the orcs, modified and adjusted over time, sometimes one theory swiftly abandoned for another (Tolkien, 1993, 408). Certain facts about the orcs do remain constant throughout the various narratives: they were made by Melkor; they were not *created* by Melkor and so had to be crafted from pre-existent materials; their purpose was to mock and oppose the elves; their evil and hatred were an intuitive component of their "nature." Tolkien chronicled the great difficulty he had working out the details beyond these basic facts in a short essay simply entitled "Orcs," which begins, "Their nature and origin require more thought. They are not easy to work into the theory and system" (Tolkien, 1993, 409).

In that essay Tolkien toys with three different possible theories that might harmonize orc metaphysics with orcish reality as written into the stories (Rateliff, 2007a, 138). The first theory is that orcs are twisted Children of Ilúvatar, either human or elvish, and therefore in possession of *fëar*. The second is that the orcs are actually Maiar, immortal spirits who have "assumed forms of Arda at will" (Tolkien, 1977, 21). The third is that the orcs do not possess *fëar* at all but are in essence animals who have been turned to their devices by a powerful spiritual will external to themselves (i.e. Morgoth or Sauron). For this third option, the orcs' power of speaking compares to that of parrots, just rather more complex (Tolkien, 1993, 410). From this point, Tolkien's essay becomes cyclical and contradictory as he continues to contemplate strengths and weaknesses for each argument. A brief separate essay suggests a fourth possibility from a hybrid of the second and third theories: that the vast majority of the orcs are bestial but are lead by a few powerful orcs which are Maiar incarnate (Tolkien, 1993, 414). Tolkien mentions that Boldog, from the war of the Jewels, as a possible "Orc-formed Maiar," and Gothmog, the captain of the orcs during the siege of Gondor, could conceivably be examples of these (Tolkien, 1993, 418).[7]

It is not the purpose of this study to rehash the "true" origin story of the orcs. Other scholars have tackled this topic *ad infinitum*, and to do so now would be tangential. Instead, the theological implications of the four competing theories are worth a closer look, shedding light on why the manuscripts show Tolkien, after seeming to finally settle on an official origin, incessantly capitulates to another. Part of the trouble is that orcs function differently on different levels, but the functions are incompatible with one another. Mythologically they function as animals—expendable, mindless ant-like hordes. Theologically they function as spiritual beings—the incarnation of demonic evil. Narratologically they function as Children of Ilúvatar—human antagonists who can think, speak, build, and make choices. None of the solutions Tolkien contrived for the origins of orcs and the presence—or absence—of their souls ever fully satisfy his late requirement of theological consistency. This is because each of the suggested theories solves one problem only to give rise to another, so the author will briefly examine the theological implications and obstructions for each.

1. Orcs are Children of Ilúvatar (either men or elves).

If the Orcs are Children of Ilúvatar, then they must be divested with not only a cosmology, but also a soteriology (plan of redemption) and an eschatology (plan for the afterlife). On separate occasions, Tolkien contradicts himself by declaring that the Orcs "have become irredeemable" and then says that calling them "irredeemably bad ... would be going too far" (Tolkien, 1993, 419; Tolkien, 2000, 195). In the 1959 essay on orcs, Tolkien suggests that perhaps dead orcs would indeed "go to Mandos and be held in prison to the End" (Tolkien, 1993, 411). These statements are the closest Tolkien ever gets to providing a soteriology and eschatology for orcs, but they are not developed, mainly because they are not tenable within the context of the stories. Orcs never behave in a manner which warrants redemption, so discussing their redemption is merely hypothetical (Cotlier, 2004, 7).[8] The Halls of Mandos are not a place of punishment but of waiting, and to turn them into a kind of "Hell" would be to change the nature of the myth altogether, creating more problems that would have forced further rewriting. Tolkien's early reticence to admit that dwarves possessed *fëar* (much less provide an afterlife for their souls) provides a model for both how seriously he considered such issues and how he resolutely redacted previous positions once his mind had been made up to harmonize the legendarium with orthodoxy (Rateliff, 2007b, 720–1). But Dwarves were an easy issue to resolve because they are largely good and moral characters. Not so the Orcs.

Furthermore, if orcs are in fact Children of Ilúvatar, then what has been done to them is an abomination, and they have been victimized beyond the pains of any other race (Rearick, 2004, 862). They are to be pitied, not hated, and evangelized, not exterminated. If it is known by Men and Elves that the Orcs are not only their brethren, but an enslaved race with millions of offspring enduring nightmare childhoods, then Men and Elves are themselves racist hatemongers (Cotlier, 2004, 4).[9] In short, the notion of irredeemable evil comes with various untenable consequences if one combines that evil with spiritual autonomy. As Anderson Rearick points out, it becomes extremely difficult to rescue Tolkien from accusations of racism if orcs are to be considered Children of Ilúvatar (Rearick, 2004, 870). For this reason, Rearick suggests that despite what Tolkien may have written in private, in the published stories, the orcs do not function as incarnate mortals but as demons (Rearick, 2004, 871).

2. Orcs are Maiar

Numerous critics note that the etymology for the word "orc" stems from OE *orcneas*, meaning "demon" in Beowulf (Atherton, 2012, 871; Rearick, 2004, 871). Rearick makes a good point that Orcs serve a demon analogue to Morgoth's Satanic analogue, so this explanation fits the theological cosmology (Rearick, 2004, 871). Theologically speaking, Maiar are like angels, used by the Valar as servants and messengers, and the demons of Scripture are often understood to be fallen angels. If the orcs are Maiar like the Istari, however, they do not behave at all like other Maiar—good or evil. Although both Morgoth and Satan seem to have battalions of rebellious spirits on hand, bringing to mind Satan's legions in *Paradise Lost*, it is inconsistent with the nature of other Maiar that they should proliferate after the manner of the orcs. Tolkien strongly hints that Maiar cannot produce more Maiar; their numbers are confined to those who entered Arda at its beginning.[10] Additionally, Maiar are immortal spirits, and if orcs are Maiar, they too are immortal, a theory which bears no fruit in the published stories. Mythologically speaking, they function as demigods, after the manner of Circe, and like demigods, they tend to be more or less attached to a single location: the Balrog of Moria and Melian of Doriath exemplify this principle, as do the Eagles of Taniquetil and Meneltarma. Also like demigods, Maiar can clothe themselves with mortal bodies, as one sees the Valar do on numerous occasions, as well as the Istari, the Balrogs, Melian, Sauron and others (Tolkien, 1977, 21). The orcs do not follow any of the above rules in any way. No hint of their spiritual nature is given and they roam freely throughout Middle Earth. Furthermore, such locally specialized spirits are by necessity scarcely used in both ancient myths and in Tolkien's legendarium. To overuse such *machina* is to create a narrative riddled with inexplicable miracles, too many *dei ex machina*. Tolkien found tampering with that principle an intolerable breach of protocol (Tolkien 2000, 271).[11]

3. Orcs are beasts (kelvar).

The third option is that orcs are beasts, without souls, and merely bent to the will of their spiritual controllers, if not outright possessed by them. Tolkien seems to briefly decide on this option in the 1959 essay: "The Orcs were *beasts* of a humanized shape ... deliberately perverted/converted into a more close resemblance to Men. Their 'talking' was really the reeling off of 'records' set in them by Melkor" (Tolkien, 1993, 410). Just as swiftly, however, he seems to abandon this decision due to the blatant fact of their independence. Animals would not have banded together to form civilizations as witnessed in *The Hobbit*. Both Morgoth and Sauron experienced periods of absence when their enemies held them in temporary captivity or similar defeat. At such times when their will was removed from their subjects, orcs who were *kelvar* would simply revert back to their mindlessness, returning to the typical, morally neutral activities of animals. But in the absence of their creators and lords, no orc ever reverts in this way. Tolkien's own narrative essentially prohibits this conclusion.

4. Orcs are controlled by Maiar

The final hypothesis suggests that the orcs could be "herded" together by a handful of orc-cloaked Maiar who could control the hordes during the absences of Morgoth or Sauron, accounting for the short list of powerful, named orcs who seem to emerge as superlative chieftains of their kind (Tolkien, 1993, 414). This concept actually has a precedence in Catholic theological history in the philosophy of Averroes, who argued that mankind shared a single intellect (Hardon, 1975, 103). Arguing for the independence of the soul, Thomas Aquinas refuted the hypothesis, declaring that such a unity would inhibit diversity (Aquinas, 1990, I.76.2).

In Tolkien's orcs, however, it may be argued that one sees just this sort of unity of intellect and, indeed, a corresponding inhibition of diversity. Tolkien seems to actually ratify this explanation at the end of *The Return of the King* when Sauron's armies disburse in despair after the destruction of the One Ring (Tolkien, 1983c, 252–3). Certainly various aspects of diabolical mind control do take place over the course of Tolkien's narratives; the *palantiri* serve as an especially obvious example. But the flaw with the specific concept of orc–Maiar controlling orc armies is that it does not explain the utter lack of unity that individual orcs display while performing their official functions. If the orcs were mindless puppets of a powerful spirit, it seems unlikely that internal quarrels would ever occur. Yet the only two views of orc-life received in *The Lord of the Rings*—between Grishnákh and Uglúk during the captivity of Merry and Pippin and between Snaga and Shagrat in the Tower of Cirith Ungol—end in disarray and murder.

In any case the goblins of *The Hobbit* do not model the Maia-mind control argument. John Rateliff argues that orcs, especially in *The Hobbit*, "seem as capable of free thought and action as any of the other races" and points out that not only do the goblins which waylay Bilbo's company in the Misty Mountains show no signs of being controlled by the Necromancer, they also have no apparent connection with him at all (Atherton, 2012, 146; Rateliff, 2007a, 139). If anything, they become more organized after the death of the Great Goblin, which counts as two strikes against any theory suggesting that orc-clad Maiar—either in the form of Sauron-as-Necromancer or the Great Goblin—are controlling the horde that wages the Battle of Five Armies.

As can now be seen, no one theory fully accounts for the appearance of independent sentience among the Orcs. The official explanation of elves—or men—twisted by Morgoth covers up some of the discrepancies but does not address them all to satisfactory consistency.[12] Because of these conundrums of orcish existence, it is nearly impossible—as Tolkien himself alludes—to settle on any one system. If the orcs are animals, they cannot be irredeemably evil, and they cannot possess intellect. If they are Children of Ilúvatar, they *are* redeemable and their souls must be provided for—requiring a soteriology and an eschatology. If they are Maiar they cannot reproduce new Maiar, and they cannot be killed. Yet sentient, irredeemable evil can only exist in a Maiar; the combination of reproduction, autonomy, and intellect can only exist in Children of Ilúvatar; and amoral expendability can only exist in animals. At the end of the discussion, unfortunately, there is no clear resolution. As a theological sub-creation, the Orcs simply fail, and it was during Bilbo's abortive journey through the Misty Mountains that they began to do so.

Oversized Animals: Eagles and Spiders

Turning to the second class of monsters found in *The Hobbit*, the number of giant, talking beasts rather outnumbers the humanoid monsters in both kind and occasion. Explaining the problem of their sentience is altogether less complicated, however, since fewer options exist with which to explain their metaphysical condition. Tolkien never made any serious consideration to include any of the talking beasts among the Children of Ilúvatar, and all are legitimately living creatures and cannot realistically be considered inanimate matter enchanted, or *golem*, as with the trolls. The only two options left is that they must be classed either as actual beasts (*kelvar*) possessing some extenuating condition or are Maiar "clothed in their own thought" (Tolkien, 1977, 21). A paragraph from Tolkien's 1959 essay concerning orcs confirms these principles: "True 'rational' creatures, 'speaking peoples,' are all of human/'humanoid' form. Only the Valar and the Maiar are intelligences that can assume forms of Arda at will" (Tolkien, 1993, 410). All of the talking animals in *The Hobbit* may be slotted into one category or another, but Tolkien himself was not so sure as to which went where until much later when the strictures of his legendarium demanded that he decide the precise nature of these beasts. Examined first will be animals which may arguably be Maiar cloaked in the "raiment of the World" (Tolkien, 1977, 21).

Chapters one and two of *The Quenta Silmarillion* spend considerable time explaining why and how certain Maiar enter Arda disguised as various plants and animals. Christopher Tolkien dates the composition of these chapters to 1958 or 1959, well after both *The Hobbit* and *The Lord of the Rings* were in print, lending support to the claim that Tolkien is attempting to redact his own narratives (Tolkien, 1994, 341). The chapter regarding Aulë and Yavanna, as already seen, tells how the Ents came to be, but it also gives Tolkien "divine" authority to put speech in the mouth of nearly any creature. The passage alludes specifically to eagles, but Eru's decree makes it possible for any natural substance, be it plant, animal, or mineral, to start talking so long as a Maia has incarnated itself within.

While Ilúvatar's ruling in Yavanna's favor only explicitly accounts for the great eagles, it does so somewhat imperfectly. Sorontor, chief of the eagles, existed in the legendarium before *The Hobbit*. He was created by Manwë to serve him and is a more-or-less independent being with the power of speech and independent thought, already busy with the various last minute rescues for which the eagles are well known (Tolkien, 1983, 176–7; Tolkien, 1986, 195; Rateliff, 2007a, 221). At first it seems as if Tolkien meant for "The Lord of the Eagles" from *The Hobbit* to be Sorontor/Thorondor himself. The article "The" in the eagle lord's title suggests that there is only one Lord, and only one "Lord of the Eagles" existed in the legendarium at the time *The Hobbit* was written. But he seems to retract that intent by invoking Thorondor's name in the published text of *Return of the King*, stating that Gwaihir and Landroval are only his "descendants," but leaving the text ambiguous as to whether Gwaihir or Thorondor is the "Great Eagle" referred to in *The Hobbit* (Tolkien, 1982b, 251). While Thorondor should be considered a Maia in the shape of an eagle, because of Tolkien's rule against Maiar reproduction, Gwaihir and Landroval cannot be (Tolkien, 1993, 410). So it remains to explain how the great eagles in both *The Hobbit* and *The Lord of the Rings* appear to possess *fëar* when they can be classified neither as Maiar nor Children of Ilúvatar. John Rateliff claims that the younger eagles are "(mortal) descendants" and moves on, but this does not satisfy the spiritual nature of their characters nor the autonomy of their personalities (Rateliff, 2007a, 223). To address the problem further, one must look next at the Great Spiders of Mirkwood.

The text of how and why the Great Spiders come to be haunting a swatch of Greenwood the Great is well documented in *The Two Towers*. They are scions of Shelob, who is the "last child of Ungoliant" (Tolkien, 1982c, 292). Her broods are described as having spread "from the Ephel Duath ... to Dol Guldur and the fastnesses of Mirkwood (Tolkien, 1982c, 292). Ungoliant herself is not identified directly as a Maia, but is unmistakably of Maiar kind. She is a spirit, originally named Moru, "the primeval night," who has taken the form of a spider, but predates the coming of the Ainur, possibly somehow "descended from the darkness that lies about Arda (Tolkien, 1983, 151; Tolkien, 1977, 73). In this way Ungoliant is like the Anarch of Chaos Milton employs to rule over the uncreated spaces of the universe in *Paradise Lost* (Milton, 1968, II.960). Regardless of her precise origin and her service as the personification of chaos and night, in the narrative, Ungoliant functions as an autonomous, "araneiform spirit" after the manner of the Ainur, able to think and act independently, but augmented with near-immortality and a supernatural ability to eat light and to weave webs of darkness (Duriez, 1992, 280; Houghton, 2007, 687). Shelob, described as "an evil thing in spider-form," possesses very similar characteristics (Tolkien, 1982c, 292). And while Shelob may not speak outright, Ungoliant and the Mirkwood spiders do.[13] It is certain that Tolkien was attempting to correlate the Great Spiders of Mirkwood to Shelob and Ungoliant via his explanation of Shelob's origin in *The Two Towers*, tying up all three loose ends with a single back story. According to Tolkien's rule concerning Maiar reproduction, one cannot properly expect Shelob or the Mirkwood spiders to be Maiar, yet all three iterations of the Great Spider brood possess will, intellect, and self-awareness, all of which are criteria named by Aquinas for the possession of soul (Aquinas, 1990, I.87.3).

So with the great spiders, as with the great Eagles, a Maiar ancestor brings forth sentient offspring that are not Maiar, but are nevertheless sentient. Tolkien never directly addresses such hybrid creatures, but a precedent for spiritual hybridity occurs on at least one other occasion: the union of King Thingol the elf and Melian the Maia. Melian bears Lúthien as her child, who is certainly not a Maia like her mother but undoubtedly possesses a *fëa,* and through her union with Beren, produces Dior, Thingol's heir.[14] This, then, appears to be unexplored territory for Tolkien. Perhaps Maiar cannot produce new Maiar, but they certainly can reproduce, and the evidence suggests that their offspring are genuine spiritual incarnates.

Oversized Animals: The Dragon Smaug

The last remaining beast who may conceivably claim to be a Maia incarnate is the dragon Smaug. Tolkien describes dragons in general as "intelligent lizards," "incarnate in time," and "able to comprise human malice and bestiality together," although he never crafted a detailed metaphysical explanation for the sentience of his own dragons (Rateliff, 2007b, 527, 543; Tolkien, 1936, 259). Instead, he draws from his readers' assumed foreknowledge of the species: that they are wily and wise, able to speak, breath fire, and have a driving lust for gold and other glistening things (Tolkien, 1986, 85). So associated with linguistic skill are they, in fact, that in the early drafts of *The Silmarillion,* Tolkien says that whoever eats "the heart of a dragon would know all the tongues of Gods or Men, of birds or beasts" (Tolkien, 1986, 85). Tolkien borrows this motif from the Norse legend of the dragon Fáfnir and the hero Sigurd, who, after slaying the dragon, tastes Fáfnir's heart and can understand the speech of birds (Evans, 2007a, 120; Rateliff, 2007b, 623).

In this light, arguing that dragons are *not* rational incarnates is exceedingly difficult. Tolkien's primary dragons—Glaurung and Smaug—possess some of the most intricately crafted personalities of any of his evil creatures. No scholar could seriously claim that these monsters do not possess autonomous will. Tom Shippey describes Smaug as "a cold, wily, superhuman intelligence," while Tolkien himself says Smaug has an "overwhelming personality" (Shippey, 2002, 37); however, to argue that they merit recognition as Children of Ilúvatar is equally nonsensical. Simply categorizing dragons as incarnate Maiar, as has been done with eagles and spiders, is likewise unavailable, because Tolkien never hints at that option for dragons. Of course, this has not stopped critics from making hints on Tolkien's behalf. Paul Kocher and John Rateliff both hypothesize that dragons most likely are "bred" from balrogs, Maiar which Morgoth corrupted into fire demons (Rateliff, 2007b, 542). Numerous problems plague this theory, chiefly that Tolkien does not permit Maiar to produce Maiar, as already demonstreated. Additionally, Maiar do not require time to grow up, yet both Glaurung and Smaug obviously experience extended periods of youthfulness. Glaurung is "young and scarce half-grown" when he first issues from Angband, and Smaug refers to himself as being once "young and tender" (Tolkien, 1977, 116; Tolkien, 1997, 224). In the earliest texts, it is claimed that Morgoth "made" the dragons. Since Morgoth could not create life, this suggests that he bent some pre-existing animal to his will (Tolkien, 1986, 85; Evans, 2007a, 128). Glaurung is name "Father of Dragons" but does not appear in Middle-Earth until well into the First Age, another indicator that he is not merely a primordial Maia in lizard shape (Tolkien, 1977, 151). While it is possible that Morgoth somehow coaxed preexisting Maiar to "possess" a living race of giant lizards, no precedent for such a possession is found in Tolkien's writings, so the idea exists only as a fan-supported theory.

There may be no satisfactory solution here that keeps the dragons grounded within the verisimilitude of the legendarium, but that may largely stem from the fact that Tolkien did not invent the dragons. They pre-date his work, and he may not have felt an ownership over their nature as he did with his own creations. Another solution may be likely, though. Dragons have been spiritually aligned with Satanic evil from time immemorial. St. John, for example, refers to dragons as the Devil incarnate (Revelation 20:2). The record of their intelligence, long life, enormous power, and evil origin far transcends, but entirely agrees with, Tolkien's use of them. Jane Chance argues that Smaug represents the monstrous sin of "venomous Envy" and that Smaug is the Devil-like adversary to the heroic everyman Bilbo (Chance, 2001, 54–5). Tolkien himself acknowledges the moral alignment of the dragon trope in his *Beowulf* essay in which he criticizes Beowulf's dragon as "a personification of malice, greed, destruction..., and of the undiscriminating cruelty of fortune that distinguishes not good or bad" (Tolkien, 1936, 259). The word "personification" is most revealing. Smaug and Glaurung may simply be personifications of evil and envy in the same way that Ungoliant is a personification of Night and Chaos. This is not an attempt to merely allegorize the tale. Instead, as a theory for explaining the sentience of Smaug in metaphysical terms, the idea helps to explain all the various contradictory data. Dragons really are tools for personifying evil incarnate in all of its frustrating and mesmerizing cleverness, and although Tolkien may not have deliberately *meant* for them to function symbolically within the legendarium, it remains that they do. Either way, Tolkien has left us with very few viable alternatives.

Personified Animals

The introduction of personification as a literary figure helps to move us to the final rung of quasi-sentient life within *The Hobbit*. The most important literary distinction to make moving forward in this section is that between anthropomorphism and personification. Talking animals may presented in one of two ways. The author may personify the animal: investing a normal animal with human traits, or the author may anthropomorphize the animal, literally transforming it into copies of humanity in animal shape. The difference between the two lies in how the animal is imaginatively conceived. A personified animal is still an animal; its appearance of humanity is imaginatively projected upon it by the author and the reader (Harmon and Holman, 2003, 377). An anthropomorphized animal functions within its story as a creature more human than animal (Harmon and Holman, 2003, 30–1). It may have a furry face and paws but will act like a human in nearly every way, including wearing clothes, living in a house, and arranging tea parties. Personification is a figure of speech whereas anthropomorphism is a narrative device. As one examines the rest of Tolkien's talking animals, it will be most helpful in deciding whether or not a creature has a soul by asking if Tolkien is personifying a creature or anthropomorphizing it.

John Rateliff makes an excellent point that Tolkien habitually *personified* numerous non-sentient things (the Cats of Betruthel, Caradhras, etc.) but none of these seem to be intentionally mistaken as rationally incarnate beings (Tolkien, 2000, 409; Rateliff, 2013). Tolkien clarifies this distinction himself when he ruminates, "What of talking beasts and birds with reasoning and speech? These have been rather lightly adopted from less 'serious' mythologies, but play a part which cannot now be excised!" (Tolkien, 1997, 117). The animals examined so far—the dragon, the spiders, and the eagles—have all, to one extent or another, been anthropomorphized. By being given human speech, intellect, and will, they have become more than merely animals. They function within the story in this specialized capacity and, therefore, must be rationalized in light of the narrative itself, which is one reason Tolkien went to so much trouble to justify *The Hobbit* with the greater legend. None are anthropomorphized to the extent that, say, Toad and Rat are in Graham's *Wind in the Willows*, nevertheless, real eagles do not wear crowns, real lizards do not horde treasure, and real spiders do not play with their food. It is, in fact, humans who do these things, which is precisely the point of anthropomorphism.

The remaining animals, on the other hand, may generally be placed in the category of normal beasts who have certain elements of humanity projected upon them without the intention that they be understood as anything other than beasts within the story itself. The most obvious example of personified animals are Beorn's livestock. Beorn has somehow trained a wide variety of animals to perform the functions that human servants would normally fill in a wealthy lord's house. His horses meet the company at Beorn's gate, staring with "intelligent faces," departing to "tell" their lord of the dwarves' arrival (Tolkien, 1997, 117). At dinner, Beorn claps his hands and speaks "a queer language like animal noises turned to talk," after which ponies appear, carrying torches in their mouths, while dogs, standing on their hind legs, set up the table, and sheep bring in plates of food on their backs (Tolkien, 1997, 124).[15] While it all seems very out of place from the relative austerity of what precedes and follows these events, Tolkien gives no indication that the reader should understand the animals to be anything other than typical beasts. Beorn has certainly trained them, and perhaps enchanted them, but his dog and pony show does not move into spiritual realms of self-awareness and autonomy. Instead, animals functioning *like* human servants, using sounds *like* speech bear the hallmarks of literary personification.

From an understanding of personification and from its most obvious example in *The Hobbit*, one may come to understand the remaining animal phenomena in the text. Tolkien obeys the principle from Aquinas that "the souls of brutes are produced by some power of the body; whereas the human soul is produced by God" (Aquinas, 1990, I.75.6). Personified animals retain their animal nature, although that nature may be magnified or exaggerated by way of the figure. Much may be made of the illusion of sentience created by the Wargs who partner with the goblins. Tolkien uses words like "plan" and "guard" to describe their actions, in addition to the fact that they speak a "dreadful language" and operate in colleague with the goblins (Tolkien, 1997, 100). This alone may warrant the suspicion that, spiritually, the wargs are more than mere beasts, especially when considering the talking hound Huan, who alone among all the beasts of Middle-earth is granted a *fëa*, and the werewolf Characaroth, who most probably is a Maia incarnate. With such precedents, one might easily begin to build a case for Warg autonomy, saying that they descend from Charcaroth and Draugluin in the same way that the eagles descend from Thorondor. In a footnote to a 1967 draft of a letter, Tolkien does refer to the Wargs as "demonic," which J. E. A. Tyler may have in mind when he describes the Wargs as "phantasms which only assumed real shapes after darkness had fallen" (Tolkien, 2000, 381; Tyler, 1976, 509). Tolkien's use of the word "demonic" certainly aligns the Wargs with evil but is hardly sufficient to claim that the wolves *are* demons in the metaphysical sense. Certainly a thing can be demonic without actually being a demon. To use such arguments to grant the Wargs full sentience denies a fundamental reality of the stories (Rateliff, 2007a, 223). The Wargs never speak the language of humans; they do not act independently; they do not possess autonomous wills or build civilizations. Instead they behave like animals. They gather; they hunt; they are ridden by the goblins, a sign of subservience that would be quite expected if the Wargs were animals and utterly surprising if they were not.[16] The Wargs' behavior, while described using the words of human activity, never transcends the bestial either in *The Hobbit* or in *The Lord of the Rings*, where they reprise their role as evil predators, but not as users of language (Tolkien, 1982a, 356). In short, Tolkien explicitly denies the Wargs all signs that would indicate that they possess souls, indicating that he has simply personified these animals.

In contrast, the thrush of Lonely Mountain presents no real difficulty in terms of sentience. Yes, it is said to speak a "language," but the twittering noises of any bird species may be labeled as "language' as a means of personifying animal sounds. Like the Wargs, the Thrush never utters a word of actual speech. Bard the bowman is said to be able to "understand" the language of the Thrush, but this, too, can be understood as a personifying metaphor. Pet owners, after long exposure to their pet's habits, will come to "understand" the animal without actually being able to translate its utterances into morphology and syntax. Aside from its linguistic prowess, the thrush never behaves as anything other than a thrush. The most one could make of its behavior is to say that it somehow has been magically altered by dwarvish art. Thorin does mention that the thrushes are "a magical breed," and John Rateliff suggests that the Thrush in question may have been placed there by the dwarves as a gatekeeper for precisely the role it plays (Tolkien, 1997, 226; Rateliff, 2007b, 490).[17] But none of that alters the bird's spiritual nature. Its appearance of sapience is just that, an appearance, an illusion caused by Tolkien's decision to personify the actions of a beast. Supporting this claim is the fact that Tolkien never bothers with the Thrush later text nor felt compelled to add a story to *The Silmarillion* explaining how the race of Thrushes got its start. Sometimes, it seems, a bird is just a bird.

The final beasts to be considered for candidacy are the Ravens of Erebor, and they remain somewhat troublesome. This is because Roäc, old Carc's son, actually delivers quite a lengthy speech "in ordinary language" to Bilbo and the dwarves (Tolkien, 1997, 256). He stands in stark contrast to the thrush and the wolves, whose linguistic deficiencies play a crucial role in their final analysis. Here, it appears, is finally a bird species that can make an authentic claim to sapience. Yet equally troublesome is Tolkien's abandonment of talking Ravens in the greater panorama of Middle-earth. This omission is curious since Tolkien's other eccentric speech makers gave him no end of worry; the speech of Roäc, on the other hand, does not appear to trouble him at all. This fact also becomes our chief clue. Tolkien would not have puzzled over the appearance of sentience if he did not believe it were properly there, indicating that once more one is dealing with a personified bird who acts in all other ways like a bird save for its remarkable gift of speech. But even this is explainable within the characteristics of a typical raven. John Rateliff helpfully compares Roäc to real-world ravens and notes that both are intelligent, live a remarkably long time, delight in "bright things" which they carry off to their nests, and are able to mimic speech like parrots (Rateliff, 2007b, 624). Most likely, then, Roäc and Carc have been enchanted by the dwarves of Erebor just as the thrush seems to have been. In Roäc's case, the enchantment merely amplified, or exaggerated, abilities already natural to the species, but nothing beyond that is occurring here.

Conclusion

Ultimately, one can attest to five various methods in which a character in Tolkien's legendarium possesses—or appears to possess—an autonomous soul. The first way is to be granted a *fëa* by Ilúvatar himself and is only available to the four species labeled "Children of Ilúvatar": elves, humans, hobbits, and dwarves. These are the orthodox species, all of whom may be "saved" and can "go to heaven" after their own manner. The second way is for a pre-existent vala or Maia to take the form of one of the Children of Ilúvatar or any of the *kelvar* (animals) or *olvar* (plants), creating the illusion that plants and animals may possess souls. This accounts for powerful beings, both good and evil, such as Morgoth, Melian, Gandalf, and Ungoliant, appearing "in the flesh." In orthodox terms, these beings are Tolkien's angels and demons. Third, and similar to the second, is if an unembodied Maia is sent into a body by a being more powerful than itself. These spirits seem to have less say in their embodiment and so warrant a different rank. This method produces the ents, the first of the great eagles, and, probably, the dragons. Fourth, an indeterminate type of spirit seems to be created when certain incarnate Maiar produce offspring. Maiar cannot produce new Maiar, and, while some certainly produce Children of Ilúvatar who possess their own *fëa,* as with Melian and Lúthien, the offspring of the likes of Ungoliant and Shelob and the great eagle Thorondor are certainly spiritual in nature but definitely do not attain the level of blessing which the Children of Ilúvatar receive. Tolkien never seems to have identified this spiritual hybrid, so its precise name cannot be given. Lastly are animals or inanimate objects who have been enchanted by a being of power who does not possess the ability or right to grant *fëar* but whose skill creates an approximation sufficient to fool the observer. This certainly accounts for Morgoth's "creation" of trolls and for the Ravens and the thrush, with the latter two appearing to have been magically enhanced by the skillful dwarves of Erebor. Within the legendarium, this device accounts for numerous instances of "soul-casting" as well, in which a powerful being imbues an inanimate object with the essence of his or her own *fëa*. Fëanor so invests the Silmarils as does Sauron the One-ring, as does, perhaps, Galadriel with her phial (Rateliff, 2013).

Not listed explicitly above, of course, are the orcs, for depending on one's perspective, they may be said to fit in multiple slots or none. As this author has previously argued, Tolkien never successfully integrated the spiritual nature of the orcs with their function in the narratives, and they remain a standing contradiction, impossible to categorize with complete satisfaction.

Of course, when Tolkien wrote *The Hobbit*, he was not thinking about whether trolls had souls, nor did he trouble himself with the trolls' cosmological origins or what would happen when they die. So the task here is clearly one of redaction. But it is redaction Tolkien himself saw as necessary, and it is important to note how much of that effort was instigated by the composition of *The Hobbit*. Without it neither orcs, trolls, eagles, spiders, nor ents would play the rich, curious roles they do within the tales. Once he saw the need to bring his vision into alignment with orthodoxy—that is, theologically consistent with Roman Catholic doctrine—he was forced to visit these issues and make provisions for those beings whose characters and natures required Providential support.

Epilogue: Peter Jackson's The Hobbit: The Desolation of Smaug

Peter Jackson tacitly waded into this debate with the film *The Hobbit: The Desolation of Smaug*. Jackson's approach to *The Hobbit* was the opposite of Tolkien's. Whereas Tolkien had no idea which shape *The Lord of the Rings* was to take when he wrote, Jackson knew precisely and took great pains to make *The Hobbit* mesh seamlessly with, what for him was, the previous work. This resulted in a darker, more edgy *Hobbit* in which all contradictions and inconsistencies had to be hammered out. The threat of war from Sauron hovers just over the edge of the horizon, and Jackson hints that most of the talking creatures are servants of the Necromancer/Sauron.

But Jackson also greatly reduces their chatty banter, and some of his decisions clearly reflect that he pondered the question of whether or not these creatures possess autonomous sapience. The giant spiders, for example, do not speak until after Bilbo puts on the ring, and even then one only hears the impulsive, animal-like utterances of ravenous bestiality. There are no jokes and certainly no songs. Their dialogue is brief and furious, and the fact that it can only be heard while Bilbo is in the Ring-realm suggests that these are merely animals who have been modified and invested with additional power from Sauron in much the way that the Nazgûl have been.

The Orcs, on the other hand, demonstrate that Jackson does accept the "official" explanation of their origin, but he goes further in depicting Orcs as Children of Ilúvatar who have been broken and twisted. In a scene of surprising emotional power, King Tharanduil and Legolas interrogate a captured Orc, offering it "freedom" if it tells them why the Orcs raided their kingdom. The Orc angrily capitulates and Tharanduil "frees" the Orc's head from its shoulders, demonstrating that Tharanduil—not the orc—is acting with cold cruelty. The implication Jackson appears to make here is that an Orc can choose to do good if it wishes. The Orc's moment of captive isolation humanizes Orcs like no other scene in book or film, and demonstrates where Tolkien could have taken his Orc concept had he been able to fully integrate them into his legendarium.

Jackson makes other clear decisions for each of the other creatures. He firmly depicts the giant animals as only *kelvar*. The giant eagles do not talk, nor do the wargs or the thrush. They are just animals. Smaug, on the other hand, undergoes a notable transformation in the other direction. Jackson lengthens his dialog and his role considerably, inserting a lengthy chase scene and extended monologue with not just Bilbo but with Thorin and the rest of the dwarves. Tellingly, Smaug's first lines exactly explain Jackson's thought process. Smaug immediately detects the presence of the One Ring and orders Bilbo to take it off, who obeys rather quickly (and irrationally). This Smaug consciously serves Sauron, and is sufficiently intimate with his plans to know of the One and its functions. In the fight with the dwarves, Smaug is visually presented very similarly to the Balrog of Moria from *The Fellowship of the Ring*, indicating that Jackson seems to imagine Smaug—and perhaps all other dragons—as Maiar who have taken the shape of great lizards; a sort of Balrog-incarnate.

Notes

1. It was surely not lost on Tolkien the philologist that the very word "animate" implies the existence of an *anima*, or spirit.

2. Curiously, Timaeus frequently refers to the Heavens themselves as "One" and "All," intending them to be understood as both a creative and mathematical unity (Plato, 1989, 31a). This is different from the idea of Ilúvatar as Eru, the One, of course, but the similarity is notable. It is easy to see how Tolkien might have been inspired by Plato but transformed the concept to fit his purpose.

3. On two separate occasions, Tolkien hypothesized that the trolls could either have originally been animals which Morgoth collected and "improved" or they could have been once "primitive human types" (Tolkien, 1993, 409, 414). These seem to be isolated conceptions and are not developed further.

4. See Thompson, *Motif-Index*, F531.6.12.2 and F455.8.1.

5. Cf. Job 12:25; Luke 11:36.

6. Treebeard's account of the Ents' awakening differs sharply, for he says that the elves awakened the Ents and taught them speech (Tolkien, *Two Towers*, 84). But as Tolkien said to Peter Hastings, "there is quite a lot [Treebeard] does not know or understand" (Tolkien, 2000, 190).

7. Lending weight to this theory is the fact that in *The Silmarillion* "Gothmog" refers to the lord of the Balrogs (Tolkien, 1977, 107).

8. Cotlicr argues that, according to Ilúvatar's original plan, orcs were never *meant* to exist, which suggests that the only way to right the wrong of their existence in an Unmarred Arda would be their annihilation.

9. One may respond that the evidence points to the idea that orcs are spawned as full-grown adults, like

insects, but this merely lends support *against* viewing them as sharing a common ancestor with Elves and/Men.

10. Melian the Maiar is able to reproduce, but does not produce another Maia as offspring; Thorondor, the great eagle, is supposed to be a Maia, but Gwaehir and Landroval are not because they are only his *descendants* (Tolkien, 1993, 410).

11. In discussing the potential overuse of the Great Eagles, themselves another example of *dues ex machine*, he warns that they are a "dangerous machine"; he says, "I have used them sparingly, and that is the absolute limit of their credibility or usefulness" (Tolkien, 2000, 271).

12. Christopher Tolkien hints that he came to regret various decisions he made when editing the published form of *The Silmarillion* (Tolkien, 1994, x). Finalizing the origin of the orcs may be one of them.

13. Tolkien permits a rare narrative shift in focus from Frodo's inner thought to Shelob's. While Shelob does not speak out loud, this transfer to her interior dialogue seems to suggest that her mind functions linguistically, if not audibly so.

14. Tolkien was not averse to inter-species cross breeding, as biologically implausible as it maybe. Men and Elves could unite to produce fruitful offspring as could, apparently, men and orcs, from which the Uruk-hai were most likely derived. Such unions do not ever seem to be ratified by Eru Ilúvatar, but they do seem to genuinely produce individuals with *fëar*, which hints at Ilúvatar's tacit acceptance, if not his approval.

15. John Rateliff labels Tolkien's tendency to make *everything* in Middle-Earth talk "The Dolittle Theme," but this label refers more to a linguistic motif rather than an expression of the theological implications of speech (Rateliff, 2007a, 266). Therefore, no detailed study of the theme is offered here since to do so would be off topic.

16. Centaurs might lend a helpful analogue. Their notorious distaste of being ridden suggests that any such creature possessing intellect would disdain similar treatment.

17. Precisely what sort of magic the dwarves might have at their disposal for such a feat is not presented by either Rateliff or Tolkien.

Works Cited

Anderson, Douglas A. 2002. *The Annotated Hobbit*. New York: Houghton Mifflin.
Aquinas, Thomas. 1990. *Summa of the Summa*. Ed. Peter Kreeft. San Francisco: Ignatius.
Atherton, Mark. 2012. *There and Back Again: J.R.R. Tolkien and the Origins of* The Hobbit. New York: I. B. Taurus.
Carpenter, Humphrey. 1979. *The Inklings*. Boston: Houghton Mifflin.
Chance, Jane. 2001. "The King Under the Mountain." *Tolkien's Art: A Mythology for England*. Louisville: University Press of Kentucky.
Cotlier, Emily. 2004. "The Unnatural History of Tolkien's Orcs." http://www.ansereg.com/TheUnnaturalHistoryofTolkiensOrcs.pdf. Accessed June 9 2013.
Dickerson, Matthew. 2007. "Ent." *J.R.R. Tolkien Encyclopedia*. Ed. Michael Drout. New York: Routledge.
Dubray, Charles. 1909. "Faculties of the Soul." *The Catholic Encyclopedia*. Vol. 5. New York: Robert Appleton. http://www.newadvent.org/cathen/05749a.htm. Accessed Aug. 21 2013.
Duriez, Colin. 1992. *The J.R.R. Tolkien Handbook*. Grand Rapids: Baker.
Evans, Jonathan. 2007a. "Dragons." *J.R.R. Tolkien Encyclopedia*. Ed. Michael Drout. New York: Routledge.
_____."Monsters." 2007b. *J.R.R. Tolkien Encyclopedia*. Ed. Michael Drout. New York: Routledge.
Grimm, Jacob. 2004. *Teutonic Mythology: Volume III*. New York: Dover.
Hammond, Wayne G., and Christina Scull. 2005. *The Lord of the Rings: A Reader's Companion*. New York: Houghton Mifflin.
Hardon, John A. 1975. *The Catholic Catechism*. New York: Doubleday.
Harmon, William, and Hugh Holman. 2003. *A Handbook to Literature*, 9th ed. Upper Saddle River, NJ: Prentice Hall.
The Holy Bible (Authorized King James Version). 1611. *E-Sword*. Vers. 10.1.0 Software.
Houghton, John William. 2007. "Ungoliant." *J.R.R. Tolkien Encyclopedia*. Ed. Michael Drout. New York: Routledge.
Lewis, C. S. 1981. *The Silver Chair*. New York: HarperCollins.
Milton, John. 1968. *Paradise Lost and Paradise Regained*. Ed. Christopher Ricks. New York: Signet.
Plato. 1989. *Timaeus. The LOEB Classical Library*. Ed. G. P. Goold. London: Harvard University Press.
Rateliff, John D. 2007a. *The History of* The Hobbit: *Part One*. New York: Houghton Mifflin.
_____. 2007b. *The History of* The Hobbit: *Part Two*. New York: Houghton Mifflin.

_____. 2013. "Tolkien's Problems of Sentience." Email to the author. 16 Aug.
Rearick, Anderson. 2004. "Why Is the Only Good Orc a Dead Orc? The Dark Face of Racism Examined in Tolkien's World." *Modern Fiction Studies* 50:4 (Winter): 861–874.
Shippey, Tom. 2002. *J.R.R. Tolkien: Author of the Century*. New York: Houghton Mifflin.
Tolkien, J.R.R. 1936. "*Beowulf*: The Monsters and the Critics." *Proceedings of the British Academy* 22, 245–295.
_____. 1977. *The Silmarillion*. Ed. Christopher Tolkien. New York: Houghton Mifflin.
_____. 1982a. *The Fellowship of the Ring*. New York: Ballantine.
_____. 1982b. *The Return of the King*. New York: Ballantine.
_____. 1982c. *The Two Towers*. New York: Ballantine.
_____. 1983. *The Book of Lost Tales: Part One*. Ed. Christopher Tolkien. New York: Houghton Mifflin.
_____. 1986. *The Book of Lost Tales: Part Two*. Ed. Christopher Tolkien. New York: Houghton Mifflin.
_____. 1988. *The Return of the Shadow*. Ed. Christopher Tolkien. New York: Houghton Mifflin.
_____. 1993. *Morgoth's Ring: The Later Silmarillion, Part One*. Ed. Christopher Tolkien. New York: Houghton Mifflin.
_____. 1994. *The War of the Jewels*. Ed. Christopher Tolkien. New York: Houghton Mifflin.
_____. 1995. *The Shaping of Middle-Earth*. Ed. Christopher Tolkien. New York: Ballantine.
_____. 1997. *The Hobbit*. Rev. ed. New York: Ballantine.
_____. 2000. *The Letters of J.R.R. Tolkien*. Ed. Humphrey Carpenter. New York: Houghton Mifflin.
Tyler, J. E. A. 1976. *The Tolkien Companion*. New York: St. Martin's.

Seeing in the Dark, Seeing by the Dark
How Bilbo's Invisibility Defined Tolkien's Vision

Michael. A. Wodzak

When Bilbo first found a ring in Gollum's lair under the Misty Mountains, even Tolkien himself was not aware that this was the One Ring. Indeed, in a 1947 letter to Sir Stanley Unwin, he wrote of his having taken the "liberty" of making "Bilbo's Ring the One Ring" (Tolkien, 1981, 122) when he started to write his *Hobbit Sequel*. All that was known at first was that the ring caused invisibility. It was certainly not apparent that, in and of itself, it caused any corruption of the person, and Gollum's behavior, his wanting to eat Mr. Baggins, in the 1937 first edition of *The Hobbit* can be understood in terms of the creature's own innate nastiness, perhaps exacerbated by his having lived for years below ground, preying on goblins. There is, in that edition of the story, no hint of any addictive power the ring has over its bearer, and the only thing that Gollum craves, far from vengeance on Bagginses, as the two part company, is Bilbo's pardon for his not having been able to personally hand over the prize he sees as the hobbit's due.

This is almost, but not quite, the whole truth of the matter. As early as that first edition, Tolkien includes what seems like an aside comment, an apparently trivial piece of descriptive commentary that was not substantially changed in subsequent revisions of the story, and that ultimately would have profound implications for the whole legendarium: "only in the sunlight could you be seen, and then only by your shadow, and that was a faint and shaky sort of shadow" (Anderson, 2002, 129). In large part, this essay is a simple exploration of the implications of this descriptive comment.

In 1955, W. H. Auden, who had written reviews of *The Fellowship of the Ring*, was asked to give a talk on the BBC Third Programme about *The Lord of the Rings*. In April the poet wrote to Tolkien, asking the author if there were any points he would like included in the talk, and if he would supply a little background information on how the book came to be written (Tolkien, 1981, 211). Although it was composed a decade after much of the writing of *The Lord of the Rings* had been completed, and so may possibly betray a certain amount of reconstructed memory, Tolkien's reply sent in June is significant. To begin with, far from affirming any notion that *The Hobbit* had little effect on the legendarium as a whole, Tolkien tells Auden that "it inevitably got drawn into the circumference of the greater construction; and in the event modified it" (Tolkien, 1981, 215). He explains, in some detail, how *The Hobbit* got drawn into that circumference:

> But if you wanted to go on from the end of *The Hobbit* I think the ring would be your inevitable choice as the link. If then you wanted a large tale, the Ring would at once acquire a capital letter; and the Dark Lord would immediately appear [Tolkien, 1981, 216].

We notice that he touches on how the *greater construction* modified both *The Hobbit* and Bilbo's Ring. The ring became the Ring, with all its spiritually corrosive properties, and the immediate consequence was that at least the story of its discovery by Bilbo had to be rewritten. The Ring was now in some sort of possession of its possessor, and it became a source of both immediate and chronic depravity, being a major contributor to Gollum's behavior and even to Bilbo's new found lack of honesty. What could not be re-written, because it was so integral to the original narrative of *The Hobbit*, was the Ring's conferral of invisibility.

Tolkien's letter to Auden is far from the only place where mention is made that *The Hobbit* had implications for the legendarium. Christopher Tolkien makes a similar point in his Foreword to *The Return of the Shadow*: "*The Hobbit* was *drawn into* Middle-earth—and transformed it; but as it stood in 1937 it was not a part of it. Its significance to Middle-earth lies in what it would do" (Tolkien, 1988, 7). Since father and son are both quite clear in asserting that *The Hobbit* somehow modified the legendarium, how the "background mythology ... had to be rewritten as well," (Tolkien, 1981, 216) it is perhaps surprising that neither in his letter to Auden, nor it would seem anywhere else, does Tolkien elaborate just what modifications the book affected, and so we must look to the stories themselves. One might suppose that what *The Hobbit* "would do," how it *modified the greater construction*, was simply to introduce hobbits to Middle Earth, and that that is modification enough. However, that assertion is not really satisfactory; the major role that a small handful of hobbits had in the career and eventual destruction of the Ring notwithstanding, hobbits do not play a significant role within the *larger circumference*. The degree of their relevance is quite quickly inferred from the fact that Treebeard can find them in none of the old lists, even though sundry minor creatures, beavers, hounds, serpents, are remembered (Tolkien, 1965c, 67). Hobbits appear in the later work because the public wanted more stories about hobbits, because Tolkien "love[s] them" (Tolkien, 1981, 121), and because they had value "in putting earth under the feet of 'romance'" (Tolkien, 1981, 215). We should infer that Tolkien's perception and intention was not so much that "mere mundane hobbits" (Tolkien, 1981, 120) were to be the stuff of legend, as that they were the connective tissue that tied the Legend to our world, and specifically to England.

On the other hand, what seems to have had a real and profound effect on the legendarium are Bilbo's Ring itself and its properties. In the same 1947 letter to his publisher, referred to above, Tolkien responds to one of the earliest recorded suggestions that his work is allegorical by telling Unwin that:

> You can make the Ring into an allegory of our own time, if you like: an allegory of the inevitable fate that waits for all attempts to defeat evil power by power. But that is only because all power magical or mechanical does always so work. You cannot write a story about an apparently simple magic ring without that bursting in, if you really take the ring seriously, and make things happen that would happen, if such a thing existed [Tolkien, 1981, 121].

What does Tolkien mean when he talks of taking the ring seriously? What are the things that would happen if such a thing existed? For all that Eä had its mythic archetypes in existing, most notably Northern European legend, the Ring itself became something unique, something completely new. Tolkien was quite adamant that, for example, it was not by any means related to the Ring of the Nibelungs, to which it bore resemblance only in as much as "both rings are round" (Tolkien, 1981, 306). That destruction and despair follow the careers of both rings is purely coincidental. That the Ring of the Nibelungs is problematic has nothing to do with its inherent nature, but rather with the curse that has been placed upon it, and that curse is external to the ring's nature. The One Ring of Sauron, on the other hand, is inherently evil. Although invisibility is a trope in the *Nibelungenlied*, the ring in that story is not its vector, rather Siegfried's cloak is. The One Ring confers invisibility, which is not an uncommon device in folk tales; the invisibility the Ring confers is not quite absolute, which is. However absolute the invisibility they bestow, rings of invisibility in Greek mythology or Arthurian romance are consequential only in so far as they confer certain advantages on their bearers. And yet Tolkien warns that such devices should be taken seriously and that, if such things existed, *things would happen*. For Tolkien, these consequences are apparently ubiquitous. At the philological level, we note that, although there are numerous times when Bilbo's fondness for "visitors" is mentioned in "An Unexpected Party," by the time Bilbo arrives at "The Last Stage" he is using the ring to avoid unwanted "callers," and of course, when he is invisible, it would be impossible for those *callers* to *visit* him. The ring makes its wearers disappear, but once it becomes the Ring, *the Dark Lord would immediately appear*. There are obvious metaphorical implications of this invisibility. In notes to himself, as he was starting the process of creating a sequel to *The Hobbit*, Tolkien realized that "it exacts its penalty. You must either lose it or lose yourself" (Tolkien, 1988, 42). If, however, we are to begin to examine the metaphorical, or the symbolic dimensions of this invisibility, we would do well to first understand the pragmatic realities of such. After all, a metaphor or a symbol is meaningless if it is not tied to something understood at the *mere mundane* level. If an object is invisible, then an observer looking in the direction of the invisible object does not see nothing. On the contrary, what the observer sees is the view on the far side of the invisible object as though the invisible being had not been there at all. Our vision transgresses the invisible, reaching that which is beyond. If it did not, we would notice the invisible being by the nothingness, the absence, we saw in its place. How does the vision of what is beyond the invisible object take place? Light from what is seen either passes through the invisible object as though it were not there, or else its path is bent around the object so that, by the time it reaches the observer, it seems as though there had been nothing intervening between the observer and what was observed. Modern technology has, in recent years, produced small scale cloaking devices that work on precisely this latter principal (Aliev, Gartstein and Baughman, 2011). If, however, we turn our attention not on the invisible object itself, but on its point of view, we have an immediate question: what does an invisible person see? Modern optical theory tells us that what we, visible beings, see are images formed in the brain caused by light striking, and being absorbed by, the retina. However, if light passes through an invisible person as though that person were not there, then no light has been absorbed by the retina; it has simply passed through, and so no image is formed in the brain. On the other hand, if light has been bent around the invisible person, then light never reached the retina at all. The Invisible Man, and the invisible hobbit, ought to be blind. If this rule of Optics were to be followed, then the undeniable convenience Bilbo took advantage of, in his adventure, of being able to disappear at will, would have been paid for by a rather considerable disadvantage; he would have been stumbling in the dark. One could easily find metaphorical meaning in this trade-off, but in considering the hobbit bearers of the Ring, that would be fruitless and irrelevant, and worse, it might quite possibly be misleading: *in the sunlight could you be seen ... by your shadow*. Light is, in fact, impeded by the almost invisible hobbits. That is precisely what causes shadows. Light can, therefore, be absorbed by the retina. Bilbo can see. But how well? How are our metaphors affected?

Literature is full of stories of invisible beings, and those stories almost never incorporate the concomitant induced blindness. J. K. Rowling's Harry Potter can see out from under his cloak, H. G. Wells' Griffin can see out from inside his bandages, and the Lydian shepherd

Gyges can see when he is wearing his ring. Why then, one might quite justifiably ask, should we look for any evidence that Tolkien was aware that invisibility came with any apparent price? There is, it would seem, no direct explicit record of his having been so aware, in that he never wrote nor is he ever recorded as specifically informing anyone that an invisible being is necessarily blind. Perhaps the comments about *shaky shadows* are simply irrelevant. Perhaps trying to use modern understandings of physical phenomena to analyze Bilbo's invisibility is to introduce a "stinking red-herring" (Tolkien, 1981, 60). Absence of evidence, however, should never be viewed as evidence of absence. Moreover, as we shall see, there does exist both quite strong circumstantial evidence to suggest the possibility that Tolkien had such an awareness of optics, and very strong textual evidence to confirm the probability that he was so aware.

Firstly, all of the modern optics included in this discussion, talk of mirrors, of refraction, of propagation of light in straight lines, was, for much of the twentieth century, standard in the physics curriculum of the lower forms of university bound boys in England and so can hardly be thought of as esoteric in Tolkien's context. Secondly, at King Edward's School, the members of the Tea Club and Borrovian Society should not be imagined as listening only to the young Tolkien's recitations of *Beowulf*. In the words of Christopher Wiseman, one of the founders of the T.C.B.S., Tolkien's interests were not seen as unusual since the group "accepted it as yet another instance of the fact that the T.C.B.S itself was odd" (Carpenter, 2000, 54). Humphrey Carpenter describes the T.C.B.S as "well-educated adolescents ... going through a stage of enthusiastic intellectual discovery" (Carpenter, 2000, 54). Tolkien scholars tend, quite naturally, to look to what Tolkien contributed to the discussions of these schoolboys, seeing his nascent interest in Old English and the Norse Sagas, but we have to accept that, as far as the group itself was concerned, each boy brought and shared his own interests with the others. These must, too, have been as accepted as Tolkien's recitations, which were by Wiseman's own account, no more than *yet another instance* of the group's oddity. Wiseman himself, for example, was knowledgeable about the natural sciences, music and mathematics (Carpenter, 2000, 54), and we should be rather more surprised if he did not bring his own interests to the discussions than if he did. Years later, when his "clubbable urge" (Carpenter, 2000, 152) led Tolkien to the Inklings, arguably an adult version of the T.C.B.S., he was again in a social setting where educated men had far-ranging intellectual discussions. Christopher Wiseman's analogue in that coterie might be said to have been the physician R. E. Havard who, on at least one occasion, seems to have set the group the problem of "the Earth as a dynamo." It is interesting to note that, when discussing this issue with C. S. Lewis, a friend notorious for not letting an unfounded claim go unchallenged, Tolkien clearly implies that he is equal to the task of posing Havard problems of a similar nature.

> I sometimes conceive and write other things than verses and romance! And I may come back at you. Indeed, if our beloved and esteemed physician is to pose us with problems of the earth as a dynamo, I can think of other problems as intricate if more petty to present to his notice—if only for the malicious delight of seeing Hugo (if present), slightly heated with alcohol, giving an imitation of the intelligent boy of the class [Tolkien, 1981, 128].

But far more compelling than any circumstantial evidence that Tolkien might have understood the optical implications of invisibility, any suggestion of his guilt of possessing scientific knowledge by association with scientifically-minded friends, is the textual evidence that demonstrates a consistent pattern of not violating the dictum that invisibility causes a loss of eyesight, of vision. Throughout *The Lord of the Rings* Tolkien is quite explicit in describing the point of view of anyone wearing the Ring. Frodo puts on the Ring to escape from Boromir and he sees the world "as through a mist" (Tolkien, 1965a, 416). Sam, thinking his master is dead, and that he must go on to complete the quest by himself, puts on the Ring, but "all things about him now were not dark, but vague" (Tolkien, 1965c, 343), and later, because "he wished to see more clearly" (Tolkien, 1965b, 175), he had to take the Ring off. Tolkien seems, moreover, to be working with these notions of invisibility and blindness almost as soon as he starts working on *The Lord of the Rings*, and we notice that, in an early manuscript fragment, someone who may be Gandalf or perhaps the elf Gildor Inglorion warns Bingo Baggins about ring-wraiths, informing him that "if the Ring overcomes you, you yourself become permanently invisible—and that is a horrible, cold feeling. Everything becomes very faint like grey ghost pictures against the black background in which you live" (Tolkien, 1988, 75). This is an unusually explicit description, and in describing a pre-electrical world where light almost invariably comes from sunshine or flame, where light and warmth are almost inseparable, Tolkien maintains a further physical consistency by including the observation that, if someone is invisible, if light has no effect on their body, then the body would be *horribly cold*. In the final version of *The Fellowship of the Ring*, Gandalf similarly tells Frodo that "a mortal [who often uses a Ring of Power] becomes in the end invisible permanently" (Tolkien, 1965a, 56), and the "nine ... Mortal Men, doomed to die" (Tolkien, 1965a, 59), the Nazgûl, would seem to be completely invisible when, as the Black Riders, they chase the hobbits from Hobbiton to Rivendell. Their black cloaks "give shape to their nothingness" (Tolkien, 1965a, 234). As in the very earliest drafts of the story, they track their prey by scent not sight, and when Merry observes this, asking Strider if they can "*see*," he is told that they "do not see the world of light as we do" (Tolkien, 1965a, 202). Further, we see hints that the Black Riders were perceived from the very beginning as being invisible: Christopher Tolkien points out that, in an early manuscript account of Bingo, Odo and Frodo's leaving the Shire, they are overtaken by a rider on a white horse. The rider turns out to be Gandalf, but initially, he is "wrapped entirely in a great cloak and hood so that only his eyes peered out" (Tolkien, 1988, 48). Tolkien evidently decided that Gandalf, however, should not make an appearance at this point in the story and made corrections to the manuscript. The horse became black, as did the great cloak and hood and, most significantly, *so that only his eyes peered out* became "so that his face was entirely shadowed" (ibid.). From the very first appearance of their clothing, the Black Riders themselves could not be seen.

An acute awareness on Tolkien's part of the physical implications of invisibility would tend to deepen and strengthen the symbolic nature of the hobbits' invisibility. Unfortunately, the thesis that Tolkien had such an optical awareness, or for that matter any serious awareness of optical principles, is seriously challenged by the observation that, in another aspect of optics, he seems to be fundamentally in error; Gollum's eyes, like cats' eyes, glow in the dark. However, when cats' eyes glow, they are reflecting what little ambient light there is, whereas, as Tolkien is quite clear, in both the original published and the final version of "Riddles in the Dark," in the caverns where Bilbo meets Gollum, there is absolute darkness: "it was just as dark [with his eyes open] as with them shut" (Anderson, 2002, 115). If they are in absolute darkness, how do Gollum's eyes glow? Conveniently, Bilbo does have his short sword with him which, since there are goblins nearby shines very faintly, and this is enough for him to see by, although by the time he reaches Gollum's lake it is shining very faintly indeed. In this very faint light, however, Gollum's eyes are simply "big, round [and] pale" (Anderson, 2002, 119). In fact, in the first version of the story, they are not described as glowing at all. It is only in later editions of the story, when the ring has become the Ring, that we see any change in Gollum's eyes; then, when he realizes what Bilbo has in his pocket, they become "two small points of light" (Anderson, 2002, 129), and as the suspicion grows, they "burned with a pale flame" (*ibid.*) that becomes a "green fire" (Anderson, 2002, 130). When Bilbo flees, he accidentally puts on the Ring. He stumbles and falls, but Gollum evidently can see neither him nor his sword, or else the hobbit would have been caught. That the sword is not to be seen implies that the two creatures are once again plunged into total darkness, and yet in that renewed absolute lack of ambient light, Gollum's eyes are like "small green lamps" (Anderson, 2002, 130), and in any case, after Gollum has passed him, Bilbo can see the glow from his eyes as Gollum moves away up the tunnels (*ibid.*). Gollum's eyes, after this episode, never seem to completely lose their incandescence, and years later in the Mines of Moria, Frodo spots "two pale points of light, almost like luminous eyes" (Tolkien, 1965a, 332). Evidently, whether Gollum's eyes glow has little if anything to do with ambient light conditions and far more to do with his own state of mind; the more desperate he is, the more depraved, the hotter the flames seem to burn, and in a particularly poignant episode towards the end of his life, when he comes "within a hair of repentance" (Tolkien, 1981, 110), he returns from an errand of his own to find Frodo and Sam asleep on the stairs of Cirith Ungol:

> A strange expression passed over his lean hungry face. The gleam faded from his eyes and they went dim and grey, old and tired. A spasm of pain seemed to twist him, and he turned away, peering back up towards the pass, shaking his head, as if engaged in some interior debate. Then he came back, and slowly putting out a trembling hand, very cautiously he touched Frodo's knee—but almost the touch was a caress. For a fleeting moment, could one of the sleepers have seen him, they would have thought that they beheld an old weary hobbit, shrunken by the years that had carried him far beyond his time, beyond friends and kin, and the fields and streams of youth, an old starved pitiable thing [Tolkien, 1965c, 324].

Friends and kin, fields and streams, are things hobbits treasure. An interior debate—whether or not to sacrifice the hobbits to Shelob—speaks of at least some moral scruples. Reaching out to caress the sleeping Frodo, reciprocating the only kindness he has been shown in centuries, all of these things show Gollum perhaps at his saddest, but also at his least depraved, and at this point, the gleam fades from his eyes. At his touch, however, Frodo stirs, waking Sam who is angered that Gollum is "pawing at" his master (Tolkien, 1965c, 324). Sam's reaction breaks the spell. Gollum loses his hobbit identity and "a green glint flickered under his heavy lids" (Tolkien, 1965c, 324). He remains resentful of Sam, "and the green glint did not leave his eyes" (ibid.). Tolkien quite explicitly answers any lingering suspicions that Gollum's eyes merely shine with feline reflection when he describes them outside the gates of Minas Morgul: "his eyes shone with a green-white light, reflecting the noisome Morgul-sheen perhaps, or kindled by some answering mood within" (Tolkien, 1965c, 314).

Douglas Anderson, in his annotations to *The Hobbit,* points out that Gollum has an antecedent in Tolkien's work. In the unpublished *Tales and Songs of Bimble Bay*, written in the 1920s, is the poem "Glip" (Anderson, 2002, 119). Glip, like Gollum, is a small, slimy creature with a penchant for gnawing bones. Moreover, like Gollum, Glip is cannibalistic, lives in a cavern close to water, and in the dark, has luminous green eyes. Tolkien himself, on the other hand, acknowledges *Beowulf* as influential on his work (Tolkien, 1981, 31), and we notice that Grendel too is a cannibalistic dweller in a cavern by water. Moreover, the Beowulf poet describes Grendel:

> him of éagumstód
> liggegelícost   léohtunfaéger·   (lines 726–27)

As he raids Heorot in the darkness, his eyes glow with an "unfair light." That there is some sort of more than alliterative descent from Grendel to Glip to Gollum is apparent. The question that concerns us at the moment is why, when he first appeared under the mountains, Gollum's eyes, unlike those of his ancestors, did not glow in the dark. Why is it that Gollum's eyes do not exhibit their genetic gleam until the ring becomes the Ring?

That Tolkien understands that the two phenomena of eyes reflecting ambient light and eyes glowing with internal light are different is evidenced in "Out of the Frying-Pan into the Fire." Not only can Gandalf's eyes be seen "gleaming in the moon as he peeped out" (Anderson, 2002, 146) from his hiding place in the pine tree, but also, when he sets light to the wolves and surrounding forest, their eyes reflect the fire "as red and fierce as the flames" (Anderson, 2002, 151). He seems, when he describes Gollum's eyes, not so much to be making a mistake in modern optical theory as to be laying modern optics aside completely and taking up ideas from the Middle Ages. Medieval scholasticism, following the views of the Greek philosophers, essentially held a pair of opposing views on how the eye worked. The Arabic scientists, on whom the medieval sholars relied to transmit Greek learning, retained everything they could from the earlier culture, but because of the destruction of the Library at Alexandria, that information was and remains fragmentary. What little evidence remains seems to suggest that it was Aristotle who was the first proponent of the optical theory of intromission, which held that light from an observed object hits the eye of the observer, causing images to be formed in the brain. This is, in essence, our modern theory of how the eye works and is the ultimate source of our argument that invisibility leads to blindness. On the other hand, philosophers such as Euclid argued that light appears to travel in straight lines, and so it would be unreasonable to expect that inanimate, insentient objects would know where an observer was and to be able to aim light towards the eyes of that observer. The sentient viewer, surely, must be doing something to direct the image of an object to the eye. Such philosophers adhered to the theory of extramission, which held that the eye sent out its own ray of light, which grasped an image of the object and delivered it to the mind of the observer. That Gollum's eyes emit light would tend to suggest that, at least some of the time, they work by extramission. Some adherents to the theory of extramission, most notably Galen, held that the image grasped was actually a material thing, the *eidolon*, a thin film of atoms, which left the surface of the observed object, traveled along the ray of light sent out by the eye, and through the optic nerve to be reformed as a simulacrum in the soul of the observer. In this way, the eyes of Grendel, Glip and Gollum have consumed something of their victims even before their mouths have. Someone who uses extramission does not passively receive images, as one does when seeing intromissively; something rather more active, and indeed acquisitive, is happening when the observer reaches out for an image. Moreover, in a practical and hence possibly metaphorical sense, extramission *imposes* the vision of the observer on the observed. It is not known where the theory of extramission originated, but the earliest description of eyes working in this way is to be found in a verse by the pre–Socratic philosopher Empedocles, who described the eye as being made of all four Elements, Earth, Water, Air and Fire. The Fire, which Empedocles explains is lit by Aphrodite, is the source of the light sent out by extramissive eyes. It is tangentially interesting to note the relationship between Aphrodite, the goddess of female sexuality, and Inanna, her Mesopotamian counterpart. In some traditions Inanna is served by Lilith; in others, as in the Sumerian story of the Hullupu tree, Lilith opposes Inanna. Nevertheless, the relationship between Inanna and Lilith is frequent and ancient. In Jewish folklore, Lilith was the first wife of Adam, the father of Cain, and when she left Adam, she became the Mother of Monsters, and so she plays the same role that Cain, the ancestor of Grendel, whose eyes burn with an *unfair light*, plays in *Beowulf.* The linking of Lilith with Adam is not, however, part of ancient mythology. Rather, it originates in the *Alphabet of Ben Sira,* dating from late in the first millennium, roughly contemporary with the writing of *Beowulf.* More significant than the perhaps tenuous link between Aphrodite and Grendel is the fact that, in "Of the Valar" we are told that the three chief male Valar—Manwë, Ulmo and Aulë—are patrons of Air, Water and Earth respectively (Tolkien, 1977, 16–18), whereas "Of the Enemies" links Melkor with Fire (Tolkien, 1977, 23).

In fact, Gollum is not the only character in Middle Earth with eyes that work extramissively. Extramission can be grasping, and it can be seen as imposing the vision of the viewer on the observed object, and so we should not be surprised to realize that Tolkien's dragons, who are acquisitive and have preternatural powers of persuasion, have eyes that are extramissive. Smaug's eyes are described this way in the scene where Bilbo returns to the dragon's lair after having stolen a cup from the piles of treasure:

> [Bilbo] was just about to step out on to the floor when he caught a sudden thin and piercing ray of red from under the drooping lid of Smaug's left eye.... Whenever Smaug's roving eye, seeking for him in the shadows, flashed across him, he trembled, and an unaccountable desire seized hold of him to rush out and reveal himself and tell all the truth to Smaug.... "Revenge!" [Smaug] snorted, and the light of his eyes lit the hall from floor to ceiling like scarlet lightening [Anderson, 2002, 278, 280].

Not only is the gaze of Smaug physically extramissive, reaching out for the hobbit in the dark, but it is also metaphorically so; it imposes a certain viewpoint, certain desires on Bilbo, the desire, in fact, to reveal himself. It grasps, and Bilbo is *seized*. Glaurung, Smaug's mythic ancestor, has eyes with very similar attributes to Smaug's, and when he and Túrin Turambar meet at the gates of Nargothrond, he attacks the warrior with his eyes, immobilizing him. Whilst he is held in the dragon's gaze, the monster's vision is imposed on Túrin, and he sees "himself as in a mirror misshapen by malice, and loathed what he saw" (Tolkien, 2007, 179). Just as Empedocles' eyes were kindled by Aphrodite, so too are Túrin's kindled by the fire-breathing dragon, and he is now able to see only what Glaurung's master Melkor wants him to see. If this is an accurate interpretation of what is happening, then the question of why Gollum's eyes did not glow in the first edition of *The Hobbit* is quite easily answered by the recognition that they simply had not been lit yet, that it would take some sort of supernatural agency to light such a flame, and that in Gollum's case, the spark emanated from the Ring. Having imposed the vision of Melkor on Túrin, the dragon releases him, but Túrin remains "blind, groping ... in a dark mist of Morgoth" (Tolkien, 2007, 255), until much later when he slays Glaurung and finally discovers that his blindness, or corrupted vision, has led him to marry his sister and to conceive a child with her. But even as the dragon lay dying, "Glaurung stirred and opened his baleful eyes and looked upon Turambar with such malice that it seemed to him that he was smitten by an arrow" (Tolkien, 2007, 239).

Sometimes, the medieval theory of extramission was explained not in terms of a ray of light leaving the eye, but by a column of pressurized air, *pneuma* or breath, which physically felt for the observed object. Shelob's multi-faceted eyes are described using both species of extramission. Quite apart from glittering in the light of Galadriel's phial, we are told that they emit something else, and that "behind the glitter a pale deadly fire began steadily to glow within, a flame kindled in some deep pit of evil thought" (Tolkien, 1965c, 329). More than this however, Sam recognizes that something is lurking even before they encounter Shelob; he could "feel something looking at [him and Frodo]" (Tolkien, 1965c, 328). A pressurized column of air emitted in order to feel for images must, in its own turn, be palpable. In this way, Shelob's eyes epitomize two different mechanisms by which the medieval scholars believed extramission to work.

Earlier it was said that the Nazgûl were both invisible and blind. This claim seems to be contradicted on the Pelennor Fields when the Witch King of Angmar is met by Éowyn and Merry, who are defending the dying Théoden.

> A crown of steel he bore, but between rim and robe naught was there to see, save only a deadly gleam of eyes: the Lord of the Nazgûl. ...[Éowyn] raised her shield against the horror of her enemy's eyes...[Merry] hardly dared to move, dreading lest the deadly eyes should fall on him.... He bent over [Éowyn] like a cloud, and his eyes glittered [Tolkien, 1965b, 115].

The exception, however, really does prove the rule in this instance; because his eyes are now visible, there is no *a priori* reason that he should be blind. The reason his once invisible and sightless eyes are now visible and can apparently see, will be addressed, but for the moment, we will simply note that he is using those eyes in a very extramissive way, not just to see his intended victims but also to cow and attack them. It is repeated that the eyes are *deadly*. This is Merry's second encounter with Nazgûl. After his first encounter, Aragorn tells him that what ails him is the *Black Breath* (Tolkien, 1965a, 186); after the second, Aragorn treats him, as just earlier he had treated both Faramir and Éowyn, with *athelas*. We are reminded, as was the herb-master at the Houses of Healing, that *athelas* is the specific remedy for exactly the same ill the young hobbit was afflicted with at Bree (Tolkien, 1965b, 141). The encounter on the Pelennor Fields is quite detailed, and yet it makes absolutely no mention of the Witch King breathing on his victims. What is quite explicitly spoken of is how his eyes are deadly. If, on the other hand, we understand his eyes to work by extramission, and in this instance to employ *pneuma*, indeed Black Breath, then the apparent narrative inconsistency is completely removed.

The gaze of Sauron also seems to be on occasion luminous and on occasion palpable. The shields of Sauron's orcs, even the backs of the flies in Mordor, are blazoned with a red eye, an image of the "flame of red, the flicker of a piercing Eye" (Tolkien, 1965b, 220) looking out from the topmost tower of Barad-dûr, and in the mirror of Galadriel, Frodo sees the Eye "rimmed with fire" (Tolkien, 1965a, 379). When Frodo is almost discovered by Sauron on Amon Hen, however, he experiences the enemy's Eye in ways that are more mechanical than optical. The emphatic italics below are mine:

> suddenly [Frodo] *felt* the Eye. There was an eye in the Dark Tower that did not sleep. He knew that it had become aware of his gaze. A fierce eager will was there. It *leaped* towards him; almost *like a finger he felt* it, searching for him. Very soon it would *nail him down*, know just exactly where he was. Amon Lhaw it *touched*. It glanced upon Tol Brandir—he threw himself from the seat, crouching, covering his head with his grey hood... The black shadow seemed to pass *like an arm* above him; it *missed* Amon Hen and *groped* out west, and faded [Tolkien, 1965a, 417].

Even the word *glance* has its etymological origins in physical movement, and the first definition given for the word in the *Complete Oxford English Dictionary*, "a swift oblique movement or impact," comes from the French *glacier*, to slip, which became in fifteenth-century English *glacen*, to strike a passing blow. It is easy to imagine how the visual meaning of *glance* could arrive as a metaphor from the mechanical meaning, and the link is easier to make in light of the word's similarity to the Middle English *glenten*, to look askance, cognate with the modern word *glint*, which Gollum does and which his eyes possess. If, moreover, as seems very unlikely, Tolkien was unaware of those origins, the word carries an obvious double meaning for anyone familiar with the game of cricket, even for someone who is not good at the game (Tolkien, 1981, 257), where a *leg glance* is a standard batsman's stroke.

Just as Sauron's master Melkor imposed his vision on both Túrin, and earlier in the story on his father Húrin, so too does Sauron impose his vision on Denethor and Saruman by means of the *palantíri*, the *seeing* stones. Vision is perilous, and the powerful can impose corrupted vision. But it should not be concluded that what is perilous is necessarily evil. It is easy to understand that, for the Catholic Tolkien, the wizards, the *Istari*, being *Maiar*, were of an order of angels, and he makes this viewpoint explicit: "they came out of the Far West and were messengers" (Tolkien, 1965b, 365). The classical Greek for *messenger*, of course, is άγελος, or, in Latin, *angelus*. But whether or not the Istari were intended to be viewed in a religious way, in a pragmatic sense they were *messengers*, "sent to contest the power of Sauron, and to unite all those who had the will to resist him, but they were forbidden to match his power with power, or to seek to dominate Elves or Men by force and fear" (ibid.). It is quite clear that the wizards are sent to bring a message, to present a vision, not to impose it, which Sauron has the *power* to do, and which power they must not match. They are sent to persuade, to counsel, not to coerce. Vision is a perilous gift, the more perilous the wider and clearer the vision is. Tolkien often symbolizes this peril with the image of the Watcher in the Tower. Sauron is an archetypical watcher in a tower. His vigilance is nothing but evil, a curse to both himself and those on whom he turns his attention. Saruman and Denethor are watchers in towers. They both possess a *palantir*, which allows them to see further than most, and this leads to their downfall. Númenor was lost beneath the Sea because, looking out from the summit of Meneltarma, the Númenoreans beheld the Undying Lands, which in envy they attacked. Húrin was punished by Melkor with the torture of being chained to a "chair of stone upon a high place of Thangorodrim" (Tolkien, 2007, 65), and having to see the world as Melkor saw it, the ultimate imposition of vision. The Witch King threatens Éowyn that he will not slay her—rather he will take the Eorling to the far worse torture waiting in "the houses of lamentation, beyond all darkness, where thy flesh shall be devoured, and thy shriveled mind be left naked to the Lidless Eye" (Tolkien, 1965b, 116). Christopher Tolkien suggests that the original version of this scene, which has an almost identical speech, except that it does not mention the *Lidless Eye*, was written quite early (Tolkien, 2000, 366). Certainly the father makes reference to the scene in letters the son received whilst he was stationed in South Africa, (Tolkien, 1981, 79) a time when we know the author was concentrating more on what would become *The Two Towers* than on what would later be titled *The Return of the King*, and the fact that Merry does not appear in that earlier version of the scene suggests that it might even have been written before Tolkien recounted how, early in his journey, when Tom Bombadil rescued him from the barrow, the young hobbit became armed with the leaf-bladed sword with which he would eventually stab the Nazgûl. The reference to the Lidless Eye, however, is certainly a later addition, and Tolkien finishes the Nazgûl's threat, in the earlier written scene simply with "thy shriveled mind be left naked" (Tolkien, 2000, 365). The final version of the scene may even have been written as late as 1946, since Tolkien seems to have left off work on his *Hobbit Sequel* for much of 1945. If this is the case, as well as having experienced firsthand the physical horrors of the trenches in the First World War, Tolkien might well have been, as he wrote of the Lidless Eye, aware of the atrocities committed in the concentration camps of the Nazis. His letters clearly illustrate his distress over the refugee lines leaving Germany and particularly the gloating of some of his compatriots over those lines (Tolkien, 1981, 111), and so we know he took an emotional interest in current events. If *The Lord of the Rings* was really an allegory of either the First or the Second World War, one might expect the Witch King to threaten Éowyn with unbearable but mundane torture, all the more horrific because, in the mid-twentieth century it could be viewed as so mundane. But for Tolkien, far worse than the war of attrition in which he took part, maybe worse even than the Holocaust, both of which might be seen to color his work, is the imposition of an evil and corrupted vision, to be left *naked to the Lidless Eye*.

Vision can be dangerous and painful, but that does not mean it is inherently evil. The Númenoreans, after all, were given their view of the Undying Lands as a blessing, a reward for their sufferings in Middle Earth, and such a reward must surely be inherently good, although this reward was eventually corrupted by Sauron. Galadriel, in fact, tells Frodo that vision is "good and perilous" (Tolkien, 1965a, 378), and it is evident that, for Tolkien, vision is inherently not just good, but even holy. If, however, we are to posit that Tolkien holds the position that vision is good but also perilous, we must ask what kind of vision he prefers and where he sees the perils. Tolkien's friend C. S. Lewis often warned of the threat of what he termed the "materialist menace," a view that science has an answer for every question, that God is not only irrelevant but non-existent, and that there is no such thing as a spiritual dimension to life. Tolkien's staunch Catholicism is well attested, and so he would have found Lewis' menace antithetical to his faith, but, in terms of addressing what kind of vision Tolkien favored, holding Faith and Science in antithesis is too simplistic. Tolkien himself had a far more subtle and complex understanding of the situation. He did not believe that science and religion were in opposition, and evidently saw science in a rather more positive light than might be understood to be the case, going so far as to say the following about the undeniably benevolent Tom Bombadil:

> But I kept him in, and as he was, because he represents certain things otherwise left out. I do not mean him to be an allegory—or I should not have given him so particular, individual, and ridiculous a name—but "allegory" is the only mode of exhibiting certain functions: he is then an "allegory," or an exemplar, a particular embodying of pure (real) natural science, the spirit that desires knowledge of other things, their history and nature, because they are "other" and wholly independent of the enquiring mind, a spirit coeval with the rational mind, and entirely unconcerned with "doing" anything with the knowledge [Tolkien, 1981, 192].

As if to contradict his own assertion that Tom Bombadil represents certain things *otherwise left out,* Tolkien also has the following to say about the Elves:

> The Elves represent, as it were, the artistic, aesthetic, and purely scientific aspects of the Humane nature raised to a higher level than is actually seen in Men. That is: they have a devoted love of the physical world, and a desire to observe and understand it for its own sake [Tolkien, 1981, 236].

To be sure, the *purely scientific* nature of the Elves is not always immediately apparent, but then perhaps, neither is that of Tom Bombadil. Elrond, certainly, displays more attributes of the natural scientist in *The Hobbit* than he does in *The Lord of the Rings*, since it is he who is able to recognize the nature of Thorin's map and of the runes written on it, and he who is able to predict when the secret way into the Lonely Mountain will be accessible. Analysis, and prediction based on that analysis, are inherently scientific actions, and Tolkien's letters make it apparent that he personally has no antipathy towards science as such. If Tolkien is not opposed to science, can it be argued that he is opposed, rather, to technology? It would be easy to jump to that conclusion since, if Elves represent, albeit imperfectly, the Good, then surely Goblins represent Evil, and Goblins are described as those for whom "wheels and engines and explosions always delighted" (Anderson, 2002, 109). However, the conclusion that Tolkien has an inherent opposition to technology also would appear to be rather too simplistic:

> The particular "desire" of the Eregion Elves—an "allegory" if you like of a love of machinery, and technical devices—is also symbolised by their special friendship with the Dwarves of Moria. I should regard them as no more wicked or foolish (but in much the same peril) as Catholics engaged in certain kinds of physical research (e.g. those producing, if only as by-products, poisonous gases and explosives.) [Tolkien, 1981, 190].

Once again, the pursuit of technology is not evil in and of itself, but rather *perilous*, and those who are the most skilled in craft (Aulë, Saruman, the Dwarves, to list only a few) are often those most in peril. Even explosions are not all bad, and we recall the hobbits' particular enjoyment of fireworks. The menace, then, for Tolkien, is neither a love of science nor even of technology, although both loves are perilous; it is a love of a particularly corrupted vision of science. What Tolkien does admit a dislike of is "scientification," as when Morton Zimmerman referred to *Lembas* as "food concentrate" (Tolkien, 1981, 274), putting an inappropriate modern, scientific and technological gloss on something that the author intended as rather more miraculous. What Tolkien is objecting to is an imposition of a corrupted vision.

The Watcher in the Tower is a particularly prevalent image in Tolkien's work, and in *Beowulf: The Monster and the Critics*, he makes it apparent that, in its uncorrupted form, the image is iconic in the religious sense of the word. Tolkien tells the parable of a man who has inherited land strewn with rocks that had belonged to earlier buildings. He uses the rocks to build a tower so that he can look out at the sea. Later people discover that the stones contain ancient carvings and so, oblivious to the purpose of the tower, they tear it down to examine the carvings. Tolkien is quite clear that he sees destruction for the sake of research as folly. All the protagonists of the parable, the watcher in the tower and the destructive researchers are, however, seeking a vision. We are left in no confusion as to which vision, and which pursuit, Tolkien favors: "he that breaks a thing to find out what it is has left the path of wisdom" (Tolkien, 1965a, 272).

It is Gandalf, of course, who tries to tell Saruman that he has left the *path of wisdom*, the way of the wizards, and his abandonment of white robes is deeply emblematic.

> I looked then and saw that his robes, which had seemed white were not so, but were woven of all colours, and if he moved they shimmered and changed hue so that the eye was bewildered.... "White!" he sneered "it serves as a beginning. White cloth may be dyed. The white page can be overwritten; and the white light can be broken" [Tolkien, 1965a, 272].

The Istari were forbidden to seek to dominate Elves or Men by force, and yet this is precisely what Saruman attempts to do, going so far as to imprison one of his own Order. They were sent as messengers, and yet Saruman's very robes *bewilder*. One cannot deliver a message if one sets out to confuse. In fact, Saruman uses the power to enchant and enthrall his listeners, matching Sauron's power to impose a false view of reality, a power he is expressly forbidden to match. He overwrites the white page, dyes the white cloth, echoing Melkor's imposition of his own theme on Eru's. Although he may have begun with a "desire of mastery," (Tolkien, 1977, 300), however, Saruman's ultimate corruption does not originate with himself. Tolkien leaves subtle clues, using more medieval optical theory, that Saruman is merely the mirror of Sauron's corruption. The white light that should be reflected off Saruman's robes has been *broken*; to use the correct optical term, it has been refracted. Tolkien evidently understands the process of refraction and uses precisely that term in his poem *Mythopoeia*, casting in that instance, in lines 61 and 62, Man as the refractor, the splinterer of white light (Tolkien, 1989, 99). The fact that he correctly uses terms from science, and in a poetic voice, speaks to a level of linguistic comfort, possibly born of familiarity, underscoring the conclusion that Tolkien's objection to *scientification* is not an objection to things scientific as such, nor to scientific terminology, but rather to the misapplication of such terms. The rainbow is arguably the most immediate example of the spectrum refracted from white light, and the medieval understanding of how a rainbow is formed is significant. It was understood, then as now, that light travelling through falling water could be broken. What was not understood so well was why a rainbow is always in front of an observer when the sun is behind. In a letter from the very beginning of 1944 to his son Christopher, Tolkien uses a very similar image to that of the rainbow, although one apparently involving unrefracted light, to explain his understanding of the concept of a guardian angel. In that image God, like the sun, is behind a person but also, like the rainbow, in front. The angel, like the sun's rays, is an intermediary (Tolkien, 1981, 66). The other physical mystery of the rainbow was its shape, a sequence of circular arcs. The Scholastics accepted Aristotle's explanation of both phenomena, which was that the sky acted as a mirror. The rain in front of the sun broke up the sunlight, but the rainbow was seen only because that light was reflected towards an observer by the sky in front of her. The fact that the sky mirror was hemispherical caused the bands of the rainbow to be circular. What is remarkable is that, from the time Gandalf and his companions arrive at Edoras until "The Scouring of the Shire," Tolkien maintains the metaphor of Saruman as the kind of hemispherical mirror that would reflect a rainbow splintered by another agency. The sky mirror is concave, and concave mirrors have certain optical properties that Saruman also exhibits. If an observer is very close to a concave mirror, the image formed is magnified. This is why modern cosmetic and shaving mirrors are always concave. The person most closely influenced by Saruman would seem to be Gríma Wormtongue, who starts by wanting to possess another human being, Éowyn, desiring her as a "price" (Tolkien, 1965c, 124). This objectification of his fellows is magnified under Saruman's influence to such a gross extent that, by the end of the story, it is at least very strongly suggested that, like Gollum, he has become a cannibal (Tolkien, 1965b, 299). As the observer moves further away from the concave mirror, there comes a point where the image is completely twisted and confused, bearing little likeness to the original, and this is precisely how we first encounter Théoden, bent in both body and mind under Saruman's influence. Removed from the fallen wizard's influence, both Théoden's mind and his body soon straighten. Finally, if the observer moves still further away from the mirror, the image seen is inverted, and so it is no coincidence that, on hearing the voice of Saruman, Gimli declares "the words of this wizard stand on their heads" (Tolkien, 1965c, 184).

Evidently at some time during 1944 or 1945 Tolkien and C. S. Lewis were in conversation about reflected light. First, in a letter dated early November of 1944 to his son Christopher, Tolkien uses the image of a dust mote in a church, suspended in a beam of sunlight to illustrate, as he had earlier in the year, his conception of guardian angels as metaphorically akin to those beams. In July of 1945, Lewis published "Meditation in a Toolshed," which starts with an almost identical image, this time of many dust motes in the beam of light, which enters through a gap at the top of a doorway of a shed. Lewis uses the image to differentiate between different ways of perceiving a phenomenon, either looking "at" it from the outside, as when looking at the beam of light, or looking "along it" from the inside, as when standing in the beam and seeing the trees in the garden outside the shed. Tolkien's description is marginally more optically accurate than that of Lewis, in as much as Lewis is not really able to look at the beam, only the dust in the beam. If there were nothing inside a ray of light to deflect it towards our eyes, we would never see the ray. On the other hand, Tolkien does not claim to see the sunbeam, only to acknowledge that it exists and to concentrate on the dust mote it illuminates and which, in turn, reveals its presence. Nevertheless, a combined vision of both Lewis' and Tolkien's understandings of the dust mote reveals important aspects of the Ring's nature.

Tolkien warned that, when the Ring acquired a capital letter, *the Dark Lord would immediately appear.* When Frodo puts on the Ring at Weathertop, he can see the Riders, and they can see him. When he flees from Boromir to Amon Hen, he is almost discovered by the searching Eye of Sauron except that he hears Gandalf's voice telling him to take the Ring off. The Ring would seem to make its wearer invisible and nearly blind in the normal senses of the words, and yet visible and sighted in some other sense. Apparently, there is some other kind of optics at play, some other kind of light by which one sees and is seen. We should not imagine that what Tolkien envisions is something as prosaic as a different *wavelength* of light. Quite apart from such a conception being a *scientification* that the author himself would surely not have approved of, it seems more plausible that what Tolkien intended is something more in the nature of corrupted light. If the nature of the Ring is to initiate vision with corrupted light, then that vision must, *a fortiori*, be corrupted vision, and we have seen that this is an evil Tolkien is particularly concerned with, illustrating it throughout the legendarium. The Ring's illumination of corrupted vision would explain why it is completely powerless where Tom Bombadil is concerned. His nature is that of a pure scientist, simply to observe the natural world as it is, and it is not in that nature for any corruption of vision to take hold, or even to be relevant. If we imagine the wearer of the Ring as a dust mote, then the view from *inside*, looking *along* the beam, as Lewis describes, is of Sauron. On the other hand, the view from *outside*, looking *at* the beam, will be of nothing. Tolkien recognizes in his letter to his son that, unless its source is directly faced, the light itself is never seen except when it is scattered by objects in its path. But the Ring does not work by ordinary light; its light is corrupted, grasping and intentional. It is not wastefully scattered. Rather it brings the image of its object back to the observer. *One ring to find them [,] and in the darkness bind them* (Tolkien, 1965a, 59). Both beam and mote are invisible. In his description, Tolkien uses the dust mote in the ray of sunshine to describe a person bathed in God's love. The sun is God, the dust is the person, and the sunbeam, as before, is the person's guardian angel, "not a thing interposed between God and the creature, but God's very attention itself, personalised. And I do not mean 'personified'" (Tolkien, 1981, 99). In the corrupted image, the Ring might well be understood as "Sauron's very attention personalised" and, being a person having something of a will of its own, as of course it does, as we first discover when Gandalf tells Frodo that Bilbo found the Ring not by accident, but "the Ring itself ... decided things ... [It was] trying to get back to its master ... when [he] was awake once more and sending out his dark thought" (Tolkien, 1965a, 65). In Tolkien's uncorrupted vision, however, the mote is "held and lit" (Tolkien, 1981, 99) by the Light, the personalization of God's attention, as clearly are all the other "millions of motes" (*ibid*). Surely, for the devoutly Catholic Tolkien, the love and attention of God is directed at the *millions of motes*, and that love and attention must, in some small measure adhere, regardless of how an individual mote receives it. It is, perhaps, significant that it is precisely and only sunlight that mitigates the effects of the Ring. Some sunlight is absorbed by the body, even a body wearing the Ring, even if all the sign of its absorption is a small and shaky shadow. Such a body might feel *horribly cold*, but surely not absolutely cold.

When Aulë made the dwarves, Eru pointed out that they would have had no life of their own, no independent being, unless He bestowed it. Otherwise, they would move only how and when Aulë willed. Initially, the dwarves were only *personalized* when they had Aulë's attention, just as the Ring is personalized when Sauron sends out his dark thought. Eru's primary creations, the Ainur, have the ability to "make" but not to create independent life. Eru does not create evil beings, but He does create beings with free will, and such beings may choose the wrong path, as Melkor does. Consequently, Eä is peopled with monsters, demons and villains. Typically, these are creatures given free will but who were led astray, or else corrupted by Melkor or later by his lieutenant Sauron. The Ainur do not have the power to create, but evil things can be made or bred in mockery of the good. Aulë is quick to assure Eru that he did not make the dwarves in mockery of any of creation, but rather out of love, whereas Melkor did breed the orcs in mockery of the elves, and Treebeard informs Merry and Pippin that trolls were "counterfeits, made in mockery of the ents" (Tolkien, 1965c, 89). Might it not be possible that, at some point during or before the First Age, some sort of corrupted light was made in mockery of natural light? If so, then we might expect that light to be acquisitive and to "pervert ... to [Melkor's] own will all that he would use" (Tolkien, 1977, 31). It would be the light of "a liar without shame"(*ibid*). In "Of the Enemies," we are told that Melkor "began with the desire of Light, but ... descended ... into Darkness"(*ibid*). There are obvious Christian allusions in casting Melkor as beginning with a *desire of Light*, recalling Lucifer, and the phrases *liar without shame*, and descending *into Darkness*, call to mind two traditional epithets of Satan, The Prince of Lies and The Prince of Darkness. But Tolkien seems to be doing something more than simply equating Melkor, his "Diabolus" (Tolkien, 1981, 195) with Satan. He is commenting on what he sees as the prime source of evil—corrupted vision, deceit, bewilderment. From this all other evils flow. In a letter describing the origins of the name *Mirkwood*, Tolkien points out that "mirce ... survives in poetry ... with the sense 'murky' wicked, hellish" (Tolkien, 1981, 369), and that it derives from the stem *merkw-, which means something like "dark." We notice that Melkor has a name that contains the *merkw-stem with a single lambdacism, but we pay particular attention to the fact that Tolkien recognizes a connection between the murky, the visually less than clear, and the hellish. Melkor takes Ungoliant to destroy the Two Trees. To get to their target unseen, Ungoliant "sucked up all the light that she could find, and spun it forth again in dark nets of strangling gloom" (Tolkien, 1977, 73). From this she weaves "a cloak of darkness ... an Unlight, in which things seemed to be no more, and which eyes could not pierce, for it was a void" (Tolkien, 1977, 74). When they reach the trees, Ungoliant destroys them, drinking their Light and from it makes a "Darkness [that was] more than a loss of light [,] a Darkness that seemed not a lack but a thing with a being of its own: for it was made by malice out of Light, and it had the power to pierce the eye" (Tolkien, 1977, 76). A careful observation of the minuscule and majuscule reveals that, initially, Ungoliant consumes light and produces darkness; at the Trees, however, she consumes Light and produces Darkness. The only capitalization in the earlier scene is of *Unlight*, absence, the *void*. But the latter Darkness is *more than a loss of light*. It is not a *lack*, a *void*, but a *thing*. Moreover, the earlier darkness was one that *eyes could not pierce*, whereas the Darkness *had the power to pierce the eye*.

A Darkness that pierces the eye, just as Glaurung's dying gaze smites Túrin like an arrow, is precisely the kind of medium by which a Ring wearer might see and be seen. The Witch King's eyes are visible in the darkness that gathers around him at Pelennor for the very reason that Darkness gathers around him. Gollum's eyes glow with the same *léoht unfaéger* as his ancestor Grendel's at those times when he is furthest from repenting. If a mortal is to become invisible in a world so defined by light and vision as Eä, then there must be mechanisms in place to corrupt or negate what Eru created and the Valar made. How else, in that mythology, could the Ring have worked? It is not the Unlight, but the Unfair Light, the Darkness that Tolkien needed to invent if he was to incorporate a simple device in a children's story, a trinket for making the wearer invisible, into a *larger tale*.

Works Cited

Aliev, A. E., Gartstein, Y. N., and Baughman, R. H. (2011). "Mirage Effect from Thermally Modulated Transparent Carbon Nanotube Sheets." *Nanotechnology*.
Carpenter, H. (2000). *J.R.R. Tolkien: A Biography*. New York: Houghton Mifflin.
Lindberg, David. (1976). *Theories of Vision from al–Kindi to Kepler*. Chicago: University of Chicago Press.
Tolkien, J.R.R. (1977). *The Silmarillion*. London: George Allen & Unwin.

_____. (1989). *Tree and Leaf Including the Poem Mythopoeia*. Boston: Houghton Mifflin.
_____. (1990). *The War of the Ring*. New York: Houghton Mifflin.
_____. (1993a). *The Fellowship of the Ring*. Boston: Houghton Mifflin.
_____. (1993b). *The Return of the King*. Boston: Houghton Mifflin.
_____. (1993c). *The Two Towers*. Boston: Houghton Mifflin.
_____. (2007). *The Children of Húrin*. Boston: Houghton Mifflin.
_____ and C. Tolkien. (1988). *The Return of the Shadow*. New York: Houghton Mifflin.
_____, and D. Anderson. (2002). *The Annotated Hobbit*. Boston: Houghton Mifflin.
_____, H. Carpenter and C. Tolkien. (1981). *The Letters of J.R.R. Tolkien*. Boston: Houghton Mifflin.

A Victorian in Valhalla
Bilbo Baggins as the Link Between England and Middle-earth

WILLIAM CHRISTIAN KLARNER

J.R.R. Tolkien was very open about the origin of Bilbo and the concept of the hobbit in general, particularly as Bilbo relates to Tolkien's authorial self (Carpenter, 2000, 179). Bilbo contained much more of Tolkien himself, the author as a person, than any other character. This created a strange paradox for Tolkien: rather than just selling a story, the popularity of his first novel was also a reflection on himself and his values. Raised at the end of the Victorian era, Tolkien was very much a product of the time in which he was schooled and the cultural context in which he lived. This might seem a self-evident subject—all authors are affected somehow by the culture which surrounds them, either as a result of joining its so-called "mainstream" cultural flow or by resisting against it—but Tolkien is a strange case. The Oxford don existed as both an example of his times and a primary point of resistance, particularly once his larger masterwork *The Lord of the Rings* was published, but even in the context of *The Hobbit*. In an effort to understand this duality another will be explored, that of Tolkien using the spirit of Victorian England in his books and writing it into the hobbits, which are so key to the popularity of his works even while Middle-earth is so much a work of medieval, northern European myth. This piece will do something, at least in part, on which Tolkien himself infamously frowned: it will examine the biographical information available about the author with the hope of giving a greater understanding of where his inspiration and work originated. This approach is always questionable, but can at least give a window into why Tolkien's works on Middle-earth touch so many. This analysis will not be of why Tolkien wrote the story, per say—rather into why the story as he wrote it can wiggle into so many hearts (Carpenter, 2000, Author's note). The larger function will be pointing out the why of that inspiration and how it translated into the figure of Bilbo, who was a thinly veiled avatar of Tolkien himself.

This essay makes the assumption (and assertion) that Tolkien's first novel, *The Hobbit*, provides the key to understanding the popularity of his works as a whole and the connection so many feel to hobbits in general. This argument functions on the idea that *The Hobbit* serves as a key narrative springboard for the larger *The Lord of the Rings*, and because it serves as the hinge on which the much more narratologically, mythological and philologically sophisticated works *The Silmarillion* and *The Lord of the Rings* turn and provides a connection between these larger examples of the mythology. The second is the use of Victorian culture and custom as an easing point into the Norse-based fantasy, which *The Hobbit* becomes after the party leaves Rivendell. Wittingly or not, *The Hobbit* has roots in the combined traditions of Norse myth and the Victorian adventure novel.

Some of this material is not new. The difference is intended to be born in how the reader relates to the book experience through Tolkien's view as author and through his narrator. The importance of Bilbo as a lens for Middle-earth cannot be overstated. He is just as shocked at the behavior of dwarves as Tolkien's polite contemporaries would be (Tolkien, 1997, 10–11). Bilbo is very much a modern view in a very ancient world, a fact which Tolkien would exploit in several ways explained below. As for Bilbo as a mirror of Tolkien himself, Humphrey Carpenter pointed out in his biography of Tolkien how the author and Bilbo have many similarities, not least that their families are similarly structured, including a famous grandfather with three beautiful daughters and parents who died while he was relatively young (Carpenter, 2000, 179).

The fact that *The Hobbit* is a novel is a nod to how his education in English literature affected Tolkien. It is written not as a long poem but in prose like *Treasure Island* and *King Solomon's Mines*. One of these at least we know he read—Tolkien makes reference to Robert Louis Stevenson's piratical masterpiece in one of his letters, discussing how it left him cold (Dickerson, 2012, 136–137). Both expressed preference, and his own written work seemed to separate Tolkien from many of his contemporaries, yet he could not help mirroring them at least a little in the construction of his fiction.

This essay will set about to convince the reader of three points: first, that Tolkien was very much a man of his times, a member of the waning British Empire. Second, that this Victorian tradition provided the bridge for so many to enter Middle-earth, in particular through both his family's history providing the base for a believable nonhuman character and through a few adeptly used narrative tricks. And third, that despite the broad picture of Nordic myth painted by Tolkien's mythology there is a strong undercurrent of modern philosophy buried underneath. These tones and themes are the key to how Bilbo eventually emerges as a fully formed, self-sufficient character at the end of *The Hobbit*, since rather than absorbing the traditions of the medieval culture all around him, Bilbo stands up for his very hobbitish values (Ibid. 76–77). All of this will require skipping back and forth across time periods—very much something Tolkien did in his everyday life, meandering from modern camaraderie at the college to the literary clubs run by he and his friends and then finally to his home and hence to Middle-earth.

Tolkien was quite open about how much Bilbo was modeled on himself. Reading about the man often calls to mind the hobbit—they even dressed similarly (Ibid.). Later in life, after financial security and much unwanted fame, Tolkien even took to acquiring decorative waistcoats much like certain of his characters. The material aspects of this mindset, while not as overpowering as with some authors, were certainly present. Even when he was financially constrained, the family employed a housekeeper and he spent time at the Bird and Baby (an Oxford bar) when simply going home might have been more frugal. This was, in part, what it meant to be a middle-class Victorian. Expenses were a part of the mindset, much the way Bilbo employs gardeners and has no clear means of employment (Carpenter, 2000, 179).

The mindset was certainly not limited to the material—much of it was philosophical. This came in part as a result of Tolkien's involvement in the First World War, and the way this changed how the public in general viewed the topic of warfare. In Tolkien's work as a whole, this is perhaps best represented by the Dead Marshes described in *The Two Towers*, which Tolkien himself admitted were probably influenced by his experience in the trenches (Tolkien, 2000, "Letter 226"). The dead bodies floating to the top, looking up out of the mud and water, is an image familiar to anyone who's studied the First World War. The modern tendency to be disturbed by warfare was not fresh to *The Lord of the Rings*, though.

The Hobbit culminates in the Battle of Five Armies, and although such climactic battles are a common theme throughout Tolkien's work, there are reasons to focus on the Battle of Five Armies to the exclusion of others here. This battle holds two important caveats: it was chronologically first, written before *The Silmarillion* was polished for publication or *The Lord of the Rings* was completed or even conceived, and its primary image is that of horror and depression at the sight of the results of war. Critics have grumbled about Tolkien's frequent battles, calling them a glorification of violence, but they miss the real point of his battle scenes (Dickerson, 2012, 36–40). They are not just culminations, but lessons. Tolkien writes about the confusion and torment, about the unpleasant aftermath. In a word, the narrator points out that Bilbo would recall it being "dreadful" (Tolkien, 1997, 283). The diminutive Bilbo was not entering the battle as a long-trained warrior or soldier, and is certainly a far cry from being the heroic Beowulf or a similar embodiment of medieval heroism. He was a single hobbit, small and weak, hailing from the peaceful Shire and thrown suddenly into a massive military engagement. Bilbo expressed confusion and fear, neither of which Beowulf would ever have admitted. Philosophically, this has far more in common with the late Victorian and early twentieth century than the earlier periods Tolkien studied in his collegiate work. While monks and others have been pacifists for time out of mind, the idea of a non-religious conscientious objection to violence is relatively recent in Western culture (Cortright, 2013).

This is not to say a distaste for the more violent aspects of warfare is anything new; rather that the balance between intellectual dislike for warfare and the continual belief in the necessity of defending one's self and others from harm. Winston Churchill expressed similar sentiments (Churchill, 6/4/1940.) Tolkien, however, was not as boisterous as Churchill or pointedly witty as Chesterton. Like the first, he went to war and watched men die, knew men that died. Like the first he seemed something of an over-thinker, and Tolkien shared Chesterton's perspective in that they were both Roman Catholic and therefore outliers in traditional English society.

Tolkien's Catholicism came from his mother, and was unquestionably one of the greatest contributing factors in his development. Most crucially, it drove him away from his mother's family, the Suffields, with whom he'd felt an enormous attachment before. Tolkien's mother Mabel, a young widow, had converted to Roman Catholicism and taken her boys with her, much to the dismay of her family. This left them, Tolkien and his mother and brother, nearly destitute. Mabel took up the education of her sons, including the instruction of various languages (Carpenter, 2000, 29). In one swift act the Suffields drove Tolkien away from the more traditional English Protestantism rather forcefully and caused him to associate both with his faith, Catholicism, and his education with his mother. These points are not new. What is perhaps most important is that this combination created not only Tolkien but his most important creation: the hobbit, Bilbo Baggins.

Bilbo is crucial because he's the meeting point between the two worlds, one with a daily postal service and tobacco, the other with goblins and dragons and massed warfare. The most sympathetic moments in Tolkien's work aren't just found in the Victorianism inherent in much of his work regarding the Shire and its hobbit residents; instead, this socio-cultural model is tossed into Middle-earth, where Bilbo rapidly finds that the absent handkerchief he bemoans is the least of his problems. It is this juxtaposition which remains the center of the appeal of hobbits. They are, all at once, part of a realm of myth and might and yet so definitely, literally small. Hobbits are very vulnerable. They are disrespected by their peers not just for their size but for the choices they make, which isolate them and the parts of their lives which they value (Tolkien, 1997, 290). Yet in the end, the two worlds meet, and Bilbo does not have to compromise his own values in the process of winning the day.

Tolkien had gone through life bearing angst against the limits placed on him, and Bilbo was his way of expressing it. *The Hobbit* is a work of emotional power, and power like that comes from somewhere—if Tolkien had just written the tale to write something, it would not have been as touching, just as "Magic for magic's sake, like art for art's sake, is found in fact to be too shallow, and to be unable to live without drawing on things deeper than itself" (Chesterton, 2011, 227). Just as he had fled, metaphorically, from the parts of social convention which opposed his mother's and his choices, Bilbo fled from the Shire out into the expression of Tolkien's two intellectual halves: English literature and Norse mythology. Humphrey Carpenter once wrote that "Really that missing piece was there the whole time. It was the Suffield side of his own personality" (Carpenter, 2000, 179). Yet without the alienation Tolkien had felt from those very Suffields, there would have been no way to access the longing for that Suffield side, and all of the parts of hobbits which have come to define Bilbo. Tolkien wrote Bilbo in longing to be part of his childhood family again.

Five years before *The Hobbit* was published G.K. Chesterton wrote "There is no reason within reason, why literature should not describe the demonic as well as the divine aspect of mystery or myth. What is really remarkable is that modern fiction, in an age accused of frivolity, in an age perhaps too headlong in pursuit of its happiness, or at least of hedonism, the only popular sort of fantasy is the unhappy fantasy." In part Mr. Chesterton wished to point out the inconsistency of social practice to snub the idea of fantasy while grasping at the tales themselves (Chesterton, 2011, 228). In effect he also pointed out part of the problematic nature of English society between the World Wars: these were people raised on the tales of British superiority, on fantasies of a world superpower, yet they could watch it all crumbling around them, so their fantasy and reality were both magnificent and obviously decaying (Overy, 2009). Tolkien was keenly aware of this; in a private letter he lamented the fall of Britain from glory and preeminence, and saw that people were still "longing for cavaliers" (Tolkien, 2000, Letter 306, 393). The British knew that their empire was failing, and sought to return to a happier time.

The commonality of this sentiment has led to some assuming that Tolkien romanticized Europe's past in much the same way Victorians took to romanticizing aspects of other cultures, as did T.E. Lawrence the Bedouin. Lawrence and men like him saw colonized cultures as ancient and proud, not necessarily barbaric; they were old Englishmen translated into another culture. Yet this also assumes that Tolkien viewed the Old Norse, Anglo-Saxons and the peoples of Middle-earth with the same patronizing glare of most Victorians (Pagden, 2008; Tolkien, 1997, 281). Tolkien had served in war, and held no romantic notions about it—the narrator in *The Hobbit* sums up the Battle of Five Armies not as something glorious, but as "very terrible" (Tolkien, 1997, 281). The dwarves and Bilbo go on a long journey which, rather than being fun and exciting, is quite miserable much of the time (Ibid. 31–32, 59). The adventure, time, place, and enemies were not fun—quite the opposite. Even the dwarves themselves, Bilbo's companions, are criticized for being gruff and greedy, and for thinking too much of their mission (Ibid. 21–22, 266–267). These are not characteristics of your typical epic—most romances and epic tales from *The Iliad* right up into modern times handle themselves with a degree of seriousness. Tolkien avoided this.

This was one of the two major ways Tolkien avoided convention in his mythopoetic tradition: the use of modern concepts. Farce is not new, but *The Hobbit* is not farce, either. Tolkien wrote an adventure which blended the old concept of the heroic epic, a story based around the actions of a hero or heroes in the face of improbable danger, yet he based it around a character of humor. The reason *The Hobbit* is not a farce is the seriousness that the reader is obviously supposed to invest in Bilbo and his companions. In a farce, the elements are all aimed at creating a conscious awareness of how absurd the action or object of the action really are. Bilbo, while occasionally humorous, obviously means to be taken seriously, not just by the Gandalf and the Dwarves, but by the reader as well. The narrator, upon looking into Bilbo's thoughts against Gollum and in the final Battle of Five Armies, finds someone struggling with regret and the realities of mortality, both his own and the end of life he could visit on others (Ibid. 86–87, 286). Bilbo's actions in this regard are quite different from even the perception of him, let alone how modern times would relate to a medieval epic.

Yet even getting Bilbo gracefully into the story is odd when the process is read over. Gandalf, in the process of recruiting Bilbo, goes from talking to an exiled king (Thorin) to essentially gossiping with a gardener (Holman, who was master to Hamfast Gamgee). The dwarves are at first offended that Gandalf had suggested such a "fatuous" burglar. Indeed if Bilbo had been placed where Tolkien said the Shire belonged, in Diamond Jubilee Worchestershire, Mr. Baggins would have been a member of the gentry (Tolkien, 2000, Letter 178). As Tom Shippey put it, there is a word to sum up Bilbo: "bourgeois" (Shippey, 2000, 9). The mythological people themselves viewed Bilbo with suspicion, even as the Victorian gentleman, used to wandering through life and reading, was stubbornly trodding alongside them into adventure. There is an awareness that Bilbo in a sense does not belong—yet this says more about their opinions than it does Bilbo's actual fitness. Bilbo was, in many ways, Tolkien himself, showing that yes, the hobbit might seem soft, but he can do great things when pressed, much as Tolkien and so many of his contemporaries had done during the First World War. Gandalf had not gone into the process with Bilbo in mind—Bilbo was, even in the history of Middle-earth, no more than a very happy accident (Tolkien, 1980, 323–326). The modern man did not belong there, but he could still contribute (Shippey, 2000, 7).

This is, again, perhaps not the most original of ideas, yet it was one central to Tolkien's early life and one his Victorian upbringing would have stressed against. Tolkien actually failed to achieve entry into Oxford on his first try, and his continued attempts to woo Edith Bratt (eventually Edith Tolkien, wife of J.R.R.) were held up time and again by outside forces (Carpenter, 2000, 179). To say Bilbo's failures mirror Tolkien's would be inaccurate; to say they mirror the trials a reader might face is less specific and more easily applied. Most people have impacted and failed to alter something in their life, just as Bilbo does by bouncing off the giants, and then gotten up to try again. Another important deviation is the multiculturalism implicit in all of Tolkien's works on Middle-earth—every race has several different cultures attached to them. The older poems, like *Beowulf*, might have different tribes, and the *Song of Roland* involves mentions of other tribes and the Muslim enemy, but neither go into the kind of depth we see Tolkien use regarding the many societies of Middle-earth. This is a much more modern feature—one of many accustomed to the stretch and breadth of the British Empire, where many nationalities and cultures were in the news, and where a whole world of wildly different ethnicities crossed on a daily basis (Wood, 2008).

The most notable way Tolkien's work varies so much from the traditional epic was his form. Most epics, including nearly all in Old Norse and Old English, were written in verse, albeit many in blank verse. Tolkien certainly made attempts at heroic verse, and published a great many of his more whimsical poems on his own (Carpenter, 2000, 72, 79). The first pieces of Middle-earth were poems derived from the material he read everyday in his work at Oxford and Leeds, and he had sufficient material to make a poem for something the size of *The Hobbit* (Cobley, 2000, 76–77). Tolkien's entire academic life—and most of his most famous criticism and courses—was spent going into great detail regarding the skill with which ancient authors handled these lengthy poems. Yet when the time came to really put down an adventure, Tolkien didn't write it out in verse, but in prose.

Prose first became the common way of telling English narrative long after Tolkien's area of expertise ended. The first real novelists appeared in the eighteenth century, and England quickly became a nation of novel-readers (Tolkien, 1997, 214–215). Much of what Tolkien read growing up was at least in prose, if not necessarily the novel, although he has noted being fond of George McDonald. Tolkien wrote a novel because he lived after the rise of the novel; this seems an overly simple statement, but for an already accomplished poet, it was not a forgone conclusion.

Skirting the edge between Norse and Victorian is the fact that Bilbo had to travel a long way to find adventure. The Vikings certainly journeyed far, and the Victorians had to in order to reach away from the safe shores of England, which didn't see foreign violence between Napoleon and Hitler. This concept, going far from home to make a fortune and find adventure or fame, was a staple of fiction during Tolkien's life and before. H. Rider Haggard's Allen Quartermain books, Robert Louis Stevenson's various pirate adventures, the Hornblower books, and many other pieces of popular literature all based themselves around finding the physical and psychological rewards of foreign adventure. For Tolkien this translated directly to some of his own expertise as well, in the form of medieval classics like *Beowulf* and *Sir Gawain and the Green Knight*. This confluence between Tolkien's subject and his contemporaries' fascination with foreign adventure is not purely contextual but provided, nonetheless, a way for the modern reader to access not only the viewpoint of a character in Middle-earth (as with Bilbo), but a way for their mind to slide into the context of the story without stretching outside their figurative, literary comfort zone.

Somewhat more telling is that once Bilbo is on the road, he becomes more and more accustomed to action, until finally he consciously enters the Norse mindset by invading the dragon Smaug's lair.

> Going on from there was the bravest thing he ever did. The tremendous things that happened afterward were as nothing compared to it. He fought the real battle in that tunnel alone, before he ever saw the vast danger that lay in wait [Dickerson, 2012, 170–171].

Technically, the above passage is not where Bilbo entered the world of Norse myth which was so dangerous—he had done that long before (Wettstein, 2002). Yet this is probably the most important choice, because Bilbo is electing to go into danger for the sake of adventure. Before this, Bilbo had taken risks to save himself or his friends, but not for the sake of treasure. While the story may have been becoming more and more adventurous all the time, this point is where the epic starts to ring through and the tale begins to be far more Norse than Victorian.

There are many original sources for the plot elements of Tolkien's works, with the most significant undoubtedly being Norse mythology (Shippey, 2000, 16). Even the name Middle-earth is a reference to the name of our world in Norse mythology, Midgard (Ferguson, 2009, 23). Tom Shippey has already pointed out the many Scandinavian connections the Dwarves have in their names and actions (Shippey, 2000, 16). So I would not be the first to say that the kind of skaldic tales and other stories and the base mythology for much of Middle-earth have at least a few elements in common, the most prominent of which is a traditional hero figure. Essentially what Tolkien did was to combine a late Victorian literary practice, the third-person prose novel, with the traditional elements of Norse myth, theoretically the kind of tale which requires a strong central figure of heroic merit. This point has already been made many times; more important to this is why Bilbo is important in breaking both molds.

Bilbo is not terribly heroic. He is, in fact, almost precisely the reverse of the prototypical Old English hero, Beowulf, and bears little in common with the Old Norse literary figures as well (Ibid.). The common route in literary tradition was to give the principal character some kind of reputation to bring in before them, much as Beowulf does when arriving at Heort. This socio-cultural capital is then spent in acquiring a place among the group with which the principal action of the story will be done (Boyd, 219–221). This is one half of the importance of *The Hobbit:* the central figure is not a returning king, or a mighty wizard, or a dragon. Rather Bilbo, whose mind the modern reader can inhabit with relative ease, instead takes the central role. Bilbo enjoys the comforts of modern life, almost all of which are foreign to the Wild, and to Middle-earth. Yet the idea of the heroic was a constant in Victorian life, from press serials about the brave actions of conquerors and soldiers in far-off lands (Rhodes and Churchill both had exalted military careers before private and political success) to the glorification of medieval history. This cultural hiccup created the perfect environment for a flourishing of literature both about adventure, like H. Rider Haggard's work, and about the medieval—with *Black Arrow*, by Robert Louis Stevenson, being only one example of a popular Victorian work set in medieval England.

Going through the most remembered stretch of the Victorian era's popular literature is, for the most part, an exercise in romanticism. The past was a fascination for many Victorians, particularly relating to the chivalric tradition. Arthurian legend became more popular again. Tolkien was not necessarily a qualifying member of that movement as a whole, but there were certainly those in the rest of the academic stream that tolerated Tolkien and other medieval linguists specifically because the culture was built to venerate England's "heroic past." Beyond this receptive state there lay a tendency to think fairy stories ridiculous, impractical or childish (Kurtz, 2013). The space between these points of view—between the veneration of a mythological past and the childish imprudence of the fairy story—has become the crux of feelings on Tolkien. To understand why it has this dual effect, two facts must be understood: the above, that Victorians and their descendants have a fascination with the idea of a heroic past (as do many cultures) and the below, that Tolkien's Middle-earth provided that mythic past not just for England but for everyone by lacing international myths throughout his legendarium.

Yet even this would not be enough but for one critical narrative device, mentioned above: social capital, a reputation. Thorin is known around Middle-earth; Gandalf even more so. Bilbo, critically, has nothing of the sort. This absence of pre-existing links to the mythological world, rather than just around the Shire, allows the reader to learn about and slip into Middle-earth alongside the nonentity that is Bilbo. Do not let this point be misconstrued: Bilbo is not a blank-slate character. Rather than relying on the reader to provide details of themselves on an amorphous protagonist, instead Tolkien placed Bilbo into a situation where the reader can sympathize: that of someone who has agreed to something they do not fully understand. Providing situations or standards familiar to the reader has long been a key component of narration, and having a protagonist from at least conceptually familiar circumstances be tossed into an again conceptually familiar situation (the journey/adventure model of storytelling) allows for an easy transition into the otherwise totally foreign Middle-earth (Boyd, 2009, 219).

These concepts are the key to the continuing popularity of hobbits, and why *The Hobbit* is in particular of great import to the rest of the legendarium. Bilbo is of paramount importance to this not only because of his initial novelty, being the first hobbit, but also because of his singularity: with few exceptions he remains the centerpiece of the narrative throughout Tolkien's first novel. This concentration enables a different set of views than the truly poly-protagonist Fellowship of the Ring. Throughout Tolkien's larger masterwork the reader learns about and sees from several different cultures. In *The Hobbit* the only two groups with any exposure are the dwarves and hobbits, who are mostly described in similar terms to Victorian British people. Which left the dwarves to be both the motivation for the quest and the focus of Bilbo's description.

As already mentioned, the dwarves in Thorin's company all have names originating in Norse literature; they are not the only members of a distinctly mythological bent to peer in on Bilbo prior to his leaving the Last Homely House. The dwarven company and Gandalf are unique only in that they intrude into the otherwise distinctly Victorian Shire. Of these only Gandalf appears during the day—a human-seeming person who is odd but not yet mythological. Bilbo doesn't mention Gandalf's magic much at first, rather concentrating on the wizard's capacity for fireworks and involving other people in his adventures. The dwarves, the first pieces of Scandinavian myth to poke in, are saved for after dark has fallen. This entry into myth foreshadows the way Bilbo will fall from Victorian children's tale to epic journey. This transition is central not only to *The Hobbit* but to the charm of Middle-earth.

The distinction between the parts of *The Hobbit* on either side of Elrond's home has been discussed already by Dickerson, who points out that the monsters after leaving Rivendell are much more serious and dangerous in tone than the single group before. Bill and the other trolls are very much in the tradition of the simpleton villains common in children's literature. The antagonists afterward are competent and dangerous—even Gollum is clearly murderous. Leaving Elrond's house becomes a microcosm for the move into violent medieval lore. Even the poems from after the break at Rivendell are of a very different caliber—the first songs in the book are about adventure and breaking Bilbo's plates, yet afterward the elves sing about the omnipresence of greed and the inevitability of death (Dickerson, 2012, 175–177). The encounter with the trolls showed Bilbo as he had been, but as he grew each new event— each notably more epic in tone— would evince how the very Victorian gentleman adapted more and more to his new environs, those of adventure and later of war.

Bilbo is also fairly useless in the encounter with the trolls, but begins to metaphorically grow once the more Scandinavian elements begin, like the riddle game with Gollum and the fight with the spiders (Shippey, 2000, 29). While he never becomes what would be typically regarded as a heroic figure, Bilbo is given some more typically heroic aspects and roles as the book advances. The riddles with Gollum, especially, are a deviation. Normally Gandalf is given the Odin symbols, like his gray cloak and staff, and certainly Gandalf is more willing to risk himself for knowledge than his compatriots just as Odin did to find the power of writing (Ferguson, 2009, 24–25). Bilbo is given the game of riddles and the Ring (Wettstein, 2002, 5). Bilbo's continued youth after acquiring the Ring could also be a reference to rings as a symbol of eternal recurrence, as well as a nod to Odin's dishonesty in acquiring the power of poetry from Utgard, since Bilbo lies about his Ring and how he acquired it at first (Ferguson, 2009, 28). The dwarven party's acquisition of the three major swords—Glamdring, Orcrist, and Sting— is a nod to the practice of raiding burial mounds in search of valuables (Ibid. 206). As Tolkien revealed more and more of Middle-earth throughout the book and got further from the Shire, the elements of the story bore less resemblance to the modern novels and more to the tales and poems he'd studied since his days in university, even sounding almost formal during his description of the Battle of Five Armies in "The Clouds Burst." Tolkien's control over his narrative eases this transition, just as it did when going from Bag End eastward. This same control allows the severe end—Thorin's death— to be a time for reflection rather than action.

Reflection of this kind is more common in modern fiction rather than older material, and Tolkien's easy applicability is in part a result of this very modern part of his writing and in particular highlights how simple and similar the Shire is, since returning home simplifies Bilbo's mental state. Bilbo survives his journey and plays such a pivotal role in the negotiations at Erebor, in part because he is true to the modern morals Tolkien instills in him (Dickerson, 2012, 3, 13, 96). Bilbo's choices regarding the Arkenstone and the Ring both connect him to a Middle-earth he was never supposed to inhabit.

Which really is what Tolkien was trying to show by combining his Victorian hobbit in his Valhallan world. "Hobbits, in putting earth under the feet of romance ... [provided] subjects for ennoblement and heroes more praiseworthy than the professionals" (Tolkien, 2000, Letter 215). Tolkien elevated this idea in The Lord of the Rings, but *The Hobbit* provided the blueprint for his later work with hobbits. *The Hobbit* taught Tolkien how to meld the Shire, which was so Victorian, with the Middle-earth of his legendarium. By slipping Bilbo into his mythology, Tolkien changed not just his legendarium as a whole but gave the modern reader a sympathetic friend in Middle-earth. By giving the reader a friend in Middle-earth, Tolkien gave access to a series of scholastic wonders and personal problems to which almost anyone can relate.

In summation, while Tolkien's cultural context provided the backdrop for his most famous invention, hobbits, it was his very alienation from that world that led to his inserting himself, in the form of Bilbo, into Middle-earth. Rather than going as a conqueror, as many of his British contemporaries went around the world, Tolkien wanted to become a part of the language and the story—and therefore made Bilbo slowly slide into Middle-earth from the Shire. In the end, that is perhaps the most striking delineation: the Victorian Shire against Norse Middle-earth. By sub-creating a place for the modern Bilbo, Tolkien gave the world a way to peek into medieval Middle-earth.

Works Cited

Boyd, Brian. 2009. *The Origin of Stories*. Cambridge, MA: Belknap.
Carpenter, Humphrey. 2000. *Tolkien: A Biography*. Boston: Houghton Mifflin.
Chesterton, G.K. 2011. "Magic and Fantasy in Fiction." In *In Defense of Sanity*, edited by Dale Ahlquist, Joseph Pearce, and Aidan Mackey. San Francisco: Ignatius.
Churchill, Winston. 1940. "We Shall Fight on the Beaches." Speech to the House of Commons, June 4.
Cobley, Paul. 2000. *Narrative*. Oxon, Oxfordshire: Routledge.
Cortright, David. 2008. *Peace*. Cambridge: Cambridge University Press.
Dickerson, Matthew. 2012. *A Hobbit Journey*. Grand Rapids, MI: Brazos.
Ferguson, Robert. 2009. *The Vikings: A History*. New York: Viking.
Kurtz, Patti J. 2013. "Understanding and Appreciating Fantasy Literature." Choice Reviews Online. Accessed December 16, 2013. http://www.cro3.org/content/45/04/571.extract.
Overy, Richard. 2009. *The Morbid Age: Britain Between the Wars*. London: Penguin.
Pagden, Anthony. *Worlds at War: The 2,500-Year Struggle Between East and West*. New York: Random House.
Shippey, Tom. 2000. *J.R.R. Tolkien: Author of the Century*. Suffolk: Clays.
Tolkien, J.R.R. 1980. *Unfinished Tales of Numenor and Middle Earth*. Boston: Houghton Mifflin.
_____. 1997. *The Hobbit*. New York: Ballantine.
_____. 2000. *The Letters of J.R.R. Tolkien*. Ed. Humphrey Carpenter. Boston: Houghton Mifflin.
Wettstein, Martin. 2002. "Old Norse Elements in the Work of J.R.R. Tolkien." October. Accessed December 5, 2013. http://www.academia.edu/228734/Norse_Elements_in_the_work_of_J.R.R._Tolkien.
Wood, Ralph C. 2008. "J.R.R. Tolkien, Our Post-Modern Contemporary." *The Ring Goes Ever On: Proceedings of the Tolkien Conference 2005*." The Tolkien Society.

Beorn and Bombadil
Mythology, Place and Landscape in Middle-earth

JUSTIN T. NOETZEL

The enigmatic Beorn of *The Hobbit* and Tom Bombadil of *The Lord of the Rings*, the shape-changing bear warrior and the nature spirit, are perhaps the two most interesting but obscure figures in J.R.R. Tolkien's vast and complex mythology. In a world largely populated by races of hobbits, dwarves, elves, and men, these two figures exist as singular entities who possess profound but geographically focused power. Both characters have their origins in the field of energy that developed between Tolkien's academic and personal lives, because they come from the combination of the medieval literature and history Tolkien studied as well as the stories that he told, wrote, and illustrated for his own children. This is a case of the sums being greater than their parts, because the mythical background, environmental focus, and narrative value supplied by Beorn and Bombadil are greater than the effect of simply adding medieval heroes and folktale spirits to adventurous bedtime stories.

Much has been written about the origins of these characters in the mythology and literature of Late Antique and Early Medieval northern Europe, but they also possess further connections to early Irish mythology. The mythical origins of the shape-shifting Beorn and the nature-loving Bombadil connect each character to his respective place in Middle-earth, because they possess a local sovereignty and an enmeshed connection with their landscape and the natural world. This essay analyzes the connection between each character and his homeland, and it defines each character using the terminology of space and place theory as a *genius loci*, a "spirit of place," who is imbued with a devout *topophilia* ("love of a place") for his respective home. Beorn fiercely loves his home and is wary of intruders, as evidenced by his stout defenses and great wooden hall, and Bombadil governs his forest cottage and the surrounding woodland with a power that rules even the natural world. In fact, the specific location in Middle-earth and the narrative function that Tolkien created with Beorn directly influences the place and role of Tom Bombadil. As Tolkien wove the fully formed Bombadil into his larger narrative of *The Lord of the Rings* in the 1940s and '50s, he also refined his notions of place and landscape. In a parallel development, the singular, insular, and warlike Beorn had an undeniable influence on the singular, insular, but peace-loving Tom Bombadil.

Even though Beorn and Tom Bombadil are (largely) individual characters in a world where fellowship and group counsel are the ways to defeat the forces of evil and achieve a peaceful existence, these two are essential for their respective narratives. They each possess an intimate connection with the natural world, and they use their environment- and landscape-oriented identities to help each book's traveling party. With his comprehensive understanding of the local landscape, Beorn protects Bilbo, Gandalf, and the dwarves from the goblins and wolves and gives them the wisdom necessary to survive the harrowing Mirkwood Forest. Bombadil possesses a similar power over his specific place in Middle-earth, and he uses his own landscape-focused knowledge to rescue Frodo and the hobbits from Old Man Willow and the Barrow-wight. In addition to these provincial victories, these environmentally conscious characters also instill wisdom and perform actions that have important ramifications for the conclusion of each of Tolkien's texts. Beorn plays a pivotal role in the combat of *The Hobbit*'s climactic Battle of the Five Armies when he charges into the fray in his bear shape, and the weapons from the Barrow-downs that Bombadil bestows on the hobbits lead directly to the defeat of the Witch-king and the rise of King Elessar at the end of *The Lord of the Rings*. These characters enter their respective stories as representatives of distinct and insular landscapes of Middle-earth, but by the end of each text, they enact a far greater role in their narrative and help the hobbits, dwarves, elves, and men achieve victory in the epic military engagement at the climax of each book.

Beorn of the Wilderland

As John D. Rateliff describes in *The History of* The Hobbit *Part One: Mr. Baggins*, one of the most important influences on Professor Tolkien's literary creation are the stories that he wrote for and told to his young children. *The Hobbit* "was originally written for a very specific audience" of Tolkien's three sons, Rateliff writes, and "while this idea is widely known as a biographical detail, few take into account the degree to which their likes and dislikes played a part in shaping the story" (Rateliff, 2007, 253–254). The boys were particularly keen on the heroic and comedic exploits of bears, and this common childhood trope shows up in *The Father Christmas Letters*, a series of letters that Tolkien wrote and illustrated in the 1920s and '30s to help his children celebrate the Christmas season. In a letter from 1933, for instance, Father Christmas describes how North Polar Bear "was squeezing, squashing, trampling, boxing, and kicking Goblins sky-high, and roaring like a zoo" (255). Such bear-related exploits, combined with the fact that Tolkien was composing *The Hobbit* at this time, reveal one of the key inspirations for the character Beorn, a hulking man with black hair and a beard who can change his form to that of a ferocious black bear. Tolkien's sons were not the only point of inspiration for Beorn, and Rateliff adds: "As so often, the figure of ... Beorn marks one of those grounds where Tolkien's scholarship and his storytelling for his children meet" (256). The most profound writing, even of a mythical world, often comes from an author's own interests and inclinations, and while Tolkien was creating these fantasies for his children, he was also reading and teaching medieval literature.

As many scholars have written, Tolkien constructed his academic career through his extensive interest in and mastery of the heroic literature of medieval northern Europe, especially (but by no means only) the Old Norse literature of Viking age–Scandinavia and post–Viking-age Iceland and the Old English literature of Anglo-Saxon England. Specifically, Beorn is a literary descendant of the Norse and English bear-like warriors Beowulf and Böthvarr Bjarki. The c. tenth-century Old English poem *Beowulf*, which Tolkien probably taught every year of his working life, describes how the Swedish warrior Beowulf defeats a series of monsters and rescues the famous Danish great hall Heorot.[1] Tom Shippey points out that Beowulf's name probably comes from "Bee-wolf," "the ravager of the bees, the creature who steals their honey, hence (as every reader of Winnie the pooh would recognize), the bear" (Shippey, 2001, 31). The hero Beowulf is named for a bear and fights in a very similar style, because his devastating bear-hugging ability nearly destroys the oversized monster Grendel:

he had never encountered in the world, in any region of the earth a mightier handgrip on another man; he became fearful in his heart and spirit... [Beowulf] stood upright and grasped [Grendel] firmly; his fingers burst; the giant was striving to escape, but the warrior stepped further. [Grendel] knew the power in that hostile grasp... The noble hall resounded; the Danes, the fortress-dwellers, the brave warriors, were filled with terror ... the hall resounded. It was a great wonder to the brave warriors that the wine-hall withstood, that it did not fall to the ground, the beautiful building; but it was firmly and skillfully forged with iron bands [Fulk, Bjork, and Niles 2008, lines 750a–775a].[2]

The honorable Beowulf fights Grendel without the aid of any weapons, and his brute strength allows him to overcome the demonic foe and wrench his arm from the socket. Beowulf's battle fury is very similar to that of Böthvarr Bjarki, the foremost of the champions of King Hrolf Kraki of Denmark in the fourteenth-century Old Norse *Hrolfs saga*. This hero's name means "Warlike Little-bear" in Old Norse, and he comes from the union between his father Bjarni (which means "bear") and his mother Bera (which means "she bear") (Shippey, 2001, 31). Bjarni was turned into a bear by his enchantress stepmother, and this supernatural inheritance gives Böthvarr the power to mentally project a warlike bear spirit in his battles for King Hrolf. In the saga's fateful final battle against a King named Hjorvard, the bear-spirit appears at the front of Hrolf's troops: "The bear was always beside the king, and it killed more men with its paw than any five of the king's champions did. Blows and missiles glanced off the animal, as it used its weight to crush King Hjorvard's men and their horses. Between its teeth, it tore everything within reach, causing a palpable fear to spread through the ranks of King Hjorvard's army" (Byock, 1998, 74).

Based on the many connections between these characters and Beorn, Marjorie Burns notes that Tolkien's character "belongs unquestionably to a Norse and pagan world. His name, his appearance, [and] his attachment to violent forms of revenge all link him to the Scandinavian or Teutonic North" (2005, 33). But, the dual-identitied Beorn, who shifts back and forth between human and bear forms, is more complex than this one-dimensional understanding. Burns adds a consideration of Beorn's flower gardens and cream and honey (but no meat) diet, and concludes that he is "a being of two extremes: both ruthless and kind, bear and man, homebody and wanderer, berserker and pacifist in one ... a highly domestic individual, a pacifist and bee-keeper, settled in the midst of rather English-sounding flower fields and gardens, but an individual who is at the same time a figure of brutal strength and violence, who belongs to an ancient, northern, and carnivorous world and lives in a Norseman's hall" (34–38). Similarly, Shippey notes that Beorn possesses a "strange combination of gruffness and good-humour, ferocity and kind-heartedness, with overlaying it all a quality which one might call being insufficiently socialized—all causes, of course, by the fact that he has 'more than one skin,' is 'a skin-changer'" (2001, 32). And as complex as Beorn appears in *The Hobbit*, Tolkien's manuscripts reveal the even greater ambivalence that went into his creation. Rateliff notes Tolkien's "considerable uncertainty" about "just what sort of being Beorn was" in passages like the following explanation from Gandalf to Bilbo and the dwarves: "No one knows [Most people disagree] whether he is a magic bear or a great man under enchantment... He is a man [an enchanter a man], one of the last of the old men who lived in these parts before the days of dragon" (Rateliff, 2007, 247). Even as he composed the formal introduction to his mysterious skin-changing character, Tolkien crossed out and rewrote his own words, revealing his evolving and revolving thought process about the exact nature of the enigmatic Beorn.

One of the most important themes in Marjorie Burns' *Perilous Realms* is the importance of the individual characters in Middle-earth. These "innate, one-of-a-kind loners, [these] honourable isolationists ... dwell in secluded domains," Burns writes, and these characters are also "distinctive, free, [and] self-reliant[,] but respectful of other lives and hostile only to those deserving hostility" (2005, 32). Like his literary kinsman Tom Bombadil in *The Lord of the Ring*, Beorn fits this category of an insular but powerful character perfectly. This fierce and mysterious warrior in *The Hobbit* is composed of two natures, and he is best described by Gandalf in the published form of the novel:

> [Beorn] is very strong, and he is a skin-changer ... sometimes he is a huge black bear, sometimes he is a great strong black-haired man with huge arms and a great beard. I cannot tell you much more, though that ought to be enough. Some say he is a bear descended from the great and ancient bears of the mountains that lived there before the giants came. Others say that he is a man descended from the first men who lived before Smaug or other dragons came into the hills out of the North. I cannot say, though I fancy the last is the true tale.... I once saw him sitting all alone on the top of the Carrock at night watching the moon sinking towards the Misty Mountains, and I heard him growl in the tongue of bears: "The day will come when they will perish and I shall go back!" That is why I believe he once came from the mountains himself [Tolkien, 1997, 106–107].

In addition to describing Beorn's otherworldly power, Gandalf's words also highlight the enigmatic nature of the character. Even the world-weary wizard, who travels far and wide across Middle-earth and has dealings with hobbits, dwarves, elves, and men, cannot reveal much about Beorn's origins and cannot say for certain whether he is primarily descended from bears or men. In this respect, Tolkien once again connects Beorn to his medieval ancestors, because the original and once famous story of the bear-warrior Böthvarr Bjarki has been lost over time. This poem, called the "Bjarkamál," can be "glimpsed today only through later versions and tantalizing references to lost manuscripts" (Rateliff, 2007, 281). Tolkien's academic and authorial careers intersected at many points during his lifetime, and one of his prime motivations in creating the vast mythology of Middle-earth was to preserve and reconstruct the ancient and medieval stories of heroes who have been lost to the ages. Shippey describes how Beorn's character, the creation of Thorin's dwarf troop, and many other elements of *The Hobbit* come from the way that Tolkien "took fragments of ancient literature, expanded on their intensely suggestive hints of further meaning, and made them into coherent and consistent narrative (all the things which the old poems had failed, or never bothered, to do)" (2001, 36).[3]

The only suitable dwelling for the enigmatic and ferocious Beorn is "a great wooden house" that is protected by "a belt of tall and very ancient oaks," "a high thorn-hedge through which you could neither see nor scramble [, and] a wooden gate, high and broad" (Tolkien, 1997, 106–107). These many layers of naturally occurring and handcrafted defense reveal the isolated and insulated nature of Beorn's homestead. Within this stratified perimeter are a "gardens and a cluster of low wooden buildings, some thatched and made of unshaped logs: barns, stables, sheds, and a long low wooden house" (107). The innermost space in the compound is Beorn's great house, and the sanctum sanctorum of this building is the hearth fire. When Gandalf and Bilbo first meet Beorn, they follow him into this structure, "a wide hall with a fire-place in the middle": "Though it was summer there was a wood-fire burning and the smoke was rising to the blackened rafters in search of the way out through an opening in the roof" (109). As Douglas A. Anderson and others have noted, Beorn's hall is purposely reminiscent of the famous Heorot (Tolkien, 2002, 170–171), the "tall and wide-gabled" Danish mead-hall that is so renowned that the "children of men should hear about [it] forever after" (Fulk, Bjork, and Niles, 2008, lines 68b–82a). Beorn's own "dim hall, lit only by the fire and the hole above it," is the epicenter of the skin-changer's culture, because it is here that he treats Bilbo's traveling party to a feast and engages in the millennia-old tradition of storytelling: Beorn relates "tales of the wild lands on this side of the mountains, and especially of the dark and dangerous wood [,] the terrible forest of Mirkwood" (Tolkien 1997, 115). And, like Heorot, Beorn's hall provides a similar protective function during the long, cold, and dangerous nights. As Marjorie Burns notes, *The Hobbit* brings "vividly to life something that came out of [Tolkien's] scholarship, offering us a re-creation of what it'd be like to spend the night in such a building" (2005, 261).

One way to map the narrative structure of *The Hobbit* is to define and understand the successive characters and cultures through their material ontology. In other words, the novel is punctuated and defined by objects and material, including fabric, stone, metal, and wood. Tolkien surrounds each culture in the novel with a distinctive materiality, and these objects and substances help identify the beliefs and values of the different populations of Middle-earth. Tolkien describes the domestic comfort supplied by the many pantries, kitchens, dining rooms, and wardrobes associated with hobbits on the first page of the text, and the comfort and warmth provided by cloth, or the sorrow at its absence, comes to define Bilbo during his long journey. Bilbo repeatedly laments the pocket-handkerchief that he left behind at Bag End, and always wears his overcoat, even over the chain mail that he receives from the dwarves. The proud and fierce dwarves, on the other hand, are defined by the hard, cold, and beautiful caverns that they carve out of stone, the precious jewels they find therein, and the metalwork that they craft at the smithy. When the dwarves finally enter the treasure chamber in Erebor, the spectacle provides a feast for their senses. As golden harps fill the space with a sweet melody, the dwarves gather as many gems as they can carry, and the kingly Thorin dresses himself in "a coat of gold-plated rings, with a silver-hafted axe in a belt crusted with scarlet stones" (Tolkien, 1997, 215).

While Bilbo feels most comfortable surrounded by his fine clothing and comfortable hobbit-hole, and the dwarves are intimately associated with their cavern architecture and metalwork, the material ontology that best describes Beorn is the "unshaped" timber of his great hall. Bilbo and Gandalf first see Beorn with his "thick black beard and hair, and great arms and legs with knotted muscles ... leaning on a large axe," and with this tool he is in the process of lopping the branches from the "great oak-trunk" beside which the wizard and hobbit find him (Tolkien, 1997, 108). Beorn's dismantling of the oak tree is a microcosm of his entire character, because his existence is one roughly hewn out of the hard landscape in the liminal space between the awe-inspiring peaks of the Misty Mountains and the dark gloom of Mirkwood Forest. The most elaborate great hall in Middle-earth is the famous Meduseld of Rohan, which features a floor of multicolored stones decorated with intertwining "runes and strange devices," and whose roof is held aloft by mighty pillars that are "richly carved [and] gleaming dully with gold and half-seen colors" (Tolkien, *The Two Towers* 1993, 116).[4] This large wooden hall stands as the cultural pinnacle of the Riders of Rohan in Book III of *The Lord of the Rings*, and it is a more decorated version of Beorn's simple and unadorned hall many miles to the north.

Beorn's place in Middle-earth and the materiality of his existence both speak to his ecological importance in the novel. Beorn lives in a human hall within a small farm, but because he also possesses a wild and animalistic nature, his buildings are built from minimally processed trees and situated far from human settlements. His "great wooden house" is situated in "an oak-wood," and this timbered essence is a central element of Beorn's character (Tolkien, 1997, 106). Instead of the handcrafted finery and architecture that populates Middle-earth, Beorn's simple hall is made of unshaped logs, and it does not possess the coziness of a Hobbit hole or the finery of a human structure. During Beorn's first conversation with Gandalf and

Bilbo, they sit on wooden benches on a "veranda propped on wooden posts made of single tree-trunks" (109). The skin-changer has built his home from timber felled and logs chopped by his own hand, and his porch sits on tree-trunk posts instead of the carved and intricate columns that are fashionable in Meduseld or Elrond's dwelling at Rivendell.[5]

Tolkien's language in *The Hobbit* further reveals the intimacy that Beorn holds to the natural world, because while the dwarves fixate on "gold and silver and jewels and the making of things by smith-craft," Beorn disdains such metal objects in favor of a natural and timbered existence. He serves the traveling company with "wooden spoons" and "wooden drinking bowls filled with mead," because "there were no things of gold or silver in his hall, and few save the knives were made of metal at all" (Tolkien, 1997, 115–116). After Beorn's fine dinner, Bilbo, Gandalf, and the dwarves relax in front of a roaring fire with "the pillars of the house standing tall behind them, and dark at the top like trees of the forest," and Bilbo is overcome by some magic (or perhaps merely the tiredness from his arduous exploits) and seems to hear "a sound like wind in the branches stirring in the rafters, and the hoot of owls" (116). Beorn's existence is so intricately enmeshed with his woodland landscape that, even within his stout and formidable great hall, the essence of the forest is present. Like Tolkien's model in Heorot, this hall is stoutly fortified and was constructed firmly and skillfully, although one suspects that Beorn's preference for timber over metal led him to use a peg-system or some other type of timber reinforcement instead of the iron bands that held the Danish hall together. Beorn's identity and homestead reveal his essential connection to his landscape and the natural world, and he presides over this small mountain and forest realm through a local sovereignty. The rough-hewn wooden buildings sit in perfect harmony among their natural surroundings, and Mirkwood forest speaks to Bilbo from a few miles away through the timber that now stands in Beorn's farm.

Furthermore, Beorn is "a model of co-operative ecology" because of his vegetarian lifestyle and enchanted animal servants (Shippey, 2001, 32). As a hybridized entity that includes both bear and human forms, Beorn is a fierce warrior, but instead of hunting or eating wild animals, he subsists on cream and the honey produced by his expansive bee-pastures" (Tolkien, 1997, 106–107). His compound is surrounded by the large patches of flowers and clover that support his bee population, and Tolkien's description of a vegetarian who lives in a flower-filled woodland resonates with the symbolism of pacifism. *The Hobbit* also describes how, when provoked, Beorn can become a fierce enemy, as evidenced by the severed goblin's head and wolf-skin that he proudly displays to Bilbo, Gandalf, and the dwarves. The skin-changer further revels in his duality because although he lives in human dwellings, he keeps animals as his companions and servants. Before he sits down to dinner with Thorin's troop, Beorn speaks to his pony, dog, and sheep servants in "a queer language like animal noises turned into talk," and they then walk on their hind legs and carry the food to the table (115).

With domesticated animals surrounding him in his forest-like great hall, consuming food served with wooden utensils and dinnerware, Beorn's identity is inextricably connected to the natural elements in *The Hobbit*. In the terminology of space and place theory, he represents a supreme form of a "placed existence" and possesses an unmatched devotion for his great wooden hall and the local countryside. Philosopher Gaston Bachelard describes this emotional connection with a specific place, or *topophilia*, as "the human value of the sorts of space that may be grasped, that may be defended against adverse forces, the space we love." Bachelard explains topophilia in his text *The Poetics of Space*, and it exists in "felicitous space" and "eulogized space," because this emotion bestows joy and is praised through both dwelling and storytelling (1994, xxxv). Beorn has such a fondness for his home, and he is so intricately connected to the landscape, that this place becomes an identifiable part of his own identity. Theologian Belden C. Lane describes this very interaction between an individual and their geography, and he states: "the construction of personal and communal identity is invariably related to primal spatial categories. Who we are, in other words, is inseparably a part of where we are ... an individual is not distinct from his place; he is that place" (2001, 6).

The comfort and security provided by the home is one of the key undercurrents in *The Hobbit*, and Tolkien repeatedly stresses the importance of topophilia for one's own home and native landscape as well as the hospitality received from both friends and strangers. Over the course of the novel, Bilbo fondly recalls of Bag End or mentions his homesickness aloud more than a dozen times, from remembering "his comfortable chair before the fire in his favourite sitting-room in his hobbit-hole" just after avoiding being eaten by the trolls, to the thought of "frying bacon and eggs in his own kitchen at home" before he encounters Gollum (Tolkien, 1997, 43 and 64). Bilbo can never escape the structuration of his home, because he is, in Bachelard's terminology, engraved within "the hierarchy of the various functions of inhabiting" (1994, 15). This pathos of topophilia arises in Bilbo before and after each of his harrowing encounters in the narrative, and such moments reveal the supremely practical hobbit nature that guides Bilbo along his journey. Even as he walks down the tunnel to the lair of the ferocious dragon Smaug within the Lonely Mountain, he thinks himself a fool for ever leaving his home: "I have absolutely no use for dragon-guarded treasures, and the whole lot could stay here for ever, if only I could wake up and find this beastly tunnel was my own front-hall at home" (Tolkien, 1997, 193). The protection and power of Beorn's home is connected to what Bilbo represents in the novel, as well as what the younger hobbits fight for in *The Lord of the Rings*. As Marjorie Burns notes, "The concept of home, in fact, not only remains a central image throughout the books but is, in some ways, the true object of the quests: the home lost and regained, the 'back again' of Bilbo's 'there and back again,' and the West to which the Elves at last return" at the end of *The Lord of the Rings* (2005, 136).

Beorn's strong wooden hall and his connection with nature are connected to his comprehensive understanding of his local landscape and his dominion over this specific place in Middle-earth. As a skin-changer who lives between the mountains and the forest, Beorn is a supremely liminal character. Liminal comes from the Latin *limen*, "threshold," and this spatial designation perfectly fits Beorn's interstitial identity and geographic location. His homestead sits between the awe-inspiring peaks of the Misty Mountains and the dark gloom of Mirkwood forest, and he is near (but not immediately adjacent to) the Old Forest Road and the Carrock in the Great River. Over this realm he holds sovereignty, but his power is defined and limited, albeit in a self-imposed manner, by his own volition. After providing refuge to Thorin's company for two days, Beorn equips Bilbo and the dwarves for the next leg of their journey from the Shire to Erebor through the imposing landscape of Mirkwood forest. As he sends them on their way, Beorn warns them of the many perils of the forest, including savage wild things and enchanted waters that await them if they stray from the path. The travelers must set out on their own, however, because Beorn can only now offer advice, as he tells them: "beyond the edge of the forest I cannot help you much" (Tolkien, 1997, 122). The skin-changer benevolently governs his animal servants and fiercely defends his homeland from the goblins and wolves that invade, but he ventures out of this realm only in the direst of circumstances.

An important piece of Beorn's provincial power is the ability to name aspects of the natural world. In describing the projection of rock in the middle of the river where the eagles set Bilbo and the dwarves down, Gandalf introduces this element of Beorn's sovereignty: "He [Beorn] called it the Carrock, because carrock is his word for it. He calls things like that carrocks, and this one is *the* Carrock because it is the only one near his home and he knows it well" (105). This designation between *a* carrock and *the* Carrock is an important one, because much of the landscape of *The Hobbit* is composed of elemental and singular geographic features—The Hill and The Water in Hobbiton, the Wild that exists beyond the peaceful borders of the Shire, the Misty Mountains, the unknown Land Beyond, The Wild River, the Long Lake, Laketown, and the Lonely Mountain. Beorn's realm, in the center of the Wild, can be a dangerous place. After his own reconnaissance mission to check on the validity of Gandalf's account of the traveling party's exploits beneath the Misty Mountains, Beorn tells them: "If you lived near the edge of Mirkwood, you would take better the word of no one that you did not know as well as your brother or better" (121). Paul W. Lewis adds, "Beorn's temperament tended towards suspicion, probably spawned and honed by his life on the edge of Mirkwood Forest" (2007, 148). The skin-changer is a fierce enemy, as evidenced by the goblin head and wolf-skin that he posts outside his gate. It is only through a clever rhetorical strategy and an exciting tale that Gandalf is even able to bring his company of dwarves into Beorn's home, as Bilbo later realizes: "The interruptions had really made Beorn more interested in the story, and the story had kept him from sending the dwarves off at once like suspicious beggars. He never invited people into his house, if he could help it. He had very few friends and they lived a good way away; and he never invited more than a couple of these to his house at a time" (Tolkien, 1997, 114).

Beorn's hard-fought existence in the wilderness has made him wary of strangers and fiercely loyal to his comrades, and his new fellowship with Gandalf, Bilbo, and the dwarves has important implications for the end of *The Hobbit*. Beorn's medieval pedigree and ecological connection to Middle-earth enhance the narrative richness and mythical depth of the overall narrative of *The Hobbit*. He proves to be an essential piece of *The Hobbit*, despite his status as a secondary character, because his symbolic and literal size allows him to be something and fulfill a narrative role that the novel's main characters simply cannot. In this respect, the oversized and menacing Beorn serves as a foil and complimentary protagonist to the small and friendly Bilbo. From the very first chapter of the novel, Tolkien describes exactly who and what Bilbo is. Although he is the eponymous protagonist of the story, Bilbo is categorically not a Hero, and he is far from the figure in mythology and epic literature who charges proudly into battle, slays dragons, and rescues damsels in distress. When the dwarves insult Bilbo and question his utility on their venture, Gandalf responds by saying: "I have chosen Mr. Baggins and that ought to be enough for all of you. If I say he is a Burglar, a Burglar he is, or will be when the time comes. There is a lot more in him than you guess, and a deal more than he has any idea of himself" (Tolkien, 1997, 19). Gandalf echoes this statement later in the text when he says that Bilbo "has more about him than you guess, and you will find that out before long," and furthermore, the hobbit is "as fierce as a dragon in a pinch" (125 and 17). His stealthiness, determination, and no small amount of good luck make him an ideal candidate to help the dwarves reclaim Erebor, because as Gandalf explains, they cannot simply charge in through the mountain stronghold's front gate:

> That would be no good, not without a mighty Warrior, even a Hero. I tried to find one; but warriors are busy fighting one another in distant lands, and in this neighborhood heroes are scarce, or simply not to be found. Swords in these parts are mostly blunt, and axes are used for trees, and shields as cradles or dish-covers; and dragons are comfortably far-off (and therefore legendary). That is why I settled on *burglary*—especially when I remembered the existence of a Side-door. And here is our little Bilbo Baggins, *the* burglar, the chosen and selected burglar, so now let's get on and make some plans [21].

As Gandalf, Bilbo, and the dwarves venture farther into the wild lands and eventually reach the Lonely Mountain, their encounter with Beorn provides a direct answer to Gandalf's sentiment about the scarcity of Warriors and Heroes. In addition to the mythical back-story and narrative gravitas that he adds to the story, Beorn's might and ferocity are essential to achieving victory at the Battle of the Five Armies. Bilbo's burglary skills and resilience serve him well throughout the journey, especially when he gains the inside information that leads to the defeat of the dragon Smaug, but he cannot kill the dragon himself or even fight in the novel's climactic battle. Instead, a true Warrior and Hero like Beorn must charge in and save the day:

> In that last hour Beorn himself had appeared—no one knew how or from where. He came alone, and in his bear's shape; and he seemed to have grown almost to giant-size in his wrath... The roar of his voice was like drums and guns; and he tossed wolves and goblins from his path like straws and feathers. He fell upon their rear, and broke like a clap of thunder through the ring. [After Thorin fell] his wrath was redoubled, so that nothing could withstand him, and no weapon seemed to bite upon him. He scattered the bodyguard, and pulled down Bolg himself and crushed him. Then dismay fell on the goblins and they fled in all directions [Tolkien, 1997, 259–60].

With the story's undersized protagonist Bilbo safely invisible, out of the way, and even knocked unconscious for most of the battle, the novel's true warrior takes center stage and fights to pull the dwarf, elf, and human army to victory.

Tolkien patterns Beorn's decisive ferocity and wrath in this episode on the martial prowess of his medieval forefathers. Tolkien's description of Beorn in battle is reminiscent of the strength of Beowulf and the weapon-proof skin and devastating destruction caused by Böthvarr Bjarki's bear-spirit, and it is also harkens back to the famous Irish warrior Cúchulainn. This hero is one of the central figures of the Ulster Cycle, a mythological codex that was first written down in eighth-century Ireland (Kinsella, 1970, ix). Cúchulainn's childhood includes many notable exploits that establish his superhuman strength and heroic character, most notably when he offers his services as the watchdog for a wealthy blacksmith named Culann. It is through this feat that he earns his famous nickname as the *Cú* of Culann, the hound of Culann, or Cúchulainn. While he is not a bear-warrior like Beowulf or Böthvarr Bjarki, Cúchulainn's martial ability is great enough that he becomes the champion warrior in the famous epic *Táin Bó Cuailnge*, or the *Cattle Raid of Cooley*, which pits Queen Medb and King Ailill of Connacht in western Ireland against Cúchulainn of Ulster, in the north. Just as Beorn's wrath in battle causes his body to grow to a giant size, so too does Cúchulainn display an Otherworldly bodily disfigurement when he charges into the fray. This "warp-spasm" seizes his body and transforms it, in Thomas Kinsella's evocative translation, into "a monstrous thing, hideous and shapeless, unheard of": this wrath causes him to "shake like a tree in the flood or a reed in the stream," his legs twist under his skin so that his feet face backwards and his calves face forwards, his hair stands straight out from his scalp, and he sucks one of his eyes into his head and pops the other one out so that it falls onto his cheek (1970, 150–151). Immediately after this awesome display of bodily ferocity, Cúchulainn steps onto his chariot and begins to systematically mow down his enemies, much like Beorn in *The Hobbit*. These two medieval warriors fight with an animalistic fury and almost single-handedly defeat their enemies, and after winning the Battle of the Five Armies, Beorn even accompanies Bilbo and Gandalf on their return journey and welcomes them into his home once more to celebrate a merry Yule-tide holiday (Tolkien, 1997, 263).

Beorn's heroism and action at the end of *The Hobbit* is necessary because it throws Bilbo's practicality and yearning for home into sharp relief—Bilbo has no idea of the heroism and ferocity needed to survive in the wild lands beyond the Shire, because goblins, dragons, and warriors are comfortably far-off from both Hobbiton and our own modern world. Bilbo's journey across the landscapes of Middle-earth and into the Wilderland brings him into a realm where monsters and heroes still exist, and his friendship with mighty men like Beorn allows the forces of good to succeed in the end. As Tom Shippey notes, Bilbo represents the modern worldview and sensibilities among the otherwise fantastic and legendary stuff of Middle-earth, and it is only through his eyes that we are able to glimpse and understand the outsized exploits of heroes like Beorn (Shippey, 2003, 71). In assessing the tone of his novel, Tolkien wrote in 1951 that *The Hobbit* is "the study of a simple ordinary man, neither artistic nor noble and heroic (but not without the undeveloped seeds of these things) against a high setting—and in fact (as a critic has perceived) the tone and style change with the Hobbit's development, passing from fairy-tale to the noble and high and relapsing with the return" (1981, 159). Beorn represents one of the narrative pinnacles of the story, and his nobility and heroism come from the medieval inspirations for his character and his connection to his landscape. For an author who idealized his childhood in the rural world of the English Midlands, it comes as no surprise that his notable character possesses such an essential connection to the flower and trees that surround him.

Tom Bombadil of the Old Forest

Professor Tolkien's narrative in *The Lord of the Rings* purposefully parallels *The Hobbit* in a number of ways, including the story's beginnings in the Shire, the central role played by a Baggins, the long and arduous journey across Middle-earth, and the climactic battle between good and evil. These similarities are also present between the thematically- and geographically-related charters Beorn and Tom Bombadil. Paul W. Lewis argues for a purposeful literary kinship between the two characters, because they both "live on the edge of a fierce and dangerous forest" and are "vastly aware of their surroundings," and they offer the security, peace, and comfort of their homes to weary travelers (2007, 153–154). Similarly, Peter Beagle states: "in a literary sense [Beorn] is the forerunner of the more deeply realized Tom Bombadil. Both are wary creatures, misliking the great concerns of other peoples. Both are their own masters, under no enchantment but their own" (1966, xii). Even though Beorn's origins are unknown to even the wisest in Middle-earth, his exact nature is clear—he is a skin-changer who takes on both human and bear shapes. Bombadil, on the other hand, embodies both an enigmatic origin and nature. Lewis comments on the importance of his origin and its relevance to his character in *The Lord of the Rings*: "The question of Tom Bombadil's background, even more so than Beorn's, can not really be distinguished from his life. 'What is he?' is intimately tied to 'who is he?' It is inseparable" (2007, 149). Scholars have put forth many ideas in an attempt to pin-down and delineate his mysterious identity, ranging from a mortal human-like creature to a spiritual or godlike being. As Wayne G. Hammond and Christina Scull note, Bombadil was originally based on a Dutch doll that belonged to the Tolkien children, and his first literary appearance was in Tolkien's poem "The Adventures of Tom Bombadil" in *The Oxford Magazine* in 1934 (2005, 124).[6] Additionally, David Elton Gay describes Bombadil's character traits in *The Lord of the Rings* as having a distinct connection to Väinämöinen, the great singer of the Finnish epic the *Kalevala* (2004, 297), while Gene Hargrove argues that Tom and his wife Goldberry are actually the Valar Aulë and Yavanna (1986, 23). Beyond these possible points of inspiration, critics often focus on the supernatural elements of this character. Most notably, Klaus Jensen and Ruairidh

MacDonald characterize Bombadil as a faerie guide who "initiates [the hobbits] into the triune worlds of faerie, childhood and myth as an indispensable prerequisite for fulfilling the Ring mission" (2006, 37).

Recent scholarship has also begun to understand Bombadil as a creature who is essentially connected with his place and environment in Middle-earth. Tom Shippey calls him a "*genius loci* ... of the river and willow country of the English Midlands," who represents, as Tolkien himself wrote, "the spirit of the (vanishing) Oxford and Berkshire countryside" (2003, 108). Lewis describes Bombadil as a primal nature spirit and an archetypal vegetation god, whose magic is part of the fabric of nature (2007, 150), and Liam Campbell calls him "a model of ecological ethics and environmental harmony" (2010, 45). Bombadil is a spirit of the Old Forest landscape because his actions, his songs, and his very identity are tied to the woods. When the hobbits first encounter him, he is sauntering through the forest and singing to himself a continuous song of rhyming couplets that mentions the wind, starling, sunlight, starlight, river, willow, water-lilies, evening, and daytime. Bombadil tells a long tale that weaves back and froth between prose and verse, so that the hobbits begin to understand "the lives of the Forest, apart from themselves, indeed to feel themselves as the strangers where all other things were at home" (Tolkien, *The Fellowship of the Ring*, 1993, 141). Additionally, when Bombadil enters his house "waving his arms as if he was warding off the rain," he appears quite dry, except for his boots, so the text subtly suggests that he has some power over the elements (140). Bombadil and his companion Goldberry are colorful creatures right out of a fairy tale, as displayed by his enormous smile, long brown beard, old battered hat with a feather stuck in it, yellow boots, and a blue coat, as well as the way that he talks to himself and others through a continuous melody. He refers to Goldberry as the "River-daughter," and her lush green gown, adorned with silver beads and a golden belt shaped like lilies and forget-me-nots, is similarly reminiscent of the natural world that surrounds their existence in the forest (134). She also possesses an elemental connection with the water of her mythical origin, because she sings a rain song "as sweet as showers on dry hills" during her washing day, which seems to have caused the downpour outside, and "the sound of her footsteps was like a stream falling gently away downhill over cool stones in the quiet of night" (140 and 136).

The nature-loving Bombadil possesses a local sovereignty over the specific realm of the Old Forest, and his command over the natural world reveals an enmeshed connection with his landscape. In the terminology of space and place theory, he represents a supreme form of a "placed existence" and possesses a devout topophilia for his cottage and the surrounding woodland. Bombadil, perhaps even more than Beorn, manifests Lane's maxim of space and place studies, which states that an individual's identity is integrated with an inextricable from their place. Bombadil possesses great power, like Beorn in *The Hobbit*, but he also displays great fondness for the plants and animals around him. Goldberry carefully describes his mastery over the forest to the hobbits: "the trees and the grasses and all living things growing or living in the and belong each to themselves. Tom Bombadil is the Master. No one has ever caught old Tom walking in the forest, wading in the water, leaping on the hilltops under light and shadow. He has no fear. Tom Bombadil is Master" (Tolkien, *The Fellowship of the Ring*, 1993, 135). She defines Bombadil's connection to the landscape as if he himself is an animal, but a proud and powerful creature that walks, wades, and leaps without fear of being captured. Bombadil maintains a very similar pacifist-unless-provoked lifestyle, and he sticks to a vegetarian diet of yellow cream, honeycomb, white bread, butter, milk, cheese, green herbs, and ripe berries with which Beorn would feel right at home.

Bombadil is also, like Beorn, a liminal being by virtue of his place in Middle-earth and his nature. The Old Forest exists on the border between the Shire and the rest of Middle-earth, and when the hobbits enter this realm in Book I of *The Lord of the Rings*, they recognize the otherworldly and threatening nature of the place. Specifically, Merry describes the forest as queer: "Everything in it is very much more alive, more aware of what is going on, so to speak, than things in the Shire. And the trees do not like strangers" (Tolkien, *The Fellowship of the Ring*, 1993, 121). The hobbits run afoul of an old and hoary willow-tree, and as they fall under an enchanted sleep, the tree snatches Merry and Pippin with its roots and traps them inside. Bombadil tells the hobbits that he knows the tune for the Old Man Willow: "I'll freeze his marrow cold, if he don't behave himself, I'll sing his roots off. I'll sing a wind up and blow leaf and branch away" (131). Bombadil threatens the tree with great harm, but his power is conveyed through words and song, and the Willow immediately complies and goes back to sleep. The end of Tolkien's chapter 6 on the Old Forest makes Bombadil's liminal symbolism even more apparent, because the last sentences shows the hobbits standing just outside Bombadil's home: "And with that song the hobbits stood upon the threshold, and a golden light was all about them" (133). Accordingly, the first sentence of chapter 7 shows the hobbits stepping "over the wide stone threshold" and blinking from the comforting light of "lamps swinging from the beams of the roof" and candles burning brightly "on the table of dark polished wood" (134). Bombadil has the same fondness for wood building materials that Beorn has, although his candles and light fixtures are a bit more modern than Beorn's roaring fire at the center of the dark hall.

When Bombadil rescues the hobbits from the menacing tree, he affirms his place as the ruler of this specific landscape and the guardian of this threshold between the shelter and protection of the Shire and the dangerous outer-world of Middle-earth. Frodo, Sam, Merry and Pippin must travel out of their comfortable native land if they have any hope of keeping the One Ring away from the enemy, and Bombadil plays an essential role in their journey from the known to the unknown and wild. The nature spirit delights in the natural earthliness of the Old Forest's riverlands, the "wood, water and hill" over which he is master, and he guards the hobbits in this liminal space as a provincially-focused substitute for the absent and globally-minded Gandalf, who is busy elsewhere (Kocher, 1972, 38). Tolkien's text portrays Bombadil as a fairie guide and nature spirit, and his sovereignty over nature and his indeterminate biological status reveals the importance of his place in the narrative. Bombadil is "too large and heavy for a hobbit, if not quite tall enough for one of the Big People"; similarly, Goldberry's fair voice strikes Frodo as "lees keen and lofty" than an elven-voice, "but deeper and nearer to mortal heart; marvellous and yet not strange" (Tolkien, *The Fellowship of the Ring*, 1993, 131 and 134). The miraculous presence of four inviting beds, four wash basins, four pairs of slippers, and four sets of earthenware dishes in Bombadil's house indicates that the hobbits have entered the realm of the faerie tale in the Old Forest. Bombadil rules over this faerie inter-space and safely conveys the hobbits on their way to the town of Bree and further, and his pastoral and utopian forest-realm represents what the hobbits must fight to protect throughout the War of the Ring.

In addition to the many influences that scholars have offered, I suggest that Bombadil, as a spiritual creature whose words contain great power, possesses a striking note of inspiration from Irish mythology. Marjorie Burns has written on Tolkien's Celtic influences, and she specifically connects the Elves of Middle-earth to the Tuatha de Danann, the euhemerized gods of the Irish Celtic Otherworld (2005, 66–67). Tolkien himself admitted a reserved recognition of Celtic material, writing in 1937: "I do know Celtic things (many in their original languages Irish and Welsh), and feel for them a certain distaste: largely for their fundamental unreason. They have naught colour, but are like a broken stained glass window reassembled without design" (1981, 26). Despite such admissions, Burns argues that Tolkien "borrowed extensively from Celtic settings, figures, attitudes, and motifs"; she adds: "If we step aside from linguistic and literary speculation and apply an unscholarly test, most of us would agree that Tolkien's Elves ... are deeply invested with Celtic ethereality and Celtic shiftings of time" (2005, 21–25). I believe that there is a similar Celtic influence on Tom Bombadil, and this influence becomes clear when two exemplary stories are placed alongside *The Lord of the Rings*.

One of Bombadil's major functions in *The Lord of the Rings* is to rescue the hobbits on the Barrow-Downs, and this episode offers a few clues to Tolkien's possible Irish source material. As some type of spiritual being, Bombadil is able to save the hobbits when they become trapped in the barrow. The supernatural foe that Bombadil vanquishes in this scene is a Barrow-wight, the spirit of a long-dead warrior that enchants Frodo and the hobbits and nearly kills them. The mythology of ancient and early-medieval Ireland has a highly developed spiritual realm commonly called the Otherworld, and this place is inhabited by fairies and spirits, demons and monsters, and even gods and goddesses. One place of connection and transaction between our world and the Otherworld was the sídh mound, the same kind of a raised-earth burial mound that was commonly called a barrow in England. During certain religiously important times of the Celtic calendar, the doorway to the Otherworld could be opened and creatures like the Barrow-wight could make their way into the world. One particularly noteworthy story where this motif is on full display is the *Echtrae Nera*, "The Adventure of Nera," another mythical Irish story from the Ulster Cycle. In this story, the hero Nera accepts a challenge from King Ailill of Ulster to leave the security of the palace and journey to the nearby crossroads, where two bodies still hang from the gallows from the previous day's executions. With this action Nera performs no small feat, because it is the uncanny night of Samain, the Celtic precursor to Halloween, and "the darkness and horror of that night were great," because demons used always to appear on that night" and the dead have the power to come back to life (Carey, 2003, 127).

Nera carries one of the newly reanimated corpses on a few errands but is understandably quick to end his harrowing ordeal, but upon returning to the palace, he finds the building smoldering and the people massacred. He then sees the army responsible for the destruction marching back into the sídh mound, because they are the merciless "army of phantoms" of the Otherworld. He follows them into the fairy realm and speaks with an oracle there who tells him that his home has not really been destroyed—what he saw was a vision of the future that will come to pass in one year if he does not act to save his kingdom. Because of the shifting of time that Nera experiences in the mound, he believes that he has spent three days in the summertime of the Otherworld, but he is able to return to the coming winter of the mortal realm without any real time lapsing. He brings *toirthe samraid* ("fruits of the summer") as proof to the king of his voyage into the Otherworld and the validity of the prophecy (Carey, 2003, 129). At the Samain celebration one year later, King Ailill musters his army and raids the sídh, returning victorious with the crown of King Brian of the Tuatha de Danann.

Just as in *The Lord of the Rings*, this Irish story features the evil and undead forces of the otherworld threatening the well-being of the living. Once Frodo and the hobbits become trapped in the barrow, they encounter the wight, a "tall dark figure like a shadow against the stars ... [with] two eyes, very cold though lit with a pale light that seemed to come from some remote distance" (Tolkien, *The Fellowship of the Ring* 1993, 151). Frodo sees, amidst piles of ancient treasure and weaponry, his companions lying unconscious on the ground with a long sword resting across their necks. Just as a long and ominous arm reaches out of the darkness and towards the sword, Frodo summons his inner strength and calls out to Bombadil. After a moment of silence, the stone-walls of the barrow crumble as Bombadil enters singing of his power: "None has ever caught him yet, for Tom, he is the master: / His songs are stronger songs, and his feet are faster" (153). Master Tom is a representative of the spirit world in Middle-earth, and he has great power over the Barrow-wight, a similarly liminal character that exists in between a truly corporeal or ethereal state. After Bombadil carries the hobbits out of the destroyed barrow, he rouses them with a cheerful waking song: "Wake now my merry lads! Wake and hear me calling! / Warm now be heart and limb! The cold stone is fallen; / Dark door is standing wide; dead hand is broken / Night under Night is flown, and the Gate is open!" (154). Bombadil's power over the Old Forest and its environs is so potent that he can even command the forces of the undead. When he delivers the hobbits from "under the knife" and back out to the cheerful, warm, and living natural world, his words demonstrate the power of songs and speech in Tolkien's Middle-earth, where they often have greater power than an arrow-shot or a sword-stroke. Tom Shippey points out the fact that even Bombadil's unsung speech contains elements of alliteration and rhyme (2003, 106–107), and Gene Hargrove adds that "Tom's inability to separate song from his other activities, speaking, walking, [or] working, suggests that it is very fundamental to his being in a profound way that distinguishes him from all other beings encountered in the trilogy" (1986, 22).[7]

While Bombadil's literary kinsman Beorn shares some connection to the warrior Cúchulainn of the *Cattle Raid of Cooley*, Tom himself displays what might be an even stronger similarity to another figure from Irish mythology. The young Cúchulainn must single-handedly fight the army of his enemy because all of his kinsmen have been incapacitated, and he becomes understandably worn out after cutting down hundreds of soldiers with each blow. The saga then reveals the forces of good that can come from the Otherworld, because Cúchulainn is joined by a mysterious "tall, broad, fair-seeming man," wearing a green cloak and a bright silver brooch, who fights gracefully and destructively with a "five-pointed spear" and a "forked javelin," and this warrior wreaks such havoc because the opposing soldiers cannot see him" (Kinsella 1970, 143). This mysterious warrior is Lug Mac Ethenn, a god from the sídh and the chieftain of the Tuatha de Danann, and he fights for Cúchulainn while the young hero sleeps and recovers his strength. The god Lug also turns out to be Cúchulainn's father, so the Irish hero has supernatural blood running through his veins like the supposed "fairy blood" in Bilbo and Frodo's Took ancestry that partially inspires them to embark on their respective adventures (Tolkien 1997, 4). After a rest of three days, Lug wakes Cúchulainn with a very Bombadil-like song: "Rise son of mighty Ulster / with your wounds made whole / a fair man faces your foes / succor has come from the sídh/ to save you in this place… / then arise my son" (Kinsella 1970, 143). Cúchulainn, like the hobbits of Middle-earth, then goes on to achieve great success in battle and achieve an ultimate victory, and his interaction with a benevolent and powerful spirit-creature teaches him much about himself and his place in the world.

Both Lug and Tom Bombadil possess supernatural powers and are ageless creatures who help mortals on earth. Bombadil is a similar being, and he lapses into the third person when describing his vast history: "Eldest, that's what I am… Tom was here before the river and trees; Tom remembers the first raindrop and the first acorn. He made paths before the Big People, and saw the little People arriving. He was here before the kings and the graves and the barrow-wights … he knew the dark under the stars when it was fearless—before the Dark Lord came from the Outside" (Tolkien, *The Fellowship of the Ring*, 1993, 142). This long existence and memory is an integral part of Bombadil's character, and in his lone time on Middle-earth he has become the master of the Old Forest, as Tolkien writes in his notes for *The Lord of the Rings*: "Tom Bombadil is an 'aboriginie'—he knew the land before men, before hobbits, before barrow-wights, yes before the necromancer—before the elves came to this quarter of the world. Goldberry says he is 'master of water, wood and hill.' Does all this land belong to him? No! The land and the things belong to themselves. He is not the possessor but the master, because he belongs to himself" (1988, 117). Tolkien further describes Bombadil as a pacifist who has taken a "vow of poverty" with no thought to his own desire for powers or control of others (1981, 178–179). He is master of the landscape of the Old Forest, but a master who dwells within and cares for this place. Such a refreshing notion of mastery is welcome in Middle-earth, where all of creation is threatened by the Dark Lord's quest for a much more destructive and enslaving form of power.

Even though Bombadil possesses a tremendous power and a connection to the natural world, his sovereignty is limited by self-imposed geographical boundaries. Gandalf describes Bombadil's strategic limitations as a potential ally of those present at the Council of Elrond by stating that "he is withdrawn into a little land, within bounds that he has set, though none can see them, waiting perhaps for a change of days, and he will not step beyond them." The ageless spirit has become unconcerned with the wider world around him, and if he were given the Ring for safekeeping, "he would soon forget it, or most likely throw it away," because such things "have no hold on his mind"; the Elf Glorfindel adds, "Power to defy our enemy is not in him, unless such power is in the earth itself" (Tolkien, *The Fellowship of the Ring*, 1993, 279). Even though Bombadil exists by choice entirely in his small corner of Middle-earth, his memory and power reach back to the very creation of the world. It is entirely appropriate, therefore, that Tolkien implants his writing with many underlying threads that relate Bombadil to episodes towards the end of *The Lord of the Rings*. Tolkien used Bombadil's mythic resonance and enigmatic character to enhance the novel's historical depth and tie the narrative together with an intricate interlacing that enriches the overall saga. Since the hobbits meet Bombadil soon after they set out, I characterize him as the front bookend of the hobbits' collective journey and the War of the Ring. The hobbits' journey is not complete and the war is not over, however, until the narrative reaches the rear bookend and Aragorn is crowned King Elessar of Middle-earth.

The foundations of the Old Forest and the Barrow-Downs date back to the first humans who ruled Middle-earth, the Men of Westernesse, who are also Aragorn's kinsmen. These Dúnedain descended from Isildur and ruled the northern part of Middle-earth for centuries, but their bloodlines largely died out and, as Tolkien writes, "there was often strife between kingdoms, which hastened the waning of the Dúnedain" (Tolkien, *The Return of the King*, 1993, 320). In this setting the Witch-king rose to power in Angmar and gathered "many evil men, Orcs, and other fell creatures" to wage war against the Men of Westernesse. Bombadil possesses such a potent knowledge of the history of his realm in Middle-earth that his story to the hobbits becomes a living entity all to itself. As he talks about the Old Forest and the Great Willow, his talk suddenly "left the woods and went leaping up the young stream, over bubbling waterfalls, over pebbles and worn rocks, and among small flowers in close grass and wet crannies, wandering at last up on to the Downs." Bombadil reveals to the hobbits the fascinating connection between his landscape and the history of their world, because he tells them how the Witch-King brought great strife to his enemies:

> There was victory and defeat; and towers fell, fortresses were burned, and flames went up into the sky. Gold was piled on the biers of dead kings and queens; and mounds covered them, and the stone doors were shut… A shadow came out of dark places far away, and bones were stirred in the mounds. Barrow-wights walked in the hollow places with a clink of rings on cold fingers, and gold

chains in the wind. Stone rings grinned out of the ground like broken teeth in the moonlight [Tolkien, *The Fellowship of the Ring*, 1993, 141].

The mounds of Tyrn Gorthad that were once revered by men as the creation of their forefathers and the burial place of their kings became infested by the Witch-King's evil spirits, and Bombadil causes the hobbits to shudder with his tale of the transformation of this holy ground to the perilous Barrow-downs.

The many victories by the Witch-king and the other forces of evil and the waning of bloodlines are why only Stewards like Denethor rule in Gondor in the south, and why Aragorn's return as the long-lost king is such a crucial component of defeating Sauron and saving Middle-earth. The Barrow-downs, the Old Forest, the Dead Marshes, and numerous other places in Tolkien's mythology can be considered *loci memoriae*, or "memory places," the concept that French historian Pierre Nora created to better understand the "history of memory" that is constructed "through the imaginary representations and historical realities that occupy the symbolic sites" that are important in forming social and cultural identity (Kritzman, 1996, ix). The burials that occurred on the ground of the Barrow-downs, and the warfare and hauntings that followed, have elevated this landscape into a symbolic and literal storehouse of the past. In fact, the Barrow-downs have become much more than a mere landscape or place on the map of Middle-earth, because this place's history of settlement, warfare, and mythologizing has shaped it into a truly sacred entity. As Lane notes, the sacredness of a culturally important place like the Barrows comes from the "history of cultural tensions and conflicting claims, [and] even ecological shifts in the terrain itself" (2001, 3–4). "Without exception," Lane adds, "the sacred place is the place rich in story," because "the enduring identity of a sacred place lies in the stories it bears and the power that these tales exert on the people who repeat them" (15 and ix). The power and enduring historical legacy of Bombadil's local landscape is almost lost to the ages, but because of luck or fate or the workings of providence, the hobbits step right into this repository for the past.

Bombadil's connection to the natural world and power over his landscape come from his comprehensive knowledge of the world around him, and he uses this knowledge to assist Frodo and the hobbits on their journey across Middle-earth. In addition to giving the hobbits a "history lesson," he also bestows upon them still potent artifacts of this history, the ancient weapons of Westernesse that the hobbits carry to war in Gondor and then back home to the Shire:

> For each of the hobbits he chose a dagger, long, leaf-shaped, and keen, of marvelous workmanship, damasked with serpent-forms in red and gold. They gleamed as he drew them from their black sheaths, wrought of some strange metal, light and strong, and set with many fiery stones. Whether by some virtue in these sheaths or because of the spell that lay on the ground, the blades seemed untouched by time, unrusted, sharp, glittering in the sun [Tolkien, *The Fellowship of the Ring*, 1993, 157].

This type of sword is mentioned many times in the poem *Beowulf*, where the poet uses terms like *bunden* ("ornamented," line 1285a), *brodenmæl* ("damascened," line 1616a), and *sceadenmæl* ("patterned," line 1939a) to describe the aesthetic of the weapon. This Old English terminology describes swords that were made of iron and steel twisted together to combine the respective metals' hardness and flexibility, and the result was a pattern on the blade reminiscent of a serpent's wavy body or a dragon's scales. With this description of the daggers from the Barrow-downs, Tolkien weaves together a host of influences and references from within his own writing and from his medieval inspiration. His language is reminiscent of *Beowulf*, the famous poem that Tolkien knew intimately and about which he delivered his famous lecture *Beowulf: The Monsters and the Critics*. Tolkien's vocabulary also calls to mind images from his own writing, such as the dragon "Smaug the Tremendous" from *The Hobbit*, the "Chiefest and Greatest of Calamities" in all of Middle-earth (1997, 200). Finally, the introduction of these weapons in Book I of the story foreshadows the famous sword Andúril that Aragorn carries into battle, the "Sword that was Broken and is forged again" that shines like a flame when it is unsheathed (Tolkien, *The Two Towers*, 1993, 36).

Despite Bombadil's focus only on his micro-landscape, he does play an essential role in the greater narrative of the *The Lord of the Rings* by helping the Army of the West achieve victory in the epic military engagement at the end of the story and on the other side of Middle-earth. Like Beorn before him, Bombadil provides the means by which a major victory is won in his text (Lewis, 2007, 156). He tells the hobbits that the "serpent-form" blades were forged by the men of Westernesse, the ancient foes of the Dark Lord, but they were defeated by the Witch-king of Angmar. In the Third Age of Middle-earth the Witch-king becomes Sauron's chief Ringwraith, the head of Nazgûl, and he would have almost certainly defeated the army of the West during the Battle of the Pelennor Fields in Book V of *The Lord of the Rings* without Bombadil's assistance. With the barrow sword that Merry carries across Middle-earth and into battle in Gondor, he strikes a powerful blow against the Witch-King, the original and ancient target for that weapon, and brings about his downfall (Shippey, 2003, 105). Just as the Witch-King is about to kill the shield-maiden Éowyn, it is the hobbit Merry who fells the monster with the sword he has carried all the way from the Barrow-downs. Tolkien tells us that the sword's creator would be glad to know that it had finally felled the "sorcerer king" of Angmar: "no other blade, not though mightier hands had wielded it, would have dealt that foe a wound so bitter, cleaving the undead flesh, breaking the spell that knit his unseen sinews to his will" (Tolkien, *The Return of the King*, 1993, 120).

Scholars discuss how the supposed coincidence of Merry's sword points to the strong interlace in *The Lord of the Rings* as well as Tolkien's sense of "cosmic order"—some fate-like power helped Bombadil rescue the hobbits and give them the barrow weapons because this providence knew the only way the evil of the Witch-King could be destroyed. And, as often happens in *The Lord of the Rings*, the forces of evil help to bring about their own demise.[8] In *The Unfinished Tales* Tolkien tells us that the Witch-King set obstacles to help find the ring before the hobbits even left the Shire: "the Barrow-wights were roused, and all things of evil spirit, hostile to elves and Men, were on the watch with malice in the Old Forest and on the Barrow-downs" (1980, 348). Providence also roused its forces of good, however, and Bombadil set in motion the events that helped to defeat the Black Captain. Bombadil acts as a bookend to the narrative of *The Lord of the Rings* because he introduces the hobbits (and the reader) to the ancient race of kings who once ruled Middle-earth, and Aragorn (the other narrative bookend) completes his own heroic journey in Book VI and ascends to become Elessar, the King of Middle Earth. When Bombadil gives the barrow blades to the hobbits, they have visions of "a vast shadowy plain over which there strode shapes of Men, tall and grim with bright swords, and last came one with a star on his brow." With this vision Tolkien gives us a glimpse of the history of Middle-earth and of the long line of kings who have ruled, with Aragorn at the end. Bombadil echoes this image, saying that, "few now remember them, yet still some go wandering, sons of forgotten kings walking in loneliness, guarding from evil things folk that are heedless" (Tolkien, *The Fellowship of the Ring*, 1993, 157). Only a tenth of the way into his vast and masterful saga, Tolkien gives us a brief inkling of the totality of his vision through Bombadil's meditative thoughts. The interlacing threads of his masterful narrative become clear when Aragorn first brandishes Andúril in Book III, where it seems to Legolas that, for a moment, "a white flame flickered on the brow of Aragorn like a shining crown" (Tolkien, *The Two Towers*, 1993, 36). Similarly, at the end of *The Lord of the Rings*, Faramir presents an ancient crown to King Aragorn that is set with "seven gems of adamant" and with a single jewel on the summit, "the light of which went up like a flame" (Tolkien, *The Return of the King*, 1993, 247).

Conclusion

Because Tolkien's narrative of Middle-earth is so heavily invested in entire races working together to defeat the forces of evil, and in heroic representatives of these races joining together in fellowship, there will always be something unusual and alluring about Beorn and Bombadil. In a vast mythology punctuated by kings and warriors, and by hidden elf cities, cavernous dwarf mines, and towering human citadels, these two characters and their small and quiet homes are remarkable for their intimacy with the local landscape and their far-reaching imprint on their respective narratives. The similar medieval origins for each character, their close connections with the natural world, their places in the landscape and in their respective texts, and their supporting but influential roles in each story indicate the strong literary influence that Tolkien's early writing had on his later creation. In fact, I believe that the singular, insular, and warlike Beorn had an undeniable influence on the singular, insular, but peace-loving Tom Bombadil. And just as Tolkien's manuscripts reveal some uncertainty over Beorn's nature and heritage, so too does Tolkien maintain the essentialness of an air of mystery surrounding Bombadil's identity. Although his character was established well before the completion of *The Lord of the Rings*, Tolkien refined his notions of place and spirituality as he wove Bombadil into his larger narrative in the 1940s and 50s. And, despite living with Bombadil as his children's plaything or a fully-animated literary character for decades, Tolkien found himself reflecting on and explaining this character even while his books neared publication. In 1954, he wrote to his proofreader: "Even in a mythical Age there must be some enigmas, as there always are. Tom Bombadil is one (intentionally) ... [he] is not an important person—to the narrative. I suppose he has some importance as a 'comment' [and] he represents something that I feel important, though I would not be prepared to analyze the feeling precisely. I would not, however, have left him in, if he did not have some kind of function" (1981, 178).

These two related characters offer a fascinating glimpse in Tolkien's medieval inspiration and the narrative methodology that he utilized in *The Hobbit* and *The Lord of the Rings*. He crafted an innovative power dynamic in his narrative with Beorn and Bombadil because these individuals stand out in a world of communities, and because their integration with their respective landscapes is a necessary development for the peaceful resolution of each book. Although they are are exotic and mysterious, even in the fantasy realm of Middle-earth, these two are essential for the achievement of Tolkien's overall literary narrative. Lewis comments on the dynamism between the center and the periphery by stating: "Bombadil and Beorn represent those aspects of tangents that always happen. They have an important impact on the final outcome, so in one sense, they are not necessarily acting enigmatically. Yet for Tolkien, it is the very nature of their enigmatic existence which makes them so important, so connected, and so essential" (2007, 157). The stakes of the War of the Ring are so high precisely because everything in Middle-earth is in peril, from the men of Gondor fighting on the front lines to the hobbits living peacefully in the Shire, blissfully unaware of the wide world around them. In summing up the many written reflections that Tolkien has left on Tom Bombadil, Jensen and MacDonald declare, "Tom Bombadil is all Tolkien ever said about him, *and* infinitely much more" (2006, 41). The nature spirit Bombadil, along with his literary ancestor the protective and fierce Beorn, receive little mention in Tolkien's writing when compared to the central characters. Despite this peripheral status, they play essential roles in the narrative that add depth to Tolkien's overall mythology and add complexity to the interconnectedness of the narrative. After analyzing these two characters in depth and revealing their true value, I believe they are worth a renewed appreciation. It falls on the dedicated scholar and reader, therefore, to renew ties with these enigmatic but inspirational creatures, and we can ask for no better exemplar than the wizard Gandalf, who states: "I am going to have a long talk with Bombadil: such a talk as I have not had in all my time. He is a moss-gatherer, and I have been a stone doomed to rolling. But my rolling days are ending, and now we shall have much to say to one another" (Tolkien, *The Return of the King*, 1993, 275).

Notes

1. Tolkien's most famous and long lasting contribution to medieval studies is a lecture he delivered in 1936 to the British Academy titled "*Beowulf*: The Monsters and the Critics." This address reveals Tolkien's dissatisfaction with much of the criticism of Beowulf, because most scholars dismantle the poem to focus on its historical figures and information, but he instead champions a focus on the poem as a unified literary work. This radical view of the poem places the monsters back in their rightful positions at the center of the poem's narrative and meaning. For the complete text and a thorough discussion of its place in Tolkien's scholarly career, see Tolkien, J.R.R. 2002. *Beowulf and the Critics*, Edited by Michael D. C. Drout. Tempe: Arizona Center for Medieval and Renaissance Studies.

2. All translations from Old English are my own. This passage from the poem uses the Old English term *middangeard* (line 751b), and although it is usually translated as "world," a more literal translation is "middle-yard" or "middle-earth."

3. The names and identities of the dwarves in *The Hobbit*, for example, come from an Old Norse poetic fragment called the "Dvergatal," the Dwarf Tally," in a larger poem called "Völuspá," "The Sybil's Vision." While the fragment exists only as a list of names, including "Bífur, Báfur, Bömbur, [and] Nóri," and what appear to be epithets, like *Eikinskjaldi* ("Oaken-shield"), Tolkien believed that some story must lie behind the tally, and so his creation of *The Hobbit* is a valiant and successful attempt at constructing a consistent and coherent narrative around the names. For more information, see Shippey, 2001, 15–17.

4. This comparison between the construction and design of Beorn's hall and that of the Riders is appropriate because, as Paul W. Lewis notes, Beorn's ancestry can be traced back in part to the same humans from whom the Riders are descended. For more information, see Lewis 2007, 145.

5. Tolkien only sparsely describes Bilbo and the dwarves' time in Rivendell in *The Hobbit*, noting simply that "there is little to tell about their stay" with Elrond and the elves (Tolkien 1997, 48). In the more complex and richly visualized *The Lord of the Rings*, however Tolkien provides greater description of the "Last Homely House east of the Sea," including a "high garden above the steep bank of the river below" where Frodo meets his fellow hobbits, and the Hall of Fire, a place of song-sing and tale-telling that has "a bright fire ... burning in a great hearth between the carven pillars upon either side" (Tolkien, *The Fellowship of the Ring*, 1993, 237–242).

6. Tolkien published a poetry collection called *The Adventures of Tom Bombadil* in 1962, and this volume included two poems on the exploits of Bombadil in the Old Forest, poems set in Middle-earth, and other poems with mythical and faerie-inspired settings and characters. This collection, along with some of Tolkien's lesser-known short stories, were published in the paperback volume: Tolkien, J.R.R. 1966. *A Tolkien Reader*. New York: Ballantine, and in the recent expanded collection: Tolkien, J.R.R. 2008. *Tales from the Perilous Realm*. Boston: Houghton Mifflin.

7. Bombadil also possesses the power to bestow names on places, things, and creatures, and this ability is matched by Beorn. In *The Hobbit* Bilbo asks Gandalf about the origins of the Carrock, the hill of stone that stands in the Great River, and the wizard replies: "[Beorn] called it the Carrock, because carrock is his word for it. He calls things like that carrocks, and this one is *the* Carrock because it is the only one near his home and he knows it well" (Tolkien, 1997, 105). Similarly, the names that Bombadil gives to the hobbits' ponies in *The Fellowship of the Ring* are the only names that the animals respond to for the rest of their lives. Shippey describes the ancient myth of these examples of "true language," where "there is a thing for each word and a

word for each thing, and in which signifier then naturally has power over signified" (2003, 106). In a world crafted with such great care by Tolkien the philologist, this ability to possess and speak true language gives great power to both Beorn and Bombadil.

8. For a complete description of the cosmic order at work in *The Lord of the Rings*, and the ways that evil brings about good, see Kocher 1972, 46–48.

Works Cited

Bachelard, Gaston. 1994. *The Poetics of Space*. Translated by Maria Jolas. Boston: Beacon.
Beagle, Peter. 1966. "Tolkien's Magic Ring." In *The Tolkien Reader*, by J.R.R. Tolkien, ix–xvii. New York: Ballantine.
Burns, Marjorie. 2005. *Perilous Realms: Celtic and Norse in Tolkien's Middle-earth*. Toronto: University of Toronto Press.
Byock, Jesse L., trans. 1998. *The Saga of King Hrolf Kraki*. New York: Penguin.
Campbell, Liam. 2010. "The Enigmatic Mr. Bombadil: Tom Bombadil's Role as a Representation of Nature in *The Lord of the Rings*." In *Middle-earth and Beyond: Essays on the World of J.R.R. Tolkien*, edited by Kathleen Dubs and Janka Kaščáková, 41–65. Newcastle: Cambridge Scholars.
Carey, John, trans., 2003. "The Adventure of Nera." In *The Celtic Heroic Age: Literary Sources for Ancient Celtic Europe and Early Ireland & Wales*, edited by John T. Koch, 127–132. Aberystwyth: Celtic Studies.
Fulk, R. D., Bobert E. Bjork, and John D. Niles, eds. 2008. *Klaeber's Beowulf and the Fight at Finnsburg*, 4th ed. Toronto: University of Toronto Press.
Gay, David Elton. 2004. "J.R.R. Tolkien and the *Kalevala*: Some Thoughts on the Finnish Origins of Tom Bombadil and Treebeard." In *Tolkien and the Invention of Myth*, edited by Jane Chance, 295–304. Lexington: University Press of Kentucky.
Hammond, Wayne G., and Christina Scull. 2005. *The Lord of the Rings: A Reader's Companion*. Boston: Houghton Mifflin.
Hargrove, Gene. 1986. "Who is Tom Bombadil?" *Mythlore* 47: 20–24.
Jensen, Klaus, and Ruairidh MacDonald. 2006. "On Tom Bombadil: The Function of Tom Bombadil." *Mallorn* 44: 37–42.
Kinsella, Thomas, trans. 1970. *The Tain*. Oxford: Oxford University Press.
Kocher, Paul H. 1972. *Master of Middle-earth: The Fiction of J.R.R. Tolkien*. Boston: Houghton Mifflin.
Kritzman, Lawrence D. 1996. "Foreword: In Remembrance of Things French." In *Realms of Memory: Rethinking the French Past*, edited by Pierre Nora, ix–xiv. New York: Columbia University Press.
Lane, Belden C. 2001. *Landscapes of the Sacred: Geography and Narrative in American Spirituality*. Baltimore: Johns Hopkins University Press.
Lewis, Paul W. 2007. "Beorn and Tom Bombadil: A Tale of Two Heroes." *Mythlore* 25.3/4: 145–159.
Rateliff, John D. 2007. *The History of* The Hobbit *Part One: Mr. Baggins*. Boston: Houghton Mifflin.
Shippey, Tom. 2001. *J.R.R. Tolkien: Author of the Century*. Boston: Houghton Mifflin.
_____. 2003. *The Road to Middle Earth: How J.R.R. Tolkien Created a New Mythology*. Boston: Houghton Mifflin.
Tolkien, J.R.R. 1980. *Unfinished Tales of Númenor and Middle-earth*. Edited by Christopher Tolkien. Boston: Houghton Mifflin.
_____. 1981. *The Letters of J.R.R. Tolkien*. Edited by Humphrey Carpenter. Boston: Houghton Mifflin.
_____. 1988. *The Return of the Shadow: The History of* The Lord of the Rings *Part One*. Edited by Christopher Tolkien. Boston: Houghton Mifflin.
_____. 1993. *The Fellowship of the Ring*. Boston: Houghton Mifflin.
_____. 1993. *The Return of the King*. Boston: Houghton Mifflin.
_____. 1993. *The Two Towers*. Boston: Houghton Mifflin.
_____. 1997. *The Hobbit: Or There and Back Again*. Boston: Houghton Mifflin.
_____. 2002. *The Annotated Hobbit*, Edited by Douglas A. Anderson. Boston: Houghton Mifflin.

Travel, Redemption and Peacemaking
Hobbits, Dwarves and Elves and the Transformative Power of Pilgrimage

VICKIE L. HOLTZ-WODZAK

On the second morning of his journey, Frodo is reflecting on the road ahead of him and thinking about Bilbo. Frodo reports that Bilbo always used to say that

> there was only one Road; that it was like great river: its springs were at every doorstep, and every path was its tributary. 'It is dangerous business, Frodo, going out of your door, ... You step into the Road, and if you don't keep your feet, there is no knowing where you might be swept off to [Tolkien, 1965a, 83].

Both *The Hobbit* and *Lord of the Rings* are travel narratives that take up this dangerous business and build plot, character, and theme around the life-changing experience of being swept off into travel. When Bilbo dashes out his front door that spring morning, without his hat or any handkerchiefs, to begin his journey with the dwarves, he has only a fuzzy notion of where he is headed, and even fuzzier notions of the dangers he will encounter on the way and how the Road will change him. Frodo's understanding is somewhat clearer. He sees an exile's journey before him. In form, both are journeys "there and back again," but as Frodo observes to Gandalf, Bilbo's journey was to find treasure; Frodo's is to lose one.

Scholars have debated the proper descriptive terms for these journeys. A variety of fruitful descriptive categories—quest, epic, adventure, allegory—have been proposed. It is the purpose of this essay to explore another way of thinking about these stories. What happens if these journeys are evaluated as pilgrimages? While I am not suggesting that this is an all-encompassing explanatory model for these works, at the same time pilgrimage seems an appropriate motif to examine, given Tolkien's ties to twentieth-century English Catholicism, to medieval literature, and given his life-long personal and professional love of language.

A conventionally Catholic definition of pilgrimage as "journeys made to some place with the purpose of venerating it, or in order to ask there for supernatural aid, or to discharge some religious obligation" (Dictionary, 2014) is not particularly helpful in understanding the relationship between the hobbits' journeys and pilgrimage. Neither one fits the religious dimension of such a definition, possibly because of Tolkien's stated principle of omitting any overt religious references (Tolkien, 1981, 172). A more useful and less overtly religious alternative offers an archetypal description of pilgrimage as "outer action with inner meaning" (Clift, 1996). According to Coggan's (1996) review of the Clifts' book, "the ritual of pilgrimage follows the same basic pattern evidenced in the hero's journey and other rites of passage, which can be broken down into three stages: (1) separation—the setting forth, (2) liminal—the journey itself, the sojourn, encounter with the sacred, and (3) return—the homecoming" (131). This description links what Dyas (2001) calls place pilgrimage and interior pilgrimage (explained below), and makes it clear that the fact of travel and the attendant adventure and hardship involved in the physical act of pilgrimage is inextricably linked to a pattern of internal changes in the pilgrim.

It should not be surprising that a pilgrimage motif would be of significance in understanding the work of an early- to mid-twentieth century Catholic like Tolkien. While religious pilgrimage had been out of favor in England for several centuries, over the course of Tolkien's lifetime it once again became an important institution in the lives of many English Catholics. One suggestive example is the restoration of the old pilgrimage destination of Walsingham as a national Catholic pilgrimage site. Walsingham was originally established in the eleventh century as a pilgrimage destination dedicated to Mary, following an apparition of the Virgin to Saxon noblewoman Richeldis de Faverches, and it became a major destination for pilgrims. In 1538, following the 1536 dissolution of the monasteries, the king's commissioners destroyed the priory at Walsingham, dismantled its shrine, and sent its statue of Mary to London to be burned. The site was sold to Thomas Sidney, who built a private mansion in its place, and pilgrimage to Walsingham was suppressed. What happened at Walsingham is typical of what happened to most places of particular significance to English Catholics, because Henry VIII's government was deeply suspicious of Catholic practices in general and regarded pilgrimage in particular as an opportunity for insurrection (Duffy, 1992, 377–504); however, the practice of pilgrimage had long been under some suspicion. Skeptics wondered why, if God was everywhere, piety required travel, and they charged that, for many, pilgrimage had more do with what Chaucer's Alison of Bath called "wandering by the weye" than with any serious religious purpose. Beginning in the fourteenth century, and as pilgrimage gained popularity as part of the affective piety of the times, these criticisms also became more common, finding expression in the Lollards' suspicions of practices they saw as tending to idolatry, and in a common popular perception that, far from being a serious religious undertaking, pilgrimage was all too often an excuse for men and women to engage in immoral activities that they would avoid at home. Members of religious orders who undertook pilgrimage came under particular suspicion, both from their religious superiors and from lay people who questioned their motives (Dyas, 2001, 144–48). So while people did manage to continue to travel to pilgrimage sites like Walsingham, and were recognized as pilgrims when they traveled to places like Rome, Champ (2000) suggests that much of the pilgrimage impulse was ultimately rechanneled into the more secular "grand tour" practices of the ensuing centuries (110–167).

English religious pilgrimage didn't really begin to recover until after the Act of Emancipation in 1829 and the influence of the Oxford Movement (Waller, 2011, 151–80). Gradually, a shift in attitude towards English Catholicism lead to the 1897 papal blessing of a new statue for the restored Our Lady of Walsingham church and culminated in the 1934 declaration of the Catholic National Shrine at the Slipper Chapel, with ten thousand Catholic pilgrims in attendance. It seems unlikely that the restored shrine and the restored practice of pilgrimage would have escaped Tolkien's notice, especially given the extensive Catholic news coverage the events received (Fedden, 1938, 15; Slipper, 1938, 12). The restoration dates of the Walsingham pilgrimage closely parallel both Tolkien's life and the dates of composition of *The Hobbit* and the early legendarium.

Pilgrimage is certainly not a new idea, and it has attributes that seem to retain currency. Dyas, in her discussion of the historical and theological heritage of medieval writers who make use of the pilgrimage motif, identifies two strands of medieval pilgrimage practices that offer a useful way of thinking about Tolkien's work. Place pilgrimage, which Dyas (2001) defines as "journeying to saints' shrines or other holy places to secure forgiveness ... to seek healing and other material benefits, to learn and to express devotion" (6), is exemplified by the sort of shrine-based pilgrimage that was restored at Walsingham or by the pilgrimage depicted in Chaucer's *Canterbury Tales*. In addition to place pilgrimage, Dyas (2001) also describes what she calls the "interior pilgrimage," which she defines as including "monasticism, anchoritism, meditation and mysticism" (6). Interior pilgrimage has been practiced over time by Christians of many stripes, and like pilgrimage of place, seems to retain some contemporary relevance. Tolkien seems to incorporate both aspects into his depiction of pilgrimage.

That the meditational and mystical aspects of pilgrimage mattered to Tolkien is perhaps suggested by his November, 1944 letter to his son Christopher, then serving with the RAF:

> I perceived or thought of the Light of God and in it suspended one small mote (or millions of motes to only one of which was my small mind directed), glittering white because of the individual rays issuing from the Light which both held and lit it.... And the ray was the Guardian Angel of the mote: not a thing interposed between God and the creature, but God's very attention itself, personalized. And I do not mean "personified," by a mere figure of speech according to the tendencies of human language, but a real (finite) person. Thinking of it since—for the whole thing was very immediate, and not recapturable in clumsy language, certainly not the great sense of joy that accompanied it and realization that the shining poised mote was myself (or any other human person that I might think of with love)—it has occurred to me that ... this is a finite parallel to the Infinite. As the love of the Father and Son ... is a Person, so the love and attention of the Light to the Mote is a person ... finite but divine: i.e. angelic [Tolkien, 1981, 89].

This moment occurred, Tolkien tells Christopher, during the *Quarant Ore*, when he was completing his half hour's share of a ritual forty hours of Eucharistic Adoration. It demonstrates that there were meditational and mystical aspects to Tolkien's practice of Catholicism, and it links his twentieth-century religious practice to Dyas' description of the medieval interior pilgrimage.

Turning from Tolkien the twentieth-century Catholic to Tolkien the medieval scholar yields similarly productive reasons to consider the pilgrimage motif. Clearly Tolkien is indebted to key medieval texts, as is well known. He refers, multiple times, to *Beowulf* as a critically important text (Tolkien, 1981, 31; Tolkien, 2006), and his reworking of such texts as *Beowulf* and Old English poems such as "The Seafarer" in *The Two Towers* is both skillfully done and apparent to any reader familiar with the works. Wilcox (2003) proposes that, for Tolkien, the "sequence of influence" from Old English texts "begins with scholarly textual engagement followed by creative linguistic manipulation resulting in fictive integration" (133). Here, Tolkien's "fictive integration" of pilgrimage draws on two literary forebears, the Old English theme of the exile and the Middle English theme of the pilgrim's journey.

The link between pilgrimage and the exile theme in Old English literature is typically grounded in the Genesis account of Adam and Eve's expulsion from the garden and in the Old Testament story of Moses and the people of Israel wandering for forty years in the desert while searching for their Promised Land. Among Christians, medieval and modern alike, these stories of exile have been seen as typologically related to the Christian journey through life to the eventual reward in heaven and are intermixed with understandings of place pilgrimage (Dyas, 2001, 173). In this view, the individual human is an exile from all that really matters and will only truly be "at home" after death. In this view, interior and place pilgrimage share destination and redemptive qualities. Writing of the pilgrimage motif in Old English literature, Dyas (2001) says that

> All too frequently the presence of [the pilgrimage motif] has been overlooked or taken for granted and its breadth and richness have gone unrecognized. So fundamental is it to contemporary Christian thought and so ubiquitous its use in Old English literature that it can fairly be described *the* key undergirding image of Christian poetry and prose in the period from the Conversion to the Norman Conquest [68]

Dyas (2001) sees the theme of exile poignantly worked out in "The Seafarer." While she concedes that there is limited scholarly consensus about this poem, she suggests that reading the experience of the speaker as an exile against the typological backdrop of pilgrimage yields a productive understanding of the poem. The lonely plight of the speaker, in this interpretation, is to be seen as typologically related to the plight of the individual Christian. Both linger in a cold world, bereft of companions and lord (68). One can see, in some respects, an extreme example of the exile in Grendel, who is condemned always to the cold and darkness away from God's light. He is an exile with no hope of home or reconciliation at the end of his life's journey. Dyas (2001) concludes that

> Pilgrimage ... should not be viewed as a single image, based on one type of human activity, but as a group of tightly knit images which make a number of profound statements about the human condition. The essential interdependence of this cluster of images is a crucial factor in assessing the extent of the use of the life-pilgrimage motif in Old English literature [69].

Tolkien's high elves are one reflection of the exilic aspects of pilgrimage. Gildor, for example, describes himself and his companions as "Wandering Companies" (Tolkien, 1965a, 94), and Galadriel, in "*Namárië*" speaks of herself and her people as "[e]lves in these lands of exile" (Tolkien, 1965a, 394).

Medieval place pilgrimage depicts a journey to holy places to give thanks or to make a request, typically for healing. For example, Chaucer's Knight travels to Becket's Shrine at Canterbury immediately after his arrival in England to give thanks for his safe return from military action; in *The General Prologue*, Chaucer explains that pilgrims seek Becket's shrine in the springtime to give thanks to the saint that "hem hath holpen whan that they were seke." While grounded in the historical reality of place pilgrimage, such trips are also frequently seen as allegories for the human journey through life and its link to internal pilgrimage. Place pilgrimage and interior pilgrimage are not mutually exclusive categories, as Dyas (2001, 173) points out. In both cases, pilgrimage offers the potential to transform the pilgrim.

In their initial conversations in chapter one of *The Hobbit*, Gandalf tells Bilbo that he is looking for someone to take part in an adventure, something Bilbo, or at least the Baggins side of Bilbo, wants no part of. Gandalf, however, has other ideas. He says sending Bilbo on this adventure will be "very amusing for me [Gandalf], very good for you [Bilbo], and profitable too, very likely, if you ever get over it" (Tolkien, 1965a, 15). The significant characteristics that Gandalf lists here are *good, profitable* and *life altering*. Of course, he could be just trying to persuade a reluctant hobbit to respond to the Tookish side of his nature and accompany the dwarves as their burglar. But I don't think so. These don't seem like sufficiently persuasive terms to overcome the Baggins love of comfort, good food, and respectability. Bilbo, writing an account of his adventure many years later has a different description of his journey. He calls his account *There and Back Again: A Hobbit's Holiday* (Tolkien, 1994, 254). Clearly, speakers of British English use the word *holiday* to indicate what speakers of American English call a vacation, and Bilbo (and Tolkien) may, just as clearly, be using the word in that sense. It is true, for example, that Tolkien and many of his contemporaries (C.S. Lewis and Owen Barfield, for example) were fond of walking holidays that may well have begun much as Bilbo's trip began, over food and beer. But Tolkien was also a philologist, and historical word play was never far from his imaginative grasp. *Holiday*, etymologically, is the Old English *halig dæg*, or holy day. Bilbo thinks of his journey as a "holy day," a journey somewhere and back again, raising the question of, in what sense, his journey was, or has become in his recollection, something holy, like a pilgrimage. It seems likely that Gandalf is fully aware of the "holy" aspects of the trip he proposes to Bilbo, and that this holiday will, in fact, be very good for Bilbo in the long run.

Champ (2000) points out that "[p]ilgrimage in the mediaeval period became formalized in the circuit of shrines to be visited and in the ritual of departure" (40). It was a ritual that involved a formal church blessing, and typically, pilgrims were given rustic garments and a staff to denote their status (Gaposchkin, 2013; Dyas, 2001, 138). In *The Hobbit*, some of the markers of pilgrimage are easy to spot and very basic. Bilbo begins his journey having just received Gandalf's pardon the previous day. In Tolkien's Catholic tradition, a *pardon* is a kind of blessing by a priest as part of the Sacrament of Confession (as it was called in Tolkien's day), and is based on the Christ's instruction: "Receive ye the Holy Ghost. Whose sins you shall forgive, they are forgiven them; and whose sins you shall retain, they are retained" (John 20:21–23). The first thing that happens to Bilbo when he joins the dwarves at the Green Dragon Inn is that his customary (and missing) hat and handkerchief are replaced by Dwalin's spare travel-stained cloak and hood. Also, like most historical pilgrims—English ones at any rate—Bilbo's journey began "one fine morning, just before May" (Tolkien, 1994, 34). To the reader familiar with Chaucer's *Canterbury Tales*, comparisons come easily: it is April; a group of travelers brought together by chance, depart an inn, having made a pact among themselves. While Chaucer's pilgrims enter into a story-telling pact, Bilbo and the dwarves are bound by a more serious pact to reclaim Thorin's heritage and inheritance and to rid the Lonely Mountain of Smaug. Bilbo's destination is Erebor, a place that is not (strictly speaking) sacred, but it is of deep ancestral importance to the dwarves, and the turning point of their experience comes on Durin's Day, the closest thing to a saint's day the dwarves have. These are small details, perhaps, but taken along with others, they seem significant.

On its surface, Bilbo's journey seems more like a crusade than a pilgrimage. He has entered into an agreement with the dwarves to travel with them as their burglar. The etymology of *burglar* strengthens the association with a crusade. According to the *Oxford English Dictionary*, the word *burglar* likely derives from *burgh-breche*, one who breaks (breaches) castles or towns. The etymological evidence, then, suggests that Bilbo the burglar is taken on this expedition with the intent that he will do something considerably more active than sit on the doorstep and wait for an opportunity, but the focus is on breaking in, not on theft. Further, the dwarves' intent, like the Crusaders', is to reclaim both lost treasure and lost homeland. Crusaders were tasked with liberating the Holy Land from Muslims in the eleventh century. Looking back in time, crusaders seem very different from pilgrims. Crusaders carried weapons and were sent on a military mission with a religious mandate. Historically, the distinction between the terms *crusader* and *pilgrim* became blurred when Pope Gregory VII transferred the term *militia Christi* from a monastic ascetic ideal and used it, instead, to describe armed soldiers commissioned to reclaim the Holy Land for Rome. Medieval writers referred to the journey of the newly-armed pilgrims as a *peregrination* (Quellor and Madden, 2000, 1–7). Madden (2002) reports that "[m]edieval crusaders saw themselves as pilgrims, performing acts of righteousness on their way to the Holy Sepulcher. The Crusade indulgence they received was canonically related to the pilgrimage indulgence" (1). In *The Hobbit*, what begins as crusade, by the end of the book, is unmistakably more like a pilgrimage, with its focus shifted from the reclamation of treasure and homeland to the redemption of Bilbo's and Thorin's fundamental values.

Bilbo is traveling with a company of exiled dwarves, reminiscent according to Brackmann, of the wandering Jews. Brackmann (2010) argues that Tolkien has unmistakably marked the dwarves as Jewish by their creation story, by their language, and she says, by some unfortunately stereotypical characteristics that betray prejudices typical of Tolkien's time. Thorin speaks of the dwarves' wandering in poverty and exile after the coming of Smaug and of their desire to return to their homes, saying

> [a]fter that we went away, and we have had to earn our livings as best we could up and down the lands, often enough sinking as low as blacksmith-work or even coal mining. But we have never forgotten our stolen treasure. And even now, when I will allow we have a good bit laid by and are not so badly off ... we still mean to get it back, and to bring our curses home to Smaug—if we can [Tolkien, 1994, 29].

Thorin's words recollecting his sorrow at their coming exile—"[we] sat and wept in hiding" (Tolkien, 1994, 29)—echo distantly the lament of the psalmist describing the longing of exiled Jews to return to Jerusalem: " Upon the rivers of Babylon, there we sat and wept: when we remembered Sion " (Douay-Rheims, Psalms 136:1).Tolkien collapses two Old Testament motifs—the wandering of Israel in the desert with Moses and the later exile of Jews in Babylon and their yearning to return to Jerusalem—into one story of loss and longing among a wandering and long homeless people.

The effect on these dwarves of pilgrimage to Erebor is life-altering. They begin the story as mean, self-centered house guests, entering Bilbo's hobbit hole with demands for food and drink and accommodations. When it is time to clean up, they sing "Chip the glasses and crack the plates!/Blunt the knives and bend the forks!/That's what Bilbo Baggins hates—/Smash the bottles and burn the corks!" (Tolkien, 1994, 19), and while they do not, in fact, damage any of his possessions, the teasing itself is unkind. At one point, Gloin states that Bilbo "looks more like a grocer than a burglar" (Tolkien, 1994, 24). On Durin's Day, when the door into the Lonely Mountain is finally open, it is clear to Bilbo that the dwarves expect him to reconnoiter, and that they have little intention of accompanying him. Tolkien explains that

> [t]he most that can be said for the dwarves is this: they intended to pay Bilbo really handsomely for his services; they had brought him to do a nasty job for them, and they did not mind the poor little fellow doing it if he would ... dwarves are not heroes, but calculating folk with a great idea of the value of money; some are tricky and treacherous and pretty bad lots; some are not, but are decent enough people like Thorin and Company, if you don't expect too much [Tolkien, 1994, 182–83].

The dwarves are also greedy and describe their planning as "dark business" (Tolkien, 1994, 23). This tendency to greed and selfishness persists among the dwarves throughout their pilgrimage. They grumble, and they complain, and they remain focused on regaining kingdom and gold. This focus seems apparent in Thorin's refusal to reveal the true goal of their journey to the elven king, and it is exacerbated by the effect of dragon fever and piled up treasure once they are able to enter the Lonely Mountain. In Smaug's absence, they enter his lair armed with torches:

> [t]he mere fleeting glimpses of treasure which they had caught as they went along had rekindled all the fire of their dwarvish hearts; and when the heart of a dwarf, even the most respectable, is wakened by gold and by jewels, he grows suddenly bold, and he may become fierce ... they gathered gems and stuffed their pockets, and let what they could not carry fall back through their fingers with sigh [Tolkien, 1994, 203].

Tolkien describes the dwarves as "bewitch[ed] by the hoard" (Tolkien, 1994, 204), and this bewitchment undoubtedly contributes to Thorin's stubborn refusal to negotiate reasonable terms with the Lake Men and the Elves of Mirkwood over compensation for the dragon's damage. By the end of the dwarves' journey, the vengeance and reclamation motif has faded and been replaced by a close analysis of the effect of wealth on dwarvish hearts. It ends with Thorin's deathbed repentance and conversion to a very hobbit-like view: "If more of us valued food and cheer and song above horded gold, it would be a merrier world" (Tolkien, 1994, 243).

Bilbo's experience of pilgrimage works similar changes. Before their journey, Bilbo is predictable, secure, and close minded. He wants no part of adventures. He says they are nasty, uncomfortable things that make you late for dinner (Tolkien, 1994, 13). The dwarves' song inspires greed in Bilbo:

> As they sang the hobbit felt the love of beautiful things made by hands and by cunning and by magic moving through him, a fierce and a jealous love, the desire of the hearts of dwarves. Then something Tookish woke up inside him... He thought of the jewels of the dwarves shining in dark caverns [Tolkien, 1994, 22].

Bilbo is not as susceptible to greed as the dwarves, and he is much more attached to the comforts of home and hearth than they are, but confronted with Smaug's treasure hoard, he succumbs again:

> To say that Bilbo's breath was taken away is no description at all. There are no words left to express his staggerment ... Bilbo had heard tell and sing of dragon-hoards before, but the splendour, the lust, the glory of such treasure had never yet come home to him. His heart was filled and pierced with enchantment and with the desire of the dwarves; and he gazed motionless, almost forgetting the frightful guardian, at the gold beyond price and count.
>
> He gazed for what seemed an age, before, drawn almost against his will, he stole from the shadow of the doorway, across the floor to the nearest edge of the mounds of treasure... He grasped a great two-handled cup, as heavy as he could carry [Tolkien, 1994, 184–85].

Bilbo teeters on the edge of succumbing to the greed that will soon overcome Thorin, and he gives in to the extent he steals the great two handled cup that both delights the dwarves and brings the wrath of Smaug down upon them and the people of Lake Town.

Bilbo's motive for stealing the cup, however, is not greed. Bilbo recalls clearly the doubts the dwarves had expressed about him long ago back in his hobbit hole—that they think he's no good, and more like a grocer than a burglar (Tolkien, 1994, 24). Despite the many things he has accomplished since that time, the assessment seems to still rankle, and it makes Bilbo vulnerable. The doubtful attitude hurts enough that he needs to prove himself. It motivates him to try to pick Bill the troll's pocket in his first adventure, to nearly disastrous end: "he could not go straight back to Thorin and Company empty handed. So he stood and hesitated in the shadows... Bilbo plucked up courage and put his little hand in William's enormous pocket... 'Ha!' thought he warming to his new work ... 'this is a beginning!'" (Tolkien, 1994, 38). The same insecurity accompanies him into Smaug's lair. After stealing the cup, "his chief thought was: 'I've done it! This will show them. More like a grocer than a burglar, indeed! Well, we'll hear no more of that'" (Tolkien, 1994, 185). Later, when Bilbo returns to the lair and converses with Smaug, he is taken aback when Smaug suggests that the dwarves knew all along that Bilbo might have trouble carrying home his fourteenth share of the profits. He hadn't considered the problem. Under the dragon's influence "a nasty suspicion began to grow in his mind—had the dwarves forgotten this important point too, or were they laughing in their sleeves at him all the time?" (Tolkien, 1994, 192). It is hard to know what motivates Smaug to plant doubt in Bilbo's mind, but inducing Bilbo to commit some sort of betrayal of the dwarves and of himself is a strong possibility.

Pilgrimage is changing Bilbo, and he is beginning to understand that he is not the same hobbit who left Bag End in the spring. When the dwarves want to send him into the Lonely Mountain he says "[p]erhaps I have begun to trust my luck more than I used to in the old days ... but anyway I think I will go and have a peep at once and get it over" (Tolkien, 1994, 182). As he makes his way down the tunnel, he scolds himself for having gotten into the situation at all, and when he detects a red glow ahead of him he stops, and "[g]oing on from there was the bravest thing he ever did... He fought the real battle in the tunnel alone, before he ever saw the vast danger that lay in wait" (Tolkien, 1994, 184). That he won the battle is clear from the fact that he continues on down the tunnel to see what has happened with Smaug. Gandalf recognizes that pilgrimage has changed Bilbo. When they meet in Bard's camp before the Battle of the Five Armies and Bilbo hands over the Arkenstone as a bargaining piece he hopes will avert bloodshed, Gandalf congratulates Bilbo for what he has done and says that "there is always more about [him] than anyone expects!" (Tolkien, 1994, 230). After Bilbo returns home, the recognition that pilgrimage has changed him is widespread, although not all of his neighbors are impressed. Gandalf remarks that "[he] is not the hobbit that [he was]" (Tolkien, 1994, 253) He is now an honored friend of dwarves and an elf friend, but he is "no longer quite respectable" (Tolkien, 1994, 254). The price for hobbit respectability is high. Bilbo would have to deny the sacred experiences of his pilgrimage, and it seems doubtful that he would be able to, or even want to, deny the changes that pilgrimage have brought about in him.

The Arkenstone, and the conflicting claims of ownership highlight the issues that Bilbo and Thorin face and overcome. For Bilbo, as he climbs Smaug's mound of treasure towards the light he sees reflected off of the stone, it begins as an attractive mystery. But then he lays guilty claim to it. What motivates Bilbo, the otherwise honest hobbit, to pocket the stone he knows that Thorin prizes above all else is unclear. He tells himself that it will be the promised fourteenth share of the treasure, but he knows that Thorin never meant to include the Arkenstone in the treasures to be divided. It appears that greed and dishonesty have, at least temporarily, overtaken Bilbo and overruled his general good sense and good intentions. For Thorin, the desire to reclaim the Arkenstone soon overtakes all other desires, and he spends hours sifting through the accumulated treasures trying to find it. His failure to find it makes him increasingly stern and possessive of what he does have, and it contributes to his refusal to consider any reasonable negotiations with Bard and the Elf King. Thorin is willing to go cold and hungry, and likely to sacrifice his life and the lives of his companions, to retain sole control of the treasure and to continue his search for the Arkenstone. Bilbo, on the other hand, reevaluates the stone and concludes that there are many things of greater value than any treasure, including a unique one like the Arkenstone. Bilbo is tired of the cold and the short rations, and he has struggled with greed, with a nagging conscience, and with a growing recognition that the likely outcome of Thorin's refusal to negotiate will be bloodshed. Significantly, he tells Bard that the Arkenstone is "the Heart of the Mountain; and it is also the heart of Thorin. He values it above a river of gold" (Tolkien, 1994, 229). The Arkenstone is the one thing that will bring Thorin to negotiations, and he agrees to ransom it, but he is furious at what he sees as Bilbo's betrayal and ejects him from the dwarves' fortifications. Greed and a stubborn desire for both revenge and recovery of his ancestral home and treasure have motivated Thorin for most of his adult life, but they cannot help him make peace with his neighbors. Thorin cannot yet see what Bilbo can see: that greed and stubbornness will not yield peace. It isn't until he approaches his own death and realizes the bloody cost of fighting over treasure that he is finally redeemed from his greed and can enjoy, briefly, the rewards of his pilgrimage.

Tolkien's use of the pilgrimage motif continues in *Lord of the Rings*. Frodo, contemplating his journey with a degree of gut-wrenching horror says

> I feel that as long as the Shire lies behind, safe and comfortable, I shall find wandering more bearable: I shall know that somewhere there is a firm foothold, even if my feet cannot stand there again... I have sometimes thought of going away, but I imagined it as a kind of holiday ... ending in peace. But this would mean exile, a flight from danger into danger, drawing it after me [Tolkien, 1965a, 71–72].

Frodo has considered going on a trip like Bilbo's, perhaps even a trip to try to find him, but he imagines a holiday. He hasn't traveled yet, and he uses the word *holiday* in its most conventional sense—a journey undertaken for fun, relaxation, or "safe" adventure. What he will undertake, he thinks, is something different—an exile. His juxtaposition of the words *holiday* and *exile* in Frodo's statement point to the continuing usefulness of pilgrimage as a construct for evaluating the journey he undertakes.

There are other indicators that pilgrimage remains a useful interpretive model for this journey. Peregrin Took's name, for example, means *pilgrim*. Dyas (2001) reports that

> [T]he etymology of the terms *pilgrim* and *pilgrimage* indicates the breadth of meaning which these words have acquired over the centuries. The Latin *peregrinus* (*per*, through + *ager*, field, country, land) denoted a foreigner, an alien, one who is on a journey, and *peregrinatio* the state of being or living abroad. *Peregrinus*, however, was also used in the Vulgate translation of the Bible to render the Hebrew *gur* (sojourner), and the Greek *parepidemos* (temporary resident), both terms which carried an additional connotation signifying the special relationship of the people of God to the world around them [1].

Within the context of The Shire, Peregrin—or Pippin—seems a well-adjusted insider. But once he leaves his home environment to travel with Frodo, he becomes a foreigner in the lands he visits.

Lothlórien's elves mourn Gandalf's death in Moria, singing "Mithrandir, Mithrandir, ... O Pilgrim Grey" (Tolkien, 1965a, 374), and Frodo's commemorative verse in the same chapter describes him as "a weary pilgrim upon the road" (Tolkien, 1965a, 375). In Dyas' (2001) etymological explanation of the pilgrim, Gandalf is "the *gur* (sojourner), and the Greek *parepidemos* (temporary resident), both terms which carr[y] an additional connotation signifying the special relationship of the people of God to the world around them"(1). Further, Tolkien seems to have retained an ongoing and shifting interest in the idea of Gandalf as pilgrim and its significance. Writing in 1954, Tolkien says that

> [Gandalf] was named among the Elves Mithrandir, the Grey Pilgrim, for he dwelt in no place, and gathered to himself neither wealth nor followers, but ever went to and fro in the Westlands from Gondor to Angmar, and from Lindon to Lórien, befriending all folk in times of need.... Mostly he journeyed unwearyingly on foot, leaning on a staff [Tolkien, 1980, 390–91].

The term *pilgrim* is doubly appropriate for Gandalf. As one of the Istari, angelic beings clothed in the form of men, he is a wanderer, and the clothes, the staff, and the apparently human body form he assumes all set him apart from his natural home. Tolkien writes,

> For it is said indeed that being embodied the Istari had need to learn much anew by slow experience, and though they knew whence they came the memory of the Blessed Realm was to them a vision from afar off, for which ... they yearned exceedingly. Thus by enduring of free will the pangs of exile and the deceits of Sauron they might redress the evils of that time [Tolkien, 1980, 390].

Not only has he undertaken a journey and an exile's status, but he has also taken on a physical form for his journey that sets him apart from his form in the Blessed Realm.

Gandalf does not emerge from his pilgrimage through Middle Earth unchanged. While Tolkien provided some information on Gandalf's pre-pilgrimage characteristics when he was the Maiar known as Olórin (Tolkien, 1980, 388–400), he provided little information on Gandalf at the beginning of his exile; he did, however, depict Gandalf at the beginning of Frodo's exile, preparing to undertake what Galadriel calls "his greatest task," and Gandalf after he has been "sent back" to complete his pilgrimage and after the ring has been destroyed. The early Gandalf, at least as he appears to some hobbits, seems crusty and intimidating. When he catches Sam eavesdropping, Sam pleads with Frodo: "'Don't let him hurt me, sir! Don't let him turn me into anything unnatural! My old dad would take on so. I meant no harm, on my honour, sir!'" (Tolkien, 1994, 73). Mr. Butterbur expects the worst from Gandalf for not having sent on his letter to Frodo, and Gandalf's account of his thoughts as he approached Bree seem to confirm Butterbur's fears: "If this delay was his fault, I will melt all the butter in him. I will roast the old fool over a slow fire" (Tolkien, 1994, 276). Gandalf is likely choosing his diction to fit his audience, but the perception still stands. Much later, after Gandalf has been sent back to complete his task, Merry and Pippin discuss whether or not Gandalf has changed. Merry reports that "'He has grown, or something. He can be both kinder and more alarming, merrier and more solemn than before, I think. He has changed; but we have not had a chance to see how much, yet'" (Tolkien, 1965b, 195).

The structure of Lord of the Rings also indicates an underlying pilgrimage motif, although it begins off balance, at least partly due to Frodo's reluctance to leave the Shire. Rather than departing in the spring, the traditional time for departure in order to take advantage of favorable weather, he delays until September and the birthday he shares with Bilbo. Bilbo notices the problem and scolds Frodo undertaking such an expedition in winter. The timing of their journey is significant: they depart Rivendell on December 25, they leave Lothlórien at the beginning of Lent, and the Ring is destroyed during the Easter season. The party is a mixed social group under no vow, blessed by Elrond in the name of all free peoples, and eventually dressed by Galadriel in specially-made cloaks. Their route takes them, on foot, through the rapidly fading (or occupied) holy places of those free peoples: Moria and Kheled-zâram of the dwarves, Lothlórien of the elves, and the Argonauth of men. The journey tests each of them, just as Galadriel's gaze tests them, and they do not emerge from their pilgrimage unchanged.

Pilgrimage offers instructive characteristics that link this pilgrimage to both Tolkien's earlier efforts in *The Hobbit* and to the larger idea of pilgrimage itself. As demonstrated earlier, Bilbo's pilgrimage with the dwarves changed them all, with the change being most evident in Bilbo and in Thorin. What emerges from *The Hobbit* is an emphasis on how pilgrimage tests and transforms Bilbo and Thorin. Pilgrimage challenges pilgrims to overcome their own weaknesses and fears. The etymological linkage of Smaug and Sméagol is illuminating here. *Smaug* is "the past tense of the primitive Germanic verb *smugan*, to squeeze through a hole" (Tolkien, 1981, 31). *Smugan* is also the root of *Sméagol* and can also mean *worm* (Gilliver, Weiner, Marshall, 2009, 191–20). The dwarves refer to Smaug as a Worm. Sméagol/Gollum seems worm-like. He lacks much body hair, he is pale and thin, he grovels and digs in the ground. The language suggests a pattern of underlying similarities. The pairing of Smaug and Sméagol and of Bilbo and Frodo suggests that each hobbit contends with specific weaknesses that pilgrimage brings to the front. Two of Smaug's clearest attributes are his greed and his well-placed mistrust of everybody. As discussed above, these are the very attributes that arise in Bilbo when he confronts Smaug and that cause him trouble with dwarves. Interestingly, Sméagol/Gollum represents the very things Frodo fears most: himself, and what the Ring is doing to him. This kinship is clearest when Frodo and Sam capture Sméagol/Gollum on Emyn Muil. Frodo is looking for a promise that will preclude treachery, and Sméagol/Gollum insists that he will promise to "be very good" on the Precious (Tolkien, 1965b, 623). Sam, watching, realizes that "the two were somehow akin and not alien: they could reach one another's minds" (Tolkien, 1965b, 623). Frodo's growing realization over the ensuing days, that he can remember less and less of The Shire and his old life and that he is slowly succumbing to the Ring, emphasizes the extent to which he is becoming more like Sméagol/Gollum. Like Bilbo's pilgrimage, Frodo's forces him to confront his own frailty, and he emerges, not like Sméagol/Gollum, but not quite whole either. He has been redeemed from the corrosive power of the Ring, but the price has been too high. It has broken him, and that brokenness will ultimately send him on another journey, this time in search of healing.

This pilgrimage, like any pilgrimage, comes with no guarantees of safe passage, safe arrival, or successful outcomes. In the case of Boromir, it fails, and it likely fails because, as was implied in Lothlórien, of the evil he brought with him. Partly, the draw of the Ring is just too strong for him, and given the choice that the pilgrimage demands of him, to turn away from his desire for the power he thinks the Ring would confer. It is not surprising that he would succumb. Boromir carries with him the hurt and fear of a man who has lived his life under the shadow of defeat, knowing that, no matter how hard he fights, the Enemy will ultimately overwhelm him. He has been a man with little hope, and to ask him to step away from the hope he thinks he sees in the Ring is too much for him. For him, the pilgrimage has brought travel and suffering, but it has not brought redemption from his desire for power or from the ways his life has been misshapen by fear and conflict.

Sam, on the other hand, is transformed by his pilgrimage. He leaves the Shire with a single clear virtue: loyalty to Frodo. And while that virtue serves him and Frodo well, it is limited and limiting. Sam has trouble imagining a bigger world than his corner of the Shire. In fact, when he, Frodo, and Pippin leave the Shire together on their first night out, he hesitates and looks back with longing as they cross over the point in the road that represents the outer limits of his experience. He is excited to meet elves, though they turn out to be, in his words, above his likes and dislikes, but he is fundamentally suspicious of everybody else. In Bree, he looks at *The Prancing Pony* with dislike. He doesn't see anything about the inn that is inviting to a hobbit and suggests that they instead ask around for a hobbit family willing to take them in for the night. And a big, weather-beaten man like Strider, he is sure, must be an enemy. Sam suspects that Strider will lead them into a remote area and attack or abandon them. It isn't until Gandalf reassures Sam in Rivendell that those reassurances combine with his knowledge of Strider's heroic actions to protect Frodo that his doubts are relieved. Sometimes his doubts and fears are rightly placed; he is right about Boromir, for example. Sam is equally suspicious of Faramir when they meet him in Ithilien. Again, he's a big man, and he bears a family resemblance to Boromir. Sam is so mistrustful that he refuses to sleep before the meal they share with him. Reasonable caution accounts for Sam's actions, but that caution is motivated by an underlying suspicion of people unlike Shire hobbits. More seriously, Sam is suspicious of Sméagol/Gollum. While Sam's suspicions are well-founded—Sméagol/Gollum is treacherous—they also blind Sam and help lead both him and Frodo to grief. The most cataclysmic instance of the impact of Sam's suspicions and his inability to see past them occurs when Sméagol/Gollum returns from Shelob's Lair. Sméagol/Gollum finds the hobbits asleep, and for a moment, the light goes out of his eyes, and he is only an ancient hobbit reaching out to Frodo in love. But Sam, startled out of his sleep and speaking on reflex, sees only a "sneak" who is "pawing at" his master (Tolkien, 1965b, 722). The redemptive moment shattered, Sméagol/Gollum reverts to his old ways, and his treachery plays out.

If Sam has a weakness, it is embedded in his loyalty to Frodo. The two hobbits are inseparable, mostly due to Sam's insistence. In Rivendell, Elrond chides Sam for coming to the Council uninvited. When Frodo decides to leave his companions and strike out across the Emyn Muil on his own, Sam realizes his plans and insists on coming with him. Frodo needs Sam, so his loyalty is essential, but it also suggests that Sam has been most comfortable as Frodo's batman. He has not been in a situation where he must strike out on his own until Frodo is immobilized by Shelob's sting, and Sam believes he is dead. He calls to Frodo, saying "'Don't leave me here alone! It's your Sam calling. Don't go where I can't follow! Wake up, Mr. Frodo!" (Tolkien, 1965b, 738). He debates with himself, resisting the conclusion that the task of the destroying the Ring has fallen to him.

> What, me take the Ring from him? The Council gave it to him.... Why am I left all alone to make up my mind? I'm sure to go wrong. And it's not for me to go taking the Ring, putting myself forward... And as for not being the right and proper person, why, Mr Frodo wasn't, ... nor Mr. Bilbo. They didn't choose themselves... I must make up my own mind. I will make it up. But I'll be sure to go wrong: that'd be Sam Gamgee all over [Tolkien, 1965b, 739].

Here, Sam comes into his own. He single-handedly frees Frodo from the orcs. Tellingly, the orcs think he is big, an elf warrior. Partly, as servants of Sauron, they respond to the presence of the Ring Sam is carrying, but partly, one suspects, they respond to his new-found independence. Sam learns that he can assume this role, and the leadership required of him to get the weakening Frodo to Mount Doom confirms it, but the role doesn't overwhelm his basic good nature: he is the only individual ever to have voluntarily passed the Ring to someone else.

One measure of how much his pilgrimage has changed Sam is his response to Rosie Cotton when he comes home. She asks him why he waited until things got dangerous in the Shire to come home, and Sam, figuring that she needed a long answer to her question or none at all, opts for short term silence. Rosie's perspective is very like Sam's used to be. She asks him "If you've been looking after Mr. Frodo all this while, what d'you want to leave him for, as soon as things look dangerous?" (Tolkien, 1965c, 287). She is concerned only with events in the Shire and is totally unaware of how close all of Middle Earth came to disaster. Sam, on the other hand, having had a central role in events, is now a beneficiary of a broadened perspective. He is also now in a position to challenge evil when he sees it. This is particularly apparent in his encounter with Ted Sandyman. In the past, Sam had been irritated by Ted but didn't confront him. After Sam's pilgrimage, he challenges the way Ted has aligned himself with Sharky, knocked down trees, apparently just for the fun of it, and installed a water-polluting mill. Prior to the pilgrimage, Sam tended to the Bag End garden, and perhaps to his Gaffer's potato patch. He was a successful gardener, but limited his efforts to home and family. He returns with a bigger sense of community and his responsibility to it, and he spends most of his first year back in the Shire traveling around with his box of dust from Galadriel, restoring as much as he can of the entire Shire.

The lessons Sam has learned about taking responsibility for solving problems are shared with Merry and Pippin. Gandalf tells them, along with Frodo and Sam, that

> [y]ou must settle [The Shire's] affairs yourselves; that is what you have been trained for. Do you not yet understand? My time is over: it is no longer my task to set things to rights, nor to help folk to do so. And as for you, my dear friends, you will need no help. You are grown up now.

Grown indeed very high; among the great you are, and I have no longer any fear at all for any of you [Tolkien, 1965c, 1009].

The hobbits Elrond had intended to send home from Rivendell, seeing them as too young for the pilgrimage they were undertaking, are now in a position to set things to rights in the Shire.

Finally, pilgrimage has a profound effect on Legolas and Gimli. Early on, the tensions between them mirror the long-standing tensions between elves and dwarves. In speaking of Nimrodel, Legolas mentions that the dwarves awakened a nameless evil in Moria. Gimli promptly leaps to the dwarves' defense. When they first arrive in Lothlórien, the elves demand that Gimli be carefully guarded and, for a time, blindfolded, leading Legolas to protest the stiff necks of dwarves when Gimli protests the blindfold, only to hear Gimli protest the stiff necks of elves when Legolas objects to sharing Gimli's blindfolded state because he is a kinsman in Lothlórien and should be trusted. Much of the tension between the two diminishes after their meeting with Galadriel. Gimli's love for her is instant and absolute, and it overcomes the basic dwarf tendency to greed and love of gold. When they are given their gifts, Galadriel shows how little she knows of dwarves. She doesn't know what would be a suitable gift. When Gimli names his desire—a lock of her hair—he explains to her that he would embed it in crystal and make it an heirloom of his house, valued for its beauty and associations, not for its material value. Gimli's love of Galadriel, and the way it reshapes his values, lays the groundwork for his friendship with Legolas. Soon, their companions note that Legolas often takes Gimli with him when he leaves the company by their pavilion in Lothlórien and spends time among the elves. By the time they leave, they are close companions, choosing to share a boat on the Anduin and hunting orcs together. Their pact to visit Fangorn and the Caves of Aglarond together—visits that themselves are pilgrimages of place— shows their growing willingness to learn about what the other values, although the visits do not necessarily change their ideas. And both offer to help Aragorn to restore Minas Tirith after war, Gimli with stoneworkers from Erebor and Legolas with Mirkwood elves who plant and tend to trees. The city cannot be whole without both, and Legolas and Gimli have come to complement each other. Finally, Tolkien writes in Appendix 3 that, after many years, and after all of the other members of the Fellowship had died, it was granted to Gimli to sail, with Legolas, to the Undying Lands, something that had never before been granted to a dwarf.

The pilgrimage motif is not something that is explicitly mentioned in either *The Hobbit* or *Lord of the Rings*, nor do I think Tolkien ever explicitly described the journeys as pilgrimages. That is not surprising. Given the close ties between pilgrimage and religious practice, it is unlikely that Tolkien would have used such language. Tolkien (1981) explained that he carefully omitted explicit religious practice or language from his work:

> The Lord of the Rings is of course a fundamentally religious and Catholic work; unconsciously so at first, but consciously in the revision. That is why I have not put in, or have cut out, practically all references to anything like 'religion,' to cults or practices, in the imaginary world. For the religious element is absorbed into the story and the symbolism [172].

Instead, pilgrimage, like religion, is absorbed as Tolkien says into story and symbolism. Writing to his son Michael in 1941, Tolkien says that "the essence of a *fallen* world is that the *best* cannot be attained by free enjoyment, or by what is called 'self-realization'; ... but by denial, by suffering" (Tolkien, 1981, 51). The story here, in both *The Hobbit* and *Lord of the Rings*, is one of great denial and great suffering, but it is also a story of attaining at least a glimpse of the best a fallen world can offer. It is that glimpse of the best that Tolkien draws on for both stories, and one of the many things that Tolkien laid out in *The Hobbit* that he returned to in *Lord of the Rings*.

Works Cited

Brackmann, R. 2010, Spring Summer. "Dwarves Are Not Heroes: Antisemitism in JRR Tolkien's Writings." *Mythlore*, pp. 85–106.

Burglar n. (n.d.). Oxford University Press, producer. Retrieved January 27, 2014, from OED Online: http://www.oed.com/view/Entry/24948?rskey=uPhGI2&result=1.

Champ, J. 2000. *The English Pilgrimage to Rome: A Dwelling For the Soul*. Leominster: Gracewing.

Clift, W. A. 1996. *The Archetype of Pilgrimage: Outer Action With Inner Meaning*. Mahwah, NJ: Paulist.

Coggan, S. 1996. "The Archetype of Pilgrimage: Outer Action with Inner Meaning." *Journal of Ritual Studiies*, 131–32.

Dictionary: Pilgrimage. (2014). Retrieved January 25, 2014, from CatholicCulture.org: http://www.catholicculture.org/culture/library/dictionary/index.cfm?id=35588.

Duffy, E. 1992. *The Stripping of the Altars: Traditional Religion in England c. 1400–c. 1580*. New Haven: Yale University Press.

Dyas, D. 2001. *Pilgrimage in Medieval English Literature, 700–1500*. Cambridge: D.S. Brewer.

Fedden, M. 1938, May 10. *Walsingham Pilgrimage 1938*. Retrieved January 24, 2014, from Catholic Herald Archive: http://archive.catholicherald.co.uk/article/20th-may-1938/15/walsingham-pilgrimage-1938.

Gaposchkin, M. C. 2013. "From Pilgrimage to Crusade: The Liturgy of Departure, 1095–1300." *Speculum*, 44–91.

Gilliver, P. E. 2009. *The Ring of Words: Tolkien and the Oxford English Dictionary*. New York: Oxford University Press.

Madden, T. 2002, April. "The Real History of the Middle Ages." Retrieved November 21, 2013, from CatholicCulture.org.

Quellor, D. A. 2000. *The Fourth Crusade: The Conquest of Constantinople*. Philadelphia: University of Pennsylvania Press.

Psalm 136, v. 1. (n.d.). Retrieved January 25, 2014, from Douay-Rheims Bible Online: http://www.drbo.org.

The Slipper Chapel, Walsingham. 1938, September 17. Retrieved January 20, 2014, from The Tablet: the International Catholic News Weekly: http://archive.thetablet.co.uk/article/17th-september-1938/12/the-slipper-chapel-walsingham.

Tolkien, J. 1965a. *The Fellowship of the Ring*. New York: Houghton Mifflin.

_____. 1965b. *The Two Towers*. New York: Houghton Mifflin.

_____. 1965c. *The Return of the King*. New York: Houghton Mifflin.

_____. 1980. *Unfinished Tales*. Boston: Houghton Mifflin.

_____. 1981. *The Letters of JRR Tolkien*. Christopher Tolkien and Humphrey Carpenter, ed. Boston: Houghton Mifflin.

_____. 1994. *The Hobbit*. Boston: Houghton Mifflin.

_____ 2006. Beowulf, the Monster and the Critics. In J.R.R. Tolkien, *The Monsters and the Critics and Other Essays* (pp. 1–48). London: HarperCollins.

Waller, G. (2011). *Walsingham and the English Imagination*. Burlington: Ashgate.

Wilcox, M. (2003). Exilic Imagining in The Seafarer and Lord of the Rings. In J. Chance, *Tolkien the Medievalist*, pp. 133–154. London: Routledge.

A Baggins Back Yard
Environmentalism, Authorship and the Elves in Tolkien's Legendarium

David Thiessen

> In all my works I take the part of trees as against all their enemies. Lothlórien is beautiful because there the trees were loved; elsewhere forests are represented as awakening to consciousness of themselves. The Old Forest was hostile to two legged creatures because of the memory of many injuries. Fangorn Forest was old and beautiful, but at the time of the story tense with hostility because it was threatened by a machine-living enemy. Mirkwood had fallen under the domination of a Power that hated all living things but was restored to beauty and became Greenwood the Great before the end of the story. ... The savage sound of the electric saw is never silent wherever trees are still found growing
>
> —*Letters* 419–20.

In his 1972 letter to the Daily Telegraph regarding the use of his name as "an adjective qualifying 'gloom'" (*Letters* 419), Tolkien explained his commitment to the environment as taking the part of trees and was generally contented with writing fiction as a means for environmental activism. Since the publication of his major works, *The Hobbit* and *The Lord of the Rings* (*LR*), the posthumously published *The Silmarillion*, and his many letters to readers, family, and publishers, Tolkien's advocacy for the environment has attracted the focus of several scholars, including Verlyn Flieger, Alfred Siewers, Cynthia Cohen, and Patrick Curry, each of whom have discussed Tolkien's works with regard to his portrayal of trees, ecology, creation myth, and the Green Movement.

Apart from Tolkien's overt statements about the savagery of the electric saw and the need for environmental protection,[1] his advocacy for nature comes through in the carefully created names and histories of the trees, forests, geographies, and locales of Middle-earth. Most readers will be familiar with Laurelin, Teleperion, the Shire's Party Tree, Mirkwood, the Old Forest, Fangorn, the Mallyrn trees of Lothlórien, and the White Tree of Gondor, descendant of Nimloth, the descendant of Galathilion. But to satisfy his desire to have guardians for the living things of Middle Earth, to protect that which cannot protect itself, Tolkien also developed several sentient (and semi-sentient) creatures, most of whom are not particularly friendly to the mortal races of Middle-Earth: Old Man Willow, Caradhras, Treebeard, the Huorns, Beorn, and Tom Bombadil form a short list of Middle-earth's environmental watchdogs.

In contrast to Tolkien's self-expressed environmentalism, Verlyn Flieger argues that Tolkien's ecological stance is not as simple as the "many book-jacket photographs of Tolkien posed in juxtaposition to a tree" ("Taking the Part of Trees: Eco-Conflict in Middle-Earth"

147) might suggest, but that it is more complicated and contradictory than most readers of his fiction may want to admit. Flieger notes a disjunction between Tolkien's treatment of trees in the episode in the Old Forest—"indeed between his portrait of Old Man Willow and those of all his other trees" (148)—and the position he takes in his letter to the *Daily Telegraph* in 1972. This paper argues that this disparity reflects the ecological positions of Tolkien's fictive authors—specifically, in this case, of hobbits—rather than of any conflict within Tolkien's personal stance. In addition, this author considers the ecological difference between a hobbit perspective and an Elven one to suggest that any analysis of Tolkien's environmentalism, as based on his fiction, must account both for the authorial tradition he created for his legendarium and for the perspectival differences that those authors' cultural ecologies generate. Seen through the various ecological perspectives of his authors, Tolkien's environmentalism provides his characters (and his readers) with an opportunity for recovery[2] of their view on nature from something familiar or trite, to something truly beautiful and alive.

Careful though Tolkien was in his fiction, Flieger sees a discrepancy between the portrayal of Old Man Willow and the Old Forest and his comments in 1972. Flieger recalls the incident between Old Man Willow and the hobbits as one of the first truly dangerous adventures that Frodo and his companions narrowly escape and suggests that Tolkien's ecological stance deserves closer investigation than it has hitherto received.[3] Flieger compares Tolkien's comments from his 1972 letter to the *Daily Telegraph*, in which he claims to take the part of trees, with the events that transpire in the Old Forest. Even from an early 1938 draft of the chapter, the negative portrayal of the Shire's border-forest remained very close to the final published form.[4] Both accounts share descriptions of the Forest as queer, not liking strangers, and how at night "things can be most alarming" (*FR* 144) under the branches of its trees. Tolkien's use of hobbit hearsay and the "old bogey-stories" that torment Fatty Bolger's sleep add to the Old Forest's negative reputation as sinister, even rivaling the infamous Barrow-downs among Shire-folk. When the hobbits catch a glimpse of the Forest's edge, the reader is told that "it was good to see a sight of anything beyond the wood's borders, though they did not mean to go that way, if they could help it: the Barrow-downs had as sinister a reputation in hobbit-legend as the Forest itself" (*FR* 149).

Flieger argues that Old Man Willow receives an even worse portrayal than the Old Forest, writing that, "he is beyond threat; he is simply evil" ("Taking the Part of Trees" 149), reminding the reader that "the first real villain to be met with in *LR* is a tree" (148). She excludes the appearance of the Black Riders on the road to Bucklebury[5] because at this point in the story they have not been met, only seen and heard. Old Man Willow, however, quickly becomes a known threat to the hobbits: "Huge, hostile, malicious, his trapping of Merry and Pippin in his willowy toils, his attempt to drown Frodo, give the hobbits their first major setback, and come uncomfortably close to ending their journey before it has properly started" ("Taking the Part of Trees" 148). Indeed, the event casts a dark shadow over the reader's conception of Old Man Willow, and when Sam proposes to burn down the great willow in rescue of his friends, it seems a proper, if desperate, choice. Flieger's suggests that this "picture of Willow-man simply does not fit with Tolkien's vision of other trees" (149). Her observation challenges an understanding of Tolkien's self-expressed and clearly discernible environmentalism in much of his other writing.

But pinning Tolkien's environmental commitments to several (or even one) of his characters' is not as straightforward as the discrepancies between portrayals of trees might suggest. Although he did self-identify with hobbits—stating in a letter that, "I am in fact a Hobbit (in all but size)" (*Letters* 288)—and planned *LR* to be "hobbito-centric" (*Letters* 237), he also donned the perspective of Elves and humans in his other tales. He explains this in a letter to Milton Waldman: "As the high Legends of the beginnings are supposed to look at things through Elvish minds, so the middle tale of the Hobbit takes a virtually human point of view—and the last tale blends them" (*Letters* 145). As to identifying Tolkien's ecological perspective with that of the hobbits, his fictional layers of authorial voices, scribes, editors, and translators ensure that he is quite distant from the discrepancies found in his characters' perspectives. In truth, the tradition that he created as a background for his legendarium, *The Hobbit* and *LR*, provides the authorial distance Tolkien needed to explore the various cultural ecologies found in Middle-earth (discrepancies and all) and use them as commentary against the savage sound of the electric saw. Tolkien's plan to write his novels as a "study of the ennoblement (or sanctification) of the humble" (*Letters* 237) creates the potential for perspectival recovery of the environment by using the perspectives of his characters' to explore an ecology typically lost to modern, industrialized societies: an ecology in which the existence of a sentient species is directly contingent on the life of the earth itself. This is the ecology of the Elves: bound to the earth, "to last while it lasts" (*Silmarillion* xv).

Tolkien aggravated the problem of identifying his own perspective when he introduced the pseudo-academic translator/philologist/narrator in the opening page of *The Hobbit* and in the "Prologue" to *LR*—a character who becomes easier to associate with Tolkien, over and above his other characters (even in the absence of direct correlation), after the appendices are read.[6] Evidently, Tolkien's interest in language and philology was shared with several of his fictive authors and functioned as a lens through which he (and his fictive authors) could trace the names and places of Middle-earth. In his article, "Tolkien as Philologist," David Lyle Jeffrey reads Tolkien's richly layered names and histories of the people and place of Middle-earth, often pointing to real-world languages and places, as a type of philological allusion. As a process of retrospection, he suggests, philology offered Tolkien a way of looking back and exploring "the etymologist's conviction that behind words, however much they might appear to be simply tags of convention, lay wider significance—indeed, basic truths about man and his world that deserved to be recovered" ("Tolkien as Philologist" 62). This conviction—that behind words lie the stories of our past—permeates Tolkien's sub-creation and can be seen in the vast number of names and histories that those names evoke. Jeffrey observes how each "name may be perceived as metonymic—a miniature myth, a poem, a story in itself," and that "Behind the Adamic playfulness ... is a high seriousness—the desire to imply or recover truths of a prior order, to engage an understanding that informs and creates history" (74). For these names to possess the kind of metonymic transference that Tolkien wanted, they needed a linguistic and literary history to which they could refer. In order to develop a convincing history for his languages, names, and tales, Tolkien needed to create a series of authors, scribes, translators, and editors through which he could trace an oral, literary, and scribal tradition right up to the present day.[7]

To garner an understanding of Tolkien's environmental commitments, then, one must understand those of his sub-created authors—elves and hobbits; for, it is through these perspectives that one can see his commitment to nature and its potential for recovery. Largely a product of Tolkien's art, the authorial tradition in his legendarium resembles something like the intricately layered "illusion of historical truth and perspective" that he describes in his lecture on Beowulf.[8] In his article "The Medievalist('s) Fiction," Gergely Nagy argues that the authorial tradition in Tolkien's texts (such as Bilbo's roles as author, translator, compiler and adaptor, Frodo and Sam as addendum authors, or the historical authors in the legendarium) functions in a similar manner to the "illusion of historical truth and perspective" that Tolkien appreciated in Beowulf. He suggests that just as Tolkien saw "the activity of the author ... as central" (31) for interpreting heroic legends "afresh in an original function" (31), so to would such an authorial tradition provide his legendarium a model with which to expand his philological fiction into a cultural one (33). For Tolkien, Nagy suggests that,

> ... culture ... seems to imply, comes into being and is maintained exactly in these acts of handing on and authoring. The texts' layers, reflecting various uses, make available a variety of voices, from the past and present of the imagined world, even if only in the very moment of their being silenced by the editor, their noninclusion, excerpting, and anthologizing [33–4].

While Tolkien argued fervently against treating Beowulf (or any poem for that matter) as an historical quarry, Nagy asserts that he recognized, nonetheless, how the "individual poem is part of a tradition and is itself a complex 'new thing,' incorporating, preserving, and rewriting previous materials" (31). To this end, Tolkien's authorial tradition includes several historical authors, such as the Elven lore masters Rúmil of Tirion and Pengoloð of Gondolin who are connected to the larger frame-narrative only in The Silmarillion and the various extant manuscripts, scribbles, and personal notes presented in the History of Middle-earth series—the existence of which demonstrates Tolkien's long commitment to this frame-narrative.

In The *Book of Lost Tales I*, Christopher Tolkien describes his father's early attempts[9] in the tale of The Cottage of Lost Play to set in order a framework of authorial transmission that would connect the myths and legends of the Eldar days to Eriol, a post–Fourth Age Anglo-Saxon mariner. Christopher Tolkien recalls how, "Eriol the mariner was central to my father's original conception of the mythology" (*Lost Tales I*:22) and was intended to satisfy his expressed desire to link his fictional world with a mythic past he wished to shape for Britain. "In those days," writes Christopher Tolkien, "the primary intention of his work was to satisfy his desire for a specifically and recognizably English literature of 'faerie'" (*Lost Tales I*:22). Tolkien expressed this in a letter to Milton Waldman:

> I was from early days grieved by the poverty of my own beloved country: it had no stories of its own (bound up with its tongue and soil), not of the quality that I sought, and found (as an ingredient) in legends of other lands. There was Greek, and Celtic, and Romance, Germanic, Scandinavian, and Finnish (which greatly affected me); but nothing English, save impoverished chap-book stuff [*Letters* 144].

Eriol was the link.[10] His voyage to Tol Erressëa and the tales he learned in the Cottage of Lost Play connected the myth of "faerie" to the history of England.[11] As Flieger explains, this was an important part of establishing a certain legitimacy for his fictive tradition, because if his real-world exemplars from Northern Europe and Iceland had, "their great manuscript books, objects of scrutiny and examination by scholars, Tolkien's Middle-earth would have the fictive equivalent" (Flieger, 2005, p. 61). In order to achieve the kind of historical depth that emerges in Beowulf, Tolkien's legendarium needed a pre-history of its own.

Recognizing Tolkien's fictive authorial tradition becomes a necessary framework through which to read his environmentalism; without it, contradictions such as the negative portrayal that frames Old Man Willow and the positive one that describes the uprising of Fangorn Forest and the Huorns' massacre of the Orcs, become not only confusing but potentially irreconcilable as Flieger notes. Needless to say, Tolkien was aware of the contrasting perspectives of his characters, however contradictory their descriptions of the environment. Rather, once his frame-narrative is understood, one can recognize that such contradictions reflect a character bias—specifically a hobbit bias in the comparison of Old Man Willow and the Ents—not the conflicted intentions of Tolkien. The *LR* was written to be "hobbito-centric" (*Letters* 237); and, from the hobbits' perspective, Old Man Willow's actions are malicious; he intends to harm, even kill them. The hobbits of Shire have little understanding of the Old Forest's "memory of many injuries" (*Letters* 419), a point made clear by Fatty's repeated objections to a proposed journey through the forest: "'But that can only mean going into the Old Forest!' said Fredegar horrified. 'You can't be thinking of doing that. It is quite as dangerous as Black Riders.' ...'you won't have any luck in the Old Forest.... No one ever has luck in there. You'll get lost. People don't go in there'" (*FR* 140). For these hobbits, as for most of the Shire-folk presumably, the Old Forest has always been menacing, and they have either never known or forgotten a time when it was not so. Not until the hobbits travel through Lothlórien does their perspective on the trees and forests of Middle-earth shift.

With consideration of his frame-narrative, the contradictory portrayals of trees in Middle-earth belong not to Tolkien but to hobbits. The Lord of the Rings is an adaptation of Bilbo and Frodo's larger tale, The Downfall of the Lord of the Rings and the Return of the King, a point explicitly described in the final chapter of *LR*:

> In the next day or two Frodo went through his papers and his writings with Sam, and he handed over his keys. There was a big book with plain red leather covers; it tall pages were now almost filled. At the beginning there were many leaves covered with Bilbo's thin wandering hand; but most of it was written in Frodo's firm flowing script. ... The title pages had many titles on it, crossed out one after another... Here Bilbo's hand ended and Frodo had written: The Downfall of the Lord of the Rings and the Return of the King [emphasis mine, *RK* 1344].

Just in case the frame was missed in parentheses is added: "(as seen by the Little People; being the memoirs of Bilbo and Frodo of the Shire, supplemented by the accounts of their friends and the learning of the Wise)" (*RK* 1344). Because it is accounted by hobbits, the story is bound to be shaped by their perspectives and biases, such as a fear and suspicion of the Old Forest—both of which were commonly held opinions among hobbits in the Third Age.[12] But these are hobbit biases, not Tolkien's. Although there is a contradiction between the interpretation and presentation of Old Man Willow and that of the Ents, it is not Tolkien's mistake. It is, rather, a hobbit error.

To overlook Tolkien's frame-narrative, is to overlook his grand effort to write himself out of his fiction. Creating a convincing oral and scribal tradition as a backdrop for his legendarium was long part of his intention to write a myth that could belong to his country. In a letter to Milton Waldman, Tolkien wrote:

> once upon a time (my crest has long since fallen) I had a mind to make a body of more or less connected legend, ranging from the large and cosmogonic, to the level of romantic fairy-story—the larger founded on the lesser in contact with the earth, the lesser drawing splendour from the vast backcloths—which I could dedicate simply to: to England; to my country [*Letters* 144].

Despite having never finished his intended scale, many of the tales' position in the legendarium were long considered, if not completed, before he wrote this letter.[13] Christopher Tolkien marks the date his father began work on The Book of Lost Tales to 1916 or 1917.[14] Long before the publication of *The Hobbit* and *LR*, then, Tolkien intended his Tales to reach back beyond the limits of human history and create a "connected legend."

In order to provide a truly convincing mythical past, one that linked real history to the history "of 'faerie'" (*Lost Tales* I:22), Tolkien needed to account for the origin of written language from a source outside human history and establish a tradition of writing on which each of his authors would be dependent, including presumably the pseudo-academic narrator of *The Hobbit* and *LR*. To do this he traced the literary history of Middle-earth through the Elves and their invention of written language.[15] In doing so, he pushed the development of literary history further into the past, removing humanity from its position as the earliest recorder of language and history, so that the farther back one delved into the history of Middle-earth, the more dependent one became on Elven rather than human (or hobbit) stories. Bilbo's "memoirs" suggest as such,[16] and according to his comments in the foreword to the second edition, Tolkien became increasingly aware of this dependence while writing *LR*:

> This tale grew in the telling, until it became a history of the Great War of the Ring and included many glimpses of the yet more ancient history that preceded it. ... the story was drawn irresistibly towards the older world, and became an account, as it were, of its end and passing away before its beginning and middle has been told [*FR* xxiii].

It would be inaccurate, therefore, to assume that Tolkien saw himself or his (mortal) fictive authors as the primary authors within the chronological history of Middle-earth. Rather, within his legendarium, words are a gift of the Elves.

Tied to any understanding of Tolkien's environmentalism as expressed in *The Hobbit* and *LR*, is the long history of the Elves, their environmentally cooperative culture, and their ecologically centered nature. Understanding the layers of Elven authorship in Tolkien's fiction is essential for an accurate reading of his environmentalism. In a letter to Milton Waldman, Tolkien explains the centrality of the Elven perspective in *The Silmarillion*, in particular, and in *LR*, generally: "As the high Legends of the beginnings are supposed to look at things through Elvish minds, so the middle tale of the Hobbit takes a virtually human point of view—and the last tale blends them" (*Letters* 145). But because Tolkien's published works, *The Hobbit* and *LR*, are "authored" by a completely different species of Middle-Earth—that is, by hobbits: Bilbo, Frodo and Sam[17]—these works fit into his legendarium in a different way. An elf perceives the world differently than a hobbit or a dwarf. While there are perspectival similarities between the races of Middle-earth, what fundamentally distinguishes the Elves from the other races is that they are intrinsically tied to the earth, for "its life is theirs" (*Silmarillion* 316); this reality provides a completely different perspective on living green. Ecology is not a science for the Elves; it is a mode of existence.

Because Tolkien chose the Elven perspective to recount the majority of known lore and history regarding Middle-earth, familiarity with their nature and its ecological implications on authorship is necessary for an appreciation of Tolkien's environmentalism. Elven nature is distinct from all other Ardan races; consequently, any understanding of the Elven perspective and how it affects authorship must begin by understanding their nature and history as ecologically rooted: to the themes of Ilúvatar, to the music of the Ainur, and to Arda, Middle-earth itself. The Elves possess two unique gifts that give to them a deeper ecological sense and history than the other races of Middle-earth. The first gift is an inherent, living connection to the earth which provides them with a kind of immortality (*Silmarillion* 316). Tolkien describes this relationship:

> The doom of the Elves is to be immortal, to love the beauty of the world, to bring it to full flower with their gifts of delicacy and perfection, to last while it lasts, never leaving it even when 'slain,' but returning—and yet when the Followers come, to teach them, and make way for them, to "fade" as the Followers grow and absorb the life from which both proceed [*Silmarillion* xv].

The Elves' connection to the earth, while providing them with immortality, burdens them to share in the earth's slowly waning fate: "to last while it lasts." It is a mixed blessing and drew the jealousy of mortals in the Second Age. The Akallabêth recalls the murmuring of the Númenóreans and their complaint of Manwë's prohibition against mortals sailing to the undying lands. In response to their complaint, Manwë's messengers speak "to the King ... concerning the fate and fashion of the world" (*Silmarillion* 315) and explain to the

Númenóreans that the source of Elven immortality is not found in the undying lands but in their connection to the earth:

> "The Doom of the World," they said, "One alone can change who made it. And were you so to voyage that escaping all deceits and snares you came indeed to Aman, the Blessed Realm, little would it profit you. For it is not the land of Manwë that makes its people deathless, but the Deathless that dwell therein have hallowed the land...."
>
> Nor can the Valar take away the gifts of Ilúvatar. The Eldar, you say, are unpunished, and even those who rebelled do not die. Yet that is to them neither reward nor punishment, but the fulfillment of their being. They cannot escape, and are bound to the world, never to leave it so long as it lasts, for *its life is theirs* [my emphasis, *Silmarillion* 315–6].

The immortality of the Elves is not dependent on place, then, but rather on their connection to the life and the existence of the earth.

The Elves' second ecologic gift, while not explicitly mentioned, is derived from the passage above. Simply, it is the cultural knowledge of their place and purpose within Ilúvatar's themes of creation. As outlined in the Valaquenta and the Ainulindalë, the Valar taught the Elves of the making of Arda, the origins of the Valar and the Maiar, and of the Children of Ilúvatar—how they were revealed in Ilúvatar's third theme of creation and "were conceived by him alone" (*Silmarillion* 7); that they are the "Firstborn of Ilúvatar" (*Silmarillion* 45); and that they named themselves the "Quendi, signifying those that speak with voices" (*Silmarillion* 45), recalling the days of their awakening in which they "had met no other living things that spoke or sang" (*Silmarillion* 45). In this respect, the Elves are unique among the peoples of Middle-earth because they alone learned of the themes of Ilúvatar, the Music of the Ainur, and the creation of Arda. The reader is told in the *The Book of Lost Tales I* that before Eriol sailed to the island of Tol Eresseä, no mortal had yet heard this history. This event is described in a linking story that occurs between The Cottage of Lost Play and The Music of the Ainur found in a single extant copy from 1918–20.[18] Simply called the Link by Christopher Tolkien, the story sets up the first telling of The Music of the Ainur to mortal ears. In conversation with Rúmil, the resident lore master of Tol Eresseä, Eriol asks to know "of the first beginnings, that [he] may begin to understand those things that are told [him] in this isle" (*Lost Tales I*:49). Rúmil answers Eriol with mention of Ilúvatar and the Music of the Ainur further prompting Eriol's curiosity: "'Tell me,' said Eriol, 'for I long to learn, what was the Music of the Ainur?'" (*Lost Tales I*:49). What follows is the first telling of the creation myth, The Music of the Ainur to mortal ears (*Lost Tales I*:49), an event that suggests only the Elves knew of the origins of Arda and the themes of Ilúvatar before this point in the history of Middle-earth. According to Lindo, one of Eriol's guides, previous mortal explanations of the Gods and creation are only "strange and garbled tales that are far from the truth" (*Lost Tales I*:45). Since their earliest days in Valinor, after learning the history of the earth from the Valar, the Elves have known where they come from, where they are going, and why as long as the earth lasts.

In contrast to the uncertain path of mortals, the Elves know their place in the world, for some still live in the Third Age since their time in Valinor. Galadriel, for one, is the daughter of Finarfin and Eärwen, grand-daughter of Finwë, King of the Noldor—she "wedded Celeborn and with him remained in Middle-earth after the end of the First Age" (*Silmarillion* 398). The Elves have among their population members who know from first-hand experience the history of their languages, politics, defeats, and victories. Thus, they do not need to search the past, as humans do, for fragments of lore, knowledge, or artifacts about their origin or their crafts, for they already know them. Tolkien makes this point in his lecture "On Fairy-stories," explaining that the complex history of fairy-stories "is now beyond all skill but that of the elves to unravel" ("OFS" 26); put simply, it is only they who really know that history. More than any other Ardan race, the Elves understand the earth, its history, its languages, and how their own culture and existence is interwoven within it.

Because the Elves' existence is contingent on the earth, they function as a benchmark for an ecologically-centered relationship between culture and environment. Their awakening at Cuiviénen marks the beginning of this relationship. In *The Silmarillion*, the reader is told that of all things the Elves first saw the stars and first heard the sound of water falling over stones,[19] and that from their initial moments of consciousness they participated with the environment, through mimesis, by the art through which they were first created—singing: "Oromë wondered and sat silent, and it seemed to him that in the quiet of the land under the stars he heard afar off many voices singing" (*Silmarillion* 45–6). That the first sound they heard was water, and that their reaction to it was to sing, illustrates the Elven proclivity for mimetic response to the environment. It is said of the Teleri, the Elves who lingered by the western shores of Beleriand in the First Age, that Ossë taught them "all manner of sea-lore and sea-music" (*Silmarillion* 57), and that they "who were from the beginning lovers of water, and the fairest singers of all the Elves, were after enamoured of the seas, and their songs were filled with the sound of waves upon the shore" (*Silmarillion* 57). Their love of water and its music connects the Elves back to the Music of the Ainur, not only because they know about the Music of the Ainur but also because they hear it in their environment. The Ainulindalë recounts that, "it is said by the Eldar that in water there lives yet the echo of the Music of the Ainur more than in any substance else that is in this Earth" (*Silmarillion* 8). Elven culture is unique in its awareness of and participation in the music that enlivens all of Arda. For the Elves, their existence is fundamentally connected to the ecology of Middle-earth. More than any other race, they are attentive to the echoes of the music of the Ainur and emulate it in their art. More than any other constructive force, it is the land and its songs that shape Elven culture.

As a benchmark for an ecologically-centered culture, the Elves reception of and emulation of nature demonstrates Tolkien's vision for a participatory model of ecology. In "Tolkien's Cosmic-Christian Ecology," Alfred Siewers explains how Tolkien derived the pattern for an "ecocentric Middle-earth" (140) from Celtic Otherworld texts and non–Augustinian patristic theology. The article explores the interwoven cultural landscape of medieval northern Europe and how Christianity was often overlaid onto the landscapes and heroes of its pagan stories. He suggests that Tolkien overlaid the Elven landscapes of Middle-earth in a similar fashion, making "True nature ... not a 'what' but a 'who' ... on Middle-earth" (148). Rejecting the possibility that Middle-earth could be viewed as mere allegorical backdrop, however, Siewers argues that Tolkien's world shares the cultural landscape of Otherworld texts that combine, rather than separate, physical and spiritual planes and thus providing a "horizontal experiential engagement of the two" (141). As such, Tolkien's world becomes "a polycentered reality, not merely an objectification of earthly reality as human desire" (141). Rather than merely pointing to divinity (as in allegory), everything—animate or inanimate, sentient or not—in Middle-earth echoes Ilúvatar's cosmic themes by analogy through participation in the creative music of the Ainur. In explanation of this, Siewers points to St. Maximus's seventh century commentary on the participatory nature of all things in God: the "Logos," wrote Maximus, "is manifested and multiplied in a way suitable to the good in all the beings who came from Him ... and He recapitulates all things in Himself.... For all things participate in God by analogy, insofar as they came from God" (149). Ilúvatar's speech to the Ainur demonstrates Tolkien's use of a similar participatory model in his cosmology:

> Ilúvatar said again: "Behold your Music!" This is your minstrelsy; and each of you shall find contained herein, amid the design that I set before you, all those things which it may seem that he himself devised or added. And thou, Melkor, wilt discover all the secret thoughts of thy mind, and wilt perceive that they are but a part of the whole and tributary to its glory [*Silmarillion* 6].

Although this first vision is just that—a vision and not yet reality—the passage describes the analogic nature of things in Middle-earth. It explains that all things were, in their beginning, sung into being and that each refers back to that music and its organizing theme. Even Melkor's great evils are described as "part of the whole and tributary to its glory." Siewers points to the songs of Tom Bombadil and the chants of the Ents as echoes of the original singing of creation, suggesting that the link between word and reality in Maximus's logoi, merging as it does the physical environment and divinity, exists also within Tolkien's fiction and that it serves to re-sacralize nature (149). Water functions in this way and is praised by the Ainur and the Elves because "in water there lives yet the echo of the Music of the Ainur more than in any substance else that is in this Earth" (*Silmarillion* 8). With their roots in a cosmology of participation, Tolkien's environmental landscapes enact an ecological vision that combines, rather than separates, the material and the divine. In doing so, Siewers writes, they "defy human objectification or control ... [yet] invite human engagement and actualization in participation with a larger mystery of the cosmos" (149–50). As participants in the ecology on which their existence depends, Elven society models a key feature of Tolkien's environmentalism.

The Elves' awareness of and connection to the Music of the Ainur in their surrounding environment enchants their dwellings with a perceptible magic to non–Elven species. In the Third Age, Lothlórien remains the hallmark of Elvendom in Middle-earth and provides ample evidence for the environmental recovery made possible through the Elves' connection to the earth. It is a magical, even perilous,[20] place for those who are ignorant of the Elves' kinship with the world: where the effects of their stewardship of the earth appears enchanting, even illusory, to those who see nature only as an object for control. But for the Elves, it is a refuge, a place where their old kinship with the earth thrives and where the weariness of the waning world is held at bay. As such, Lothlórien provides a window onto an older, yet younger, world. For Frodo, standing on Cerin Amroth,

> It seemed to him that he had stepped through a high window that looked on a vanished world. A light was upon it for which his language had no name. All that he saw was shapely, but the shapes seemed at once clear cut, as if they had been first conceived and drawn at the uncovering of his eyes, and ancient as if they had endured for ever. He saw no colour but those he knew, gold and white and blue and green, but they were fresh and poignant, as if he had at that moment first perceived them and made for them names new and wonderful [*FR* 456].

The reader is told that as the wind blows upon Cerin Amroth it transcends the bounds of time, repeating the forgotten sounds of "great seas upon beaches that had long ago been washed away, and sea-birds crying whose race had perished from the earth" (457). Lothlórien embodies a vision of the world as it appeared in the days of its youth, and illustrates the symbiotic relationship of the Elves and the earth.

Evidently, the perceived magic of the Elves comes not from their technology but from their art. In a letter to Milton Waldman, Tolkien explains that

> Their "magic" is Art, delivered from many of its human limitations: more effortless, more quick, more complete (product, and vision in unflawed correspondence). And its object is Art not Power, sub-creation not domination and tyrannous reforming of Creation [*Silmarillion* xiv].

Elven arts only appear magical to the hobbits (and other mortals) for whom such skills represent a secret learning or arcane techné. While the learning of the Elves does reach back to a younger Arda, granting them a special knowledge of the earth and its elements, in practice their knowledge serves rather than controls, as is the case in Lothlórien. But a question remains regarding the Rings of Power and the technology for crafting them that they learned from Sauron. Although Sauron's scheme was malicious (and deceitful) from the start, the Elves desired only understanding, making, and healing (*Silmarillion* 344–5), and their hiding of the rings by concealment and non-use demonstrates discipline of a need to control. It is true that Galadriel's ring, Nenya, protects Lothlórien's verdancy from fading, but the power there, as in Rivendell or the Grey Havens, is more a product of the Elves' care for the earth, binding them closer together, than of a controlling technology: the Rings of Power grant wisdom for making and healing, not for dominion and control. In comparison with Saruman's industrialization of Orthanc and his treachery against Fangorn Forest, or more generally with Sauron's desire to conquer all of Middle-earth and enslave its peoples, the Elves represent Tolkien's vision of the best use of technology: namely, that it be a tool for the benefit of the earth rather than for mere human gain. The Elves' use of technology furthers their appreciation for the natural world as it positions its users in service of the earth.

The most potent aspect of Lórien's magic is its potential for environmental recovery, and their "gifts of skill to order all the lands and heal their hurts" (*Silmarillion* 49) help recover the hobbits' environmental awareness. For the hobbits, Lothlórien is magical but only in so far as they lack knowledge of the Elves' history and experience of their ability to heal and order the earth. Sam experiences this history, even feeling the echoes of the Music of the Ainur, in his expression, "I feel as if I was inside a song" (*FR* 457), though he does not really understand why or how. Additionally, he observes the Elves' existence as a kind of timeless ecology, a belonging: "They seem to belong here, more even than Hobbits do in the Shire. Whether they've made the land, or the land's made them, its hard to say.... If there's any magic about, it's right down deep, where I can't lay my hands on it" (*FR* 469). Sam's comparison of the sense of belonging between Elves and Hobbits exhibits his new awareness of the deep connection that Elves (and to an extent hobbits) share with the earth. Frodo's experience changes his awareness of and sensitivity to nature, resembling even an Elven empathy for the life within trees:

> he laid his hand upon the tree beside the ladder: never before had he been so suddenly and so keenly aware of the feel and texture of a tree's skin and of the life within it. He felt a delight in wood and the touch of it, neither as forester nor as carpenter; it was the delight of the living tree itself [*FR* 457].

These descriptions contrast sharply with the hobbits' earlier account of the Old Forest as "queer" (*FR* 144) and Frodo's description of Old Man Willow as "beastly" (154). But here, in the long-cared for realm of Lothlórien, their perspective changes as they begin to understand how life permeates the inanimate things of Middle-earth and extends deeper than the stories told in the Shire.

In addition to Merry and Pippin's experience in Lothlórien, their ecological perspective further changes in Fangorn Forest after they meet Treebeard. Merry and Pippin do not speak much during their interaction with Treebeard besides some questions concerning Middle-earth's forests, the Entwives, and Saruman. Treebeard's statement—"I am not altogether on anybody's side, because nobody is altogether on my side, if you understand me" (*TT* 615)—opens the hobbits to an awareness of a political and environmental reality far greater than the concerns of the Shire. But it is in Pippin's question regarding the Entwives, "Why are there so few, when you have lived in this country so long?" (*TT* 618), and in the subsequent telling of how the Ents lost the Entwives, that one sees a shift forming in the hobbits. Merry's confession that "the songs [of the Entwives] have not come west over the Mountains to the Shire" (*TT* 619) reveals a new awareness in him of how isolated Shire-hobbits have become. Bregalad's touching account of the felled Rowan trees near his home reinforces to the hobbits that the categories of living beings go beyond themselves and "the Big Folk" (*FR* 1), causing them to realize that the trees of Middle-earth are more than timber, branch, and leaf.[21] For Merry and Pippin, their experience in Lothlórien is reinforced and furthered by Treebeard in Fangorn Forest.

Because of their ecological connection, the Elves' perspective of the environment is different from the other races of Middle-earth and demonstrates two crucial aspects of their interpretive framework: first, their connection with the earth explains the magic of the Elves without diminishing its enchanting allure—just as the hobbits, readers are enchanted by the Elves' mode of existence and want to experience the world, at least in part, as the Elves do. In his lecture "On Fairy Stories," Tolkien affirms that the Elves' relationship with the earth is desirable because it fulfills the "old ambitions and desires [of humanity] ... to which they offer a kind of satisfaction and consolation" (66) and explains that the Elves also fulfill our "profounder wishes: such as the desire to converse with other living things" (66):

> On this desire, as ancient as the Fall, is largely founded the talking of beasts and creatures in fairy-tales, and especially the magical understanding of their proper speech. This is the root, and not the "confusion" attributed to the minds of men of the unrecorded past, an alleged "absence of the sense of separation of ourselves from beasts." A vivid sense of that separation is very ancient; but also a sense that it was a severance: a strange fate and guilt lies on us [66].

Treebeard explains how, "They always wished to talk to everything, the old Elves did" (*TT* 610), and that it was the Elves who first woke up the trees and taught them to speak: "the Elves began it, of course, waking trees up and teaching them to speak and learning their tree-talk" (*TT* 610). In contrast to the human desire to overcome its severance from the environment, the Elves provide others opportunities to commune with the environment and its creatures in a way that is difficult (if not impossible) for others to achieve on their own. For the Elves this enchantment is neither magical nor peculiar; for them, it is the meaning of life.

To understand Tolkien's environmental commitments one must read his fiction while remembering the biases and perspectives that are embedded within the fictive authors who wrote each tale. Using as he does both Elven and hobbit perspectives, Tolkien not only provides a "good-use" model as an ideal for interacting with the environment, but also illuminates a pathway towards achieving it. The hobbits learn that their earlier convictions regarding the trees and forests of Middle-earth did not consider the ecological impact of their culture's perspective. As understood by the Elves, Arda exists for purposes beyond the desires of Elves, hobbits, dwarves, and humans. Reading *The Hobbit* and *LR* without awareness of the authorial tradition that enlivens its story is not enough to develop a cohesive comprehension of the perspectival layers that Tolkien so carefully crafted: layers which, when accounted for, enchant his fiction with an environmental awareness that is both ethically responsible and culturally conscious.

Notes

1. See also *Letters* 319–21.
2. I use this word, "recovery," as Tolkien describes it in his lecture "On Fairy Stories": "Recovery (which includes return and renewal of health) is a re-gaining—regaining of a clear view. ... I might venture to say

'seeing things as we are (or were) meant to see them'—as things apart from ourselves. We need, in any case, to clean our windows; so that the things seen clearly may be freed from the drab blur of triteness or familiarity—from possessiveness. ... This triteness is really the penalty of 'appropriation': the things that are trite, or (in a bad sense) familiar, are the things that we have appropriated, legally or mentally. ... They have become like the things which once attracted us by their glitter, or their colour, or their shape, and we laid hands on them, and then locked them in our hoard, acquired them, and acquiring ceased to look at them" ("OFS" 59).

3. See Flieger, "Taking the Part of Trees: Eco-conflict in Middle-earth," 147–8.

4. See *The Return of the Shadow*, where Christopher Tolkien explains that despite redistribution of some of the actions to different hobbits, "the old text is very close to the final form" (113).

5. See chapter three of *The Fellowship of the Ring* (*FR*), "Three is Company" (*FR* 98–99).

6. The fictional editor of the appendices shares Tolkien's philologic interests found in his early academic articles, "The Devil's Coach-Horses: Eaueres," *The Review of English Studies*, 1.3 (July 1925): 331–336; and, "Some Contributions to Middle-English Lexicography," *The Review of English Studies*. 1.2 (April 1925): 210–215. Consider, for example, the meticulous attention given to the proper use of dwarves, Orc, and moon-runes at the beginning of *The Hobbit*, or "Appendix E" to *LR*, in which one can find a detailed course on two systems of Elven phonology and typography; additionally, there is the shared tone of the academic historian, as seen in "The Note on Shire Records," in the "Prologue" to *LR*, and in appendices A through D.

7. See Flieger's excellent study on how Tolkien developed this fictive tradition in her work *Interrupted Music: The Making of Tolkien's Mythology*, chapter five, "The Artifice."

8. Tolkien argues that, "The illusion of historical truth and perspective, that has made Beowulf seem such an attractive quarry, is largely a product of art" ("Beowulf: The Monsters and the Critics" 105).

9. See Christopher Tolkien's description of his father's "High School Exercise Books," dated from 12 Feb. 1917 (*The Book of Lost Tales I*:13).

10. For more on the development of Eriol as the link between worlds, see Flieger, *Interrupted Music*.

11. See "The History of Eriol or Ælfine and the End of the Tales" (*Lost Tales II*: 290–94) where Christopher Tolkien suggests a possible narrative of Eriol's life: from the coming of the Eldar and Noldoli to Tol Eressëa to the conquering of that island by Eriol's Anglo-Saxon sons, Hengest, Horsa, and Heorrenda, and renaming it "England."

12. Such as Fatty Bolger's comment "I wish you were not going into the Forest. I only hope you will not need rescuing before the day is out" (*FR* 144), or Pippin's question—"Are the stories about it true?"—and Merry's answer: "the forest is queer. Everything in it is very much more alive, more aware of what is going on, so to speak, than things are in the Shire. And the trees do not like strangers. They watch you ... [and] at night things can be most alarming, or so I am told" (*FR* 144).

13. In his comments on this letter, Humphrey Carpenter explains that even though the letter is not dated, it was probably written late in 1951 (*Letters* 167).

14. For specific dates of these earliest "Tales" see *The Book of Lost Tales* vol. I & II and *The Lays of Belleriand*: The Cottage of Lost Play and The Music of the Ainur, 1916–17 (*Lost Tales I*:13,45); The Tale of Tinúviel, Turambar and the Foalókë, and The Fall of Gondolin, 1917 (*Lost Tales II*:3,69,144); The Lay of the Children of Húrin, 1926 (though an envelope note to the "Sketch of the Mythology with especial reference to 'The Children of Húrin'" shows a beginning of 1918) (*Lays* 3); and the Lay of Leithian that tells the story of Beren and Luthien, 1925–1931 (*Lays* 150).

15. Rúmil of Tirion is credited with the achievement of finding "fitting signs for the recording of speech and song" (*Silmarillion* 63), though this passage points to an earlier origin, mentioning that it was the Noldor who, blessed with great skill and knowledge, "first bethought them of letters" (63). Fëanor later improved Rúmil's design and created the letters that bear his name, the Fëanorian Letters, which were used ever after by the Elves (*Silmarillion* 64). (cf. *LR* Appendix E II).

16. See "Note on Shire Records" ("Prologue," *FR* 19), where Tolkien's narrator/philologist/translator explains the manuscript history of Bilbo's memoirs, named the Red Book of Westmarch, and the scribal tradition through which it descended. In origin Bilbo's private diary during his time in Rivendell, Frodo brought it back to the Shire to write his account of the War of the Ring. To it was annexed Bilbo's gift to Frodo: "three large volumes, bound in red leather" (*FR* 19). And to these four volumes a fifth was added that contained commentaries, genealogies, and other hobbit lore that concerned the members of the Fellowship (*FR* 19). This "note" explains also that, although the original Red Book was not preserved, several copies were made. The most important of these was the Thain's Book written in Gondor by the scribe Findegil; for it alone contained "the whole of Bilbo's 'Translations from the Elvish'" (*FR* 19): material that was "almost entirely concerned with the Eldar days" (20). Presumably, it is this copy that became the source of the appendices attached to The Lord of the Rings as we have it. Without Bilbo's diary, the earliest histories of Middle-earth and its peoples would have been forgotten.

17. After completing his own tale, Frodo makes clear to Sam that, "The last pages are for you" (*RK* 1344).

18. Christopher Tolkien explains that, "in another notebook identical to that in which The Cottage of Lost Play was written out by my mother, there is a text in ink in my father's hand ... entitled: Link between Cottage of Lost Play and (Tale 2) Music of Ainur" (*The Book of Lost Tales I*:45). Evidently, his father had written it during his work on the Oxford English Dictionary from 1918–1920: cf. *Biography* pp. 99, 102.

19. "Their eyes beheld first of all things the stars of heaven ... and the first sound that was heard by the Elves was the sound of water flowing, and the sound of water falling over stone" (*Silmarillion* 45).

20. Boromir first calls Lothlórien "perilous" (*FR* 440) while on the outskirts of it borders: "now we must enter the Golden Wood, you say. But of that perilous land we have heard in Gondor, and it is said that few come out who once go in; and of that few none have escaped unscathed."

21. For further information on Tolkien's various categories of trees, see Cynthia M. Cohen's study, "The Unique Representation of Trees in The Lord of the Rings," *Tolkien Studies* 6 (2009): 91–125.

Works Cited

Carpenter, Humphrey. 1977. *Tolkien: A Biography*. Boston: Houghton Mifflin.
_____, ed. 1981. *The Letters of J.R.R. Tolkien*. Boston: Houghton Mifflin.
Cohen, Cynthia M. 2009. "The Unique Representation of Trees in The Lord of the Rings." *Tolkien Studies* 6: 91–125.
Flieger, Verlyn. 2000. "Taking the Part of Trees: Eco-Conflict in Middle-earth." In *J.R.R. Tolkien and His Literary Resonances*. Ed. George Clark and Daniel Timmons, 147–58. Westport, CT: Greenwood.
_____. 2005. *Interrupted Music: The Making of Tolkien's Mythology*. Kent, OH: Kent State University Press, 2005.
Jeffery, David Lyle. 2004. "Tolkien as Philologist." In *Tolkien and the Invention of Myth*, ed. Jane Chance, 61–80. Lexington: University Press of Kentucky.
Nagy, Gergely. 2005. "The Medievalist('s) Fiction: Textuality and Historicity as Aspects of Tolkien's Medievalist Cultural Theory in a Postmodern Context." In *Tolkien's Modern Middle Ages*, ed. Jane Chance and Alfred K. Siewers, 29–41. New York: Palgrave Macmillan.
Siewers, Alfred K. 2005. "Tolkien's Cosmic-Christian Ecology: The Medieval Underpinnings." In *Tolkien's Modern Middle Ages*, ed. Jane Chance and Alfred K. Siewers, 139–153. New York: Palgrave Macmillan.
Tolkien, J.R.R. 1982. "On Fairy-stories." In *Tree and Leaf, Smith of Wootton Major & The Homecoming of Beorhtnoth*, 11–79. London: Unwin.
_____. 1985. *The Lays of Beleriand*. History of Middle Earth Series, vol. 3. Ed. Christopher Tolkien. Boston: Houghton Mifflin.
_____. 1986. *The Book of Lost Tales: Part I*. History of Middle Earth Series vol. 1. Ed. Christopher Tolkien. London: Guild.
_____. 1986. *The Book of Lost Tales: Part II*. History of Middle Earth Series vol. 2. Ed. Christopher Tolkien. London: Guild.
_____. 1990. *The Return of the Shadow: The History of The Lord of the Rings Part One*. Ed. Christopher Tolkien. London: Unwin.
_____. 1999. *The Silmarillion*. Ed. Christopher Tolkien. London: HarperCollins.
_____. 2002. "Beowulf: The Monsters and the Critics." In *Beowulf: A Verse Translation*. A Norton Critical Edition, ed. Daniel Donoghue, 103–130. New York: W.W. Norton.
_____. 2007. *The Fellowship of the Ring: Being the First Part of The Lord of the Rings*. 50th anniversary edition. London: HarperCollins.
_____. 2007. *The Return of the King: Being the Third Part of The Lord of the Rings*. 50th anniversary edition,. London: HarperCollins.
_____. 2007. *The Two Towers: Being the Second Part of the Lord of the Rings*. 50th anniversary edition. London: HarperCollins.

Polytemporality and Epic Characterization in The Hobbit: An Unexpected Journey
Reflecting *The Lord of the Ring*'s Modernism and Medievalism

JUDY ANN FORD *and* ROBIN ANNE REID

Peter Jackson's *The Hobbit: An Unexpected Journey* proves to be both more consistent with the canon of J.R.R. Tolkien's fiction and more infused with the conventions of medieval epic than might have been expected from an adaptation of the novel *The Hobbit*. These two qualities are related, as the later Tolkienian texts on which the film draws are more resonant with medieval epic than is the novel that provides the film's title as well as its main plot line and characters. The film embeds its story in the broad, rich historical drama of Tolkien's Middle-earth, drawing on its history that was largely unwritten at the time of the publication of *The Hobbit*, and in so doing captures the echoes of European history, medieval and modern, that imbue Tolkien's *The Lord of the Rings* and *The Silmarillion* with the polytemporality that distinguishes those works from thinner, less embodied fantasies.

The influence of the medieval languages and literatures that were Tolkien's scholarly passion on his literary work is well known, as is the fact that the majority of scholars publishing on Tolkien's literary work during the past fifty years are medievalists. In recent years, however, a growing body of scholarly articles have explored the influence of World War I and II on *The Lord of the Rings* (Chrism, Croft, Flieger, Garth, Jackson, Livingston, Long, Murnane, Simonson). Additionally, John Garth's 2003 monograph, *Tolkien and the Great War: The Threshold of Middle-earth*, is an extended biographical study drawing on archival materials from the British Army, Tolkien's own papers, and letters and other papers by his close friends to analyze the influence of World War I on *The Silmarillion*, parts of which Tolkien began writing during his time in the army. The majority of the scholarship on Tolkien's modernisms focuses on the influence of the world wars on Tolkien's later fictions, which are embedded in the polytemporal history of Arda, a history which is increasingly coming to be understood as being influenced by both the medieval and the modern.

This essay argues that *An Unexpected Journey* serves as a more congruent prequel to *The Lord of the Rings* than does the book *The Hobbit* because it draws on Tolkien's later work to a great extent. This film foregrounds two elements that do not play important roles in the novel *The Hobbit* but are integral elements of Tolkien's *The Lord of the Rings*. First, the film focuses on political and military themes that echo the history of twentieth-century Europe, particularly the era of the two world wars. Second, the film employs the conventions of medieval epic, specifically those of epic masculinity, especially in respect to the construction of the characters Thorin and Bilbo, who are changed from the comic fairy-tale (in the childish sense of the word) figures of the first half of Tolkien's novel. These two elements of the film are grounded in its incorporation of the material generated by J.R.R. Tolkien during his later revisions, and his commentary about *The Hobbit* in what John Rateliff calls the post-publication phases of revision, including Tolkien's consideration of a complete revision of the published text.

In a very real way, Peter Jackson's film continues the project begun by Tolkien of revising *The Hobbit*, his earliest novel, to make it more consistent with his later, more mature conceptions of Middle-earth. The inconsistencies between the two works emerged from the process of their creation. Tolkien did not originally intend to publish *The Hobbit*, still less a series of related books about hobbits, and he certainly did not expect the resultant popularity. When publisher Stanley Unwin asked him for a sequel to *The Hobbit* in 1937, Tolkien's first response was that he did not have anything more to say about hobbits (Carpenter and Tolkien, 1995, 24). Instead, he submitted some of his earlier writings about Middle-earth, including the "Quenta Silmarillion," and an unfinished poem about Beren and Lúthien for consideration. When that material was rejected, he would eventually begin work on a story that he called the sequel to *The Hobbit* which would ultimately become *The Lord of the Rings* (Carpenter and Tolkien, 1995, 25–6).

Despite Tolkien's use of the term "sequel," it is problematic as a way of describing the relationship between these two novels as they were originally published because of the inconsistencies between them: specifically, the different tones and genres. Although *The Hobbit* and *The Lord of the Rings* are part of a broadly continuous sequence of events that is now understood as part of Tolkien's Legendarium, they were not initially created for the same audience. The book *The Hobbit* is a children's story and *The Lord of the Rings* is not, as Tolkien acknowledged in letters to his publisher which described *The Lord of the Rings* as "more grown up" and *The Hobbit* as "matter from the great cycle susceptible of treatment as a 'fairy-story,' for children" (Carpenter and Tolkien, 1995, 42 and 159). Another inconsistency relates to content, specifically the nature of Gollum's ring. The discrepancies between the ring in the different works came to bother Tolkien to the degree that he rewrote a chapter of *The Hobbit* and sent it to his publisher shortly before the publication of *The Lord of the Rings*. This act led to a second edition of *The Hobbit* being published, a highly unusual step to take for a book that had first appeared in print more than a decade earlier.

The authors argue that Tolkien subjected the 1937 published version of *The Hobbit* to a process that is known as "retconning" in the comics industry, in other words, creating retroactive continuity between the two works. John Rateliff, in his extensive and careful detailing of *The History of The Hobbit*, has analyzed its manuscripts and additional materials in order to identify different phases in its composition. The first three phases consist of the drafts Tolkien created before publication, separated by periods of time during which he could not work on the novel. The first phase was a thirteen page opening; the second was an extensive and "nearly complete" version; and the third was a fairly complete "home copy" for circulation amongst family and friends. Then a submission copy was prepared for publication (Rateliff, 2007, xxiii–xxv). The fourth phase identified by Rateliff is the start of the retcon. Rateliff identifies this stage as taking place after the book appeared in print, when Tolkien revised it to "better suit his evolving conception of Middle-earth and the role which the story of Bilbo's adventures played in it" (Rateliff, 2007, xxvii).

These fourth-phase changes were published in the 1951 edition and are also documented in Douglas Anderson's *The Annotated Hobbit*. The plot of *The Lord of the Rings* required a very different ring from the one Bilbo originally found in *The Hobbit*, so significant changes were made to Chapter 5, "Riddles in the Dark," when Bilbo meets Gollum and acquires the ring (Rateliff, 2007, xxvii). The key alterations are Gollum's wretchedness and attachment to the ring; in the original version, Gollum offers to give Bilbo a present, a magic ring, if he won, and agrees to show Bilbo the way out when the ring is discovered to be missing, without any concern over the fate of the ring (Tolkien, Anderson, 2006, 128). There is a striking contrast between Bilbo walking along with Gollum to the passage on the way out in the original edition and the revision, which highlights Gollum's threat and Bilbo's growing heroism as well as his decision to spare Gollum's life. The revised chapter marks a distinct turning point in the novel where the lighthearted and comic tone of the first part shifts to incorporate the darker and older, elements of Germanic heroic epic which came to dominate the second half of the novel. Rateliff also includes in phase four the 1954 composition of "The Quest of Erebor," a chapter written to provide Gandalf's explanation of why he chose, over the Dwarves' objections, to include Bilbo in the quest to the Lonely Mountain. "The Quest of Erebor" integrates the events of *The Hobbit* with those of *The Lord of the Rings*, and explains how important the results of "There and Back Again" were to the outcome of the later events, creating retroactive continuity. While Tolkien hoped to include "The Quest for Erebor" among the appendices of *The Lord of the Rings*, only a summary of the key information ultimately appeared.

Creating a narrative of Middle-earth characterized by internal consistency was clearly important to Tolkien although he was not able to achieve it. Rateliff identifies a fifth phase, the 1960 version, during which Tolkien began to revise the entire novel to match *The Lord of the Rings,* getting as far as Chapter 3 before stopping the project. Nevertheless, Rateliff's analysis of the manuscript history makes it clear that Tolkien wished to make the two works more congruent in style as well as content. And even though he did not pursue a complete revision of *The Hobbit*, he constructed a framing narrative which explained them, rather than leaving the earlier one to be read as evidence that its author changed his mind. Tolkien used the Prologue to *The Lord of the Rings* to explain that the first published version was a lie told by Bilbo to Gandalf and the Dwarves. His decision to conceal the truth about his acquisition of the ring in his original story is diagnosed by Gandalf in *The Lord of the Rings* as the first working of the evil of the ring on Bilbo. Thus the discrepancies are explained by the translator-narrator as an artifact of the process by which the original manuscript of the *Red Book of Westmarch*, written by Bilbo and given to Frodo, then Sam, to finish, includes Bilbo's lie. Later versions of the manuscripts, copied by different scribes, of the *Red Book*, contain Frodo's version of Bilbo's acquisition of the Ring. The revised, and, according to the narrator, truer version of events, is presented as having been written by Frodo and Sam who completed the *Red Book* with the events of the War of the Ring, and translations from the Elvish which Bilbo did at Rivendell—Tolkien's reference to *The Silmarillion* manuscript. Bilbo's false version remained the original manuscript, however, since neither Frodo nor Sam deleted it, and other copies and variants were prepared with the true events. Since Middle-earth has no printing press, variants of the *Red Book* exist in different places, paralleling the situation in the Primary World in which different editions of *The Hobbit* have different versions of Chapter 5.

An Unexpected Journey can be understood in the context of the project, begun by Tolkien, of revising *The Hobbit* to make it more consistent with his later ideas of Middle-earth. This project includes both a re-imagination of the characters that shapes them in the fashion of medieval epic conventions, as well as a reframing of the story of Bilbo and the Dwarves to integrate it in the more complex narrative of the struggle to save Middle-earth from rule by Sauron. The film draws upon the 1951 edition of *The Hobbit*, "The Quest for Erebor" of 1954, and the appendices to *The Lord of the Rings* published in 1955 for the material used in the reframing, and in doing so introduces the polytemporal echoes of modern Europe at war that add so much resonance to *The Lord of the Rings*. Much of this material focuses on the subject of the Necromancer.

Little information is given in *The Hobbit* concerning Gandalf's reasons for leaving the dwarves and Bilbo at the eaves of Mirkwood, to reappear only after the defeat of the dragon in the camp where Bilbo tries to negotiate with the leaders of the Elves and Men. In the final chapter of the novel, both Bilbo and the reader learn that when Gandalf left the company at the Edge of the Wild he attended a council of authorities in good magic and the wise which had driven the Necromancer from his stronghold in the southern part of Mirkwood (Tolkien, 1989, 299). Although Gandalf's departure serves as an important plot element, providing a reason for the wizard to leave Bilbo and the dwarves to their own devices, the novel devotes very little space to this council and provides no direct narration of its activities. In contrast, in *An Unexpected Journey*, the first installment of Peter Jackson's film adaptation, a meeting at Rivendell in which Gandalf and other members of the White Council discuss the Necromancer takes up an entire sequence of dialog-heavy scenes.

The differences between the book and the film in regard to the treatment of the Necromancer contribute to the creation of a different tone in these works. Far from being a children's story, *An Unexpected Journey* focuses on the adult themes of politics and war. The sequence depicting the meetings of Gandalf and members of the White Council in Rivendell serves to contextualize the journey to the Lonely Mountain as part of the larger effort to prevent Sauron from taking control of Middle-earth. It establishes Bilbo's story as part of a war story, a story about politics, duplicity, strategy and tactics.

The scenes in *The Unexpected Journey* showing Gandalf meeting with Elrond, Galadriel, and Saruman at Rivendell to discuss the threats of the Necromancer are drawn from information in the appendices of *The Lord of the Rings* and "The Quest of Erebor." Appendix B to *The Lord of the Rings*, "The Chronology of the Westlands," provides a longer history for the White Council than does *The Hobbit* and offers a few more details about its business. It was formed, according to this appendix, in 2463 of the Third Age, about the same time as Sméagol acquired the ring (Tolkien, 1955; 2013, 406). The entry on the formation of the White Council immediately follows one for 2460 which announces that the Watchful Peace ends and Sauron returns with increased strength to Dol Guldur. The chronology lists three more meetings. At the meeting in 2851, Gandalf attempts to persuade the Council to attack Dol Guldur but is overruled by Saruman, who, unknown to the others, is already trying to find the One Ring and possess it himself. He hopes that the presence of Sauron might induce the Ring to reveal itself (Tolkien, 1955; 2013, 409). The White Council meets again in 2941, and this time, Saruman agrees to an attack on Dol Guldur because he believes that the servants of Sauron are too close to finding the ring and wishes to distract them. Sauron is forced to abandon Dol Guldur. The chronology places this third meeting of the council between the time when Bilbo finds the ring and the Battle of the Five Armies; it is clearly the meeting that Gandalf attends after leaving Beorn's house (Tolkien, 1955; 2013, 408). The next meeting, which is described as the final meeting of the While Council, takes place in 2953, and is devoted to a debate about the rings (Tolkien, 1955; 2013, 409).

In *The Unexpected Journey*, members of the White Council, namely Gandalf, Elrond, Galadriel, and Saruman, hold a meeting at Rivendell. The dialog revolves around Gandalf's attempt to persuade the others that Sauron is plotting and has some connection with an evil presence at Dol Guldur. The film is thus telescoping events in the appendices to *The Lord of the Rings* to move the 2851 meeting into the timeframe of the events of *The Hobbit*. Although the chronology is telescoped, the ideas expressed at the council meeting in *An Unexpected Journey* tie it closely to Tolkien's later ideas.

The purpose of the meeting at Rivendell in the film is an inquiry into Gandalf's decision to help Thorin Oakenshield and the other dwarves to retake Erebor. Gandalf explains that he is motivated by a concern that the dragon Smaug, although currently unaligned, might in future form an allegiance with Sauron. This motive seems to have been taken from Appendix A, which in turn summarizes a conversation among Gandalf, Frodo, Pippin, and Gimli from "The Quest of Erebor" set after Aragorn's coronation.[1] One of the themes of the conversation is strategy. In "The Quest of Erebor," Gandalf makes it quite clear that, although he felt sorry for Thorin and believed him to be deserving of help by his own merit, the wizard's primary reason for providing aid was that Thorin was unwittingly caught up in Sauron's sinister strategies (Tolkien, Anderson, 2006, 370). Gandalf explains that he was motivated by a concern for tactics, describing himself as a captain who was a member of a War Council (Tolkien, Anderson, 2006, 370). He feared that Rivendell and Lórien were vulnerable if Sauron succeeded in taking Angmar: only the Dwarves of the Iron Hills and the small number of men at Dale would stand between him and Rivendell. Smaug, Gandalf explains, might have been used to "terrible effect" enabling Sauron to retake the north (Tolkien, Anderson, 2006, 370). Gandalf describes the effort to take Erebor as a mission against Smaug in defense of Rivendell, and explains that only when this mission was launched did he feel sufficiently safe to turn his attention to persuading the Council to attack Dol Guldur before Sauron could attack Lórien (Tolkien, Anderson, 2006, 370). "The Quest of Erebor" ties Gandalf's actions in *The Hobbit* directly to those in *The Lord of the Rings*.

Gandalf in *An Unexpected Journey*, like Gandalf in Tolkien's revised version of the story from the 1950s, aids Thorin as part of a larger strategy to resist the rising power of Sauron. At the meeting of the members of the White Council at Rivendell, Gandalf argues that Thorin should be aided in his attempt to return to the Lonely Mountain because it would disturb Smaug who might be used by the enemy to "terrible effect," the same phrase found both in the appendices of *The Lord of the Rings* and in "The Quest for Erebor." Gandalf also tries to persuade the others that Sauron is connected with an evil presence in Dol Guldur. He presents his motives as strategic and tactical.[2]

One substantial difference between the film and the novel is that, in *An Unexpected Journey*, Gandalf only suspects, albeit very strongly suspects, that Sauron is trying to return and end the "watchful peace," a descriptive phrase that appears in Appendix B of *The Lord of the Rings* as well as in the film, whereas in *The Hobbit*, Gandalf states that he already knew, before he met Thorin, that a Necromancer had taken up residence in Dol Guldur. As Gandalf explains in the chapter "An Unexpected Party," he tried without success to rescue Thorin's father, Thrain, from the dungeons of the Necromancer and barely escaped (Tolkien, 1982, 26). Even though the Necromancer is not explicitly identified as Sauron in *The Hobbit*, in the novel Gandalf knows about him from the start as an enemy far beyond the powers of the dwarves (Tolkien, 1982, 26). In the film, Gandalf does not learn about existence of the Necromancer until he and the dwarves are already on their journey, and does not have any prior knowledge of his powers.

A reason why Gandalf in *An Unexpected Journey* might have been drawn as less well-informed may have to do with the order in which the films appeared.[3] In the appendix to *The Lord of the Rings*, Saruman merely overruled Gandalf when he first proposed an attack on Sauron in Dol Guldur. It would be difficult for Jackson to replicate that decision because his *The Hobbit* follows his *The Lord of the Rings*. The likelihood that many of the viewers will have seen *The Lord of the Rings* means that the audience has seen graphic images of the destruction that Sauron wreaked on Middle-earth. It would be difficult for a film-maker to ask such an audience to believe that the council would allow Saruman simply to overrule Gandalf if all the members were actually sure that Sauron was already active and had established himself in Dol Guldur as the Necromancer. Instead, in the film, while the other members of the White Council implicitly accept Gandalf's argument that, if Sauron were to try to rebuild his strength, he should be resisted, they contest the evidence that he has done so. Lacking the certain knowledge that Gandalf possessed in *The Hobbit*, the meeting at Rivendell becomes a debate over Gandalf's evidence.

In the debate over the question of Sauron's re-emergence, Sarumon acts as leader of the council yet his authority is revealed to be in doubt. At Sarumon's first appearance in *An Unexpected Journey* he is acknowledged by Elrond as the one who summoned the meeting. Sarumon takes the lead in interrogating Gandalf, asking if he expected his schemes to go unnoticed. As Gandalf had described Sarumon the White earlier in the film as the greatest of the wizards, even those in the audience who do not know him from either Tolkien's books or Jackson's earlier films might expect him to take the lead. Yet the film also signals that members of the council lack confidence in his leadership. Gandalf's initial greeting of Sarumon is noticeably stiff and uneasy. Furthermore, during their debate, the volume of Sarumon's voice is lowered and overlain by a telepathic dialog between Gandalf and Galadriel. This technique indicates to the audience not only that the other members of the council are not giving Sarumon their full attention, but also that Galadriel may not trust Sarumon sufficiently to make her opinions known to him.

An Unexpected Journey uses this debate between Saruman, insisting that Middle-earth is at peace and will remain at peace, and Gandalf, arguing that there is mounting evidence that Sauron is preparing for war, to open a polytemporal space, allowing echoes of Britain between the wars to be heard. In the years after World War I there was a powerful anti-war sentiment. As historian K. W. Watkins writes, "...both politicians and people who had lived through the First World War were haunted by the ghosts of the earlier holocaust. It was not the theoretical pacifism of a minority, but a deep-rooted desire for peace, for peace at almost any price, that permeated nations" (Watkins, 1963, 71–72). Avoiding military conflict, no matter what the provocation, became a prime objective of the British government. A Foreign Office memorandum of 1926 summarized this attitude: "Our sole object is to keep what we want and live in peace ... whatever else may be the outcome of a disturbance of the peace, we shall be the losers" (Adams, 1993, 6–7). The rise of Fascist governments in the 1930s did not, at first, alter the general refusal to consider military action as a possibility. In February of 1933, two weeks after Adolf Hitler had become Chancellor of Germany, the Oxford Union Society, a renowned debating club, sustained the following motion by a vote of 275 to 153: "That this House will in no circumstances fight for its King and Country" (Adams, 1993, 9). Many working in the British government refused to see anything but peaceful intentions from Fascist leaders. For example, Deputy Secretary to the Cabinet Tom Jones wrote in 1936, and later published in his *Diary with Letters* (1954), "But Hitler does not want war with us. He seeks our friendship" (Watkins, 1963, 91). During Neville Chamberlain's tenure as British Prime Minister (1937–1940), the policy of conciliation towards the National Socialists, often described as one of appeasement, had a broad base of supporters. There was also a small number of bitter critics, including the man who was to follow Chamberlain as Prime Minister, Winston Churchill. Those who opposed appeasement tried to offer evidence that continued peace was not possible. In April 1939, in response to the Italian invasion of Albania, Leo Amery, former M.P. and Secretary of State for the Colonies, wrote "Another blow has fallen. Another proof has been given that friendly and peaceful relations are as impossible with Signor Mussolini as they are with Herr Hitler" (Watkins, 1963, 90). The vocal minority forced debate and were often dismissed as trouble-makers. In October of 1938 *The Anglo-German Review*, an English publication, described Winston Churchill as "unquestionably the biggest war-monger in the world to-day" (Watkins, 1963, 89). Up until the moment that news broke, in March of 1939, that Hitler had invaded Czechoslovakia, the British people were bitterly divided over foreign policy (Rock, 1966, 202).

The debate at Rivendell in *An Unexpected Journey* resonates with the British experience between the wars. The film presents Saruman as eager to thwart Gandalf's plans to remove the threat of Smaug. Saruman tries to label Gandalf as a meddler, a trouble-maker, an instigator, echoing both the charges made against the anti-appeasement politicians and the charges made against Gandalf when he entered the Golden Hall in *The Two Towers*, another situation in which Gandalf's attempts to raise forces against Sauron are resisted by Saruman (Tolkien, 1954, 125–25). The resonances with both Britain between the wars and with *The Lord of the Rings* makes this sequence a superb example of the polytemporal effects achieved in this film. Throughout the meeting at Rivendell, Saruman attempts to persuade the others that Gandalf is creating trouble in an otherwise peaceful situation. Saruman insists that the Enemy was obliterated, saying "What enemy? The Enemy was destroyed. He will never be able to regain his full strength." Elrond reminds the Council that there has been peace—a "watchful peace"—for four hundred years. Viewers familiar with *The Lord of the Rings* will be aware that Saruman is being duplicitous because in Jackson's *The Fellowship of the Ring* he attempted to persuade Gandalf that it would be wise to form an alliance with Sauron. In the context of the meeting at Rivendell, Saruman pretends to agree that an active Enemy should be opposed. The issue under debate is the validity of Gandalf's evidence that the Enemy is actually active.

Gandalf presents three pieces of evidence. The first is that orcs and trolls are appearing in places they had formerly avoided, attacking Thorin's company. In Tolkien's *Hobbit*, Gandalf does not need to tell Elrond about the trolls on the main road because he was himself warned about them by Elrond's people, but in the film they become part of the contested evidence (Tolkien, 1982, 44). Gandalf's second offer of proof is that the Greenwood has been encroached upon by dark forces, evidence based on reports from human woodsmen and the wizard Radagast the Brown. Saruman dismisses the movement of orcs as an aberration and disparages Radagast's character, using an *ad hominem* attack to undermine his reports. He does not argue against the fundamental idea that dark forces become bolder as Sauron gains strength, and indeed, that idea is present in Tolkien's writing. Appendix A of *The Lord of the Rings* twice describes such things happening earlier in the Third Age. The text explains that other evil things are prompted to stir by the signs announcing that Sauron is regaining his power, and describes Sauron's re-emergence as a shadow in Greenwood (Tolkien, 1955; 2013, 359 and 388).

Gandalf's third piece of evidence, and the one that occupies the longest segment of the meeting at Rivendell, is that a Necromancer who can summon the dead has taken up residence in Dol Guldur. Gandalf appears to categorize the Necromancer with the orcs and mountain trolls as signs that the Enemy is rebuilding. His description of the Necromancer is based on Radagast's report, bolstered by a dagger he recovered there. Both Elrond and Galadriel identify the weapon as one buried with the Witch-king of Angmar, a character who does not appear in the novel *The Hobbit* but who is an important servant of Sauron in *The Lord of the Rings*. In the film, Saruman refuses to attach any importance to the weapon and claims that there is no proof that it was taken from the Witch-king's tomb. Elrond, in contrast, appears to be convinced that the dagger recovered by Radagast is actually a Morgul weapon and appears to be at the point of agreeing with Gandalf when the meeting is interrupted and ended by the news that the Dwarves had already left Rivendell to continue their journey. The fourth member of the Council, Galadriel, explicitly supports Gandalf's decision to aid the Dwarves, but as much of her communication with Gandalf concerning this matter takes place telepathically or in private after the Council meeting ends, it is not known if Saruman is aware of her position. The meeting ends with the strong possibility that Gandalf could, at some future point, persuade the majority that something must to be done. *An Unexpected Journey* leaves no doubt that that the attempt to retake Erebor is part of the larger narrative of the effort to defeat Sauron.

The expansion of the context of the story of *The Hobbit* from the relatively confined world of a short novel intended for children to the vast panorama of a looming war with the potential either to plunge Middle-earth into darkness or to preserve freedom and goodness for another age inevitably alters the way in which the characters may be read. As the larger issues at stake render the tone of the work more epic, either the characters must be adjusted to the new background or run the risk of appearing satiric—photo-negative Don Quixotes incapable of realizing that they are actually in an epic. The film, although retaining some of the novel's comic elements, begins in a more epic mode than the novel, with two openings, one of which parallels the opening of Jackson's *The Fellowship of the Ring*: the first is a prologue, starting with Bilbo writing in the *Red Book*, and narrating in a voiceover the story of Erebor and Smaug's destruction, a narrative that he states has not yet been told to Frodo. The prologue is polytemporal, incorporating the epic and legendary tale of Erebor, and situating Bilbo as the narrator of the part of his tale that becomes a part of this story, as well as connecting it to the "future" of Bilbo's eleventy-first birthday party, with Frodo present on the day of the party. Bilbo's epic prologue parallels Galadriel's prologue in *The Fellowship of the Ring* although there are significant differences: the attack of Smaug on Erebor, the greatest of all the dwarf kingdoms of Middle-earth, results in the fall of a great kingdom and the loss of the last remaining Dwarven ring. Unlike the alliance of Men and Elves against Sauron, however, there are no allies to come to the aid of the Dwarves. Additional epic framing for the film is provided by Balin's narrative about the Dwarves' attempt to retake Moria and the origin of the conflict between Thorin and Azog, who kills Thror, shown in a flashback experienced by Thorin as Balin relates the tale to the younger dwarves and Bilbo.[4] The history of conflicts between Orcs and Goblins and the Dwarves, and between the Elves and Dwarves that Tolkien created and used in *The Lord of the Rings*, and which is hinted at in his *Hobbit*, is foregrounded in Jackson's film, presumably to build up to the Battle of the Five Armies in the final film.

The more light-hearted events that follow immediately after the tale of Erebor's fall, specifically Gandalf's conversation with a flummoxed Bilbo and the unannounced arrival of multiple dwarves for an unexpected dinner party, complete with the comic dishwashing song and Bilbo's treasured china flying through the air, are similar to the opening of the novel. The film does retain the construction of the Shire that dominated Jackson's first film, a place that is very much set apart from the rest of Middle-earth, unaffected by the evil that is threatening, and much more modern in material and social culture than the other lands. Tom Shippey has pointed to all the ways in which the Shire, and the Hobbits, are anachronisms in the medieval world of the rest of Middle-earth, ranging from the regular postal deliveries to their modern diction. They are a necessary anachronism, allowing the reader to learn about the cultures and histories of the rest of Arda along with the hobbits (Shippey 2002, 5–7). Shippey, however, does not consider the ways in which the masculinity of the hobbits is also connected to a more modern culture. David Craig analyzes the extent to which the values and gender roles of Tolkien's Shire reflect mainstream British culture during the period between the two world wars, claiming that "although inter-war culture was conservative on sexual questions, by the standards of pre-war heroic and masculine values, it was rather 'feminine'" (Craig, 2001, 11). Craig focuses primarily on *The Lord of the Rings*, but his argument concerning the valuing of the domestic and 'feminine', that is, "anti-heroic values" such as "food, drinking, and smoking" applies equally to Bilbo (Craig, 2001, 11). Jackson's film shows viewers the domestic Bilbo, including, in the Extended Edition, his trip to the local market to buy his dinner which he prepares beautifully for himself, only to have to turn it over to Dwalin as any good host would.

The tone of the film changes back to epic with Thorin's arrival, however, which is handled quite differently than in the novel. When Gandalf notices that they are missing one Dwarf, Dwalin assures him that Thorin will come, that he is attending a Dwarven council. With the shift to a more epic tone, constructions of masculinity shift as well, from comic to heroic, not only in respect to the Dwarves, especially Thorin, but also with respect to Bilbo although not to the same extent. Tolkien's novel has a similar shift in characterization for the dwarves, from comic to heroic, but it occurs near the close of the novel, with the entrance of Thorin and Company to support the Elves and Men at the Battle of the Five Armies and the heroic deaths of Thorin, Fili, and Kili. Bilbo's standing amongst the Dwarves shifts after his rescue of them in Mirkwood from the spiders, and the Elves' dungeons, which gains him their respect, but not to the much greater extent that *An Unexpected Journey* shows, with Bilbo using Sting to kill an orc before he can kill the nearly-unconscious Thorin.

The change in the characterization of Thorin is apparent from his entrance in *An Unexpected Journey*. In the novel, Thorin is part of a group pratfall, ending up on the bottom of a pile of dwarves in Bilbo's front hall, underneath Bifur, Bofur, and Bombur. Thorin's lengthy and rather pompous speech after the songs is rudely interrupted by Bilbo's shriek. In the film, Thorin is a seasoned war leader and dwarf prince who comes on his own from a meeting with the leaders of the seven kingdoms of the Dwarves bearing the news that the other dwarves, including Dáin and the Dwarves of the Iron Hills, will not join their quest. Thorin's language is terse, fragmented at times, and his diction is straightforward and simple. His first question to Bilbo concerns his choice of weapon, and Thorin is the one to deliver the comment that Bilbo more resembles a grocer than a burglar. The table below compares Thorin's dialogue, transcribed from Chapter 1, "An Unexpected Party," with Thorin's dialogue transcribed from the film covering the same narrative span. Thorin's dialogue in the film has 19% of the total number of words, and 54% of the total number of sentences. Additionally, the average sentence length (number of words) is only 34% as long.

Table 1: Comparison of Thorin's Dialogue in Book and Film

	Chapter 1	*Film*
Total words	1392	263
Total sentences	74	40
Av. sentence length (#words)	18.8	6.57

(UAM Corpus Tool)

Beyond his language, other aspects of Thorin's characterization are constructed in the heroic mode from the start of the film: he is a prince, heir to Erebor, which Bilbo describes as the greatest kingdom in Middle-earth before its fall. He leads the dwarves against Smaug, and rescues Balin and Thror from the dragon. He takes up leadership after the death of his grandfather in battle, wounding Azog, and then as Balin notes, he leads his people to the Blue Mountains after the battle at Moria which took so great a toll. Thorin's quest to return to a lost homeland, and reclaim a lost kingship have parallels to Aragorn's story, parallels that do not exist in Tolkien's *Hobbit*.

The Dwarves who accompany Thorin are also presented as epic warriors, far more than in most of the novel. Tolkien's description of the Dwarves as they enter Bilbo's home, calling variously for food and drink, focuses more on the colors of their hooded cloaks (green, scarlet, blue, purple, grey, brown, white, and yellow) and their multiple instruments than their weapons. As Corey Olsen notes in *Exploring Tolkien's* The Hobbit, the encounter with the Trolls shows the dwarves are apparently unarmed and unprepared at the start of their journey, since Thorin has to pick up a burning stick to fight the Trolls (Olsen, 2012, 49). In contrast, the costumes and weapons of Thorin's Company in Jackson's film show very clearly that these Dwarves are ready to fight, and have experience fighting, although there are differences among them, with Ori (the youngest) being armed only with a slingshot in contrast to Dwalin's multiple axes and Fili's multiple knives. Robert C. Woosnam Savage, the Curator of European Edged Weapons at the Royal Armouries Museum, Leeds, argues in "The *Matériel* of Middle-Earth: Arms and Arms and Armor in Peter Jackson's *The Lord of the Rings* Motion Picture Trilogy," that Jackson's goal of emphasizing the historicity of the races of Middle-earth through their material culture is supported in the design of the arms and armor for Jackson's film (Bogstad and Kaveny, 2011, 139). Weta Workshop, run by Richard Taylor, worked on *The Hobbit* and has published two volumes on the art, design, creatures and characters of the first film (Falconer, 2012, 2013). In the first *Chronicle*, extensive information on the design of the Dwarves' clothing and weapons is given, along with sketches, paintings, and photographs of the material and the characters, including the numerous and individualized weapons each Dwarf carries, consistent with their biography and history. As Woosnam-Savage notes, the fact that so much of the academic scholarship on Jackson's film comes from literary scholars may explain the neglect of the material culture in the films; so his essay covers the seven years of production that went into Weta's process of designing and production (Bogstad and Kaveny, 2011, 139), evaluating the quality of the physical artifacts created which are themselves of museum quality, and are being exhibited in museums around the world. Tolkien acknowledged his own disinterest in material culture, especially clothing, and the physical appearance of his characters in a letter written to Miss Beare where he says he sees "with great clarity and detail scenery and 'natural' objects, but not artefacts" (Carpenter and Tolkien, 1995, 280). A film, of course, cannot leave such details to the imagination of the viewers, and the quality of the Dwarven weapons, and the fight choreography done for the film, all work visually to show the Dwarves as embodying epic masculinity.

To an even greater extent than Thorin, Bilbo's characterization is changed from the novel's version. In the early chapters of the book, Bilbo is a comic figure, described by the narrator in sometimes quite condescending ways, squeaking and scurrying about, unable to climb a tree or keep up with the Dwarves in the goblin tunnels. While Tolkien shows a change in Bilbo that takes him from an ineffectual burglar to a leader acknowledged by the Dwarves, especially after the fight with the spiders in Mirkwood and his rescue of the Dwarves, Jackson's film heightens that change, beginning earlier in the narrative, starting with Bilbo's decision to join the Company which is made on his own without any help from Gandalf. While that decision is regretted and nearly rescinded, when he attempts to return to Rivendell, he commits to the quest again when he follows the Dwarves after they have been taken captive, and then, free of the goblin caves, chooses to take off the Ring and join them rather than trying to return to Rivendell, or home on his own. This change is explained as his understanding of what their loss of a home means; throughout the film, Bilbo consistently denies any identification with or interest in being a burglar. For example, he does not try to steal the troll's purse, but is the first to urge the rescue of the ponies. His promise is to help the Dwarves regain their home, not their treasure. The first scene in *The Desolation of Smaug*, showing the meeting between Thorin and Gandalf in Bree a year before the events of the main narrative, establishes the importance of the Arkenstone in the film's plot: Thorin must have the Arkenstone, the symbol of kingship, to defeat Smaug and reclaim Erebor because the Dwarves have sworn only to follow the one who holds the Arkenstone. Finally, at the end of the first installment of the film, Jackson creates an original scene in which Bilbo attempts to defend Thorin, with a number of visual parallels to Aragorn's attack on the Orc attacking Boromir in *The Fellowship of the Ring*. Despite this climactic scene of epic heroism, in which Bilbo is soon supported by the Dwarves entering the fight, two original scenes in *The Unexpected Journey* undercut the construction of Bilbo as an epic hero and maintain the thematic importance of Bilbo's decision not to kill Gollum. The first is an original scene written for the film, a warning from Gandalf after he gives Bilbo Sting, telling him that true courage may lie in saving rather than taking a life, a scene that strongly parallels Gandalf's speech to Frodo in Moria about the importance of pity. Since that speech, adapted from the original in Tolkien's chapter, "The Shadow of the Past," concerns the importance of Bilbo's first act upon taking the Ring being mercy rather than murder, Gandalf's words to Bilbo have a prophetic power. The second scene does not involve Bilbo at all, but is Gandalf's response to Galadriel's question of why he chose a hobbit for the quest: here, Gandalf does not mention finding a burglar but explains his reason in a speech that corresponds strongly to Tolkien's own language in his letter to Milton Waldman. Gandalf says that he has come to believe that it is "the small things, everyday deeds of ordinary folk, that keeps the darkness at bay," instead of the great power that Saruman espouses. In his letter, Tolkien says that *The Lord of the Rings* is: "a study of a simple ordinary man, neither artistic, nor noble and heroic, but not without the undeveloped seeds of those things, against a high setting" (Carpenter and Tolkien, 1995, 159). These two scenes foreshadow and lead to Bilbo's decision not to kill Gollum in order to escape from the goblin caves. In the first film of the trilogy, the heightening of Bilbo's heroism in defense of Thorin is balanced by the original scenes, as well as by the fact that despite his courage, he is simply not very good with his new blade. The final analysis of the changes in Bilbo's characterization will have to wait for the release of the remaining two films in the trilogy, to see how Jackson handles Bilbo's rescue of the Dwarves in Mirkwood, his encounter with Smaug, the theft of the Arkenstone and the negotiations before the Battle of the Five Armies.

In 1977, *The Silmarillion* was published posthumously. Although J.R.R. Tolkien was not even able to decide on a publishable edition, he worked on variants of the mythic and historical narratives of the First Age until his death. *The Silmarillion* describes in detail the creation of the rings and the resulting war between Elves and Sauron, filling out the history that Gandalf and Elrond introduce in *The Lord of the Rings*. It also includes the origin story for dragons, who were created by and associated with Morgoth, the evil lord whom Sauron served as a lieutenant. In these later texts, Gollum's ring is transformed into a key element of Tolkien's vast, multi-book, multi-poem, legendarium and serves to connect *The Hobbit* to a millennia-long war waged by elves and men against Sauron and Morgoth. *The Hobbit* becomes one thread among many in Tolkien's legendarium, its narrative woven back into what Tom Shippey has argued is a narrative structure that is interlaced not only with *The Lord of the Rings* but with *The Silmarillion* as well (Shippey, 2001, 102–11).

The multiple versions of Bilbo's story (along with the multiple versions of the narratives of *The Silmarillion*) may be understood in the context of Tolkien's desire to create a "mythology" for England, as he famously expressed in a letter to Milton Waldman, a mythology that had to be "re-created" by a medievalist because the stories of the early medieval northern European peoples, with very few exceptions, had not survived in writing (Carpenter and Tolkien, 1995, 143–60). A body of myth is not a single, coherent narrative: it is a huge corpus of materials created by different, often anonymous sources, existing as oral tradition before being captured, at least in part, by writing. Most of Tolkien's mythology may be found in *The Silmarillion* in its various versions, and in his poetry, some of which as Garth notes, pre-dated his novels. But that mythic foundation not only underlies *The Lord of the Rings*; it surfaces slightly in *The Hobbit*, as for example when the swords are found in trolls' cave that were made in Gondolin, one of the Elven cities whose growth and fall is related in *The Silmarillion*.

In 1937 *The Hobbit* was published and marketed as a stand-alone children's story; the 1951 *Hobbit* was published and marketed as a prequel to *The Lord of the Rings*, a relationship Tolkien attempted to legitimate through revisions and appendices. The publication of *The Silmarillion* enlarged the story much further, expanding it through the epic scope of *The Lord of the Rings* into the wide realm of myth. Based on this reconstruction of the history of *The Hobbit*, it is clear that there are many ways in which a film adaptation of the story might be made, depending on which stage of Tolkien's development of the tale of the finding of a ring on the way to Erebor was chosen.[5] The novel published in 1937 is one version, but not the only one Tolkien created. *An Unexpected Journey* does not represent an attempt to make a children's film from a children's novel, nor does it attempt to dramatize the mythic background Tolkien eventually provided. *An Unexpected Journey* attempts to capture the epic tone and the focus on combat and strategy with polytemporal echoes of the two world wars, in the first of which Tolkien served and in the second of which his sons Christopher and Michael served, while Tolkien was creating *The Lord of the Rings* during the late 1940s and early 1950s. The authors believe that Jackson's film not only works as a prequel to his earlier one, but that *An Unexpected Journey* is imbued with the modern echoes of World War II and the epic heroism of Tolkien's medieval sources, capturing a sense of polytemporality with a considerable degree of success and reflecting Tolkien's later understanding of the wars and histories of Middle-earth.

Notes

1. The first scene of *The Hobbit: The Desolation of Smaug* (2013) is a dramatization of Gandalf and Thorin's meeting at the Prancing Pony at Bree to discuss taking back Erebor, and the need for a burglar to help recover the Arkenstone

2. In the Extended Edition of the Film (December 2013), an additional scene is added to the Council meeting in which Gandalf asks Saruman, Elrond, and Galadriel if they are not concerned with the fact that the last Ring of the Seven given to the Dwarves is unaccounted for, being lost with Thrain after the battle to retake Moria.

3. Another reason, as Brian D. Walter argues in "The Grey Pilgrim: Gandalf and the Challenges of Characterization in Middle-earth," is that the reduction in Gandalf's omniscience and power allows for development of other characters and more dramatic tension in Jackson's *The Lord of the Rings*." Thus, it is possible to argue that there is a consistency in the characterization of Gandalf in Jackson's *The Hobbit*.

4. The film has changed the Dwarves' fight to take back Moria, which resulted in Dáin killing Azog, to emphasize Thorin's participation and to leave Azog, wounded but alive, to pursue his vengeance against Azog.

5. The 1977 Rankin Bass animated musical version of *The Hobbit* was clearly created as a film for a younger audience.

Works Cited

Adams, R. J. Q. 1993. *British Politics and Foreign Policy in the Age of Appeasement, 1935–39*. Stanford, CA: Stanford University Press.
Bogstad, Janice M., and Philip E. Kaveny. 2011. *Picturing Tolkien: Essays on Peter Jackson's* The Lord of the Rings *Film Trilogy*. Jefferson, NC: McFarland.
Carpenter, Humphrey, and Christopher Tolkien, eds. 1995. *The Letters of J.R.R. Tolkien*. Boston: Houghton Mifflin.
Chism, Christine. 2003. "Middle-Earth, the Middle Ages, and the Aryan Nation: Myth and History in World War II." In *Tolkien the Medievalist*, ed. Jane Chance, 63–92. Routledge Studies in Medieval Religion and Culture (Routledge Studies in Medieval Religion and Culture): 3. London: Routledge.
Craig, David. 2001. "'Queer Lodgings': Gender and Sexuality in *The Lord of the Rings*." *Mallorn* 38, 11–18.
Croft, Janet Brennan. 2011. "The Hen That Laid the Eggs: Tolkien and the Officers Training Corps." *Tolkien Studies: An Annual Scholarly Review* 8: 97–106.
Falconer, Daniel. 2012. The Hobbit: An Unexpected Journey *Chronicles: Art & Design*. New York: Harper Collins.
_____. 2013. The Hobbit: An Unexpected Journey *Chronicles II: Creatures and Characters*. New York: Harper Collins.
The Fellowship of the Ring. 2003. Dir. Peter Jackson. New Line Cinema.
Garth, John. 2003. *Tolkien and the Great War: The Threshold of Middle-earth*. Boston: Houghton Mifflin.
_____. 2007. "'as under a Green Sea': Visions of War in the Dead Marshes." *Myth and Magic: Art According to the Inklings*. Eds. Segura, Eduardo and Thomas Honegger. Cormarë Series (Cormarë): 14. Zollikofen, Switzerland: Walking Tree. 285–313.
_____. 2008. "Tolkien, Exeter College and the Great War." *Tolkien's the Lord of the Rings: Sources of Inspiration*. Eds. Stratford Caldecott, Thomas Honegger and Frances Cairncross, 13–56. Cormarë Series (Cormarë): 18. Zollikofen, Switzerland: Walking Tree.
_____. 2011. "Robert Quilter Gilson, T.C.B.S.: A Brief Life in Letters." *Tolkien Studies: An Annual Scholarly Review* 8: 67–96. Print.
The Hobbit. 1977. Dir. Jules Bass and Arthur Rankin, Jr. Warner Bros. Family Entertainment.
Hobbit: An Unexpected Journey. 2012. Dir. Peter Jackson. New Line Cinema.
The Hobbit: An Unexpected Journey. Extended Edition. 2013. Dir. Peter Jackson. New Line Cinema.
The Hobbit: The Desolation of Smaug. 2013. Dir. Peter Jackson. New Line Cinema.
Jackson, Aaron Isaac. 2010. "Authoring the Century: J.R.R. Tolkien, the Great War and Modernism." *English: The Journal of the English Association* 59 (224): 44–69.
Livingston, Michael. 2006. "The Shell-Shocked Hobbit: The First World War and Tolkien's Trauma of the Ring." *Mythlore: A Journal of J.R.R. Tolkien, C. S. Lewis, Charles Williams, and Mythopoeic Literature* 25.1–2 [95–96]: 77–92.
Long, Rebekah. 2005. "Fantastic Medievalism and the Great War in J.R.R. Tolkien's the Lord of the Rings." *Tolkien's Modern Middle Ages*, eds. Jane Chance and Alfred K. Siewers, 123–37. New Middle Ages (Nemia). New York: Palgrave Macmillan.
Murnane, Ben. 2012. "Frodo's Band of Brothers: Myth, Morality, and Reality in J.R.R. Tolkien and Stephen E. Ambrose." *Seven: An Anglo-American Literary Review* 29: 5–16.
Olsen, Corey. 2012. *Exploring J.R.R Tolkien's* The Hobbit. New York: Houghton Mifflin.
Rateliff, John. 2007. *The History of* The Hobbit, one volume edition. Boston: Houghton Mifflin.
Rock, William R. 1966. *Appeasement on Trial: British Foreign Policy and Its Critics, 1938–1939*. North Haven, CT: Archon.
Shippey, Tom. 2000. *J.R.R. Tolkien: Author of the Century*. Boston: Houghton Mifflin.
Simonson, Martin. 2005. "The Lord of the Rings in the Wake of the Great War: War, Poetry, Modernism, and Ironic Myth." *Reconsidering Tolkien*, ed. Thomas Honegger, 153–70. Cormarë Series (Cormarë): 8. Zollikofen, Switzerland: Walking Tree.
Tolkien, J.R.R. 1954; 2013. *The Lord of the Rings: The Two Towers*. New York: Ballantine.
_____. 1955; 2013. *The Lord of the Rings: The Return of the King*. New York: Ballantine.
_____. 1982. *The Hobbit or There and Back Again*. Rev. ed. New York: Ballantine.
_____. 2004. *The Lord of the Rings*. New York: Houghton Mifflin.
_____. 2006. *The Annotated Hobbit: Revised and Extended Edition*. Annotation by Douglas Anderson. New York: Houghton Mifflin Harcourt.
Walter, Brian D. 2011. "The Grey Pilgrim: The Challenges of Characterization in Middle-earth." In *Picturing*

Tolkien: Essays on Peter Jackson's The Lord of the Rings *Film Trilogy,"* ed. Janice M. Bogstad and Philip E. Kaveny, 194–215. Jefferson, NC: McFarland.

Watkins, K. W. 1963. *Britain Divided: The Effect of the Spanish Civil War on British Political Opinion.* Westport, CT: Greenwood.

Woosnam-Savage, Robert C. 2011. "The *Matériel* of Middle-Earth: Arms and Arms and Armor in Peter Jackson's *The Lord of the Rings* Motion Picture Trilogy." In *Picturing Tolkien: Essays on Peter Jackson's* The Lord of the Rings *Film Trilogy,"* ed. Janice M. Bogstad and Philip E. Kaveny, 139–68. Jefferson, NC: McFarland.

The Wisdom of the Crowd
Internet Memes and
The Hobbit: An Unexpected Journey

MICHELLE MARKEY BUTLER

Internet memes—recurring images with different captions[1]—are a relatively new form of entertainment, emerging in the last decade and a half. They have rapidly spread, developing into a subculture that exists primarily, but not exclusively, on the web.[2] Given the recent emergence and technological birthplace of this subculture, it is interesting and perhaps a bit surprising that memes frequently reference the works of Tolkien, arguably more often than they do newer literary works which are also the subject of contemporary film or television adaptations. Harry Potter, the Game of Thrones, and Twilight do appear regularly in memes. But the works of Tolkien, despite being decades older, hold their own with them in the cutting-edge culture of memes. While most other research on memes has focused upon the methods by which they spread, the ways in which memes are measures of cultural affinity and production, or the characteristic elements of successful memes,[3] my handling of memes deals with their rhetorical functions.[4] Among these, as I have argued elsewhere, is crowd-sourced literary criticism.[5] This essay will argue that memes are a vehicle through which a broad community thoughtfully engages with and presents nuanced critiques of Jackson's films. This is true for both the *Lord of the Rings* movies and *Hobbit: An Unexpected Journey*, but the focus here will be upon the first Hobbit movie.

Lord of the Rings memes have been part of meme culture since its inception. While the Lord of the Rings as Meme Subculture submission remains under evaluation at Know Your Meme, the submission entry describes how memes have circulated since the release of the first of Peter Jackson's film adaptations in 2001.[6] This chronological fact points to a related observation about the type of literary analysis that appears in *Lord of the Rings* memes; it tends towards comparative analysis of the book and its movie adaptations. Of course, not all Lord of the Rings memes participate in crowdsourced literary analysis. Indeed, many do not. Some are merely humorous, or employ LOTR elements for other objectives such as social critique. A rough estimate would be that one in ten engage in literary analysis of *Lord of the Rings*. But those LOTR memes that do carry the function of literary analysis by and large do so through the method of comparative consideration of the book and Jackson's film versions.

In contrast, memes about *The Hobbit: An Unexpected Journey* have thus far focused almost exclusively on the movie. Memes that appeared before the film was released express anxiety about its potential handling of the book and question why the book was adapted into three movies. One meme,[7] for instance, unfavorably compares Jackson's strategy for adapting *The Hobbit* with his approach to *Lord of the Rings*. The meme make its argument by showing first a photo of the *Lord of the Rings'* volumes with the caption "3 movies" and a copy of *The Hobbit* with the same caption, "3 Movies." This photo is followed by one of Peter Jackson with his hands up in the History Channel "Aliens" meme with the caption "Money" (WeKnowMemes.com, 2012). The meme is arguing that while adapting three books into three movies is a reasonable artistic decision, adapting one book into three movies is not. The real reason for this decision, the meme asserts, is financial, making this claim of financial motivation using the Aliens meme, a choice which allows the meme to imply that a monetary incentive for a three-movie adaptation of *The Hobbit* is as crazy a notion as the claim that aliens might have visited the earth. Anxiety and skepticism about the upcoming *Hobbit* films are evident.

Not all memes that express concern about the *Hobbit* movies do so with as much wit and subtlety as the 'Jackson Money' meme. Another meme, for instance, uses the Questioning Picard image, which shows Jon Luc Picard (of *Star Trek: Next Generation*) with his arm outstretched, hand raised. "Why the Fuck" appears at the top of the image, followed by "Is *The Hobbit* a Trilogy?" at the bottom (Memegenerator.net, 2012). While there's moderate cleverness on display here in the crossover SF/F usage of the Picard meme to comment upon the *Hobbit* movies, the question is posited straightforwardly—one might be tempted to say bluntly—and without any particular answer being suggested.

Memes criticizing the decision to adapt *The Hobbit* into three movies[8] usually employ images drawn from SF/F fandom cultures, most commonly LOTR, as might be expected. But not exclusively. Meme culture is not limited to the SF/F fan community. Indeed, memes can draw upon a variety of pop culture images and references, and Hobbit memes are no exception. One meme employs a Skeptical Gymnast image with the upper caption "*The Hobbit* as a Trilogy?" and the lower caption "We'll see..." (3goldensisters.com, 2012). It is not the more famous Maroney Not Impressed picture of gymnast McKayla Maroney which became the basis for many memes, but draws upon cultural awareness of that image to make its point while employing a different gymnast picture that better suits the meme's purpose. While the Maroney picture shows only one skeptical-looking gymnast, this meme's image contains several, suggesting the many fans anxiously awaiting the release of the movies to assess their success or failure. Unlike the previous two memes, which argued that *The Hobbit* movie trilogy was a bad idea, this one expresses concern ("*The Hobbit* as a Trilogy?") but promises to reserve final judgment until viewing the films ("We'll see...").

Another meme ironically posits that the decision to adapt *The Hobbit* into three movies originated as a dare. Challenge Accepted is a meme deriving from a *How I Met Your Mother*, beginning as a catchphrase spoken by Barney, who is played by Neil Patrick Harris (Accepted, 2012). Hence the meme has a rare dual image existence: the image of Neil Patrick Harris and a stick figure, although the stick figure version appears more commonly in Rage Comics, in which a challenge is considered in a series of frames and then accepted or rejected. This particular memes employs the Neil Patrick Harris picture with the upper caption "Turn 1 Book into 3, 3-Hour Movies?" and the lower caption "Challenge Accepted!" (Fletchword.blogspot.com 2012) Challenge Accepted memes, both in general and in the particular Hobbit example discussed here, have at their core the premise that the proposed activity is difficult but not necessarily worth the effort.

These two Hobbit memes appear far less commonly than the Jackson Money meme discussed above. They are, however, important indicators of the widespread appeal of and interest in the *Hobbit* movies after the success of the LOTR films, and the resulting widespread anxiety about how the *Hobbit* adaptations would turn out. In another meme likewise drawing upon a non SF/F image, the Skeptical Third World Kid is shown with the upper caption "So You Are Telling Me" and the lower caption "You Can Make the Hobbit into 3 Movies?" (Hutchinson, 2012). While the two previous memes clearly did not circulate widely, appearing seldom in a Google image search, this meme was chosen by Moviefarm.uk.co as its number one pick in an article entitled "Top 10 Tolkien Inspired Memes," published just before the release of the first Hobbit movie. The meme itself is a fascinating usage. This is Skeptical Third World Kid (Kid n.d.), a meme image typically employed to question first world approaches to helping disadvantaged countries (or claiming to), but also to question elements of western culture which are normalized to those living within it but can seem odd to an outside perspective. The meme implicitly argues that adapting *The Hobbit* into three movies is so questionable that even a disadvantaged child from outside western culture can see its flaws. Whether drawn from pop culture or from other sources, the variety of images used in memes critiquing the decision to adapt *The Hobbit* into three movies suggests a broad-based community of interest.

There are more than a few other memes that critique the decision to make three movies from *The Hobbit* but one more example will suffice to give an overview of how such memes go about questioning that choice. Possibly the most common meme to circulate before the first *Hobbit* movie was released was a version of a popular LOTR meme, "One Does Not Simply Walk into Mordor." Like the memes cited above, this meme in its many variations, questions the directorial decision to make three *Hobbit* movies. In this case, the meme employs the popular LOTR meme "One Does Not Simply Walk into Mordor" to convey suspicion about Jackson's decision. The usual image of Boromir from the Council of Elrond scene is used, with the upper caption "One Does Not Simply" and the lower caption "Make Three Films Out of a Book as Short as The Hobbit" (Memegenerator.net, 2012). The result is a particularly effective meme, marrying the "One Does Not Simply Walk into Mordor" meme, one of the most popular LOTR memes[9] with the skepticism about the decision to make *The Hobbit* as a trilogy of movies. Boromir's line from *The Fellowship of the Ring* film was an example of ironic understatement (interestingly, much like the Old English poetic concept of litotes) and was picked up a meme as shorthand for ironic understatement, with the related usage of questioning ideas that should be obvious or the obviousness of a foolish idea. Using "One Does Not Simply Walk into Mordor" to question *The Hobbit* trilogy decision makes the argument that the idea should have seemed foolish from the outset.

Memes that emerged before any of *The Hobbit* movies were released raise questions about the strategy for adapting the book into film. Three movies from such a small book? Another trilogy? To be released annually? But the memes do not simply raise questions. They suggest answers, posit motivations, and take positions. Using a variety of images and rhetorical techniques, memes engage in thoughtful analysis and nuanced critique of Jackson's choice to adapt *The Hobbit* into three films.

Within hours of the release of *The Hobbit: An Unexpected Journey* in December 2012, memes drawing upon images from the film began to appear and indeed, evaluate the movie, functioning in essence as crowd-sourced critique. The earliest and most prevalent of these memes—I'm Going on an Adventure, Majestic Thorin, and Never Have I Been So Wrong—focus upon moments and elements of the movie that engender strong reactions, either positive or negative, and analyze those reactions.

Snippets of the I'm Going on an Adventure scene had already been revealed in a trailer released in September 2012 (Adventure 2012) (Adventure I. G., 2012). Yet while the image that is the basis for this meme was present in the trailer, memes featuring this moment did not appear until after the movie's release. The meme community became interested in this line when it appeared in the context of the movie, rather than in the relative isolation of the trailer, as would be expected if memes function as crowdsourced analysis of the larger work.

Unlike the two other pervasive memes that emerged following the release of *The Hobbit: An Unexpected Journey*, I'm Going on an Adventure memes are overwhelmingly positive in their characterization of the scene. In one example, for instance, the first frame of the meme shows a stack of videogame cases. The second frame is the usual meme image of Bilbo running from his home, contract dangling from his hand, with the upper caption "I'm Going" and the lower caption "On an Adventure!" The third frame shows a man lounging on a couch in his underclothes, wearing a headset and holding a game controller CITATION Img13 \l 1033 (Memecenter, 2013)*obHobbit*. The juxtaposition of the first two images suggests that getting new videogames feels just as exciting, just as much the beginning of an awesome adventure, as Bilbo setting out with a group of dwarves to steal treasure from a dragon. However, the juxtaposition of the second and third images critiques the actual experience of those games. Whereas Bilbo in fact goes on an adventure, playing the videogames leads nowhere but sitting on the couch in your underwear. Not exactly the same as encountering trolls, fighting giant spiders, riddling with Gollum—and Smaug—and finding the One Ring. The meme makes an argument about the limitations of virtual entertainment through (perhaps ironically) comparison with a fictional (albeit presented as real) adventure. Such an analysis, however, is beyond the scope of our concern at present. For our purposes, it is enough to observe that the meme employs the "I'm Going on an Adventure" moment in an unambiguously positive manner. The movie scene is used to provide a point of reference, and a preferential basis of comparison, both of which rely upon a favorable estimation of the scene itself.

Similarly, let's consider a second example of a meme that depends for its meaning upon a positive view of the "I'm Going on an Adventure" moment. In this one, the first frame is a picture of a nicely dressed man sitting with a suitcase beside him with the upper caption "How I should act." The second frame is a screenshot of an existing I'm Going on an Adventure meme with Bilbo running from his home with the lower caption "I'm Going on an Adventure!" This meme has added an upper caption to the second frame, "How I actualy [sic] act" (Adventure I. G., 2012).[10] The meme implies that the narrator believes that as an adult, he should take a level-headed, even casual, approach to travel, but in reality he sees it like Bilbo sees his journey—an exciting adventure.

There are far too many examples of "I'm Going on an Adventure" memes to consider even a small percentage of them here, as a quick Google image search reveals. There are literally hundreds on Memegenerator.net (Adventure B. B., 2013) alone.[11] The examples discussed above provide a representative sample of the more successful versions. It is worthwhile to pause to consider what 'successful' means in meme culture. On most meme sites, anyone can create and submit memes, but not all memes are featured by the websites. Most have a voting system that factors into determining which memes become featured (often called "making the front page.") Memegenerator, for instance, has ranked categories of memes, depending upon how they were received by the community ("God Tier," "Demigod Tier," "Legendary Tier," "Top Tier," "Fascinating Tier," "Meh Tier," "Lame Tier," and "Fail Tier.") Memes, then, function as crowdsourced literary criticism (among other rhetorical purposes, as discussed above) both due to the open submission format and because successful memes are those chosen by the community. Memes are, thus, peer-reviewed.

The popularity of "I'm Going on an Adventure" memes carries several interesting implications. First, the widespread interest in such memes, both creating and choosing them, suggests that movie audiences identified this moment as one to which they had an intense response. For images or moments to become memetic, they must be immediately recognizable—important, meaningful, or in some way striking enough to have formed an accessible memory in the viewer's mind (Shifman, 2014). The widespread presence of the "I'm Going on an Adventure" meme thus suggests that this scene was indeed such a moment. Secondly, the handling of the scene in the meme suggests that audience reaction was in general a positive one. As seen in the examples discussed above, the "I'm Going on an Adventure" moment appears in memes as the desirable option in a comparison. The film clearly intends the scene to be a moment of high emotion and engagement (witness the filmic techniques employed as well as the swell of the musical score). From the evidence of the memes, we would have to conclude that it was successful.

While meme communities' responses to the "I'm Going on an Adventure" scene were positive, other elements of the film did not fare as well. "Majestic Thorin" is a meme that points up the mixed results of the film's adaptation of the characterization of Thorin. In the book, Thorin is a middle-aged dwarf whose overriding character trait is pomposity, most clearly seen in his tendency towards long-winded speeches filled with big words. Like most elements of the book, Thorin is not taken entirely seriously; at times his pomposity is played for humor. Nonetheless, the book handles that aspect with a light touch, never undercutting Thorin so much as to disable his ability to be seen as a courageous, albeit flawed, figure. We take his status as king seriously, we regret his bad decisions, we applaud his repentance, and we mourn his death, none of which would be possible—or at least would be considerably different—if the book presented him purely as a figure of humor.

The movie, in contrast, portrays Thorin as young, good-looking ("hot" would be more accurate), laconic, and most importantly, intensely serious. Perhaps *too* serious, the memes suggest. For instance, one meme uses an image of Thorin the pine trees, staring down, with the caption "Everyone stay back. I'm about to unleash my MAJESTY" (Thorin, 2012). The movie clearly intends to characterize Thorin as a "chip on his shoulder," "tough as nails" dwarf prince out for revenge—a "badass," in internet parlance. But memetic attention to this element is not necessarily positive. Nor is it overwhelmingly negative. "Majestic Thorin" memes question the portrayal, not utterly condemn it.

One problem with it, the memes suggest, is that the difference between the characterization of Thorin in the book, and, perhaps more importantly, the rest of the dwarves in the movie, might be too wide. Consider, for instance, another Majestic Thorin meme. In this one, we see Thorin, and over his shoulder, Kili. The upper caption reads "That guy? Oh, yeah, no, I am aware he is watching me. He does that a lot." The lower caption reads "He just cannot handle my majesty. Just let me know if he starts openly weeping in awe. Again" (Thorin 2012)(Thorin, 2012). The meme's argument is that Thorin is so much more awesome than even his closest dwarf competition that Kili is often reduced to tears of frustration at his inadequacy.

The situation is similar in nearly all Majestic Thorin memes. In another, we see Oin, Fili, Kili, and Bombur staring off into the distance (Thorin, 2012). The positioning of the captions on the image form them into a narrative:

> Kili: "Fili. Fili. Fili."
> Fili: "Omg, what."
> Kili "Do you think Thorin is ... real?"
> Oin: "Omg, shut up and listen to him you unmajestic excuse for a dwarf. You don't even have a beard."

As with the example above, this meme argues that the gap between the movie's attention to and characterization of Thorin compared with its presentation of the other dwarves is too extreme. The movie lavishes Thorin with markers that we are to understand that he is the only really important dwarf, that he has legitimate grievances to avenge, that we are to give our full sympathy to him. None of the other dwarves, even Kili, come close. This particular meme takes a bonus swipe at the movie's presentation of Kili, noting that he lacks the most definitive of dwarvish characteristics, a beard.

A final example of Majestic Thorin demonstrates how extreme the meme community finds the characterizations to be. In this instance, the image employed is of all the dwarves in a line with Thorin in the center (Thorin, 2012). Here also, the placement of the captions create a narrative:

Kili: "Thorin, Thorin, look at me. I have a giant sword. Thorin look. Uncle, **pls**."
Bifur: "Kili, you are at the end for a reason."
Thorin: "I am too majestic to look at any of you. So very majestic."

This meme is particularly effective at making the argument that the movie goes too far in elevating Thorin above the other dwarves. It picks up on Thorin's characteristic gesture throughout the movie of staring into the middle distance, clearly brooding upon the injustices he's experienced and how he intends to get vengeance. The meme argues, though, that this is not the reason for his continual middle-distance contemplation. Rather, he looks away from the other dwarves so much because he's too majestic for their presence and can't stand to look at them, even to the point of ignoring his nephew Kili, who begs like a child to be noticed. Everyone loves a brooding good guy intent on punishing those who wronged him, the meme argues, but *The Hobbit: An Unexpected Journey* goes too far in trying to make Thorin the sole dwarvish object of our affection. We love the other dwarves too (especially Kili) and would prefer to feel as if we do so because of the movie's presentation of them and not despite it.

Unlike most memes[12] 'Majestic Thorin' does not have a dominant image, instead making use of numerous stills from the film. This variation suggests that the meme is indeed about the overall portrayal of Thorin, not simply how he appears in a particular scene. Majestic Thorin memes consistently draw attention to the potentially over-the-top characterization of Thorin, but do not (at least not yet) mercilessly mock that characterization. In addition to suggesting that the characterization gap between Thorin and the other dwarves is too wide, the memetic attention of Thorin also questions whether Thorin's majesty is problematic not because it is his most defining characteristic but because it is largely his *only* characteristic. By focusing upon Thorin's majesty, the memes suggest that while viewers did not necessarily dislike the characterization of Thorin, they came away from the film with concerns that the brooding, appearance-based presentation was limiting, ultimately resulting in a nice-to-look-at but underdeveloped character.

An underdeveloped portrayal of Thorin might go a long way towards explaining memetic communities' ambivalent response to a later scene in the film. Far and away the most prevalent meme deriving from *The Hobbit: An Unexpected Journey* is Never Have I Been So Wrong/I Have Never Been So Wrong. Thorin's actual line in the movie is "I have never been so wrong in all my life," but versions of the meme exist using both the shortened real line and the variant phrasing, "Never have I been so wrong." Quotations have an observed tendency to distill or distort as they become widely known.[13] In this instance, it is interesting to note that the change makes the phrasing more formal, arguably more consistent with the film's characterization of Thorin as aloof and proud, bordering on arrogant. Inverting his words gives the phrase a more formal, more archaic, and more elevated feel.

The Never Have I Been So Wrong meme nearly always employs the same template, a juxtaposed pair of images. In the first frame, we look over Bilbo's shoulder at Thorin. In the second, we look over Thorin's shoulder at Bilbo as they embrace. These images derive, of course, from the climactic scene near the end of the film in which Thorin changes his mind about whether bringing Bilbo along was a good idea—after we see Bilbo risk his own life to save Thorin.

As with the "I'm Going on an Adventure" scene, the film clearly intends this scene to be a moment of high emotional engagement for the audience. Unlike the earlier scene, it is not at all certain that the scene succeeds in being so; indeed, the consistent irreverence with which the scene is handled in memes suggests that it does not. Whereas "I'm Going on an Adventure" memes nearly always reference the scene positively, "I Have Never Been So Wrong" memes employ the scene at best ambivalently, and at worst, mockingly. For instance, we see examples of the meme using the typical images but with the following captions:

> Upper: I thought it was just a fart
> Lower: Never have I been so wrong [n.d.]

> Upper: I thought being older would be fun
> Lower: Never have I been so wrong [n.d.]

> Upper: I thought I could put aftershave on my balls after shaving them
> Lower: Never have I been so wrong [Wrong 2012–2013]

> Upper: I thought the history channel would teach me some history
> Lower: Never have I been so wrong [Wrong 2012–2013]

> Upper: I thought staying up late in college was fun
> Lower: Never have I been so wrong [Wrong 2012–2013]

The widespread popularity[14] of the "Never Have I Been So Wrong" meme seems to result from at least two elements. The meme is highly adaptable, lending itself to commentary about a wide variety of topics, as the examples above show. While that is demonstrably true, it seems insufficient to explain the meme's popularity and longevity. Within that flexible meme resides a core of commentary about the movie—that *An Unexpected Journey* aims to bridge the lighter, more playful world of the *Hobbit* book with the more solemn and dangerous world of LOTR, both as text and as movies, but is not entirely successful—a conclusion that viewers arrived at not long after the film's release and about which they have not changed their minds.

Never Have I Been So Wrong is the most common Hobbit movie meme to emerge, most likely because the scene in many ways encapsulates the film as a whole, and audience reaction to this moment is representative of viewer reaction to the movie as a whole. This scene, like the movie itself, aims at a serious, high-concept reaction from viewers but does not fully succeed, resulting in a moment that partially deconstructs itself, teetering on the edge of self-parody. That teetering is what "Never Have I Been So Wrong" memes draw attention to. We react strongly to this moment, but we're not certain how or why, or whether our reaction tracks with what the film meant to provoke. When Thorin confronts Bilbo, the seemingly-intended seriousness does not entirely hold together; the moment does not ring fully true. It is this partial failure of dramatic persuasiveness that memes have picked up on, the moment that almost, but not quite, unravels into unintentional self-satire, and employs it repeatedly for precisely that purpose—mocking partly serious, partly ludicrous, situations. Of which, it turns out, we encounter many in our lives, hence the meme's continued vibrancy.

As much as audiences wanted to like *The Hobbit: An Unexpected Journey*, they struggled to do so. There was concern and skepticism about the decision to adapt the book into three movies, and memes reflected this, but there was also goodwill towards the films and a profound hope that they would turn out well. Parts of *An Unexpected Journey* were well received, as we can see from the emergence of the I'm Going on an Adventure meme and its favorable handling of the scene. Other memes, however, suggest that while audiences recognized the filmmakers' goal of incorporating *The Hobbit* into the more developed and darker world of *Lord of the Rings*, that goal has been incompletely met, at least as evidenced in *An Unexpected Journey*. The desire to make Thorin a more serious character came at the expense of him being a more fully realized character, as the Majestic Thorin meme's insistence upon drawing attention to the movie's portrayal of Thorin as a laconic, brooding badass, and *only* that, suggests. Most crucially, what is clearly met to be the film's climatic scene of repentance and redemption is so unsuccessfully rendered that instead it becomes a meme for critiquing moments that are half-serious and half-ridiculous. Each of these issues were raised either implicitly or explicitly in the memes themselves and demonstrate how the broader meme community engages in thoughtful, nuanced critiques of Jackson's films. With this in mind, it will be interesting indeed to watch the meme communities when *The Desolation of Smaug* is released, to see what memes emerge and what they tell us about viewers' analysis of the film.

Notes

1. While the originator of the term "meme," Richard Dawkins (Dawkins, 1976) has objected to this (and other) expanded usages of the term, arguing that they distort its original intent (Burman, 2012), it is indisputable that in popular culture "meme" usually conveys this meaning.

2. It's not uncommon to see memes make the leap from the web to the real world. There are examples of memes adapted, printed, and posted to chastise litterers, notify management of a malfunctioning vending machine, beg that a lunch at work be left alone, and request a neighbor to keep quieter.

3. See for example "Competition and Success in the Meme Pool: A Case Study on Quickmeme.com" (Coscia, 2013), which provides both a good synopsis of earlier studies on how memes spread as well as its own study of how collaboration and competition contribute to the propagation of memes.

4. See "Online Memes, Affinities, and Cultural Production" (Knobel & Lankshear, 2007) for a consideration of memes as a social phenomenon. They argue that the characteristics of successful memes include humor, intertextuality, and juxtaposition of anomalous images. Their work approaches but does not overlap with mine, as I am looking not at the characteristics that determine a meme's success but about the rhetorical functions observable in successful memes. Most commonly, these rhetorical functions include humor, one-upmanship, participation in the wider culture, participation in sub-cultures, macro level reflection (social critique), micro level reflection (introspection), and engagement with significant works of cultural meaning and relevance, among them books, films, and artwork, one result of which is crowdsourced literary criticism of such works. See also Limor Shifman's recently released *Memes in Digital Culture* (Shifman, 2014). Shifman has begun a nice consideration of the rhetorical purposes of memes and makes a persuasive argument for serious scholarly attention to these elements of seeming ephemera, but focus attention largely upon the political purposes to which memes are employed.

5. (Butler, 2013).

6. (Network, Know Your Meme, 2013). In the current study, I am focusing largely but not exclusively upon memes found with the Cheezburger network.

7. Due to concerns about potential objections from the copyright holders of the images employed in the memes discussed in this chapter, we have elected not to reproduce the memes here. They can viewed on my website, www.michellemarkeybutler.com/hobbitmemes.

8. Intriguingly, memes critiquing the decision are easy to find. Memes in support of it, however, are almost non-existent. This fact is most likely indicative of widespread fan anxiety about the decision, but it might also be a function of the nature of public communication and humans. We're more likely to complain when we dislike something than we are to express praise when we like something, as all customer service organizations know.

9. See the "One Does Simply Walk into Mordor" entry at KnowYourMeme (Mordor, 2012). This meme has proven so popular that it has spawned a "snowclone" version of itself; that is, a generic template derived from but more general than the original meme. In this case, "X does not simply Y."

10. Typo sic. Typos are in reality fairly rare in memes; misspellings, grammatical errors, and factual errors indeed invite mocking responses in both comments and response memes. Misusing memes tends to invoke a similar response. That the internet culture that Nicholas Carr claims is making us stupid (Carr, 2011) has a high enforcement of proper grammar and spelling is one reason, among others, that I take issue with his conclusions, but that discussion is beyond the scope of this essay.

11. Not that they're entirely straightforward to find. Memegenerator.net's search function is inadequate.

12. Intriguingly, it is also a rare meme that can be traced to a particular source, a discussion on Tumblr by users mistlethalia and jackietastic in December 2012 (Thorin, 2012).

13. See, for example, the list of misquotations at (Wikiquote, 2003).

14. And I do mean widespread popularity. There are hundreds, if not thousands, of "Never Have I Been So Wrong" memes.

Works Cited

Aliens. *Know Your Meme*. 2012. http://knowyourmeme.com/memes/ancient-aliens, accessed November 22, 2013.

Bilbo Baggins Adventure. 2013. *Memegenerator.net*. http://memegenerator.net/Bilbo-Baggins-Adventure, accessed November 30, 2013.

Burman, Jeremy Trevelyan. 2012. "The Misunderstanding of Memes: Biography of an Unscientific Object, 1979–1999." *Perspectives on Science*, 75–104.

Butler, Michelle Markey. 2013. "Tolkien Memes: Crowdsourced Literary Criticism?" *Presented at MythCon 44*. East Lansing, MI.

Carr, Nicholas. 2011. *The Shallows: What the Internet Is Doing to Our Brains*. New York: W.W. Norton.

Challenged Accepted. 2012. *Know Your Meme*. http://knowyourmeme.com/memes/challenge-accepted, accessed November 2013.

CheezburgerNetwork. 2013, November. *Failblog*. http://failblog.cheezburger.com, accessed November 2013.

CheezburgerNetwork. n.d. *Template5919614*. http://cheezburger.com/template/5919614, accessed November 30, 2013.

Coscia, Michele. 2013. "Competition and Success in the Meme Pool: A Case Study on Quickmeme.com." *Association for the Advancement of Artificial Intelligence*, http://arxiv.org/abs/1304.1712.

Dawkins, Richard. 1976. *The Selfish Gene*. Oxford: Oxford University Press.

Fletchword.blogspotwww. 2012, December 12. http://fletchword.blogspot.com/2012/12/the-hobbit-at-48fps-230.html, accessed November 22, 2013.

Hutchinson, Paul. 2012, December 13. *Moviefarm.co.uk*. http://moviefarm.co.uk/2012/12/13/top-10-tolkien-inspired-memes/, accessed November 2013.

I'm Going on an Adventure. 2012. *Know Your Meme*. http://knowyourmeme.com/memes/im-going-on-an-adventure, accessed November 29, 2013.

I'm Going on an Adventure. 2013, February. Memecenterwww. http://www.memecenter.com/fun/1228309/im-going-on-an-adventure, accessed November 29, 2013.

Knobel, Michele, and Colin Lankshear. 2007. "Online Memes, Affinities and Cultural Production." In *A New Literarcies Sampler*, edited by Michele Knobel and Colin Lankshear, 199–227. New York: Peter Lang.

Know Your Meme. November 2013. http://knowyourmeme.com, accessed November 2013.

mandroppings.blogspotwww. 2012, August. http://mandroppings.blogspot.com/2012/08/mckayla-is-not-impressed.html, accessed November 23, 2013.

Memegenerator.net. Pandawhalewww. 2012. http://pandawhale.com/post/11319/the-hobbit-memes, accessed November 22, 2013.

Never Have I Been So Wrong. 2012–2013. *Memegenerator.net*. http://memegenerator.net/Never-Have-I-Been-So-Wrong/images/popular/alltime/page/9, accessed November 30, 2013.

One Does Simply Walk into Mordor. *Know Your Meme*. 2012. http://knowyourmeme.com/memes/one-does-not-simply-walk-into-mordor, accessed November 23, 2013.

Shifman, Limor. 2014. *Memes in Digital Culture*. Cambridge, MA: MIT Press.

Skeptical Third World Kid. n.d. *Know Your Meme*. http://knowyourmeme.com/photos/334344-third-world-success, accessed November 23, 2013.

Thorin, Majestic. 2012, December. *Know Your Meme*, accessed November 30, 2013.

3goldensisterswww. 2012. http://3goldensisters.com/memes/hobbit/, accessed November 22, 2013.
WeKnowMemes.com. 2012, December. WeKnowMemeswww. http://weknowmemes.com/2012/12/why-the-hobbit-is-going-to-be-three-movies/, accessed November 22, 2013.
Wikiquote. *Wikiquote.* 2003, July. http://en.wikiquote.org/wiki/List_of_misquotations, accessed November 30, 2013.

About the Contributors

Damien **Bador** is a French aeronautics engineer who studied at the Massachusetts Institute of Technology. He edited *L'Encyclopédie du Hobbit* and regularly publishes articles on the use of language in Tolkien's legendarium.

Michelle Markey **Butler** is an instructor in the College of Information Studies at the University of Maryland College Park. Her research is internet memes as literary criticism.

Jane **Chance** is the Andrew W. Mellon Distinguished Professor Emerita in English at Rice University and holds an honorary doctorate of letters from Purdue University (2013). Author of 22 books and more than 100 articles and reviews on Old and Middle English literature, medieval women, mythography and medievalism, she founded the Tolkien at Kalamazoo symposium.

Bradford Lee **Eden** is dean of library services at Valparaiso University. He publishes in the areas of metadata, librarianship, medieval music and liturgy, and J.R.R. Tolkien.

Verlyn **Flieger** is a professor emerita at the University of Maryland. Her books on Tolkien include *Splintered Light*, *A Question of Time*, *Interrupted Music*, and *Green Suns and Faërie*, and editions of Tolkien's essay *On Fairy-Stories* and his short story *Smith of Wootton Major*. She co-edits the journal *Tolkien Studies*.

Judy Ann **Ford** is a professor of history at Texas A&M University–Commerce. She specializes in medieval religion and society, and she works with popular medieval sermon collections.

Gregory **Hartley** teaches English and humanities at Johnson University, Florida. His primary research is the integration of theology and literature, extending to film, and world, medieval and renaissance literature.

Vickie L. **Holtz-Wodzak** teaches literature and writing classes at Viterbo University in La Crosse, Wisconsin. She holds a Ph.D. in medieval literature from the University of Missouri–Columbia.

Sumner Gary **Hunnewell** is a Tolkien fandom historian and has worked with Marquette University to microfilm his collection. As a teen he founded the New England Tolkien Society. Since 2010, he has abstracted Tolkien-related items found in fanzines.

Gerard **Hynes** teaches at Trinity College Dublin where he was awarded a Ph.D. for a thesis on ideas of creation and sub-creation in J.R.R. Tolkien's works. He has been published in *Tolkien Studies* and co-edited, with Helen Conrad-O'Briain, *Tolkien: The Forest and the City*.

William Christian **Klarner** earned a bachelor's degree from Loyola University Maryland and has worked in writing and editing. He is a graduate student in English literature.

Kristine **Larsen** is a professor of astronomy at Central Connecticut State University, where her teaching focuses on science pedagogy, the history of science, and the use of science in popular culture. Her work on Tolkien has appeared in *Tolkien Studies*, *Mallorn*, *Silver Leaves*, *Amon Hen*, *The Classroom Astronomer*, and *Mercury*, and in numerous chapters in book-length collections.

Justin T. **Noetzel** is an instructor in the English Department at Saint Louis University, where he teaches British literature and English composition. His research interests include manuscripts, Anglo-Saxon and Viking literature, modern British fantasy, travel and nature writing, and environmental studies.

John D. **Rateliff**, an independent scholar, spent many years researching among Tolkien's manuscripts. Out of this grew *The History of* The Hobbit, his edition of Tolkien's original manuscript. He has written for *Tolkien Studies, Mythlore, VII,* and the volumes *Tolkien's Legendarium, Tolkien and the Study of His Sources, Picturing Tolkien*, and the Shippey festschrift *Tolkien in the New Century*.

Robin Anne **Reid** is a professor of literature and languages. She teaches creative writing, critical theory (stylistics, cultural studies, gender and queer theory), and marginalized literatures. She has published stylistic analyses of Tolkien's work, and is in the early stages of the Tolkien Corpus Project. She edited *The Encyclopedia of Women in Science Fiction and Fantasy*.

David **Thiessen** is a doctoral candidate in English literature at the University of Waterloo. His research examines the expressed and assumed cognitive roles of the body in late fourteenth century literature. He is specifically interested in how authors and readers have used the body and its cognitive operations as an interconnecting horizon across spatial and temporal distances.

Michael A. **Wodzak** is an associate professor of mathematics at Viterbo University in La Crosse, Wisconsin. He holds a Ph.D. in mathematics and has taught mathematics and physics on three continents.

Index

Ainur 90–92, 115, 127, 149, 200–4, 206–7; *see also* Eru/Iluvatar, Valar
Arkenstone 7, 16, 22–23, 85, 87, 92, 104, 160, 188, 218
Arthur/Arthurian 2, 71–76, 138, 158
Auden, W.H. 80, 136–37
aventure 2, 70–76

Balrog 107, 117, 119, 125, 128, 133
Bard the Bowman 15, 23, 53, 61, 72, 85, 106, 131, 188
Barrow-Downs 162, 173, 175–77, 196
Barrow-wight 162, 173–75, 177
Battle of Five Armies 15, 23, 74, 88–89, 106, 126, 154–56, 159
Beorn 3, 14, 25, 60, 62, 83, 88–89, 105–6, 130, 161–73, 174, 177–79, 195, 211; comparison with Bothvarr Bjorki 162–64, 169; comparison with Cuchulainn 169, 174
Beowulf 28, 80–82, 87, 124, 129, 139, 141–42, 147, 154, 156–58, 162–63, 169, 176–77, 183, 197–98
Brothers Grimm 1, 20, 27–28, 35, 79, 118

Caradhras 129, 195
Carc/Roac 3, 66, 106, 131
Celtic 52, 60, 70, 93, 172–73, 198, 202
Chesterton, G.K. 82, 154–55

Dead Marshes 153, 176
Dol Guldur 127, 211–14
Dragons 82, 87–88, 99–100, 103, 116, 128–29, 132–33, 143, 154, 164, 168, 170, 218; *see also* Glaurung, Smaug
dwarves 1, 6–37, 74–75, 83–93, 101, 103, 105–6, 109, 114, 116, 118, 120, 122, 124, 130–33, 146–47, 149, 153, 155–157, 159, 161–69, 181, 184–88, 190–91, 193, 205–6, 210–12, 215–19, 225–27; connections to Jewish people 32–33, 44–45, 52, 63–65, 186; Nibin-Noeg 1, 34; portrayal in *Hobbit* 10–13; portrayal post-*Hobbit* 13–16; portrayal pre-*Hobbit* 7–10; "Quest of Erebor" 75, 210–12; Thorin 4, 11–15, 17–18, 22–24, 26, 32–33, 40, 42–43, 45, 53, 56, 59 62, 64 66, 72, 83, 85, 87, 99, 101–3, 105, 109, 116–17, 120, 122, 131, 133, 146, 156, 158–59, 164–67, 169, 185–88, 190, 198, 209, 212, 214–19, 224, 226–29

Eagles 3, 6, 74, 88–89, 101–3, 114, 116–17, 125–30, 132–33, 167
Elrond 7, 23, 40, 59–60, 74–75, 91, 99–104, 106, 109, 146, 159, 166, 175, 190, 192–93, 211, 213–14, 218, 224
Ents 114, 116, 119, 121–22, 127, 132, 150, 198–199, 203, 205; *see also* Giants; Huorns; Treebeard
Eriol/Aelfwine 9, 108–9, 198, 201, 206
Eru/Iluvatar 10, 13–15, 21, 33, 90–92, 114–17, 121–24, 126–28, 131–34, 147, 149–50, 200–3; *see also* Ainur; Valar

Faerie 7, 70–72, 74–75, 79, 81–83, 89–90, 92, 171–72, 179, 198–99, 233
Father Christmas Letters 42, 103, 111, 162
fea/hroa 114–16, 119, 121–24, 127–28, 130–34; *see also kelvar*; *olvar*
Finnish 85, 170, 198
Fotheringham, John Knight 2, 46–51, 54

Galadriel 34, 75, 101, 132, 143–44, 146, 184, 190, 192–93, 201, 204, 211, 213–15, 218
Gandalf 23, 43, 53, 59–60, 62, 72, 74–75, 83, 86, 88–89, 92, 102, 105, 109, 113, 120–21, 132, 140, 142, 147–49, 156, 158–59, 161, 163–69, 172, 175, 179, 181, 184–85, 188–92, 210–19
Giants 3, 10, 21, 72–73, 82, 88, 103, 110, 114, 117–22, 156, 164; *see also* Ents; Treebeard
Glaurung 15–16, 128–29, 143, 150; *see also* Dragons: Smaug
Goblins 3, 6, 9, 11, 20, 22–23, 25, 72, 74, 83, 88–89, 101, 103, 105, 113–14, 116, 119–20, 122–23, 126, 130, 136, 140, 146, 154, 162, 167, 169–170, 215
Gollum 3, 26, 72, 75–76, 80, 84, 86–87, 106, 108, 113, 136–37, 140–44, 148, 150, 156, 159, 167, 190 92, 209 10, 218, 225

The Hobbit: An Unexpected Journey (film) 4, 208, 222–25, 227, 229; *see also* Jackson, Peter
Huorns 195, 198; *see also* Ents

Istar(i) 83, 88–89, 92, 105, 124–25, 145, 147, 189; *see also* Wizards

Jackson, Peter 1, 4, 56, 132, 208–9, 211, 217, 222–23; see also *The Hobbit: An Unexpected Journey* (film)

Kalevala 79, 85, 170
kelvar 115–16, 119–20, 122, 125–26, 132–33; *see also fea/hroa*; *olvar*

Lang, Andrew 1–2, 20, 26, 78, 80–83, 92–93
Legend of Sigurd and Gudrun 2, 78, 80–81
Lewis, C.S. 72, 120, 139, 146, 148–49, 184
Lewis, Paul W. 168, 170–71, 178–79
Lothlorien 189–91, 193, 195, 199, 203–5, 207

MacDonald, George 81, 113, 157, 171, 178
Maia(r) 86, 89–90, 92, 114, 116, 122–28, 130–34, 145, 190, 201
Melkor/Morgoth 9–11, 13–15, 21, 25, 33, 41, 49, 91, 98–100, 103–4, 106–7, 109, 114–15, 119, 121–26, 128, 132, 143–45, 147, 149–50, 203, 218
Middle English 3, 64–65, 71, 75, 79, 93, 144, 183
Mirkwood 22, 25, 66, 74, 98–100, 102–3, 110, 114, 127, 150, 162, 165–68, 187, 193, 195, 211, 216–18
Moria 17–18, 23, 34, 45, 52, 55–56, 65, 101, 117, 119, 125, 133, 141, 146, 189–90, 193, 215, 217–19
Morris, William 1, 20, 26, 80
music 1, 14, 22, 72, 90–92, 139, 198, 200–4, 226; *see also* song

Nazgul/Black Riders 3, 10, 133, 140, 143–45, 177, 196, 199
Necromancer 7, 23, 86, 104, 120, 126, 132, 175, 211–14
Nibelungenlied 28, 137–38

235

Index

Ogres 10, 21, 121
Old English 3, 28, 80, 82, 92–93, 106, 108, 121, 139, 155–56, 158, 162, 176, 183–85, 224
Old Forest 100, 167, 170–72, 174–77, 179, 195–96, 199, 204
Old French 70–71, 75
Old High German 28
Old Man Willow 162, 172, 195–96, 198–99, 204
Old Norse 1–2, 28, 30–31, 78–81, 87, 92–93, 155–56, 158, 162–63
olvar 115, 122, 132; *see also fea/hroa; kelvar*
"On Fairy-Stories" 2, 40, 51, 70, 78–82, 90–91, 93, 201, 205
Orcs 3, 8–9, 13, 21, 33–34, 74, 89, 102, 104, 107, 113–17, 122–26, 132–33, 144, 150, 175, 192–93, 198, 214–15

Plato/Neoplatonic 3, 90, 115, 130, 133
polytemporality 4, 208, 219

quest 3, 25–26, 40, 75–76, 118, 140, 159, 167, 175, 181, 210, 216–18

retconning 4, 209
Rivendell 40, 53, 59, 102–4, 109, 140, 152, 159, 166, 190–93, 204, 210–15, 217–18

Saruman 4, 89, 144–45, 147–48, 204, 211–15, 218–19
Sauron 86–87, 89–90, 102, 104–5, 117, 119–120, 123, 125–26, 132–33, 137, 144–49, 176–77, 189, 192, 204, 211–15, 218
Shelob 127, 132, 134, 141, 143, 191–92; *see also* Spiders; Ungoliant
Shire 3, 62–63, 76, 88, 103, 106–7, 140, 148, 154–56, 158–60, 167–68, 170–72, 176–78, 189–93, 195–96, 199, 204–6, 215–16
Smaug 3, 10, 13–14, 16, 22–23, 25, 53, 61–62, 83–88, 92, 101–2, 104–6, 113, 117, 128–29, 132–33, 143, 157, 164, 167, 169, 177, 185–88, 190, 212, 214–16, 218–19, 225, 229; *see also* Dragons; Glaurung
song 1, 3, 14, 22, 25–26, 34, 36, 88, 91–92, 100, 133, 141, 156, 159, 171–72, 174, 179, 187, 202–6, 215–16; *see also* music
Spiders 3, 6, 74, 83, 103, 114, 116–17, 126–30, 132–33, 159, 216–17, 225; *see also* Shelob; Ungoliant
Sturluson, Snorri 29–30, 36

Thomas Aquinas 3, 115–16, 125, 127, 130
Tom Bombadil 3, 145–46, 149, 161–62, 164, 170–79, 195, 203
Treebeard 3, 114, 117–19, 121, 137, 150, 195, 204–5; *see also* Giants; Huorns
Trolls 3, 23, 31, 53, 63, 72–74, 83, 89, 91, 101, 103, 107, 113–14, 116–21, 123, 126, 132, 150, 159, 167, 214, 217, 219, 225

Ungoliant 127, 129, 132, 150; *see also* Shelob; Spiders
uvanimor 10, 13, 21, 114, 121

Valar 25, 33, 41, 49, 55, 89–90, 99, 105, 116, 124–26, 143, 150, 170, 201; *see also* Ainur; Eru/Iluvatar
Volsunga Saga 30–31, 80, 82, 87

Wagner, Richard 1, 7, 28
Wargs 89, 104, 117, 130–31, 133
Welsh 60, 71, 106, 172
Witch-King 144–45, 150, 162, 175–77, 214
Wizards 4, 74, 86, 88–89, 92, 99–100, 102, 104–6, 109, 145, 147–48, 158–59, 164–65, 179, 211–14; *see also* Istar(i)

www.ingramcontent.com/pod-product-compliance
Ingram Content Group UK Ltd.
Pitfield, Milton Keynes, MK11 3LW, UK
UKHW050533150426
5217IPUK00026B/1920